Investing for Beginners

5 Books in 1:

Stock Market Investing for Beginners

Dividend Investing

Day Trading for Beginners

Forex Trading for Beginners

Options Trading Crash Course

© **Copyright 2020 - All rights reserved.**

The content contained within this book may not be reproduced, duplicated or transmitted without direct written permission from the author or the publisher.

Under no circumstances will any blame or legal responsibility be held against the publisher, or author, for any damages, reparation, or monetary loss due to the information contained within this book. Either directly or indirectly.

Legal Notice:

This book is copyright protected. This book is only for personal use. You cannot amend, distribute, sell, use, quote or paraphrase any part, or the content within this book, without the consent of the author or publisher.

Disclaimer Notice:

Please note the information contained within this document is for educational and entertainment purposes only. All effort has been executed to present accurate, up to date, and reliable, complete information. No warranties of any kind are declared or implied. Readers acknowledge that the author is not engaging in the rendering of legal, financial, medical or professional advice. The content within this book has been derived from various sources. Please consult a licensed professional before attempting any techniques outlined in this book.

By reading this document, the reader agrees that under no circumstances is the author responsible for any losses, direct or indirect, which are incurred as a result of the use of information contained within this document, including, but not limited to, — errors, omissions, or inaccuracies.

Stock Market Investing for Beginners

The Essential Guide to Make Big Profits with Stock Trading: Best Strategies, Technical Analysis and Psychology to Grow Your Money and Create Your Wealth

Table of Contents

Introduction 11

Chapter 1: Stock Marketing Basics 12

    Ways of Investing

    What Are Stocks?

    Different Types of Stocks

    Choosing the Best Stocks

    The Minimum Capital to Start with

Chapter 2: How to Start Trading 20

    Invest in a Stock from Home

    Starting Your Investment in the Stock Market

    How to Learn to Play in the Stock Market

    How to Operate on the Stock Exchange

    How Investments in the Stock Market Work

    Investment Strategies

    How Much Can You Earn?

Chapter 3: Financial Leverage for Experts 32

    Fundamental Analysis Rules

        Establish a Baseline

        Consider Worldwide Issues

        Put It All Together

        Understand the Relative Strength of Any Given Trade

    Quantitative Fundamental Analysis

        Balance Sheet

        Income Statement

        Cash Flow Statement

Finding the Details
Qualitative Fundamental Analysis
  Competitive Advantage
  Changes to the Company

Chapter 4: Technical Analysis 40

Price Charts
  Line Chart
  Bar Chart
  Candlestick Chart
  Point and Figure Chart
  Trend or Range
Chart Patterns to Be Aware of
  Flags and Pennants
  Head Above Shoulders Formation
  Gann
  Cup and Handle Formation
  Trend Lines
  Moving Averages

Chapter 5: Mindset 51

Traits That Set You Apart from Those That Have Failed
  Rise Early and Shine
  Prior to the Market, Do Some Research
  Ensure That Trade Plans Are Followed
  Investors Know That Trading Every Day Is Not Necessary
  Reflect on the Trades That You Have Purchased
  Small Losses Happen — Embrace Them
  Consider Your Next 100 Trades
  Reduce Your Risks to Fight Back the Fear

    Fear That They Are Missing Some Great Move

    The Loving Feeling That Those Who Succeed Experience and Now Create a Need to Continue That Feeling

    Use Your Excitement for Good

    Consider What a Newbie Would Do and Then Snatch Them at the Low

    Look for Those Ticks

    High Five Equals Sell

  Traits That Will Ensure You Succeed as a Day Trader

    There Are Several Enemies That We Do Not Even Recognize and Most of It Is Ourselves

    There Is Power in Awareness

    Bias Sensory-Derived

    Vagueness and Ambiguity Are Avoided

    The Anticipation Is Tangible

Chapter 6: Stock Trading Strategies.................................64

  Trading vs. Investing

    What Is Trading?

    What Is Investing?

  How to Find Good Stocks to Invest in

  Technical Analysis — Short-Term Trading Strategies

    Really, What Is Technical Analysis?

    Charts

    About Technical Indicators

  Simple Short-Term Trading Strategies

    Trending Markets

      Trading an Uptrend

      Trading a Downtrend

Sideways Markets

    Trading a Wide-Ranging Market

    Trading a Narrow-Ranging Market

Chapter 7: Mistakes to Avoid..77

Mistake No. 1: They Add to 'Losing Positions'

Mistake No. 2: Making Those Trades Out of 'Boredom'

Mistake No. 3: They Keep Moving from One Strategy to the Next

Mistake No. 4: They Don't Have an Exit Plan

Mistake No. 5: They Go in for Impulsive Trading

Mistake No. 6: They Lack the Much-Needed Discipline That Is Needed for Swing Trading

Mistake No. 7: They Don't Have a Strategy at All

Mistake No. 8: They Overestimate How Much They Should Invest at Any Given Time

Mistake No. 9: They Listen Too Much to Those 'Pundits' Out There

Chapter 8: Tips for Becoming a Successful Top Trader..81

Determine Your Current Level of Skill

Decide How Much Risk Is Right for You

Prepare Yourself

Understand When You Will Want to Get While the Getting Is Good

Find the Right Place to Start

Make Sure That Your Goals Are S.M.A.R.T.

  Specific

  Measurable

  Attainable

  Relevant

  Timely

Track Your Progress
Chart Your Success
Results That Matter Most
   Net Profit
   Profit Factor
   Percent Profitable
   Trade Average Net Profit

Conclusion..94

Introduction

Thank you so much for purchasing the book *Stock Market Investing for Beginners*! In this book, not only will we show you how to get started with stock market investing, but we will also help you to get started with your trading endeavors.

Keep in mind that for you to make money with trading stocks, you need to have excellent knowledge of many techniques and tricks. This will help you to figure out how it can be done profitably. With that being said, we will also help you to figure out how it is that many people fail with investing their money into stocks. You need to understand the main reason why mistakes happen. We will help you to eliminate any errors. Overall, this book would be an excellent guide for people interested in making money, whether it is sitting at home or if they want to make money on the side.

It is totally up to you how you would like to make money from these tips. We will also show you how much money can be expected of you to make when starting investing. Stock investing, when done right, could perhaps be the key to ultimate freedom. With that being said, make sure that you will take massive actions after you are done reading this book. The main reason why most people see success when trading would be the fact that people take action—and hopefully, you do the same.

Chapter 1: Stock Marketing Basics

Have you ever heard the word "investing" before, but you have never understood what it really means? It's actually quite simple—it means making your money work while you do what you want. Basically, it's a different way of thinking about how to make money. While growing up, most of us have been taught that we can only earn an income by finding a good job—and that's exactly what most of us do. However, there is a big problem with this—if you want more money, you have to work longer hours. However, there is a limit to the number of hours a day we can work on—not to mention the fact that having a lot of money is not fun if we do not have the time to enjoy it. This is why rich people do not have a job—they have businesses that work for them.

Think about it—you have a job that allows you to earn over 2000 dollars a month, but that takes you over 13 hours a day, 6 days out of 7, so about 11 remain—and usually, the hours of sleep should be at least 7–8 (for a healthy lifestyle). Considering also the displacements and the time lost to go to work, you have 3 to 4 hours left, where you most likely will use 2 for dinner in the evening. In the end, there are 2 actual hours of time per day, which do not allow you to enjoy life to the fullest. You will find yourself having a 2000-dollars-a-month salary (which, nowadays, is nothing) that will continue to accumulate, as you will not absolutely enjoy them in any way. This is what is often called the "rat race."

Is there a solution? Yes, it exists, and it is to take part of your money and invest it properly in the financial markets. By doing so, you are letting it work for you. The possibilities are scary and extremely profitable. Do you want one example? Take a look at Apple's stocks.

Apple's stocks have risen at a frightening rate in the last 10 years, from $10 to about $100. This means that with an investment of only $ 1,000, you would now have over 10 thousand dollars. This is the power of online investing—it allows you to grow your money in a totally automatic way.

Unfortunately, there is no duplication of self to increase the time at work, but instead, you can create an "extension" of yourself—that is, your money—and put it to work. In this way, while you are working for your employer, or while you are at the bar with friends, you can still earn at the same time—thanks to the investment you made. In a very simple way, therefore, you can make your money useful, thus maximizing your earning potential, even if you do not receive an increase in your pay, or even if you do not decide to make an extraordinary one, or you are looking for a more remunerative job.

Ways of Investing

There are many ways to do this. This includes investing your money in stocks, bonds, mutual funds, forex, CFDs or real estate (and many other things), or even starting your own online business (like affiliate marketing). Sometimes, people refer to these options as "investment vehicles," which is just another way of saying "a way of investing."

Each of these vehicles has positive and negative aspects, and the best is undoubtedly the investment on a binary options broker, which allows you to start even with only 10 dollars to invest in the forex market, stocks, and commodities. The point is that no matter what method you choose to invest your money, the goal is always to put your money to work so that you always earn an extra profit. It may seem difficult, but today, with the internet, it's really easy—and brokers are different players that allow you to build a diversified portfolio of stocks, currencies, indices, and commodities. Can beginners invest and earn in the financial markets? Absolutely yes, they can—given that they can employ the right broker.

What Are Stocks?

A company, to function, needs capital—in joint-stock companies, the shareholdings of the shareholders, and therefore capital, are represented by the shares. Each has an identical nominal value, which multiplied by the total number of shares represents the company's share capital.

The stock, therefore, represents a title of participation in the company, that is, by purchasing a share buy a piece of the company. In fact, the shares give rights (and obligations) of various kinds—for example, voting at meetings, management control, options on new shares or convertible bonds, and participation in the dividend. As Warren Buffet once said, "The quickest way to get a Lamborghini is to own a piece of that company."

The stocks do not guarantee the return of the invested capital, since by buying them, you have lent money to the company, without guarantees. If the company thrives, your shares will grow in value, but if they have problems, your capital may be reduced to zero. It is quite evident that no entrepreneur wants to reduce his company on the pavement and wants to see how much he has invested, so it will do everything to avoid loss of value. However, it is equally evident that every company is included in a larger system called the market, which dictates certain rules. If you are not competitive, if you do not renew processes and products, if you do not have a catchy brand (and I could continue for a long time), the company may risk being excluded from the market itself.

Different Types of Stocks

There are ordinary shares, which are the most widespread and of which we have spoken so far, preference shares, savings shares. The preference shares give the right to a preference in the distribution of profits or the repayment of capital. Savings shares do not have the right to vote but have patrimonial privileges established by the company's deed of incorporation. If you have bought an action, you also have the right to receive an annual dividend—that is, the company profit divided among all the participants in the so-called "risk capital." High dividends are very attractive to investors, but it is not guaranteed that they are distributed every year or even that they are constant, for budgetary reasons or for company policies that do not provide for profit distribution to favor the company's capitalization, for example.

The market value of a share is that which results from the official price lists, if listed and may be different from the nominal value and the asset value (net equity divided by the number of shares), according to some variables. By simplifying, a solid company with good growth prospects will be associated with high potential and, therefore, a high value of the shares issued; on the other hand, a company with financial problems and with prospects of de-growth will be associated with a low value of its shares. Even the performance of the economy, politics, and speculation can influence the market value of an action.

Choosing the Best Stocks

But which actions to choose? Upstream of this choice, there must be a careful study of their tolerance to risk, also taking a cue from past behavior. Once you have decided how much to invest in shares, based on all the reasoning you have to do, you have to decide what to buy.

To this end, many theories come in handy—the main ones are fundamental analysis and technical analysis. The fundamental theory tells when to buy, hold, or sell a share, based on the prospects for growth over competitors, budget data, price, dividend. However, the financial statements of companies do not always correspond to reality, since it is sufficient to insert an active or passive contingency to see the final result change. There are also the emotions of the market, so even under ideal conditions, it is possible that the value of action remains very low for a long time, perhaps falling below the purchase price.

Technical analysis, on the other hand, deals with the historical price trend, and purchase (or sales) decisions are made by forecasts. In reality, it is not so simple. What complicates things? The fact that even the market (companies, private investors, and institutional investors) probably uses the same tools, is observing and reacting—sometimes logically, and sometimes in an illogical way.

The Minimum Capital to Start with

What is the minimum capital that you need to trade? This is one of the most recurring questions that are asked me by those who would like to begin to dedicate themselves to this activity. The answer, as we shall see, depends on many factors—and in this section, I would like to clarify some aspects that affect the choice of initial capital.

Let's start immediately by saying that the amount we decide to allocate to the trading activity, whatever the objective we want to achieve, must not be a capital we need to 'live' or for the needs of every day. It must be, as I like to call it, an 'available capital.'

In other words, since investing is a risk activity (and so it's trading), like any other financial transaction, the money we devote to trading—if it is lost—must not, in any way, move our and our family's economic balance.

The question we must ask is, if we lose the money we have decided to dedicate to investing, do we compromise our family serenity in some way? If yes, you can either reduce the amount up to the parameters of 'tranquility' or avoid dedicating yourselves to this activity, at least until you are in a position to have a minimum capital aside that meets the required requirements.

Recently I happened to meet a gentleman who, wanting to follow my own course during a discounted 'launch' offer to start trading using my system, asked me if I could keep the offer for a few days, to give him time to release his savings invested in accumulation plans in his bank. Since those were his only (and small) savings, I calmly advised him to let go of the course and the real operation, at least at the time, and in the meantime to start studying in free time waiting for better times (read: pending to have an 'available capital'). This, I think, should be the philosophy of all those who want to devote to what is defined by many as one of the most beautiful professions that can be dedicated.

After this first 'rock,' we try to understand what the minimum capital to devote to trading can be. Which, as we said at the beginning, depends on many factors. Unfortunately, the generation that is approaching only now for the first time to trading is the result of misleading advertising that magnifies the achievement of wealth or, in any case, earnings to many zeros starting from a few hundred dollars.

Although it is true that with the advent of CFDs - which offer an excellent leverage on almost all financial instruments - and cryptocurrencies (which, in some cases like Ripple made over 16,000% in 2017) today it is possible to trade even a few hundred dollars, it is clear that starting with a small capital we cannot seriously think about to become rich, or even less, to have an extra monthly income worthy of the name.

Instead, we can reasonably think, so to speak, of 'biting ourselves' on real markets by acquiring the necessary experience. Only once we have obtained stable results, we will be able to use more capital and aim to have an extra monthly income to add to our income from work (which, in the meantime, I advise not to abandon).

So, we start to put stakes—if we have an 'available capital' that is around €500, this amount can be enough to start if and only if our goal is to check our attitudes to trading and to check if we can achieve positive and constant results. In other words, it can be seen as a "testing capital," used to gather experience rather than profits.

But beware—we must not run the risk of using exaggerated leverage. This means that we will have to open up transactions (and CFDs give us this opportunity) with very small lots and be content with small gains (and have small losses). Otherwise, using maximum leverage, we would risk burning the amount with very few transactions. If you want, you can go further into the topic in my article on leverage.

If, and when, the objective will instead be to have an extra monthly income, then the amount to devote to trading (and we always talk about 'available capital' in the indicated sense) must be at least 3,000/5,000 dollars. Of course, the operation cannot always be dedicated to instruments such as CFDs because it would be unthinkable, with this capital, to operate on different instruments that require margins far higher than those required by CFDs.

With 3000 or 5000 dollars—of course, once you have acquired the necessary experience and a good trading method—we can set ourselves the goal of having an extra income that is around 200 or 300 dollars per month while maintaining a low-risk profile. They might seem few in absolute terms, but if we consider the percentage return on 'risk capital,' it is a respectable ratio.

Chapter 2: How to Start Trading

We have already spoken extensively about how to invest in the stock market and how this activity can generate very high profits. Precisely because of a large number of profits that can be obtained, many are those who aspire to become stock traders—but how do you learn to invest in the stock market?

The point is that the exchange is not a game—every time someone uses the term "play in the stock market" is taking you on the wrong path, as it is not a game—it is about investment. The best way to learn how to invest in the stock exchange is to start investing with an intuitive and easy-to-use broker. What's the best solution, in my opinion? It's definitely *24option*. Among other things, those who register for free at *24option* also get free excellent trading alerts with which to invest in the stock market is much easier.

Invest in a Stock from Home

The first characteristic of the investment in the stock market that immediately jumps to the eye is that it is an investment that can be made directly from home. It is no longer necessary to go to the Bank to hand over the purchase orders to the employee on duty. With a little nostalgia, the old traders remember those bank branches that had become a bit of a meeting place for the oxen park, considering the large number of traders who met and exchanged information and observations. On the one hand, it is a positive thing, since investing in the stock market through an Italian bank is the best way to get skinny off of commissions and to lose money, given the inadequacy of the tools offered.

The only positive aspect of these oxen park meetings was the possibility of transmitting the necessary experience to those who were starting to invest in the stock market. Learning to invest in the stock market using the comments and experiences of older people is something that is difficult to do if you work from home. To solve this problem, it is obviously possible to attend discussion forums and try to establish a dialogue with the most experienced users. It is also advisable to always go very carefully on the forums because not all the information there is correct. Add, however, that investing in the stock exchange from home, using tools such as binary options or contracts for difference, is great more convenient than going to a bank branch physically.

What are the best platforms to invest in home exchange? There are a few platforms that are truly reliable and affordable. Among the best platforms to invest in the Stock Exchange, we can report:

- Plus500: safe and reliable; it is a truly professional platform. Plus500 is a difference trading (CFD) trading platform that allows you to invest in thousands of shares listed in all major world markets.
- 24option: a truly safe and reliable binary options broker, perfect for investing in the stock market.
- IQ Option: This is one of the most innovative binary options brokers. It is very safe and reliable. It offers a free unlimited demo account in time and quantities. IQ Option is the only platform for trading on the stock market that allows you to start investing with just 10 dollars.

Starting Your Investment in the Stock Market

The first step to start investing in the stock market is to know what the stock exchange is. It might seem obvious, but it's not like that—many traders start stock trading without even knowing what it is. The Stock Exchange is the regulated financial market on which shares are exchanged, which represent securities owned by listed companies. Each share gives the right, as the case may be, to receive a dividend (a portion of the company profits that are redistributed) and to participate in the ordinary and extraordinary meetings of a company.

Usually, however, it is not advisable to invest in the stock market through the shares. The best way to start investing in the stock market is to focus on derivative contracts that have underlying shares. In this way, you get the advantage of increasing earnings and, above all, earning both when stocks go down and when they go up, obviously making the right prediction.

How to Learn to Play in the Stock Market

At this point, you may ask how to learn how to play the stock market? The title of this paragraph is a provocation because we know that we must not talk about gambling but about investing. In any case, how do you start? How do you learn? The best way to start is options. These derivative instruments, in fact, are very simple to use and understand. In fact, binary trading is very easy—if we choose a stock listed on a World Exchange (one of the main ones, of course), we only have to indicate whether the price of the asset will be increased or decreased at the end of a period of time. It does not count the level of variation; only the sign counts. This is perfect for learning because the aspiring trader can concentrate only on a few fundamental factors, leaving out all the details. It must be said that options trading can produce profits so high that many traders are choosing to trade options only, although they do not need a simplified approach.

How to Operate on the Stock Exchange

We have already seen that in order to operate on the stock exchange, it is convenient to use derivative instruments; binary options are better to start with and, later, CFDs can also be adopted (contracts for difference). Another important choice to make to invest in the Stock Exchange, especially at the beginning, is to focus exclusively on the best stocks, i.e., those of large companies listed on the world's major stock exchanges.

Among other things, the major options brokers and CFDs provide access to all the big stocks but not too small listed companies, perhaps in secondary stock exchanges like the one in Milan. In fact, these titles are usually extremely dangerous, and the novice trader who should choose them would be at serious risk of losing money.

How Investments in the Stock Market Work

For completeness of information, I try to make a global overview of the functioning of investments on the Stock Exchange. In general, it is possible to invest in the stock market with the direct purchase of listed shares or with the purchase of derivatives. In general, for those who have the problem of how to start investing in the stock exchange, the recommended choice is that of derivatives, in particular, binary options. For those who want to buy the securities directly, the process is slightly more complex—you have to open an account for the custody of shares, and on this deposit, you, unfortunately, pay a salty stamp.

Moreover, this type of investment usually passes for Italian banks and involves high fees and poor service. Vice versa, for those who choose to invest in the stock market with binary options or CFDs, there are zero commissions and a service that really works very well.

Another way to invest in the stock exchange is made up of mutual funds. Investments of this type do work through the purchase of a share of the fund. The managers then use the money obtained through the sale of shares to invest in the stock exchanges. This is an indirect investment that delegates all responsibilities to fund managers. In some cases, good profits can be made, but it has often happened that investment funds, especially if managed by Italian companies, have led to very strong losses. Moreover, the tax treatment of this type of investment is strongly penalizing.

Investment Strategies

It is much better to do it yourself, then. But when you work with options or CFDs on the stock exchange, you need to have investment strategies that work well. In general, we can say that there are very simple strategies that allow us to predict the market trend based on the direct observation of the graphs. It is also possible to predict the market trend also based on the news relating to the various listed companies. Finally, for those wishing to delegate to others the choice of strategy without incurring the costs of investment funds, it is always possible to subscribe to trading signals services—in practice it is another trader (or group of traders) that indicates by e-mail, SMS or integration with the trading platform, what is the right transaction to do at the right time.

How Much Can You Earn?

The questions of those who aim to invest in stocks always stand identically from the day the stock market is born, and I would like to respond to these in-depth. Example queries:
- How much do you earn on the stock market?
- How to start playing on the stock market?
- How do you earn in the Foreign Exchange?
- How much can you earn by investing in the stock market?
- I lost everything in the bag.

The last one will seem strange, but it is one of the many searches that many users make. They are traders who lose their investment in the stock exchange, and we should try not to fall into the same mistakes studying the financial markets and investing with a non-high risk profile and a diversified portfolio.

There is no time, in fact, that an investor does not ask how much you earn by choosing to invest in the stock market. To this question, it has never been possible to assign a precise answer. Most professional traders, in fact, know perfectly well that the amount of gain that can be obtained on the stock exchange is also linked to subjective factors. It is these latter that really determine what is then called gain.

The return on an investment in the stock exchange is also linked to a series of elements circumscribed over time. Investing today in the stock market is certainly not the same thing as an investment that took place over 10 years ago. In fact, then, it was in full expansion. The FTSE MIB, remaining at the Italian stock exchange, had reached very high levels, and the performance of the individual shares seemed to improve continuously.

That era is officially over for some time. Investing in the stock market today means charging a series of risks unthinkable up to 10 years ago. Not only. Entire sectors of the stock market, such as the banking sector, are subject to an erosion of the price that seems unstoppable. This is another element to take into consideration when trying to understand how much you can earn on the stock market. Compared to the past, investing today in the stock market means to be aware that there are securities whose relaunch still seems very far away.

All the factors listed belong to the determination of how much you earn with the stock exchange. It is a variable sum linked to contingencies. But there is a way to calculate when to invest in the stock exchange and when not? In other words, is it possible to determine a minimum sum above which the investment was successful?

The minimum gain that can be obtained on the stock exchange to be able to talk about a successful investment is the result of a kind of summation. By removing the field from possible misunderstandings, it is always important to highlight that the factors to be added do not concern the subjective sphere of the investor. Instead, these are purely objective elements. The first, and most important, concerns inflation. When choosing to buy stocks, it is hoped that, at the end of the investment, the increased capital will not be lost with the increase in the consumer price index. Now, it is clear that, when starting to invest in the stock market, the inflation rate is not known but only reputable. During the investment, however, we have all the information available to quantify what would have been the natural increase in the amount invested in light of the trend of inflation.

Assuming that there are zero risk investments on the market (a postulate rather than a reality), investing in the stock market is worthwhile if the yield is higher than that obtainable with the risk-free security. To do this calculation, you can take into consideration the government bonds of a highly developed country. The yields of these bonds, clearly low, must then be compared with those of the investment on the stock exchange.

The interest rate that is paid by this risk-free security must, therefore, be added to the index relating to the trend in consumer prices. Thus, we obtain data first, which, however, is still incomplete. To define what is the expected gain of the investment on the stock exchange, a third element must be added. At this point, one enters the field of subjectivity. The third variable is an additional margin that compensates for the risk invested by the investor. Quantifying this third element is not at all simple. Traders, however, are used to quantifying the risk run in a couple of percentage points.

The definitive summation to determine how much you earn by choosing to invest in the stock market can be summarized as follows: inflation + return on capital + additional margin → 11 percentage points.

The 11 percentage points of return obtainable by investing in the stock market are gross. It is, therefore, necessary to subtract all the items of expenditure, including taxes. Furthermore, this is a level that is supported by a normal trend in the consumer price index. It is obvious, on the other hand, that today with low inflation, that minimum level tends to fall further. The summation alone, however, provides a partial picture of how much money should be earned "at a minimum" on the stock exchange.

A very important factor is the duration of the investment. In this case, the rule is very clear—to obtain interesting returns, hold shares for very long periods. This happened over 10 years ago. In fact, at the time, economic growth seemed to be unlimited, and the trend in inflation was positive too. In those years, the same stock indices improved continuously. But that picture has failed today. Paradoxically, to be able to earn on the stock exchange, based on the model mentioned, it would take an even longer period of time than 10 years ago.

All the major analysts say that investing today in the stock market makes sense only if the shares can be maintained for 10 years. It takes time to succeed, so, year after year, to accrue an interesting return. But over time, it also serves a lot of confidence in a restart.

The example of banking sector securities is just the tip of an iceberg of what is happening on the stock exchange. If you look at the prices of many stocks in recent years, you notice the total absence of lasting restart. It is true that this situation is taking root, especially in recent years, but who says that the picture will improve in a few years? This is the real breaking point compared to the past.

Today the balance risks/opportunities hang, and not a little, on the first course. The factors to be taken into consideration are many starting from systemic risk. The stock market trend, in fact, has to deal with the macro framework of reference, and it is pitiless. The global economic recovery, in fact, does not take off.

As for the domestic market, the underlying picture is even more deteriorated. For this reason alone, investing in Italian shares is already a less advantageous step than an investment in US equities. All reports of the International Monetary Fund do not leave much hope in this regard—the difficult situation is bound to last in the future. The overall risk is then increased as further elements of concern have been inserted into this framework. The examples, in this sense, are the Brexit but also the serious crisis of Italian banks.

Therefore, investing in long-term stocks remains a bet for strong hearts. The fact that the long-term risks have increased, however, does not mean that it is impossible to gain on the stock market today. There is a way to avoid being overwhelmed by these fears. The road is to focus on the short term. The means to travel this way is to rely on binary trading and Forex & CFD Trading.

Alongside the various factors that we have mentioned as elements of risk to be reckoned with by choosing to invest in the stock market today, there are also purely economic considerations that advise against the long term. That 11% that we have indicated as the minimum sum that can be earned, in fact, is gross. In that percentage, in fact, various expenses are charged that derive from being a shareholder.

Those who choose to buy shares are subject to a series of taxes and are obliged to respect a lot of duties. It is obvious that if this happens at a time of financial expansion, then it is not a problem. On the other hand, if it starts at a time of crisis, then it is a further factor that discourages the long term.

Investing today on the stock exchange means relying on binary trading and CFD trading. In fact, only these two financial instruments make it possible to obtain a profit that is not subject to the many risks of the long term. With binary options and Contracts for Difference, it is possible to bet on the progress of stock even for very short time intervals.

This is especially true in the case of binary options. Investing in the stock market with options trading means betting on what is the direction that our action will take even in the 60 seconds following the opening of the trade. It is obvious that if the mechanism of operation of binary options is this, then all the talk about the risks of long-term investment makes no sense.

Options trading, on the other hand, is a way to defend against the high uncertainty that is ultimately characterizing the markets.

These same considerations apply in the case of CFD trading. The latter very closely resembles the traditional purchase of shares. With CFD trading, it is possible to buy instruments that are linked to the performance of specific actions. You earn and lose in relation to the trend of listing but with a substantial difference compared to the stock exchange.

In fact, when you buy CFD, you do not charge any duty. Also, the expenses as a commission are certainly not like those of the shares. Earnings, on the other hand, can be immediate. In this case, too, short-term investments can be carried out.

But where can you trade online today? In recent years there has been a boom in authorized platforms. This talk covered both binary trading and CFD trading. The list below shows the best brokers to earn trading with the stock market. It is good to remember that the use of these instruments can lead to the loss of capital. For this reason, before betting on online trading, it is always better to practice on demo platforms. These allow simulating the trading activity without risking losses.

All the best trading platforms give this possibility that it is exercisable without time limits. By joining the practice on the trading platform also a study on technical analysis and fundamental analysis, it is possible to create a valid alternative to the investment on the stock exchange. How much you earn today with online trading is definitely higher than what you earn on the stock market. Testing with a demo account costs nothing. Today, however, the role of inflation has become secondary. The curve of consumer price trends leaves no room for misunderstanding. Inflation is increasing nowadays slowly, and indeed, the risk of deflation remains around the corner. This is why we need other elements to define what we earn today in the stock market.

Chapter 3: Financial Leverage for Experts

While it should come as no surprise that you are going to need to gather as much data as possible in order to make the best trades—regardless of what market you are working in—it is important to keep in mind that if you don't use it in the right way, then it is all for naught. There are two ways to get the most out of any of the data that you gather, the first is via technical analysis, and the second is via fundamental analysis. As a general rule, you will likely find it helpful to start with fundamental analysis before moving on to technical analysis as the need arises. To understand the difference between the two, you may find it helpful to think about technical analysis as analyzing charts while fundamental analysis looks at specific factors based on the underlying asset for the market that you are working in.

The core tenant of fundamental analysis is that there are related details out there that can tell the whole story when it comes to the market in question, while technical analysis believes that the only details that are required are those that relate to the price at the moment. As such, fundamental analysis is typically considered easier to master as it all relates to concepts less expressly related to understanding market movement exclusively. Meanwhile, technical analysis is typically faster because key fundamental analysis data often is only made publicly available on a strict and limited schedule, sometimes, only a few times a year—meaning that the availability for updating specific data is rather limited.

Fundamental Analysis Rules

The best time to use fundamental analysis is when you are looking to gain a broad idea of the state of the market as it stands and how that relates to the state of things in the near future when it comes time to actually trading successfully. Regardless of what market you are considering, the end goals are the same, find the most effective trade for the time period that you are targeting.

Establish a Baseline

In order to begin analyzing the fundamentals, the first thing that you will need to do is to create a baseline regarding the company's overall performance. In order to generate the most useful results possible, the first thing that you are going to need to do is to gather data both regarding the company in question as well as the related industry as a whole. When gathering macro data, it is important to keep in mind that no market is going to operate in a vacuum, which means the reasons behind specific market movement can be much more far-reaching than they first appear. Fundamental analysis works because of the stock market's propensity for patterns, which means that if you trace a specific market movement to the source, you will have a better idea of what to keep an eye on in the future. Furthermore, all industries go through several different phases where their penny stocks are going to be worth more or less overall based on general popularity. If the industry is producing many popular penny stocks, then overall volatility will be down while at the same time liquidity will be at an overall high.

Consider Worldwide Issues

Once you have a general grasp on the current phase you are dealing with, the next thing you will want to consider is anything that is going on in the wider world that will after the type of businesses you tend to favor in your penny stocks. Not being prepared for major paradigm shifts, especially in penny stocks where new companies come and go so quickly, means that you can easily miss out on massive profits and should be avoided at all costs. To ensure you are not blindsided by news you could have seen coming, it is important to look beyond the obvious issues that are consuming the 24-hour news cycle and dig deeper into the comings and goings of the nations that are going to most directly affect your particular subsection of penny stocks.

One important worldwide phenomenon that you will want to pay specific attention to is anything in the realm of technology as major paradigm shifts like the adoption of the smartphone, or the current move towards electric cars can create serious paradigm shifts.

Put It All Together

Once you have a clear idea of what the market should look like as well as what may be on the horizon, the next step is to put it all together to compare what has been and what might to what the current state of the market is. Not only will this give you a realistic idea of what other investors are going to do if certain events occur the way they have in the past, you will also be able to use these details in order to identify underlying assets that are currently on the cusp of generating the type of movement that you need if you want to utilize them via binary option trades. The best time to get on board with a new underlying asset is when it is nearing the end of the post-bust period or the end of a post-boom period depending on if you are going to place a call or a put. In these scenarios, you are going to have the greatest access to the freedom of the market and thus have access to the greatest overall allowable risk that you are going to find in any market. Remember, the amount of risk that you can successfully handle without an increase in the likelihood of failure is going to start decreasing as soon as the boom or bust phase begins in earnest, so it is important to get in as quickly as possible if you hope to maximize your profits.

Understand the Relative Strength of Any Given Trade
When an underlying asset is experiencing a boom phase, the strength of its related fundamentals is going to be what determines the way that other investors are going to act when it comes to binary options trading. Keeping this in mind, it then stands to reason that the earlier a given underlying asset is in a particular boom phase, the stronger the market surrounding it is going to be. Remember, when it comes to fundamental analysis, what an underlying asset looks like at the moment isn't nearly as important as what it is likely to look like in the future, and the best way to determine those details is by keeping an eye on the past.

Quantitative Fundamental Analysis
The sheer volume of data and a large number of varying numbers found in the average company's financial statements can easily be intimidating and bewildering for conscientious investors who are digging into them for the first time. Once you get the hang of them, however, you will quickly find that they are a goldmine of information when it comes to determining how likely a company is to continue producing reliable dividends in the future. At their most basic, a

company's financial statements disclose the information relating to its financial performance over a set period of time. Unlike with qualitative concepts, financial statements provide cold, hard facts about a company that is rarely open for interpretation.

Here are some of the important financial statements:

Balance Sheet

A balance sheet shows a detailed record of all of a company's equity, liabilities, and assets for a given period of time. A balance sheet shows a balance to the financial structure of a company by dividing the company's equity by the combination of shareholders and liabilities in order to determine its current assets. In this case, assets represent the resources that the company is actively in control of at a specific point in time. It can include things like buildings, machinery, inventory, cash, and more. It will also show the total value of any financing that has been used to generate those assets. Financing can come from either equity or liabilities.

Liabilities include debt that must be paid back eventually while equity—in this case, measures the total amount of money that its owners have put into the business. This can include profits from previous years, which are known collectively as retained earnings.

Income Statement

While the balance sheet can be thought of as a snapshot of the fundamental economic aspects of the company, the income statement takes a closer look at the performance of the company exclusively for a given timeframe. There is no limit to the length of time an income statement considers, which means you could see them generated month to month, or even day to day; however, the most common type used by public companies are either annual or quarterly. Income statements provide information on profit, expenses, and revenues that resulted from the business that took place over a specific period of time.

Cash Flow Statement

The cash flow statement frequently shows all of the cash outflow and inflow for the company over a given period of time. The cash flow statement often focuses on operating cash flow, which is the cash that will be generated by day to day business operations.

It will also include any cash that is available from investing, which is often used as a means of investing in assets along with any cash that might have been generated by long-term asset sales or the sale of a secondary business that the company previously owned. Cash due to financing is another name for money that is paid off or received based on issuing or borrowing funds. The cash flow statements are quite important as it is often more difficult for businesses to manipulate it when compared to many other types of financial documents. While accountants can manipulate earnings with ease, it is much more difficult to fake having access to cash in the bank where there is none that really exists. This is why many savvy investors consider the cash flow statement the most reliable way to measure a specific company's performance.

Finding the Details

While tracking down all the disparate financial statements on the company that you are considering purchasing stock in can be cumbersome, the Securities and Exchange Commission (SEC) requires all publicly traded companies to submit regular filings outlining all of their financial activities including a variety of different financial statements. This also includes information such as managerial discussions, reports from auditors, deep dives into the operations and prospects of upcoming years, and more. These types of details can all be found in the 10-K filing that each company is required to file every year, along with the 10-Q filing that they must send out once per quarter. Both types of documents can be found online, both at the corporate website for the company as well as on the SEC website. As the version that hits the corporate site doesn't need to be complete, it is best to visit SEC.gov and get to know the Electronic Data Gathering, Analysis, and Retrieval system (EDGAR), which automates the process of indexing, validating, collecting, forward and accepting submissions. As this system was designed in the mid-90s, however, it is important to dedicate some time to learning the process as it is more cumbersome than 20 years of user interface advancements have to lead you to expect.

Qualitative Fundamental Analysis

Qualitative factors are generally less tangible and include things like its name recognition, the patents it holds, and the quality of its board members. The first thing that you are going to want to do when you catch wind of a company that might be worth following up on is to check out its business model, which is more or less a generalization of how it makes its money. You can typically find these sorts of details on the company website or in its 10-K filing.

Competitive Advantage

It is also important to consider the various competitive advantages that the company you have your eye on might have over its competition. Companies that are going to be successful in the long-term are always going to have an advantage over their competition in one of two ways. They can either have better operational effectiveness or improved strategic positioning. Operational effectiveness is the name given to doing the same things as the competition but in a more efficient and effective way.

Strategic positioning occurs when a company gains an edge by doing things that nobody else is doing.

Changes to the Company

In order to properly narrow down your search, you will typically find the most reliable results when it comes to companies that have recently seen major changes to their corporate structure as it is these types of changes that are likely to ultimately precede events that are more likely to see the company jump to the next level. The specifics of what happened in this instance are nearly as important as the fact that statistically speaking, 95 percent of companies that experience this type of growth started with a significant change to the status quo.

Chapter 4: Technical Analysis

When working with technical analysis, you are always going to want to remember that it functions because of the belief that the way the price of a given trade has moved in the past is going to be an equally reliable metric for determining what it is likely to do again in the future. Regardless of which market you choose to focus on, you'll find that there is always more technical data available than you will ever be able to parse without quite a significant amount of help. Luckily, you won't be sifting through the data all on your own, and you will have numerous technical tools, including things such as charts, trends, and indicators to help you push your success rates to new heights. While some of the methods you will be asked to apply might seem arcane at first, the fact of the matter is that all you are essentially doing is looking to determine future trends along with their relative strengths. This, in turn, is crucial to your long-term success and will make each of your trades more reliable practically every single time. Understand core assumptions:

Technical analysis is all about measuring the relative value of a particular trade or underlying asset by using available tools to find otherwise invisible patterns that, ideally, few other people have currently noticed. When it comes to using technical analysis properly, you are always going to need to assume three things are true. First and foremost, the market ultimately discounts everything; second, trends will always be an adequate predictor of price; third, history is bound to repeat itself when given enough time to do so. Technical analysis believes that the current price of the underlying asset in question is the only metric that matters when it comes to looking into the current state of things outside of the market, specifically because everything else is already automatically factored in when the current price is set as it is. As such, to accurately use this type of analysis, all you need to know is the current price of the potential trade and the greater economic climate as a whole. Those who practice technical analysis are then able to interpret what the price is suggesting about market sentiment in order to make predictions about where the price of a given cryptocurrency is going to go in the future. This is possible due to the fact that pricing movements aren't random. Instead, they follow trends that appear in both the short and the long-term.

Determining these trends in advance is key to using technical analysis successfully because all trends are likely to repeat themselves over time, thus the use of historical charts in order to determine likely trends in the future. When it comes to technical analysis, the "what" is always going to be more important than the "why." That is, the fact that the price moved in a specific way is far more important to a technical analyst then why it made that particular movement. Supply and demand should always be consulted, but beyond that, there are likely too many variables to make it worthwhile to consider all of them as opposed to their results.

Price Charts

Technical analysis is all about the price chart, which is a chart with an x- and y-axis. The price is measured along the vertical axis, and the time is measured via the horizontal axis. There are numerous different types of price charts that different types of traders prefer; these include the point and figure chart, the Renko chart, the Kagi chart, the Heikin-Ashi chart, the bar chart, the candlestick chart, the line chart, and the tick chart. However, the ones you will need to concern yourself with at first are going to be included in any forex trading platform software and are the bar chart, the candlestick chart, the line chart, and the point-and-click chart, which is why they are outlined in greater detail below:

Line Chart

Of all the various types of charts, the line chart is the simplest because it only presents price information in the form of closing prices in a fixed time span. The lines that give it its name are created when the various closing price points are then connected with a line. When looking at a line chart, it is important to keep in mind that they will not be able to provide an accurate visual representation of the range that individual points reached, which means you won't be able to see either opening prices or those that were high or low prior to close.

Regardless, the closing point is important always to consider, which is why this chart is so commonly referred to by technical traders of all skill levels.

Bar Chart

A bar chart takes the information that can be found in a line chart and expands upon it in a number of interesting ways. For starters, the chart is made using a number of vertical lines that provide information on various data points. The top and bottom of the line can then be thought of as the high and low of the trading timeframe, respectively, while the closing price is also indicated with a dash on the right side of the bar. Furthermore, the point where the currency price opened is indicated via a dash and will show up on the left side of the bar in question.

Candlestick Chart

A candlestick chart is similar to a bar chart, though the information it provides is much more detailed overall. Like a bar chart, it includes a line to indicate the range for the day; however, when you are looking at a candlestick chart, you will notice a wide bar near the vertical line, which indicates the degree of the difference the price saw throughout the day. If the price that the stock is trading at increases overall for the day, then the candlestick will often be clear—while if the price has decreased, then the candlestick is going to be read.

Point and Figure Chart

While seen less frequently than some of the other types of charts, a point and figure chart has been around for nearly a century and can still be useful in certain situations today. This chart can accurately reflect the way price is going to move, though it won't indicate timing or volume. It can be thought of as a pure indicator of price with the excessive noise surrounding the market muted, ensuring nothing is skewed. A point-and-figure chart is noticeable because it is made up of X's and O's rather than lines and points. The X's will indicate points where positive trends occurred, while the O's will indicate periods of downward movement. You will also notice numbers and letters listed along the bottom of the chart, which corresponds to months as well as dates. This type of chart will also make it clear how much the price is going to have to move in order for an X to become an O or an O to become an X.

Trend or Range

When it comes to using technical analysis successfully, you will want to determine early on if you are more interested in trading based on the trends you find or on the range. While they are both properties related to price, these two concepts are very different in practice, which means you will want to choose one to emphasize over the other. If you decide to trade according to trend, then you are more interested in going with the flow and choosing stocks to trade while everyone else is having the same idea.

Chart Patterns to Be Aware of

Flags and Pennants

Both flags and pennants show retracement—that is, deviations that will be visible in the short term in relation to the primary trend. Retracement results in no breakout occurring from either the resistance or support levels, but this won't matter as the security will also not be following the dominant trend. The lack of breakout means this trend will be relatively short term.

The resistance and support lines of the pennant occur within a larger trend and converge so precisely that they practically form a point. A flag is essentially the same except that the resistance and support lines from the flag will be essentially parallel instead. If you are looking for them, both flags and pennants are more likely to be found in the mid-section of the primary phase of the trend. They can last up to two weeks before being absorbed back into the primary trend line. They are typically associated with falling volume, which means that if you notice a flag or a pennant and the volume is not falling, then you are more likely actually seeing a reversal, which is an actually changing trend instead of a simple retracement.

Head Above Shoulders Formation

If you are looking for indicators of how long any one particular trend is likely to continue, then looking for a grouping of three peaks in a price chart, known as the head above shoulders formation, can indicate a bearish pattern moving forward. The peaks to the left and to the right of the primary peak, also known as the shoulders, should be somewhat smaller than the head peak and also connect at a specific price.

This price is known as the neckline, and when it reaches the right shoulder, the price will likely then plunge noticeably. The inverse head and shoulders (or head and shoulders bottom) is a sign that the price of the security in question is about to rise in the face of an existing downward trend. It typically forms at the lowest overall price of the trend. Based on the analysis of the peak-and-trough pattern from the Dow Theory, an upward trend is then seen as indicative of a series of successive rising troughs and peaks. Meanwhile, a downward trend is indicative of a series of lower peaks and deeper troughs. If this is the case, then the head and shoulders pattern represents a weakening of an existing trend as the troughs and peaks deteriorate. The head and shoulders top forms at the peaks of an upwards trend and signals that a reversal is often forthcoming through a process of four steps. The first of these starts with the creation of the far-left shoulder, which can be formed when the cryptocurrency reaches a new high before dropping to a new low. This is then followed by the formation of the head, which occurs when the security reaches an even higher high before retracing back to the low found in the left shoulder. Finally, the right shoulder is formed from a high that is lower than the high found in the head, countered by a retracement back to the low of the left shoulder. The pattern is then completed when the price drops back below the neckline. The inverse head-and-shoulders pattern is the exact opposite of the head-and-shoulders top, as it signals that the security is set to make an upward move. Often coming at the end of a downtrend, the inverse head and shoulders are considered to be a reversal pattern, as the security typically heads higher after the completion of the pattern. In both instances, the price dipping below the neckline signals the true reversal of the trend in question, which means the security will now be moving in the opposite direction. This breakout point is often the ideal point to go either short or long depending. It is important to keep in mind, however, that the security is unlikely to continue smoothly in the direction the pattern suggests. As such, you will want to keep an eye out for what is called a throwback move.

Gann

While not universally trusted, Gann indicators have been used by traders for decades and remain a useful way of determining the direction a specific currency is likely to move next. Gann angles are used to determine certain elements of the chart include price, time, and pattern, which makes it easier to determine the future, past, and even present of the market as well as how that information will determine the future of the price.

While you could be forgiven for thinking they are similar to trend lines, Gann angles are actually a different beast entirely. They are, in fact, a series of diagonal lines that move at a fixed rate and can likely be generated by your trading program. When they are compared to a trend line, you will notice the Gann angle makes it possible for users to determine a true price at a specific point in the future, assuming the current trend continues at its current strength. Due to the fact that all times exist on the same line, the Gann angle can then also be used to predict resistance, support, and direction strength as well as the timing on bottoms and tops as well. Gann angles are typically used to determine likely points of support and resistance, and it is easy to get started with as it only requires the trade to determine the proper scale for the chart before drawing in the relevant Gann angles from the primary bottoms to the tops. Essentially, this means that they make it less complicated for the trader to properly frame the market and thus makes it easier for them to predict the way the market is likely to move in the future based on the way it is currently moving in the predetermined framework.

Angles that indicate a positive trend determine support and angles that show a downward trend outline resistance. This means that by understanding the accurate angle of a chart, the trader can more easily determine the best time to buy or sell far more simply than what could otherwise be the case. When utilizing Gann angles, it is crucial that you keep in mind all the different things that can potentially cause the market to change between specific angles.

Cup and Handle Formation

The "cup and handle" formation most commonly appears if given security reaches a peak price before dropping off significantly for a prolonged amount of time. Sooner than later, however, the security will rebound, which is the perfect time to buy. This is an indicator of a trend that is rapidly rising, which means you are going to want to take advantage of it as soon as possible before you miss out. The handle will form on the cup when those who purchased the security at the previous high-water mark and couldn't wait any longer begin to sell, which makes new investors interested who then begin to buy as well. This type of formation does not typically form quickly, and indeed, has been known to take a year or more to become visible. Ideally, you will then be able to take advantage of this trend as soon as the handle starts to form. If you see the cup and handle forming, you will still want to consider any other day to day patterns that may be interfering with the overall trend as they are going to go a long way when it comes to determining the actual effectiveness of buying in at a specific point.

Trend Lines

Trend lines represent the typical direction that a given underlying asset is likely to move in and, thus, can be very beneficial for traders to highlight prior to trading.

This is easier said than done, though, due to the high degree of volatility that assets of all types experience on a regular basis. As such, you will find it much more useful to consider only the highs and lows that the underlying asset experiences as this will make it far easier to determine a workable pattern. Once you have determined the highs and the lows for the underlying asset, it then becomes much easier to determine if the highs are increasing while the lows are decreasing or vice versa. You will also want to remain alert to the possibility of sidewise trends, where the price doesn't move much of anywhere, as this is a sign that you should avoid trading for the time being. When watching the trend lines, you will likely notice that the price movement of a given underlying asset tends to bounce off the same high and low points time after time.

These are what are known as resistance and support levels, and identifying them makes it easier for you to determine the supply and demand of the coin in question. The support level is the level that the price is unlikely to drop below because there are always going to be traders who are willing to buy at that point, driving demand back up. Once the price reaches the point where traders feel the price is unlikely to go any higher, they start to sell, and a level of resistance is created.

Moving Averages

The most commonly used confirmation tool is one that is referred to as the moving average convergence divergence or MACD for short. This tool measures the amount of difference that there is between two averages that have been smoothed to minimize ancillary noise. The difference between the two results is then further smoothed by the process before then being matched against the moving average that it relates to as well. If the resulting smoothed average is still greater than the existing moving average, then you can be sure that the positive trend you were chasing exists. Meanwhile, if the smoothed average ends up below the existing moving average than any negative trends will be confirmed instead. The moving average convergence divergence indicator is a type of oscillating indicator that primarily moves between zero and the centerline. If the MACD value is high, then you can assume the related underlying asset is nearly overbought, and if the value is low, then the stock is nearly oversold. The MACD chart is typically based on a combination of several EMAs. These averages can be based on any timeframe, though the most common is the 12-26-9 chart. This chart is typically broken into multiple parts, the first of which is the 26-day and 12-day chart. Mixing up the EMAs will allow you to more accurately gauge the level of momentum that the trend you are tracking is experiencing. If the 12-day EMA ends up above the 26-day EMA, then you can assume the underlying stock in on an uptrend, and the reverse indicates a downtrend. If the 12-day EMA increases more quickly than the 26-day EMA, then the uptrend is going to be even more well-pronounced.

However, if the 12-day EMA moves closer to the 26-day EMA, then you can safely assume that it is starting to slow, and the momentum is waning, which means it is going to take the trend with it. The MACD uses the EMA by considering the difference between them once they are plotted out. If the 26-day and the 12-day are the same, then the MACD equals out to 0. If the 12-day ends up at a higher point than the 26-day, then you can assume the MACD is positive; if not, it will be negative. The greater the difference between the two, the greater the difference between the MAACD line and zero. From there, you will then want to take into account the 9-day EMA as well. The 9-day EMA is different in that it determines the trend of the AMCD line as opposed to that of the stock price. As such, if the 9-day EMA smooths out the movement of the MACD line, the results are going to be far more manageable. If the result then generates a trend that indicates a negative amount of divergence, then you can be quite certain that the positive trend that is currently taking place is ultimately going to hit a level of resistance that it simply won't be able to overcome.

Chapter 5: Mindset

Day traders have specific character traits that make them prosperous and able to handle the stress that comes from dealing with the stock market and the fast-paced environment. It is not a secret that this job is hard and stressful, but what is a secret are the character traits that are needed by a broker so that they do not crack under pressure. 90% of the investors who trade on the stock market as a day trader will not make it.

Traits That Set You Apart from Those That Have Failed

Winning traders have several character traits that help them be successful. Below, I will go over a few of these traits that can set you apart from those that have failed miserably.

Rise Early and Shine

Waking up at an early time is very crucial to your day trading abilities. You do not want to rush your routine for your pre-trading hours. When doing day trading, you are able to make quick decisions when faced with pressure, and it is very crucial for you to be fully awake as well as an alert when the market opens. When you go on a walk an hour prior to working, this will increase your endorphins and give you a natural high that will carry you through the day with extra energy. This gets your blood moving and helps you get alert quickly.

Prior to the Market, Do Some Research

If you have stocks that have just been added to your watch list, then you will need to do the research prior to the market opening. To trade a stock, you should be fully informed about why it is moving. Being inadequately prepared can show up in how you trade for that day. You should trade with confidence and a little less uncertainty, especially if you prepare yourself completely prior to investing or trading the stocks. You need to know the key support levels as well as the intraday resistance that is listed on the charts daily.

Ensure That Trade Plans Are Followed

Prepare a plan for all the scenarios that could arise with the stocks that are on your watch list. They are well informed of where they will stop out, enter, and take profits all before they enter for the trade. Without a trading plan, you will be more stressed out, and it will present as a more difficult accomplishment. You will need to prepare in advance.

Investors Know That Trading Every Day Is Not Necessary

A winning trader can tell you that every day will not be positive, and some days are not good for trading opportunities. If you cannot recognize these days, then you will fail. When trading, you can win or lose, knowing when to step back is necessary.

To grow your account, it's just as much about avoiding the losses as well as the wins. Recognize the criteria that make it an A+ stock opportunity. This helps you to recognize when to sit on your hands.

Reflect on the Trades That You Have Purchased

If it does not get measured, then it does not get improved. Successful traders will track their trades religiously. Examine the wins and see what each one has that connects them. Then, use that analysis to replicate this for future purchases. For those trades that are losses, you will need to analyze the common connections and avoid making those same mistakes. Eliminate the habits which lead you to the losing trade, which is outside your plan of trading. Not every single losing trade is an actual bad trade. It is unavoidable for a losing trade not to happen, so remember that it will happen—just make sure you are prepared for it. If you lose due to a rule of trading, then you will need to figure out why, and then you can make changes to prevent it from continuing to happen. Now that I have gone over ways that successful day traders stay successful, I will discuss other ways that show the mentality of a successful day trader and how to fix the mental game that is helping them increase their profitability.

Small Losses Happen — Embrace Them

When working as a day trader, you will deal with losses. This is customary; however, you need to be able to handle it. Losses can impact your emotional stability, and it can make a big dent in your confidence. You must recognize the triggers that lead to loss and can create a revenge trade, as well as some micro-managing that will influence us to make improper procedure changes or even dump a stock that we should hold on to. By embracing small losses, you will be able to fix the trigger of loss. A small loss simply means that you are testing the waters and doing something right. If the losses are sandwiched between some bigger wins, you will be able to handle them easier.

Consider Your Next 100 Trades

Many traders can live or die by the actions of their trades, or the need to make their next trade. Over long-term trade should be analyzed for the overall focus, and this should not be connected to the gains or losses of that time period, but the overall time period that you own the stock. Do not stress out because of the loss that you receive. In the grand picture of building your trading portfolio, one loss can be meaningless. Instead, consider obsessing about those 100 trades that come next. This can keep you focused on something that is not pertinent. The short-term is what you should be focusing on; however, you would be focusing on the process. When trading for probability, you will experience losses for good trades. If you experience a drawdown, then you are not poorly trading your stocks. Do not let a positive trade with short terms that are poor impact the results of the psychology of the trade.

Reduce Your Risks to Fight Back the Fear

Placing trades can be scary. When you place your cash in the hands of another, you are stressed and worried. It is hard to trust that you will not lose it. Anyone that has been practicing trading, who then goes out on their own, must know how it feels to fear losing money. Fear can manifest into your trading strategy and keep you in a losing streak. It makes it harder to pull the trigger on a trade than it would be if you were not so fearful. Reduce your risk if fear is showing up for you when trying to trade. If your loss is small, then you will be less scared to trade. If your normal risk is $200 per trade, then you will need to have a lower $100 trade to feel less pressure and fear. Once you start to do this without fear, you can increase your trade amount by up to $200 again. All these tips show how the mental psyche of a day trader works its best.

You also need to put into context things that can negatively affect the day trader within his own mindset belief system. Below, I have included several mindset beliefs that can affect how the day trader will negatively impact their trading accouterment.

Fear That They Are Missing Some Great Move
As a day trader, they are conditioned to stalk the market for fear of missing some big break; however, they become more like a two-year-old who does not want to go to bed. They sit and sit, with fear that they will miss some amazing experience that will take place on the market. They fear that while they are away, the market will continue to run without them, and this creates anxiety about the loss of opportunity. Due to this fear, the day trader may find themselves jumping into a buy simply because he fears the loss. This can also happen when the market does free-fall.

This is an easy-to-notice point on the chart with the high or low within the print of the day. It is just not enough, even $250. The day trader is churning out a profit of $250 a day from his $10,000 account. This is due to his steady strategy and system that he has been implementing; although he is managing and trading for the good, he is not happy. He considers that $250 is not enough and that $500 would be much better for him. This is the point that greed becomes the deciding factor in his future profits. At this point, greed takes the wheel and starts to decide what to buy and when to sell. This creates a trigger in his brain that ripples into making all kinds of trading mistakes. He overtrades and stops sticking to his parameters.

He experiences rampant emotions that resemble an angry football enthusiast, such as yelling at the screen. This is the culminating downfall of a lot of day traders. This is the time that a day trader will refuse a profit of $300 simply because it is not bigger and better. At this point, his winning trades start to turn into losing trades, and his $10,000 account decreases to $5,000 in a matter of months.

The Loving Feeling That Those Who Succeed Experience and Now Create a Need to Continue That Feeling

For instance, let's say that the day trader has an amazing day on the market. Everything is going their way. They are having episodes of minimal stress elevation. This day is amazing in all ways.

This overwhelming feeling of joy and warmth can create a feeling that is addictive. The day trader rarely feels this kind of emotional high, so they try to recreate it over and over again. They begin to add to their already existing positions. They double and triple the investment. This is similar to many who are super happy with his family. He enjoys their company, and it brings him boundless joy. He decides that he needs to feel this more, so he heads out to find another family to add to his already existing joy. As we all know, this can only end badly, so the resulting factor of over joyful and ecstatic for a day trader can create a need to feel that over and over again and loses it all trying to reach that high. So how can you use these negative triggers to your advantage? Below, I have included a breakdown of how to use this to your advantage, whether it is you who are experiencing these emotions or someone else you trade with.

When someone losses in a trade, the money from the trade simply goes to another trader's account. What this means is that these negative emotional, mental blocks can become your payday.

Use Your Excitement for Good

Instead of doubling or tripling down your investment, create a double stop to block these urges. This can be used in many ways. For instance, consider how much time you could spend in a private villa on a tropical island. Then, place your trailing point stop 2 for 20 contracts. Then, double the size of the position you are currently in. This means that as long as that trade is going higher, you will stay; however, if the market turns, I am removed from the position with a nice profit, and I get short on contracts that total 10.

This will use the market dynamics for emotions and take a clear and clean advantage. This sell-off will only occur from the trades of another day that succumbed to the emotional reactions for buying at the top because they feared losing out on the move altogether. It can also be contributed to the fear of missing the euphoria that you get in a win and when you have that winning position. After the market turns, the day traders that bought will be the fuel that needs to move down, and they will dump the position once the loss is too great.

Consider What a Newbie Would Do and Then Snatch Them at the Low

Visualize what the newbie day trader would be doing at this exact position. For instance, you entered at a specific point, at what point is the pain point for a newbie? If the S&P movement was 6 points with no retracements that were meaningful, then this would become UNCLE for the majority of day traders. Imagine that this is the pain point of the newbie, and after this point, swoop in and buy up the stocks.

Look for Those Ticks

Watch for those ticks that will come along. If the readings are over +1000 tick readings or -1000 tick readings below, then you will need to fade out your moves. If there is a +1000 tick move and I have already gone, then I start to exit the move with a short position. However, the reverse of this is also true for a stopping point of 4 ½ and a target point of 3. If neither is hit after 25 minutes, exit this trade at the price that is current.

High Five Equals Sell

When I see traders going around the room giving others a high five for a good trade, I take that as my cue to sell.

This is a signal that I have noticed comes from extreme emotional euphoria and means that the market is in a good spot.

Traits That Will Ensure You Succeed as a Day Trader

So how can you ensure that you will be successful at day trading? And what does it take to be successful? There are 3 psychological quirks that will have an enormous impact on your day trading. As a day trader, we can face some troubling problems, and most of these are going to be ones that we do not even know we have. Some of our human characteristics will affect how we trade and, in the end, our bottom line. Although there are several that can affect us, the five most important and detrimental are listed below, with a breakdown of how they do affect us with our day trading. These can place a block in the way of us achieving the goals that we have set for our finances.

There Are Several Enemies That We Do Not Even Recognize and Most of It Is Ourselves

When you deal with day trading, there will be moments that we will err, and this can be fixed, but only if we analyze it and make attempts to adjust the err. If you have exited from a trade too early, you will find that by adjusting your criteria, you will be able to make a better decision. Make adjustments to this error by looking for an indicator that is different or takes a longer amount of time to make the trade. If your trading strategy is solid, but you still find yourself losing some money, you will need to examine yourself and the psychology that we apply to the solution. When dealing with your own inner workings, your view is often skewed due to being so personally connected. You may not have the ability to fix the problem that is creating the loss. Your true problem could be created by a clouded mindset that is biased at best. There may be some trivialities that are superficial, and they are creating the discrepancies within your trading ability. For example, you have a trading strategy but never stick to it. So, this person is on a continuous adjustment period, and nothing is working because it is not given the proper time to work nor the right amount of credit. By sticking with a strategy, you will be able to check your resolve for solving the equation. Your success record will increase by applying one specific approach that has a solid framework and foundation.

There Is Power in Awareness

Being aware of the possibilities that could be creating the issues will help us to adjust them later. By creating actions which we can adjust over time, we can begin to see how each action is creating loss and change the habits that are contributing to this loss. We will overcome the problems that arise and be able to eliminate these problems. Since there is no magic plan that will make everyone a winner, this is where knowing who you are and adjust non-serving traits will come in handy. Psychology states that by being aware of our pitfalls, we can adjust them and improve upon who we are. This rings true for the day trader as well. Changing our habits and creating a profit will help us to be better at our day trading.

Bias Sensory-Derived

By compiling information from the experiences around us, we gain opinions, and this can create a bias with which will dictate how we operate. This will allow the investor to function as well as learn behaviors. However, as we understand that this is forming behaviors or opinions that would be factual in bases and evidence shows, it is often not the case. For instance, a trader who watches the news and bases his knowledge on the reports will believe he has stripped the opinions from the broadcaster and is going on pure facts when he, in fact, is not. If our sources are all biased, then how can we expect our own thoughts and opinions not to be biased based. There are always two sides to every story, and biased is the basis with which these stories have differences. Constant exposure to a biased opinion can, in turn, make you believe that this biased opinion is your own truth, even if it is not factual. Those raised to believe that dogs are scary will, no matter what, always believe that dogs are scary even if there are no bases for the truth. Since there is no counterevidence to dispute the bias, the opinion becomes their truth as it is the only available information that has heard, even if it is biased.

Vagueness and Ambiguity Are Avoided

This can also be known as the fear of the unknown. The avoidance of what is possible to occur, even if it has not. The avoidance of things that is not clear to our thoughts. This avoidance can prevent even a seasoned investor from doing things that would increase their profit line and keep them locked in that state of loss. Some traders have actually found that they fear the process of making money, and this rings true for many entrepreneurs as well.

This is not a conscious fear; it is something that is deep within. The fear of the taxes that they will owe can be so daunting that they will fear themselves into losses. Expanding the zone with which they are comfortable can create blocks and worry that sends them into downward spirals of loss. This creates patterns of sabotage that is done by self. This can also create a bias about which industry they will enter, making them fear trading in any other industry than the one they are most familiar with. The fact that this industry is declining will be irrelevant to them. They will simply continue to pump money into a dead horse. They avoid the chance of winning a profit by staying in familiar investments and associate this with uncertainty.

This can also be seen when the investor holds onto winners less time than they should and sells the loser way later than they should have. If the price fluctuates, they struggle to face the facts of the movement and then fail at determining the appropriate action. They also will fear the experience of loss and begin to make drastic and risky decisions that will place them in jeopardy of losing it all. When they deviate from the rational, they will then become irrational and start acting accordingly. This then causes the investor to miss the gains that potentially could make them increase their wealth.

The Anticipation Is Tangible

Anticipation is immensely powerful and can create stress as well as worry and excitement. Since anticipation is connected to "I want" or "I need," the mentality is self-serving. Most of the time, our anticipations will take place way in the future, and sometimes, they will take place within a few weeks. Although these can be far in the future, they create an emotional enjoyment that becomes addicting. This addiction can become the focus of how we want to feel always, and this becomes the achievement instead of the reaction. This can limit our ability to see that the payout is now and block us from taking the payment with anticipation that there is a bigger one coming, and eventually, we lose the money altogether or make ways less than we should have. Easy money can find its way to our door.

It is more than likely that it will be grabbed by the ones that think calm and collected about their trading values. We can begin to fall into an anticipatory feeling that becomes the consolation and not the reaction to the prize. Watching the changing of hands for billions of dollars can be exciting, but if the confidence is not there, we can miss our opportunity to benefit from this changing of hands. This is like us subconsciously telling ourselves that we are better off dreaming and that this dream is better than the real thing. Wanting to become profitable has become the goal instead of actually being profitable. By understanding what is affecting our trading, we can begin to make changes for the better. The psychology of day trading can be an extensive research project in and of itself, but awareness of how we respond and what our actions are can bring us to understand better why we are at this point. One way to adjust our psychology is to remove the bias that is influencing our decisions.

Use charts, since they do not lie. Remain objective and become focused on the strategies that will bring profit instead of the movement of price. Avoid others' well-thought-out opinions and create some of your own. Gain knowledge of how the market moves and shakes. This will help you overcome the fear and the greed that will arise during a day trading career. Unknown territory can create mistakes, so avoid the unknown by researching and gaining knowledge. Base all of our actions on an objectively sound decision that is made with knowledge instead of fear.

Chapter 6: Stock Trading Strategies

Investing successfully over a lifetime requires the use of strategy. Why? It's because participating in the financial markets is never a sure thing. There is an inherent risk involved. Sure, you could gamble every now and then—but you can never expect to get lucky in the markets every time. You need a proven methodology that can stack the odds of success in your favor. And that is what this section focuses on. We will discuss everything you will need to know about strategy as well as a few good ones that you can use. You will also take a small test designed to help you identify the best strategy you can apply to your stock market investment. Let's go.

Trading vs. Investing

Let me first begin by explaining the difference between these two. This is important because your approach to the stock markets will fall under these two; every strategy out there is either one that belongs to trading or investing. Therefore, it is important that you are able to tell the difference.

What Is Trading?

Trading is what I have referred up to this point as speculation. It is a way of seeking short-term gains from the financial markets by attempting to predict the future movement of prices of a financial instrument such as a stock. Traders are not concerned with the intrinsic value of an asset or its long-term performance. The only concern of a trader is how he or she can make a profit from the movement of prices.

Since traders are mostly concerned with the movement of prices, the classic tools used are technical analysis tools and trading systems (we will look at technical analysis later on). A trader will rely on things like charts, trend lines, moving averages, and many others. These tools are built into any trading software you will get out there. The beauty of becoming a trader or speculator is that you can make a profit whether the market goes up or down; a trader can buy or go long when the market is going up and sell or go short when the market goes down. Since traders operate with this kind of flexibility, they are thought to have access to more opportunities as compared to investors. Based on the time a trader can hold an investment alone, traders can be put into four different categories.

They are:

- Position traders: These are traders that hold positions in the market for months to even years on end.
- Swing traders: Swing traders can hold a position in the market for weeks or even months.
- Day traders: These are traders who hold positions for no longer than a day.
- Scalpers: Scalpers get in and out of positions within minutes and, sometimes, even seconds. Scalpers can execute several transactions in a typical day – sometimes, even more than a hundred.

What Is Investing?

Investing, on the other hand, is very different. Unlike traders, investors are more concerned with the long-term performance of an asset. If it is a company, as is the case in stocks, they will be looking to see how the company will perform in the next five years, ten years, or more. They are not interested in making a profit by the end of the day, week, or month. Investors also tend to operate in only one direction – the buy-side. It is rare that an investor will look to short a market. The belief of a trader is that even though a market may move up and down if the asset is a good one, it will eventually go up. So investors tend to sit through up and downward price movements with the hopes of eventually turning a profit. Another difference between investors and speculators is that investors tend to rely on fundamentals to perform their analysis. Technical analysis has little value to investors since they don't make their decisions based on price. They are interested in the intrinsic value. So you will find an investor paying more attention to the profit earned this quarter instead of something like prices breaking below a trend line. It is important to note that since traders need to track prices more frequently, there is more work involved in trading. So many independent traders take up trading either as a full-time job or part-time. But the job needs focus and high competence. Investing, on the other hand, is a more passive income activity. If you are busy, you may want to choose to invest since you will rarely need to stay in touch with prices every single minute, hour, or day. If your plan is to exit your investment in 10 years, tracking prices the way a speculator does is a waste of time. You are better off taking a vacation or focusing on your day-job. There you have it. Now, you know the difference between the two. Let us now take a look at how you can find good stocks to invest in using both fundamental and technical analysis.

How to Find Good Stocks to Invest in

In the stock marketplace, there are both good and bad places to put your money. Your main job as someone who wants to make money in stocks is to come up with an appropriate strategy that helps you select the best opportunities that are more likely to turn a profit for you. I say "likely" to highlight an important point. As a stock market participant, you can never expect to make money on all your transactions. Some will make money, and some won't. Nobody ever makes money 100% of the time. Not even the best of the best. A good strategy is that which helps you make more money than you lose. That said, let us start with technical analysis.

Technical Analysis — Short-Term Trading Strategies

Previously, I mentioned that technical analysis is mostly used by speculators. Investors may use it at times, but that happens on very rare occasions and for very specific reasons – such as when designing an exit strategy. I am going to give you a short introduction to technical analysis. Technical analysis is a deep subject that could actually take up a whole book on its own, but I am guessing you have little interest in that. You are only interested in knowing what is necessary to help you get started in trading as quickly as you can. After covering the basics, I am going to show you a few simple technical trading strategies that you can use to make money in the markets. So let's start from the beginning.

Really, What Is Technical Analysis?

Technical analysis is simply a way of evaluating an investment and spotting opportunities that makes use of patterns identified from the statistical analysis of price movement. These patterns are identified using technical tools such as charts and technical indicators.

Charts

Charts are the most basic way of representing price information about a particular financial asset such as a stock. And when it comes to that, there are three main types of charts that you will need to know of as an investor or speculator. These charts are found on literally every trading software in existence.

About Technical Indicators

Charts by themselves don't provide you with much to work with. If you intend to develop a reliable trading strategy - or system, as it is sometimes called – you will need to add technical indicators as well.

So what are technical indicators, really?

They are simply tools that rely on mathematical equations and calculations and are used to evaluate price data about a particular financial instrument. In my experience, indicators mainly serve as confirmation signals in technical trading systems. There are many indicators out there—hundreds of them—perhaps even thousands. Knowing all about them is never important. You simply need to get acquainted with a few common ones that can help you design the strategy or system that you want. Let's look at them:

- Trend lines - The first indicator is a trend line. I wouldn't label it as an indicator, per se, as it isn't constructed using mathematical calculations. A better term would be a charting tool. So, what is it? A trend line is simply a line that is usually drawn across two or more points across a trading chart. It is one of the simplest and most common tools in trading, and certainly one of the most important. The goal of drawing this line is to determine the predominant trend in a particular market. As you can see from the diagram below, the trend-line has been drawn, indicating that the trend is upwards. Such a trend line is always called an "Uptrend line" It is important to note that trend lines are usually drawn below the wicks of the candlesticks for accuracy reasons.

- Moving averages - Then, we have a class of indicators called moving averages. These are indicators used to calculate the averages of the prices of a stock or other security over a certain period of time. They are frequently used as "automated trend lines" in many trading strategies. They are automated because the computer calculates the averages for you and plots the line. You must know that there are two types of moving averages: simple moving average (SMA) and the exponential moving average (EMA). Simple moving averages track the averages over a much longer period of time, while exponential moving averages track prices that are more recent. When it comes to tracking the trend, EMAs are considered to be much more effective than SMAs. For example, here is a chart showing an EMA with a period setting of 200 tracking an uptrend on the stock of General Electric.

- Commodity Channel Index (CCI) - We also have an indicator called the commodity channel index. This indicator is mostly used to track overbought or oversold conditions in the market. Such signals are especially important when trading momentum-based or range-based systems in the markets. Using it is pretty simple; when the line in the indicator window moves above the +100 mark, you are looking at an overbought condition. On the other hand, if the line crosses below -100, you are looking at an oversold condition. Take a look at the chart below. The CCI crossed above the +100 mark at about the time when the market was breaking from a tight range. This could be used as a signal to go long on a particular stock.

- Relative Strength Indicator (RSI) - Then, there is the Relative Strength Indicator (or RSI). This is an indicator that works in a similar way to the CCI. It is designed to be a momentum indicator. It is displayed as a line graph in a window, and the y-axis marked from 0 to 100. To use this indicator, you need to keep your eye on two numbers 70 and 30. If the line crosses below 30, it denotes and undersold situation. But, if the line crosses above 70, it indicates an overbought situation. Check the chart below. In this case, you are looking at a sideways range-bound market. When the price gets closer to the previous high, the market reverses. This is a great shorting opportunity.

The same happens when the price gets to the previous low, indicating a great buying opportunity. As you can see, the RSI is behaving accordingly. As you now have the basics of fundamental analysis under your belt, let us look at some simple short-term trading strategies that you can apply.

Simple Short-Term Trading Strategies

You have just learned that, in order for you to operate successfully in the financial markets, you must implement a strategy. And when it comes to that, there are countless strategies out there. Some are good, and some aren't that good. Some are simple, and some are downright difficult to work with. Teaching you a few basic but workable strategies that can quickly get you started in the markets is one of my most important goals in this book. Many people are under the impression that you need a complicated strategy to be successful – you don't. You just need to find a simple strategy that works. Then, you can stick with that strategy for as long as it works. Let us look at what some of those strategies are.

Trending Markets

Making money in a trending market is one of the most popular and time-tested ways of making money in the financial markets. It's also remarkably simple. For us to begin, a trending market is that which prices seem to move in a certain direction with only a few retracements in the move. This direction can either be up or down. A market that is trending upwards is said to be in an Uptrend. Conversely, a Downtrend describes a market that is trending downwards.

Trading an Uptrend

The basic idea in trading an uptrend is to buy into the lows (also called the pullbacks or retracements). A market can never go straight up; even the strongest trends retrace at some point. Your goal as a trader is to buy or go long at these retracements. Then, when the movement is back on track, you stand to make a profit. Do this consistently, and you stand to make quite some nice profits. Therefore, what you need to do is first draw trend lines. A valid trend line is that which connects more than two retracements on the chart. Well, you can rely on one that connects only two, but having at least three past retracements connected by your line is better. The expectation is that a good retracement to buy into will develop close to the trend line or above the trend line. Once you spot any of these situations, you have a green light on placing your trade. However, refrain from trading retracements that appear below the line. When the market does this, you are supposed to assume that the market has broken the trend and is either reversing its direction or transitioning into a sideways direction. As you can see from this other chart, when the market broke the trend line, it transitioned to a downtrend. Another consideration you have to make in this strategy is the location of your stop-loss order. A stop-loss order in trading is an order that protects you from losing all or most of your capital should the market fail to act in your favor. It does this by automatically selling and closing your position. It is the most basic form of risk management you can ever implement in your trading.

Don't forget that regardless of how good is your strategy, you can never assume that any given trade will work out. The best you can do is be prepared for such a scenario and avoid losing a significant portion of your capital. This gives you the chance to take another opportunity that could work in your favor next time. Putting a stop-loss order on every trade that you place is the best way of ensuring that. So, the best location to put your stop-loss order is just below a retracement. The areas marked red are your best areas to place a stop-loss order in such a market. As the market keeps moving in your favor, you keep on raising your stop-loss order to the next retracement so that you lock in on profits and protect your investment. This is always known as "trailing a stop." In addition to a stop-loss order, you will also need a "take-profit" order; every good trading strategy has one. This order automatically sells your investment so that you pocket a profit, should the market hit your profit target. And just like the stop-loss, you can also move this order as the market moves in your favor so that you pocket even more profit. The best place to put your take-profit order is at a distance that is at least twice that which is between your entry price and the stop-loss order. This gives you a risk-reward ratio of 1:2. If the trend is a good one, this profit target should be hit. As you now know how to trade an uptrend, let's look at how you can trade a downtrend.

Trading a Downtrend

Trading a downtrend is easy. Once you know how to trade an uptrend, it's simply a matter of repeating the same concepts, just in reverse. As you well know by now, a downtrend is a market where prices keep moving downwards with some minor retracements. The idea is to short the market at the retracements; the market never goes straight down. These retracements offer you the best chance of selling. So, as always, you begin by drawing a downtrend line, as shown by this chart. The retracements that occur at or below the line are your best entry signals. The stop-loss order needs to be placed just above the retracements and the take-profit order, at a distance twice that between the entry price and the stop-loss. Now, you know how to trade and profit from trending markets. Let's look at sideways markets.

Sideways Markets

The market only moves in three directions – upwards, downwards, and sideways. It is a known fact in the world of trading that the market trends only 40% of the time. The rest of the time, it moves sideways. So, knowing how to trade both trending and sideways markets gives you a significant advantage when it comes to spotting market opportunities. There are many ways to trade sideways markets. But, for the purposes of this book, we will look at two simple strategies, each targeting two main sideways market setups.

Trading a Wide-Ranging Market

The first sideways market set-up you will encounter is that of a market that seems to be stuck in a wide range. It isn't always clear to someone who isn't used to looking at charts because patterns in the market aren't always exact. But if you focus your eyes a little bit, you should be able to spot it.

In fact, training your eyes to see certain things is one of the most important skills you could ever arm yourself with. If you are keen enough, you should be able to notice that prices are bouncing-off in both directions at some imaginary line. It's as if there is something that is preventing them from going further, once they reach a certain point. Take a look at this chart. The main idea in this kind of setup is to plan on shorting the market at the highs (also called resistance) and going long at the lows (support), as illustrated in this diagram. Doing this gives you the best chance of profiting from this kind of market. So the first thing you do is draw the horizontal lines connecting the highs and lows. These lines help you identify the main "decision levels." Then, plan your entries and exits. To help you confirm your entry and exit signals, you could use a momentum indicator such as the RSI, CCI, or stochastics.

Once the indicator signals overbought, you can look to short the market. At the same time, you can look to close out any long open position you might have. When the indicator signals oversold, you can look to place a buy order or seek to cover any open short position you might have. The chart below best illustrates my point. And when it comes to the stop-loss orders, common sense should dictate that they are to be placed above the highs for the shorts, and below the lows for the long positions. Take profits are to be placed at or near the support and resistance lines.

Trading a Narrow-Ranging Market

The next type of sideways market setup is that of a narrow-range market (also called a consolidation). Here, the prices always seem to be stuck within a narrow range.

Fundamentally, this could indicate indecision amongst market participants. Most of the time, this happens when traders are anxious about a particular news event that could rock the prices in the market. So they lie quietly in wait for the outcome. When the news comes out, the market either does rally or fall sharply. This is always called a breakout. A good breakout offers a tremendous opportunity for profit. So to begin, you need to be able to spot such a setup. This chart below shows a good example of a market in a consolidation phase. The next thing you do is draw horizontal lines marking the levels of support and resistance, as shown. This helps you identify the levels at which you will need to make decisions on whether to buy or sell. The idea is to exploit a breakout situation such as the one illustrated by this diagram. Please note that this doesn't mean that prices always break downwards. This is just one of the two scenarios that could occur. Prices could break upwards or downwards. You should be prepared for both. If prices break upwards, you go long; if they break downwards, you go short. It is important to keep in mind that you are not to delay this decision. You are supposed to have your finger on the trigger at the opportune moment. Execute your trade the moment prices break past the point you are watching.

Do not even wait for the next candle to open. The reason for this is because prices tend to break rapidly during consolidation breakouts, so if you are not fast on your fingers, you may execute when it's too late, and most of the profit potential of the trade is already gone. Also, executing when it is too late places you at a high risk of getting whipsawed. You get whipsawed when prices move rapidly in one direction only to suddenly reverse, taking you out of a trade incurring significant loss. So, trading breakouts requires a degree of finesse. But if you are alert, very little can go wrong. The stop-loss order for going long is to be placed *below* the consolidation. Conversely, the stop-loss order for going short is to be placed *above* the consolidation. The take-profits are to be placed at a distance that is equal to twice the width of the consolidation pattern. If you need confirmation to add value to your decision, you can use an indicator such as the "volume." When trading volume is high, the bars become long, and when the trading is light, the bars are short.

Chapter 7: Mistakes to Avoid

Now that we've taken a look at the proverbial list of 'to-dos,' as far as rookie traders such as yourself are concerned, let's take a look at the most common 'mistakes' that are made by beginner traders in an attempt to rectify them and move along the path towards success in our stock trading endeavors.

Mistake No. 1: They Add to 'Losing Positions'

It's most common for rookie traders out there to add to 'losing positions' in an attempt to turn things around, but that might just be the last thing that they needed to do. Solution: If you really need to turn things around, you need to do more of what is working and less of what does not in order to make sure you don't drive yourself deep into a loss.

Mistake No. 2: Making Those Trades Out of 'Boredom'

Sometimes, new traders find themselves unable to even sit for a moment without making a trade, simply because they find it too 'boring' to do nothing, considering the fact that up until now, they have been most active in the trading process. As a result, they make a trade without doing the appropriate and most essential research behind it. Solution: You cannot afford to be in a position where you make those trades simply because you have been habituated to so doing. It's much better to be bored and wait things out until the right moment comes to invest again, which will be sooner than you expected.

Mistake No. 3: They Keep Moving from One Strategy to the Next

Of course, if you kept on making money all the time through the process of your newfound trading activity, you wouldn't find yourself in a situation like this at all. If things are really going askew for you, it is certainly not prudent to keep juggling your way through various strategies. Solution: Things might not be all that rosy at times, but if you have the discipline to stick to the strategy that you have implemented, it will be well worth your while in the end. You have to give your strategy enough time to work and banish that losing streak!

Mistake No. 4: They Don't Have an Exit Plan

This is the commonest mistake that a lot of new traders make. They don't have an exit plan and just keep those losing stocks for far longer than they should have ever kept them. That just results in them ending up as 'dead stocks', something that is most clearly detrimental to your business of stock trading. Solution: The thing you need to do whenever you buy a stock is to put in your stop loss once you get your 'fill.' This means that you will know when you are going to be getting out. That means having a proper exit plan, which will entail just how much money you are prepared to lose right before buying the stock itself! Of course, this exit should be based on a logical method of thinking, such as determining that whenever it falls below that support area, it should no longer be held and therefore gotten rid of.

Mistake No. 5: They Go in for Impulsive Trading

While it is advisable to stay with the trends most of the time as we have discussed already in the previous chapter as far as stock trading is concerned, it might not really be the best thing to do, to end up trading rather impulsively simply because there is a trend in the market out there that you need to 'follow'. Oftentimes these trends are not backed by good solid research. Solution: No matter which way the trends point, you have to make sure that you do the requisite market research on your very own before you actually go towards following that trend in an attempt to garner more profits.

Mistake No. 6: They Lack the Much-Needed Discipline That Is Needed for Swing Trading

What they do is, more often than not, wait too long or too short before they make their entry or exit. This only results in getting that 'market timing' wrong, which then causes it not to end up doing as well as they might have expected. Solution: You need to have the discipline to wait for just the perfect market conditions and make trades that are high in probability in order to avoid those huge losses that you might if you push those limits too much.

Mistake No. 7: They Don't Have a Strategy at All

A few points earlier, we just discussed how it is most wise not to have too many strategies where it comes to the process of that stock trading business of yours, but the worst possible thing you could do is to not have a strategy at all in the first place. Solution: You need the patience to work on a strategy that seems plausible enough to work in an environment that is indeed most competitive out there. Otherwise, you will simply find yourself short of having any sense of direction at all and lose your way in the dark.

Mistake No. 8: They Overestimate How Much They Should Invest at Any Given Time

They take position sizes that are too large for their portfolio. What compounds the problem is when they don't use stop losses in the trades that go against them. Solution: You need only to take on that which you are capable of taking on. That way, you will always find yourself in a most realistic situation, one that has stop losses as well in order to ensure that when things do go wrong, they do not go terribly askew.

Mistake No. 9: They Listen Too Much to Those 'Pundits' Out There

There are so many people out there advising you on what to do when it comes to maximizing profits in stock trading, but that might just not be the perfect advice for you, as you might find out rather harshly later on. Solution: Stick to your own strategy and zone out the world outside. The 'pundits' are in all probability not actively trading themselves; besides, when things go wrong, it's really 'you' that will have to find a way out of the mess, not them.

Chapter 8: Tips for Becoming a Successful Top Trader

It is important to determine your personalized trading plan. Create a plan. The fact of the matter is that there is simply no way you can expect to be successful in the long term when it comes to day trading if you don't have a plan that has been personalized based on your very own strengths and weaknesses. While skipping this section, finding a generalized trading plan online may probably be the fastest way to start trading as soon as possible.

Determine Your Current Level of Skill

In order to ensure that you create a plan with a realistic chance for success, the first thing that you are going to want to do is determine what your current competencies are when it comes to trading, in general, as well as the underlying asset you are hoping to focus on specifically.

The more experience you have, the more elaborate and ambitious your plan can be, but it is important to determine your level of experience honestly as overestimating your experience is only going to make it more difficult for you to start turning a profit in the first place. During this step, you are also going to want to catalog your general strengths and weaknesses as they relate to trading in general and options trading specifically. It is especially important to be honest with yourself when it comes to your strengths and weaknesses, especially when it comes to your ability to maintain your composure when properly, your emotions are running high. Remember, this isn't a test that you can either pass or fail; it is simply an examination of the ways you can be the most effective trader possible. As such, if you fudge the results, then the only person who is going to be losing out is you. With enough forethought, you can maximize your strengths and minimize your weaknesses, leading to overall greater success in both the short and the long term.

Decide How Much Risk Is Right for You

When it comes to determining how much risk is the right amount, the final solution is going to be different for each trader. This is because there is no singular amount of risk that is perfect for everyone; the risk is more individualized than that. To get started figuring out the perfect amount of risk for you, the first thing that you will want to do is to determine how much capital you are going to allot solely to trading, as well as what that amount means to you. If you have saved a few thousand dollars in a month or so to give something new a try, then your overall risk is going to be little. If you saved that same amount over nearly a year of dedicated saving, then that same amount might represent a much higher risk. Regardless, it is important never to put more into a single trade than you can ever afford to lose. A good rule of thumb is that each individual trade should encompass no more than 5 percent of your total options trading fund to ensure that a small mistake doesn't end up costing you dearly. What's more, when it comes to deciding to take chances on potential trades you are only going to want to pull the trigger when you have a reasonable suspicion that the trade in question is going to end with you making three times as much in profit as what you originally put in prior to paying any related fees. To determine this amount, all you need to do is take the potential payout and divide it by the buy-in amount; if the result is greater than three, then you can move ahead with the trade with a clean conscience. This advice is what is known as the risk/reward ratio, and it is key to trading in options successfully. Besides the financial realities of your situation, you are also going to need to consider how much time you ultimately plan on spending concentrating on options trading to the exclusion of all else along with the amount of profit you hope to see in the process.

If, after determining the amount of time you hope to spend trading your financial estimates aren't as high as you might like, you can then either change the amount of time you are planning to spend or the amount of risk you are willing to put up with, there are only these three variables to work with. Be wary when it comes to raising your risk too high as major amounts of risk are as likely to lead to major losses as they are too major windfalls.

Prepare Yourself

Ideally, you will be spending the early hours of the day reading up on the likely state of the market for the moment when it opens so that you can take advantage of your planning as much as possible. As such, when it comes to creating your plan, it is important to understand how much time you realistically have to commit to maximizing your trade advantage and what other parts of your life are going to interfere with this preparation.

There is certainly money to be made by trading options at less regular hours, but the only way that you will be prepared to do so is if you know about the discrepancy ahead of time and work to minimize its impact as much as possible. In addition to the daily preparations that will be required of you, you will also need to be aware of various important due dates, both for your underlying asset of choice as a whole, as well as any holdings you might have specifically. Earnings reports of all types are sure to have a noticeable effect on the market, and if you are caught unaware, you have no choice but to take a loss that, in many cases, can be quite serious. You will also need to be aware of when any dividend payments are coming due for any options that are related to stocks that you might own. Owning an option does not entitle you to a dividend, so you must know when to exercise your options if you hope to maximize your profits at all times.

Understand When You Will Want to Get While the Getting Is Good

When it comes to creating a successful strategy, it is important that you take the time to determine exactly when you are going to want to exit every trade that you make, no matter what. Choosing this point means considering your acceptable level of risk and will ultimately serve to limit your losses, though also doing the same to your profits. Specifically, this means that when scenarios arise such as when a stock drops out of the money from a previously profitable position, you will always want to be realistic about the situation and understand that the best thing to do is to sell rather than to wait for it come back around, risking even greater losses in the interim. This logic is flawed, and what's worse, will lead to future negative habits if you are lucky enough for it to work out in your favor the first time as it will always result in a loss in the long run. Instead, you will want to determine what the best strategy is for you and your holdings based on numerous personal factors, including other trades you are currently pursuing, what you believe to be an acceptable level of risk and how closely you plan to micromanage each individual trade. Essentially, what this means is that the specific details behind the exit strategy that you choose don't matter, what does matter is that you plan out what it is going to be, before you make your first move, and then stick with it no matter what, even if every emotional cell in your being is telling you to change horses midstream and do something that is almost certainly stupid.

To keep your losses to a minimum, you are going to want to use what is known as stop losses. Stop losses are a way to automatically buy or sell options based on a predetermined set of specifications. As such, they are not terribly useful when it comes to trading in options that are likely to move a great deal in both directions over a short period of time but can be extremely useful in other, more stable situations. It doesn't matter if you are the holder or the writer, stop losses are a must for everyone involved in the interaction. You will also find that secondary stop orders are also useful when it comes to securing a predetermined amount of profit while still ensuring that you can take advantage of any ongoing positive trends as well. This is done thanks to what is known as a price target, which is the amount you feel is realistic to expect to make from the trade in question. You then simply set your first stop loss at this point and then set a second stop loss much higher. This way, when the first level of profit is reached, you can sell off half of your holdings while still retaining the rest in case the positive trend continues in a big way.

Find the Right Place to Start

Once you know when you are going to get out of any trade that you place, the next thing that you will need to consider is the right time to capitalize on the trend of a specific option. The best way to go about doing this is to consider the amount of risk that you deem acceptable before considering what type of purchase you want to make when you come across an option that meets your criteria for purchase based on your earnings goals and your risk assessment. As a new options trader, what you are going to be the most interested in is making a single option purchase per trade. While this might not seem like a lot, it is important to keep in mind that each option is going to be worth 100 shares, which means that it only takes a little bit of movement from the underlying asset to cause significant gains or losses for any trades that you make. This means that you are going to want to be discerning when it comes to choosing the right entry point, one that is relaxed enough to ensure that you aren't waiting days between trades and strict enough that every option you come across doesn't automatically qualify.

Make Sure That Your Goals Are S.M.A.R.T.

It is important to ultimately consider what goals you have for trading and how likely each trade is to help move you one step closer to achieving them. A good way to do so is to determine if each of your goals related to options trading is not only realistic but SMART. The first SMART goal that you set should be one that is at the same time straightforward enough to more or less ensure your success while at the same time being relevant enough to your day to day life that actually succeeding will be a moment that you can easily recall in the future when success on a future goal is not nearly so assured. This way, you will start forming the right type of neural pathways as soon as possible, which will then form into patterns that will eventually become habits. With this in mind, you want to start off with a goal that is, at least, tangentially connected to the negative pattern that you are the most anxious to start to change. You don't need to have an exact goal in mind at this point, just the start of an idea that you can build into something larger later on.

Consider the following to ensure that you are on the right track. SMART goals are:

Specific

The best goals are the ones that you will always be able to determine where you stand in relation to the goal. The goal should then have a clearly defined fail state as well as state that will clearly let you know when you have crossed the finish line. Specific goals are also going to be much easier to chart out over time as their specificity will lend to clear sub-goals that can be linked to their success or failure. When you choose a specific goal, you are going to want to guarantee that you have a clear idea of the following details to ensure that you have chosen a goal that is truly specific enough for your needs.

- Who you will need to work with so as to make the goal a reality
- What you will need to do in order to get started on completing the goal
- Where you will need to go in order to see the goal through to completion
- Why you wanted to get started completing the goal in the first place
- When you can realistically expect the goal to be completed
- How you will go about completing the goal in various steps

Measurable

A good goal is one where progress towards success can easily be measured, giving you a feeling of accomplishment and a serotonin boost every time you take another step in the right direction. With your first few goals, it is extremely important to keep them measurable in order to nurture the growth of the proper neural pathways.

To determine the metric of success you should be using, start by determining the easiest criteria by which you can measure success. This metric can either be one that is based on achieving certain predetermined outcomes or one that is based on cold, hard facts; the important thing is that there are clearly defined points that can be used to ensure you are always on the right track. Early goals tend to work better when a success metric is a number that can be easily defined as it helps to be able to see a stream of new progress unfolding constantly. Once you know how you will be able to tell if you have achieved a specific goal, it is important to keep a visual record of your progress that you can look back on in times of hardship to snap your mind out of trying to make excuses. The visual proof of effort already exerted can be a powerful motivator when it comes to silencing excuses and making goals seem more attainable, which in turn keeps motivation high throughout the ordeal. This is especially true once you have reached the halfway point as everything after that is downhill when compared with the effort you have already put in. Keeping detailed notes of your progress can be as simple as charting your progress on a graph or as complicated as keeping a detailed journal of your experiences. Try various methods of keeping track of your progress and see which works best for you.

Having this record will help to keep the entirety of the goal in the appropriate perspective as well as helping to mitigate any concerns and excuses you might have about not making any headway to your ultimate goal.

Attainable

SMART Goals are always attainable. Ideal scenarios are nice, but including goals that have only a slim probability of materializing is doing little more than wasting your time. This is not saying that complicated or difficult goals should be avoided; rather, it is about knowing your limits and when they can be expanded. Setting long-term goals is good for the self-image of the business, and it can help every member of the team grow in an attempt to reach them.

Relevant

It is important that the goal you choose is relevant to your current situation, as well as being simply something that is attainable with only a reasonable amount of effort. Relevance is key to turning the SMART goal system from a one-time thing into a pattern and eventually a lifelong habit that you can rely on to help you meet the challenges of life no matter what they may be. Remember, you want these early goals to be as meaningful as possible so that you think back on them regularly and fortify the neural pathways as quickly as possible, so they become your brain's default way of acting.

If you take it slow, you will find that completing part of the task related to achieving your current goal will become a habit just like anything else, which will then make it easier to work on even more complicated tasks in turn. As with everything else described above, when working on cementing SMART goals in your life, you will want to remember that practice makes perfect.

Timely

Studies show that you are statistically more likely to continue to works towards the completion of a complicated or difficult task if it has a deadline associated with it. What this means is that you will want to determine what your ultimate goal will be, determine a timeline for completion, and then do the same for each of the sub-goals you set as well. When it comes to setting a due date for your goals, you will want to consider periods of time that are long enough to allow you to experience a few setbacks along the way, without being so lax that you never actually get around to accomplishing anything. What you are shooting for is something that will force you to stop dreaming about financial freedom and start working towards it, not something so strict that you have no realistic chance of success.

Track Your Progress

Instead of being in a rush to look into how effective your plan is or setting daily trading goals that are, frankly, completely unrealistic, especially so early on, you will want to make a point of sticking to the plan that you created and keeping detailed notes on every single trade that you make, what the results are and what all of the relevant details turned out to be. To determine the metrics that are most relevant to your overall success, you are going to want first to ask yourself what type of trader you are. If you are someone who is always hunting for big risks and bigger rewards, then you will be much better served by finding out how successful you have been overall in a given time period (starting with one month of data) as opposed to the number of successful or unsuccessful trades. On the other hand, if your overall number of trades is very low because you only make extremely safe moves, then you will want to ensure that each trade you make is as profitable as possible.

Chart Your Success

After you have waited long enough that you have some data that can be genuinely useful to you, the next thing you are going to want to do is chart out how effective your initial trading plan has been so far. Charting out this type of data will make it easier for you to see if all of the rules you are basing your trading decisions on hold up to a critical analysis. This will help you to determine if the plan that you are working with is going to be reliable, moving forward to help to assure yourself that it is going to continue to line up with the goals you have for profit generation. This is also a way to create the baseline for future historical volatility analysis. Once you have charted out the data that you have so far, the next thing you are going to want to do is to create a summary that reflects the details in the data that you have generated so far. You will want this summary to include all of the details of every single trade that you made in your first month of trading. Seeing all of this data, clear of any daily biases, will make it much easier for you to see the forest, not the trees.

This broader focus will, in turn, make it easier to determine not just how profitable your venture has been thus far but also to illuminate patterns ultimately related to either failure or success that may be hiding in the apparently random data. The more you study your results, the more likely it is that you will be able to turn apparently random instances of good luck into a repeatable pattern of success.

Results That Matter Most

If you have been following along as suggested, then by now, you will certainly have all the data you could ever need when it comes to determining the efficacy of your system. Luckily, you aren't going to need to use all of it regularly, and can instead rely on a few important indicators that will tell you what you really need to know.

Net Profit

To determine the total net profit that you have brought in by trading options thus far, all you need to do is add up all of the profitable trades that you have made thus far and compare that number to the total number of trades where you lost money and determine which number is higher. This is the most basic and broad determination of whether or not your plan is successful if the number you end up with is negative, it is time to go back to square one and find a more profitable plan, anything else is akin to burning money.

Profit Factor

Once your total net profit is facing the right way, the next thing you are going to need to consider how much you are likely to make on your plan per dollar spent assuming everything else remains equal. To find this number, you take your total profit number and divide it by the total amount of any losses you had. This number needs to be above 1 to indicate an effective plan, and anything higher is hugely profitable.

Percent Profitable

You can think of the percent your project is valuable as how likely you are to win at any given trade. To determine what the number is, you take the name of trades that ended in success and divide it by the total number of trades that you attempted. There is no target number in this scenario, as the right amount depends on whether you prefer significant gains and higher risks, in which case you should aim for few trades with higher margins, or you will want a high number if you prefer lots of small, safe trades.

Trade Average Net Profit

The trade average net profit is the amount that you are likely to make on each trade that you complete, given your history of trading. To find this number, all you need to do is divide the total amount of profit you made by the total number of trades, regardless of whether or not they were ultimately successful. This number should be positive, and ideally, the higher, the better. If the number ends up being negative, then you need to stop trading until you come up with a plan that is somewhat more effective. When finding this number, it is important to leave out any trades that you may have made that were extreme outliers compared to all of your other trades, as they can skew this number to the point of irrelevance.

Conclusion

Thank you once again for purchasing Stock Market Investing for Beginners: The Essential Guide to Make Big Profits with Stock Trading — Best Strategies, Technical Analysis, and Psychology to Grow Your Money and Create Your Wealth. As you can tell, we talked extensively about stock investing and how you can make it happen for yourself.

Many people do not see the results that they're hoping to get just because they don't apply the tips and tricks provided to them. It is essential for you to exercise everything you learn, as that is how you will succeed in your future endeavors. Nonetheless, the topics we talked about will help you to not only become good at stock investing but to take you to the next level. Even though this book has been geared toward beginner investors, advanced people can still reap the benefits of this book.

Many investors have not touched the information provided to you. This is why you will see amazing results once you start using the tips in this book, as you will have the edge over other people. Also, if you're having trouble with any of the chapters, then make sure that you read it once again.

Dividend Investing
Step-by-Step Guide for Beginners to Create a Passive Income and Find your Way to Financial Freedom Through Dividend and Stocks Investments

Table of Contents

Chapter 1: What Is Dividend Investing............................101
   The Pros of Dividend Investing
      Regenerating Cash Flow
      The Benefit of Trade-Off
      Security With Dividends
      Tax Benefits
      Consider Yield Spikes
   Dividend Investing vs. Index Investing
   How Dividend Investing Can Fit into Your Retirement Goals
   What Is Dividend Investment?
      So, How Did It All Start?
   Terms to Know in Dividend Investment
   Rules of Dividend Investments
      Always Go for Quality!
      The Bargain Principle
      Always Play Safe
      Reinvest Your Dividends
      Understand Your Tax Laws
      Do not Make Dividends Your Only Priority
      Watch Out for Value Traps
      Always Look out for Special Dividends
      Use the Survival of the Fittest Principle

Chapter 2: Types of Dividend, Plus Key Technical Terms, Rules, Analysis, and System Best Strategies............120

   The Income Statement
      Revenue
      Operating Expenses
      Income From Continuing Operations
      Non-recurring Events
      Net Income
   The Balance Sheet
      Assets – Liabilities = Owner's Equity
      Current vs. Non-Current
      Assets
      Liabilities
      Equity
   Additional Attributes to Consider When Selecting Dividend Stocks
      Dividend Yield
      Payout Ratio
      Cash Flow
      Moving Forward

Chapter 3: Dividend Investing for Passive Income............152

   Benefits of Dividend Investing
   How to Pick Dividends
      Profits in the Company
      Size of Payouts
      The health of the Company
      History of Problems
   Some Tips for Dividend Investing

Chapter 4: The Right Mindset..............................159

Preparation and Planning

  Outlook

  Goals

Continuing Success

Financial Risk Management

Growing and Maintaining Your Income

  Save It

  High Interest

  Spend It

  Invest It

  Try New Things

  Put It Back In

Chapter 5: Beginner Mistakes to Avoid..............................169

The Biggest Mistakes to Avoid When Growing Your Portfolio

  Ignoring a Variety of Growth Factors

  Showing Favoritism to the Home Market

  Focused Toward Those Blue Chips

  Giving Macro Factors More Weight

Chapter 6: Examples of Success..............................175

Always Contribute to Your Portfolio

Seek a Dependable Dividend

Focus on the Quality, Not Necessarily the Quantity

Create a Diversified Portfolio

Reinvest Wisely

Chapter 1: What Is Dividend Investing

The idea of dividend investing is considered one of the best ways for investors to collect steady and consistent returns. There are several people who invest in these dividend stocks to take advantage of that dependability before utilizing some of those incoming funds to invest back into more shares of stocks. It is kind of like playing with some house money after winning a few rounds of blackjack at the casino. The main difference is that if you make smart investing decisions, you'll have a better chance at yielding some gains than beating the dealer. Because there are many dividend-paying stocks that represent different organizations that are considered a safer bet for investments. The prices might increase over time, which leads to bigger gains for shareholders. Additionally, those companies will raise dividend payments over time, such as providing a 3 % dividend after one year at about 2.5 %. At the same time, those are never set in stone.

But, a company that builds a profile and gives its shareholders dependable, increasing dividends will do everything possible to continue pleasing their investors. There are companies that will pay consistently increasing dividends; they are usually considered financially healthy, generating a dependable return on investment on the different dividends. Stable companies usually feature any falling stock prices to make it less alarming for the shareholders in the general market. Because of this, they can be considered less of a risk than the companies that do not pay those dividends and, in turn, see more sharp ups and downs in the price. With a lower risk for the investors of these dividend stocks, they can be a more attractive option for a variety of investors, such as the young bucks who are hoping to get more income over the long haul and for those who are looking to build up their retirement fund. Even those already in retirement use the money from dividend investing in providing a regular income while they are not working. Another reason that these dividend stocks have built confidence among dividend investors is the correlation between the share prices and the yield of gains from the dividends. When one rises, the other follows. There is also the consideration for the power of compounding your investments, which is taking the generated earnings and putting them back into the stocks that will continue to build more and more.

In other words, the money you have generated from your earnings will generate additional earnings, and the generated earnings will continue to multiply as the investor continues to reinvest in the long run. This process can hypothetically turn one penny into a very large sum of money after about a month. If you take that one penny and continue to double your account every day for 30 days, you could see your money grow from a few cents to a few dollars. Ten dollars becomes $20, which becomes $40, then $80, $160, $320, $640, up to thousands and, eventually, millions. Sure, there are a lot of things that have to happen, and it requires a little luck. But in theory, it can happen, even if it is a bit unrealistic. This is not to say that any investor can expect to see their money grow when they begin to utilize dividend investing. But it shows that money can, and likely will, grow in a process that Albert Einstein once called the eighth wonder of the world. Many who enter the world of dividend investing will see the eventual rise of their rate of return as they continue to reinvest the money that comes in their returns on investment. Let us say that you have 100 shares of a stock that sells at $50 per share. This is an investment of about $5,000. In that first year, the company offers a 2.5 %dividend that provides an income of $125. If the investor continues to see dividend growths of 5 % each year, that $5,000 initial investment will be valued at more than $11,200 after about 20 years. This is with the assumption that there will be no change in the stock price, and there is the reinvestment mentioned earlier.

Now let us have that same company pay a quarterly dividend rather than one that pays annually. That $5,000 investment will grow to a little more than $11,650 in two decades for a gain of about 133 %. Because of the process of compounding, a $50,000 investment can become a $116,500 sum after that same period of time during which there are reinvestments into the dividend folder.

The Pros of Dividend Investing

Regenerating Cash Flow

There are moments when a company will declare that they offer a special dividend, which on paper, does not necessarily bring a benefit to the investor. In this case, a company usually gives the money back since they feel there is no use for it, thinking you could probably get a better return in another way. That could be a sign that the company does not have any new products, or they are in the middle of a saturated marketplace with a minimal chance for growth. If a company is prepared to grow, they retain the earnings so that they can be reinvested back into the company's expected expansion, but companies with minimal growth potential usually give the money back to their shareholders.

Dividends are best when a company has products and services that can help generate a cash flow that comes in a dependable fashion. Investors want to see the company they have shares in replenishing a dollar cut to its stock price for every dollar paid in dividends. The goal is to bring as much surplus money from one fiscal quarter to the next. This regenerative flow of money usually comes from companies that have minor debt and a little more experience as a business.

The Benefit of Trade-Off

Every investor should keep the potential trade-off in mind whenever they decide to invest in dividend stocks.

While you are receiving that consistent and steady flow of income, there is generally a lost opportunity in the growth of the stock, and a market that becomes hot can easily do better than the percentage gains an investor receives from their dividend investments. But even if the stock market has that sort of turnaround—a change of pace from what it has been in the past decade—an allocation that brings gains of 20 % or more, which can come with dividend stocks, can go a long way in increasing the performance of an investor's stock portfolio. By doing so, it also gives an investor a little bit of extra money that can be reinvested at times when there is a pullback from the market. This allows the investor a chance to gather up any other stocks that have grown at a discounted cost to purchase.

Security With Dividends

Despite the chances that a dividend can be trimmed or suspended, investors have to be certain that the company from which they have bought stocks will continue to pay them for the long-term. But the good news is that there is a long list of safe, dependable options to choose from. One of the easiest ways to start is to look into mature large caps like the choices found within Russell 1000 Index. Those 1,000 companies usually offer yields that range from 1 to 5 %, sometimes even more. There is even stronger dividend security found among what are affectionately called "Dividend Aristocrats." These are companies that have been consistent in how they pay their shareholders and have increased regularly for at least 100 fiscal quarters, which equals about 25 years.

That type of longevity is what attracts the investors the most and makes dividend investing a very popular choice.

Now, there are some pitfalls since everything in the world is not sunshine and lollipops. Sometimes, you have to take the good with the bad.

Tax Benefits

The folks at the Internal Revenue Service are known for always looking for another income to tax, which also includes any money made from those that come from the dividends. There are even dividends that are taxed as much as three times in a majority of jurisdictions. The first comes from about a federal withholding tax at about 20 % of the dividend's earnings, which comes out as soon as there is a payment made to your account. After this, 80 % of that amount is considered your income and is taxed twice for federal and state income taxes. So maybe, there is not that much left of that initial dividend payment you were thinking about. On paper, this looks to be a negative circumstance that might make you question whether or not you should invest in dividends, especially when you consider that the money lost is coming from the stock. For every dollar paid in dividends, the stock value falls a correlative dollar while allowing a collection of only 50 cents. So how do you counter that?

Consider Yield Spikes

This can be a scary possibility when you think you have found a great booming company before it, all of a sudden, burns out and drops before you have a chance to sell, potentially losing a larger gain. Either you could learn how to monitor and have the ability to sell as soon as you see any inkling of a decline, or you could focus more on investing within those more established companies that offer a more consistent payout and have almost no yield spikes.

An investor might become a victim of the yield spike if they have conducted a search for the different stocks in the marketplace, sorted what they found based on the highest yield of a specific time frame, and then picked the top three or four payers, doing so with the highest of expectations. Oftentimes, an investor may find yields that show an increase of 20 %, 30 %, and even up to 50 %. But recent performance may show a stock price drop, and that the most recent dividend payment was made between a few weeks and a month ago. This combination means that the yield percentage reached a high that it probably will not be sustainable for the long-term road. The drop in the stock price is usually a sign that the next dividend payment is going to see a big decrease as well, and that is if it is not suspended, like many companies in this predicament have done in a way to give itself time to sort things out. It is something to look out for when looking at the market.

Dividend Investing vs. Index Investing

While dividend investing focuses on the ability to maximize cash that is then distributed among the shareholders of each stock, index investing is a passive approach that hopes to generate the same return rate that correlates with the market index.

In other words, it hopes to replicate the performance of specific equity or fixed-income index through things like index funds or exchange-traded funds. Not every larger company pays its shareholders in dividends as growth investors are usually found on the other end of the spectrum from those who focus on dividends. A company that pays a dividend is usually one that already has a track record of having yearly profits and has a belief that the real money is in identifying the stocks that have the best potential to grow fast and provide advantages in the open market, usually in smaller companies that are taking a small risk and paying minimal to no dividends. The difference between the two goes back to the fact that there are two ways to make money in the stock market. A stock can see an increase in value titled capital gain, or you could have a dividend. There are mixed opinions on which one will make the most money, depending on the different criteria and tax situations. Let us first consider the facts of what differentiates index investing:

There is plenty of money that is on the line within the stock market, so much of which attracts several intelligent investors to collect it. Because of this, there are very few strategies that still work today that do not copy some of the characteristics of thousands of other plans and strategies tried by other people.

What works today is quickly copied tomorrow and, eventually, reduces any advantage that it once had. One of the biggest challenges of trying to come up with a unique index investing strategy is being able to understand it and applying it to work within an investor's portfolio. For both of these, most people have a hard time adjusting, which means index investing is usually a good route for them. At the same time, investors for both index and dividends have several commonalities, which include having the same approach regarding the buying and holding of stocks for a longer period of time. Those who invest using either of them will usually have a portfolio of larger, stable companies that provide steady cash flow and are not too much of a big risk to the investor. But what makes dividend investing an attractive option? One is that investors can pick out their stocks that have a higher chance of outperforming the average market numbers by using formulas and growth statistics based around dividends. The only argument is that more will eventually follow the same path and begin to make similar stock moves that will begin to level the competitive market again. There is also a constant line of dividends, which can become an income that is more tax-efficient to the investor. On the other hand, if stocks remain in registered accounts, such as a Tax-Free Savings Account (TFSA), a Registered Retirement Savings Plan (RRSP), or a Registered Education Savings Plan (RESP), the advantage is almost void. But if those registered accounts are all filled up, that could be extremely beneficial for the investor. Finally, dividends are considered a good option to boost an investor's self-esteem to stay in the market, especially if the stock market, all of a sudden, takes a big hit and moves down the graph. Being able to have that mental boost can be beneficial when other investors are in a panic to sell off their stocks, giving you a good chance to buy cheap for larger money gains later.

At the same time, stocks are usually arbitrary to pick regardless of the approach used, so there are still no guarantees in the competitive market. Every investor is going to have their own opinion on the correct way to pursue the big dollar signs they see in the stocks stashed away in their portfolios. Of course, there is plenty of strategizing and studying that can lead to making the best choices possible, but even then, there is still at least a tiny bit of risk that can foil your plans. The question becomes whether you want to take a big risk in exchange for the bigger reward or play it safe and have a low-to-moderate income with the thought of "something is better than nothing."

How Dividend Investing Can Fit into Your Retirement Goals

The concept of retirement can be mentally draining. You are already working as hard as you can to provide for your family, and then you have to have money after work.

That is not to say that you are in a career where you have to be forced into retirement, but everyone looks forward to the idea of being able to sit on a porch with lemonade on a sunny day rather than put on a suit and go to a busy office. Alas, to be able to reach that dream, you have to have enough money saved up to live on for years, and many folks use an individual retirement account (IRA), which come in various forms because the right type of investments can lead to building up that stockpile of money. That, in itself, is a challenge that can overwhelm a good number of people. First, let us look more into the Roth IRA that people prefer to use to build toward their retirement goals. These IRAs are savings and investment vehicles that have some tax benefits that are more beneficial than a typical investment portfolio.

While a traditional IRA provides an opportunity for an investor's contributions to be made with income deposited before tax is taken out, those distributions are taxed as any other form of income you that would earn from the 40-hour workweek. But when you consider a Roth IRA, those contributions into the stocks are taxed, and the money that is returned to the investor is free of any taxes. Roth IRAs are usually free of taxes when the time comes to get the return on the investments with income that has hopefully built up over time with the power of compounding interest. This means there is a chance to have dividend stocks in the portfolio that pay well and are not being harvested by the greedy IRS tax people. Sure, you have to pay more to get into the party, but the benefits are too great to pass up. So how does the process of dividend investments fit into your retirement goals? A good, dependable dividend investing plan can be the right choice when looking for a portfolio that can build long-term wealth to eventually provide the income to enjoy retirement without any worries of being able to afford not working. One of the biggest factors that attract some retirement planners is the ability to use the power of compounding interest that is found in dividend investment strategies.

Compounding the interest by reinvesting the money you gain regularly requires being able to have a good starting amount of money to be the initial capital, and then investing it in strong equities and letting the price appreciation to be shared and the dividend payments to grow to the point of providing a good base to live on when you do actually retire. Because you are making your dividend investments through something like a Roth IRA, the earnings from those investments are exempt from any taxes that usually hit the money you earn, in many cases, taking out as much as 30 % between state, federal, and an additional federal withholding tax. That is one of the main reasons that people like to use dividend investing as part of their retirement plans. Since Roth IRAs have these tax-free distributed payouts to the shareholders, those returns are more than just the key contributors to the wealth built up for a person's retirement.

Let us add to the fact that the income that comes from the withdrawals of those dividend returns is tax-free. But these IRAs have one disadvantage—of course, there's always a catch—in the sense that these accounts mandate contributions that come from taxable, earned income. On the other hand, the rewards that come from sticking to the plan for several years of dividend investing within a Roth IRA will outweigh those shorter-term costs that one would have to pay upfront. But is the Roth IRA a perfect fit? Well, there are a number of things to consider when choosing between tradition and Roth IRAs: A traditional IRA provides tax-free contributions, while the Roth IRAs offer tax-free income. Roth IRAs provide an advantage in withdrawal taxes since they are not taxed like traditional IRAs. You cannot take out funds without penalty from a Roth IRA until you turn 59-and-a-half years of age, and the IRA has been established for five or more years. A traditional IRA has the same rule, but the money must be withdrawn before 70-and-a-half before a 50 % penalty. There are no limits on contributions within a traditional IRA, but Roth IRAs have a few restrictions, such as the limit on the number of contributions each year if you make more than a certain level of income. Regardless of which IRA type, you will have until April 15 each year to make up the contributions from the prior fiscal year. Overall, those who expect to be taxed at a rate higher than the current income tax when you are expecting to retire—based on tax bracket levels—consider opening a Roth IRA. In the end, different individuals will have their own needs when it comes to how they plan for their retirement. Not everyone can just start at age 18 or in their early 20s. A lot of it depends on their current and potential financial situations down the road, which can affect whether investing in a Roth IRA is the best option for an individual's retirement plan. One way to help in the decision is to know where a person may end up within the tax brackets when they do decide to retire because the Roth IRA may prevent an opportunity to stay away from the higher income tax rates later on. But whatever decision is made on the type of IRA that will form a retirement plan, the main goal is being able to find the best type of investment strategy that can make those golden years of comfortable and relaxing retirement more achievable, which is easily possible with dividend investing within a Roth IRA.

What Is Dividend Investment?

Generally speaking, dividends are referred to as the distribution of the after-tax earnings of a company to shareholders in relation to the number of shares they hold. Mind you, there are 3 parts to this definition, and each one is equally important. Firstly, dividends are paid from profit and not from any other source of equity, for instance, paid-in surplus. Secondly, dividends must be in the form of real assets, and this part is quite tricky. It is a common habit for companies to pay out dividends in the form of cash, checks, or more stocks since these are convenient. However, it would be quite difficult and nonsensical for an airline company like Boeing to offer the right-wing of a 747 to a major shareholder as dividends. Nevertheless, during high levels of inflation, we have seen corporations pay dividends in the form of products that they sell. Finally, the third part of this definition states that every shareholder has a share in dividends irrespective of the number of shares that they hold in the company.

So, How Did It All Start?

You might wonder: how did companies start paying dividends, and who started the whole concept? Well, dividend-paying stocks have been around for hundreds of years, and it has provided an infallible source of passive income to investors for many generations. Here is the outline of the history of dividend-paying stocks.

1250 — A French bank called Société des Moulins du Bazacle was the first company to pay out dividends.

1602 — Nearly 400 years later, the Dutch East India Company became the second corporation in history to pay out dividends. Over the course of its 200-year existence, this company paid out 18 % of its capital.

1682 — Dividend investment finally came to North America officially. The Hudson Bay Company is arguably the first to pay dividends; the first dividends were paid about 14 years after the inception of the company in 1670 and were worth half of the stock value.

1910 — In the early 20th century, many investors were only interested in stocks paying dividends. During this period, stocks were expected to have higher dividend yields than bonds in order to compensate investors for the risks that come with most equities.

2003 — After 28 years of growth, the tech giant, Microsoft, declares its first dividend payment.

Today, about 420 companies out of the 500 company stocks on the S&P 500 pay a dividend. This includes giant corporations like Chevron, McDonald's, and Wal-Mart.

Terms to Know in Dividend Investment

Before we proceed to the countless benefits of dividend investments as a passive income, here are a few terms you first need to get familiar with. These terms will not help you to breach the world of dividends but will enable you to make better financial decisions during investments.

1. Cash Dividends

    Cash dividends are cash payments made to shareholders as part of the company's accumulated earnings or current profit. This is a way for the company to return profits to investors for the shares they hold. Companies pay out dividends monthly, quarterly, or yearly. Besides normal dividend payouts, shareholders can also receive special cash dividends after legal settlements or one-time cash distribution.

2. Declaration Date

This is the date on which the board of directors in a corporation announces the next dividend payment. Also referred to as the announcement date, the board of directors announces the ex-dividend date, the dividend size, and the payment date.

3. Dividend Cover Ratio

    The Dividend Cover Ratio is the ratio between a company's net dividend to shareholders and its earnings. This is an analytical tool used by investors to gauge if a company's earnings can sufficiently cover its dividends to investors. You can calculate this by dividing the earnings per share by the dividends per share.

4. Dividend Reinvestment Plan (DRIP)

    This is a plan offered to investors by dividend-paying corporations to reinvest their cash dividends. The DRIP is an amazing strategy that you will come across in the course of this book. By re-investing your cash dividends into more shares, you will earn higher dividend payouts. Furthermore, most Dividend Reinvestment Plans allow investors to buy additional shares at a discount and without commission. However, most DRIPs do not allow a reinvestment that is less than $10. If your company does not offer a DRIP, you can set one up with a major brokerage firm.

5. Dividend Yield

    Dividend yield is a term you definitely need to add to your repertoire. It is a financial ratio that, in relation to its share value, depicts the amount a company pays out in dividends each year. You can measure the dividend yield by dividing the yearly dividend per share by the share price. This term represents the total amount of return from an investment, and it is the perfect tool to measure potential investments. Here is how to calculate a dividend yield. Let us assume that Company ABC is trading at $40 per share, and the company offers a yearly dividend of $1.5 per share. Therefore, the dividend yield would be at 3.75 %. You may have noticed that the share price and dividend yield move in the opposite direction. If we selected a higher share price of $60, for example, the dividend yield would decrease (1.48 dividend ÷ $60 per share equals to 2.45 % yield).

Therefore, you can earn more dividend income if the share price is lower.

6. Record Date

    Companies determine their shareholders on the record date.

7. Ex-dividend Date

    The ex-dividend date is one of the four main important dates to dividend investors. This is the fixed duration, after which a security is traded without a formerly announced distribution or dividend. Additionally, it is also the date on which the seller of a stock will be entitled to a recently declared dividend.

8. Payment Date

    This is the date on which a stock dividend is scheduled to be paid to shareholders. You should know that only those who bought their shares before the ex-dividend date can receive dividends on the payment date.

9. One-time Dividends

    Also referred to as special dividends, these payments are larger than the conventional dividends paid out to shareholders.

Rules of Dividend Investments

Dividend investments, just like any other niche, comes with its own set of rules. Think of these rules as shortcuts to avoid making common mistakes. These rules are backed by academic research and principles from some of the world's greatest investors. Mind you, do not think of these rules as infallible since there will always be an exception. Nevertheless, it is good to integrate these rules into your everyday investment decisions.

Always Go for Quality!

Long-term orientation is one of the best advantages an investor could ever have. It is a rule to invest in businesses that have stability, profit, and a proven track record of showing growth. Why should you go for a mediocre business when you can invest in a high-quality business? As a financial rule, you should rank stocks by both their dividend and corporate history length, and the longer they are, the better.

The Bargain Principle

It is a rule to invest in businesses that pay you the most dividends for the cash you invest. Remember, the higher the dividend yield, the better. In addition to this, avoid investing in overpriced securities.

You should only deal with stocks trading below a decade historical average valuation multiple, which is the average value of stocks calculated over a ten-year period.

Always Play Safe

Avoid businesses that pay all their income as dividends, as this means that the business has no margin of safety, and dividends can be reduced at any time.

Reinvest Your Dividends

This is definitely one rule you must never break. The power of reinvesting your dividends cannot be undermined. In fact, putting your dividends back to work can do wonders for your portfolio. What's more? You can make use of reinvestment programs, which often enable you to reinvest your payouts automatically without paying a commission fee.

Understand Your Tax Laws

Warren Buffet once said that he is taxed less than his secretary. So, how does he do it? Well, most of his income comes from dividends, which are indeed often taxed, though lower than standard income. So, try to become familiar with the tax structure for dividends and take note of any changes resulting from a new company or government policies.

Do not Make Dividends Your Only Priority

Dividends are an indispensable part of investing. However, dividends are not the all-mighty metric to abide by. Investors need to pay attention to different fundamentals that are often at play in investments. Fundamentals like profits, price actions, and earning growths are just a few of the features you need to pay attention to. Remember to look beyond high-dividend yields and make sure you understand the company's growth pattern and future prospects.

Watch Out for Value Traps

Many investors jump at seemingly lucrative stocks without realizing that they are value traps. A value trap is a phenomenon where a dividend yield is increasing, and stock prices are reducing. When faced with this phenomenon, most investors think they have hit the jackpot. However, they fail to realize that the stock prices were reducing for a legitimate reason. So, how can you detect this trap before it is too late?

Here is the first sign to watch out for. When you see a company that pays out far more than its peers in the sector or market index, this indicates a value trap. In addition to this, falling cash flows with stable yields also indicate a value trap.

Always Look out for Special Dividends

One of the perks of dividend investments is the ability of corporations to initiate a one-time dividend payout. When looking for stocks to purchase, these one-time dividend payouts often mislead investors. During one-time dividend payments, a company's stock might seem rosier than normal. A good example is Microsoft (MSFT), which issued a one-time dividend payment in 2004. It was a sharp contrast to the normal dividend payouts. Microsoft's normal dividend payouts varied from $0.3 to $0.5, while the one-time dividend payout was a whopping $3 per share. Many resources calculate the one-time dividend payment as an annual yield. If we were to include the special dividend payout, Microsoft's annual yield for 2004 would have been 13.78 %, instead of the 0.38 % payout from normal dividends. As you can see, the figure was enough to confuse investors who had not checked and analyzed the yield statistics.

Use the Survival of the Fittest Principle

Sell your stocks when your dividend payouts are reduced or cut short—it's that simple. Research carried out between 1972 and 2017 showed that stocks that cut or reduced their dividend payouts had a 0 % recovery. If your dividends are reduced or stopped, this obviously goes against the principles of generating passive income. In fact, it is the opposite of what we are aiming for. Any business that cuts its dividends has lost its competitive advantage. Therefore, you want to reinvest the proceeds of your sale into a more profitable stock.

Chapter 2: Types of Dividend, Plus Key Technical Terms, Rules, Analysis, and System Best Strategies

Picking stocks is a skill that is honed over time. As investors develop this skill, they conform to a style that matches their personality. Some prefer value, while others prefer growth. Some subscribe to fundamental analysis and make investment decisions based on what they believe to be a company's intrinsic value. Others subscribe to technical analysis and make decisions based on analyzing charts. And while it is easy to apply labels to different styles, when you get down to it, there are as many different variations to picking stocks as there are investors who pick them.

The wealth of literature devoted to each of the different styles allows investors to learn from their predecessors and incorporate existing knowledge into their approach. We all have our own idiosyncrasies, and even when we subscribe to a specific school of thought, we can still be influenced by other techniques. The dividend investor is only different from other investors in the sense that we adopt our own take on what we consider a safe dividend. And safety is important because our goal is to hold our stocks for an extended period of time, all the while being prepared to move into a different stock should the forecast change. Our goal is not to invest in stocks simply because of high dividend yield, but to invest in quality stocks that offer an attractive yet sustainable distribution. If the yield is both sustainable and exceeds that of the market, and the stock possesses other attributes that suggest good performance over a period of at least five years, then the stock should be a candidate for inclusion in the portfolio. With the right stocks, we can increase the benefits of compounding without risking too much, if any, in terms of capital gains. It is important to take your tolerance for risk into consideration when deciding how much, if any, of your portfolio should be invested in individual stocks. At the same time, your individual selections should not infringe on the amount invested in other markets, such as bonds and real estate.

If, for example, your desired asset allocation is 50 % stocks, 25 % bonds, and 25 % REITs, and you want to dedicate 5 % of your portfolio to individual stocks, then you should reduce your investment in stock funds to 45 %. This will give you a combined portfolio allocation of 50 % stocks and allow your bond and REIT allocations to remain at 25 % apiece. Stock picking is as much an art as it is a science. While covering every aspect of a stock that one could conceivably analyze is well beyond the scope of Dividend Investing, I'm going to present some basic attributes that every investor should consider before purchasing a stock, followed by a host of attributes that are particularly important to the dividend investor.

Yes, we are going to dive into the financial statements, but do not think you need to be a CPA in order to read these statements. We are going to look at some high-level attributes that every investor should be familiar with. And I firmly believe that reading footnote disclosures and understanding all of the subtle intricacies of earnings and valuation are not essential in order to feel comfortable with a company's financial position. If the company was able to trick their audit firm, then they will not have much trouble tricking their investors. So you do not need to understand everything that the CPAs wade through when they audit the financial statements. A basic understanding of what the financial statements mean is sufficient. If you find financial statements intimidating, you should not. We will review them at a high level, and while deeper analysis is often beneficial, it is not crucial when it comes to picking a winning stock. I strongly believe that the most important attribute you can look for in a company is its competitive advantage. Is there something they are doing that can't easily be replicated? You will not get this from reading the financial statements. What you will get is a feeling of whether or not the stock is fairly priced, given this competitive advantage. You will also see that the indicators for a safe dividend are very straightforward. There are plenty of resources available online that provide the basic attributes of a stock. Yahoo! Finance is a particularly popular site that is both free and easy to follow. They publish stock statistics that will save you the trouble of crunching numbers. This allows you to devote your time to analyzing the numbers rather than calculating them.

They also publish full financial statements, and these generally include both the most recent year and two or three prior years. For the dedicated investor who wants to dive deeper, I recommend going to the company's website to download the annual 10-K reports, or you can search for the report at sec.gov. If you are not familiar with the 10-K report, it is an annual report required by the U.S. Securities and Exchange Commission (SEC). Publicly traded companies are also required to file quarterly reports (10-Qs). These are public documents that hold the financial statements, and many of the statistics available on Yahoo! Finance are derived from these reports. The documents also provide very thorough explanations of the amounts reported in the financial statements.

This is a great resource when further investigation is warranted.

The Income Statement

The income statement can be used to analyze a company's revenues (or sales) and the expenses that are not only attributed directly to those sales but the overall operations of the company. In general terms, it allows us to analyze how effectively the company generates sales and how efficiently it manages expenses. Look for a copy of the Apple Inc. (AAPL) income statement for a specific fiscal year and you might find it helpful to use as an example as we review each section of the income statement.

Revenue

At the top of the income statement is revenue. Comparing revenue from the current year to prior years will provide an indication as to whether or not the company is growing. Ideally, we want to see a revenue increase from one year to the next. Obviously, the bigger the year-over-year increase, the better. And any increase that scarcely keeps pace with inflation should not be considered an increase at all. Revenue is metrics for demand. It speaks directly to the number of sales generated by the company. It does not tell us anything about how efficiently the company generated those sales. If revenue is decreasing and the company makes corresponding cuts to their expenses, the bottom line (net income) may very well increase. And while such a situation would actually increase profits (for the year), it is an indication that growth has stagnated. For a stock to be an attractive investment, we do not just want to see an increase in net income, but we also want to see revenue increasing each year.

- Cost of Revenue – While revenue alone is a good metric for measuring sales, it tells us nothing about how much those sales cost. What we also want to know is what kinds of expenses did the company incur in order to generate sales? The cost of revenue speaks directly to the cost of manufacturing and delivering a product or service. It ignores costs that the company incurs, irrespective of its output, and focuses on labor costs, commissions, materials and supplies, and related overhead. It is a measure of costs that fluctuate with the level of output, which should increase as sales increase. A company with low cost of revenue as a percent of total revenue is thought to be in good financial position.

- Gross Profit - Gross profit is a company's revenue minus its cost of revenue. It is beneficial to see this number increase, along with the revenue, meaning that the company is not increasing costs by too much in order to generate additional sales. If sales are increasing, the gross profit will tell us if the company was able to increase those sales by more or less than the corresponding increase in the cost of sales.

  To compare gross profit between different companies, calculate as a ratio the following: Gross Profit / Revenue = Gross Profit Margin

This type of comparison is most meaningful when made between companies in the same industry. The higher the margin in comparison to that of the company's competitors, the better.

Operating Expenses

Operating expenses include necessary expenses to support the company's operations. Unlike the cost of revenue, these expenses will not fluctuate directly with output.

Operating expenses include rent, research and development, the cost of equipment, administrative payroll, insurance, and a large host of expenses that a company incurs, regardless of that quarter's production run. Generally, a company will attempt to reduce these costs as a means of staying efficient and competitive, or if the company is struggling, they will reduce them just to stay alive. An increase in operating expenses could be an indication of coming improvements in the quality or innovation of their products or services. Or it could mean that they are slipping in terms of efficiency.

Income From Continuing Operations

This figure tells us if the company is profitable as a result of its primary income source. That is, did net income go up because there is a demand for the company's product or service, or did they put themselves in the green by selling something extraneous like a piece of real estate? It can also be referred to as income before interest and taxes. It is the culmination of everything we discussed above, but it excludes interest, taxes, extraordinary items, and other non-recurring events.

Companies acquire all sorts of assets in order to produce and market a product or service. And while they may eventually sell those assets at a profit (or loss), this income is outside the scope of their general operations and is not included in income from continuing operations. While such sales may affect a company's financial position, seeing continued improvement in a company's income from continuing operations is a sign of strength and stability. It means that they are growing as a result of their core business purpose, rather than having stumbled into an amazing one-time real estate deal. It is desirable that, on average, the bulk of a company's net income is derived from its continued operations, though unrelated gains are certainly welcome. Like gross profit, we can also derive a ratio off of income from continuing operations in order to make comparisons between companies: Income from Continuing Operations / Revenue = Operating Margin

Again, the higher the margin, the better. And the comparison is most meaningful when made between companies in the same industry.

Non-recurring Events

Sometimes, a company looks really good in certain areas, yet for some reason, it has negative net income for the year. Or maybe, they underperformed in terms of sales, but net income still went up. In either case, you will want to take a look at the numbers booked under non-recurring events. These are one-time happenings that impact the bottom line. That amazing real estate deal alluded to above is a non-recurring event. It is also an example of the company making money. Another year, there might be a natural disaster that destroys one of their plants. This, of course, would produce a loss. If a non-recurring event leads to a loss, you definitely want to dig deeper. It might be necessary to wade through the 10K and review the footnote disclosures.

But if it is a large company with heavy coverage, then a Google search might be an easier way to see what is going on. It could be a write-off of bad debt with no expected impact on future performance. Or it could be the result of litigation against the company, and depending on the nature of the litigation, there could be a residual effect that hurts their reputation and impacts future sales. If the company has discontinued operations, it could explain why sales have fallen. But it could also be a sign that they are taking steps to improve efficiency. The numbers are just that—numbers. The interpretation is up to the investor. Reading financial statements in conjunction with articles published on the company often provides the needed insight. In this regard, larger companies with plenty of press coverage are much easier to evaluate. A non-recurring event will not always influence your perception of the company, but if they have non-recurring events each year, and the losses are significant, it is a sign to stay away.

Net Income

Net income, often referred to as the bottom line, is basically sales (of all kinds, not just for the product or service that the company specializes in) less every expense incurred, from those required to produce or provide their product or service down to the cost of financing their operations and the interest and taxes they incurred in this endeavor. While it is important to review the bottom line, an understanding of how the above pieces feed into net income is far more important. When reviewing a large number of companies, it might be tempting to start with net income and move on to your next candidate if you do not see year-to-year improvement. I recommend starting with revenue instead. Look, first, for companies that have increased their revenue for at least three years straight, and do not waste any time with companies that haven't. If they pass this requirement, then keep reading and see if you are still interested by the time you have worked your way down to net income. If you are, then it is time to review the balance sheet. Just as we did with gross profit and income from continuing operations, we can express net income as a percentage of revenue in order to make comparisons across companies: Net Income / Revenue = Net Income Margin

As before, we are looking for a high ratio relative to that of the company's competitors.

The Balance Sheet

While the income statement is our source of information for earnings, the balance sheet tells us about the company's overall financial position. How many assets has the company accumulated? What kind of debt is it currently holding? And do assets exceed liabilities in order to provide a positive equity position? These are the types of questions we will be asking. The entire balance sheet should be reviewed before making an investment. But different companies will show different types of assets and liabilities, especially if they compete in different industries. If one company manufactures a good while another provides a service, there will be items on their balance sheets that are not comparable. For this reason, we are going to hone in on an assortment of key items that every investor should be familiar with. We will look at both assets and liabilities, knowing that in an accounting sense, the true worth of the company is net assets or assets held in excess of liabilities.

Assets − Liabilities = Owner's Equity

The owner's equity represents the value of the company, but this measurement is different from how the company is valued on a stock exchange.

On an exchange, the company is worth whatever the investors are willing to pay for it (or, more specifically, what the most recent investor paid for it). The current selling price multiplied by the number of shares outstanding determines the market capitalization. But accountants are not concerned with what investors are willing to pay for the company; they want to know the valuation of what the company owns, less the obligations they have incurred but have yet to pay. If we take owner's equity and divide by the number of shares outstanding, we get the book value per share. This, of course, will differ from what a share of stock sells in an exchange. In most cases, market price per share will exceed the book value per share. And this is perfectly fine. Most value investors do not mind paying more than book value. Ben Graham, the father of value investing, advocated buying stocks with a price-to-book ratio of 1.5 or less, meaning he was only willing to pay 1.5 times the book price for a share of stock. Given this criterion, if we find a stock with a price-to-book ratio less than 1.5, or even less than 1, it should be a candidate for investment. Other attributes, such as a solid profit margin or a strong outlook for growth, are likely more important than book value. So when you find a stock with an attractive price-to-book ratio, consider it icing on the cake. If you are unfamiliar with Ben Graham, you might want to become acquainted with his book, The Intelligent Investor. It is not geared toward building a portfolio around dividend-paying index funds, but it is an excellent resource for any investor who likes to pick her own stocks. A lot has changed since it was first published in 1949, but it will forever hold its place as the foundation that value investing was built on. To this day, many investors consider it their primary handbook. It's important to note that the income statement provides earnings results over a period of time, usually a year. But the balance sheet displays the company's financial position as of a specific date. It does not report on all of Apple's fiscal year 2018 but rather shows what their position was on the very last day of their fiscal year.

Current vs. Non-Current

You probably noticed that some of the assets and liabilities are designated as current, while others are simply included in the total. A current asset is a liquid asset that the company expects to convert to cash within the next year. An example would be all of the accounts receivable that the company expects to collect on within 12 months. A current liability is an obligation that will be paid in the coming year, such as accounts payable that will be remitted within 12 months under the normal course of business. A comparison of current assets to current liabilities is important as we evaluate the company's ability to sustain current operations, where a review of non-current items, such as long-term debt, comes into play as we forecast on the company's value and ongoing profitability. The distinction is also important in terms of dividend payment, particularly as we forecast the company's ability to increase the payment on an annual basis.

Assets

Cash and Cash Equivalents

Cash is king. There's no way around it. Good sales and low expenses are important. It is the earnings per share that analysts most frequently make projections on, and it is the company's ability to beat those projections that send the stock higher. But not every sale is collectible, and if the company is not bringing in cash, it's going to catch up with them. As dividend investors, we really want to know if there is enough cash to maintain the dividend during an economic downturn. If the company is heavily debt-financed with very little cash reserves, it is a cause for concern. Creditors take precedence over shareholders when companies are liquidated. Even the lawyers get paid before the shareholders. But beyond the fear of liquidation, a low cash position means that the company could be forced to cut their dividends in order to pay back loans. Some investors view too much cash as an indication that the company is not putting their capital to use effectively. As dividend investors, this is a secondary concern. We want to buy financially stable companies, and a strong cash position is a good indication of stability. It keeps our dividends safe through both the ups and downs. In addition to cash as reported on the balance sheet, it also pays to take a look at the statement of cash flow. This statement shows all cash activity, and it basically reconciles the change in cash position from one year's balance sheet to the next. If income from continuing operations is increasing, you want to make sure that cash flow from operating activities is also increasing. This will not happen in exact proportions. Sometimes, a sale made this year will not be collected until next year. But over time, you want to see a smoothing out that brings these numbers together.

Accounts Receivable
This is what the company is owed due to sales generated in the normal course of business. Changes to accounts receivable can tell us a number of things about the company. If it increases with time, it could be the result of increased sales. Similarly, if it decreases with time, it could be

an indication that sales have declined. By reviewing accounts receivable in conjunction with revenue, it is easy to gauge whether or not it is increasing or decreasing proportionately to changes in sales. If it's not, further evaluation is necessary. There is also the possibility that the company is just getting better or worse at collecting on their accounts. Or perhaps, they have expanded into a new territory or marketplace that comes with different challenges. There is no hard and fast rule with accounts receivable. It needs to be reviewed in terms of what the company is doing. But if it increases or decreases dramatically without a corresponding trend in sales, it is a cause for further investigation. A common ratio used to compare accounts receivable between companies in the same industry is accounts receivable turnover: Revenue / Accounts Receivable = Accounts Receivable Turnover to express as a factor of days: 365 / Accounts Receivable Turnover = Accounts Receivable Turnover expressed in days. This is a ratio that we want to be as low as possible, as a low ratio indicates timely collections.

Inventory

With inventory, we really want to analyze trends. How does it change over time? And do the changes make sense based on whether or not the company is growing? When sales go down, we should expect an immediate increase in inventory. But after this has happened, we want to know if the company adjusted its production accordingly. If inventory keeps rising, it's a sign of poor management. At the same time, is a sudden boost to the net income the result of increased sales, or is the company depleting inventory from prior periods? This all ties into how efficiently the company is run, and a company that keeps tight controls on their inventory is desirable, not just because it costs money to produce inventory, but also because it costs money to store inventory. A common ratio to compare inventory management between companies in the same industry is the inventory turnover ratio: Cost of Revenue / Inventory = Inventory Turnover Ratio

The result represents the number of times that a company turns over its inventory throughout the year. The more it turns over, the better.

Property, Plant, and Equipment

PP&E is just what the name implies. These are the large assets necessary to conduct business. The land has the potential to appreciate in value and, therefore, is reported at current market value. All other PP&E is initially reported at cost and then depreciated over time. When evaluating stocks, where the book value is less than market value, PP&E is important because these are big assets that will fetch the most in the event of liquidation. It means the company still has something of value should everything else go horribly wrong (though, we will not be investing in a company if we have reason to believe that all else will go horribly wrong). Land and buildings could conceivably be sold for a gain over the purchase price, where most other PP&E will sell for a loss, but hopefully, fetch something in the neighborhood of its depreciated value. An increase in PP&E is often observed during times of expansion. Steady decreases to PPE&E will likely correspond to the company's depreciation schedule and should not be a cause for concern.

Goodwill

Not every asset on the balance sheet is a monetary or physical asset. Goodwill is more or less synonymous with brand recognition. Or, more especially, brand recognition that was purchased from another company. When a company produces goodwill internally it does not appear on the balance sheet. The expenses incurred to build and market the business are, of course, recorded on the income statement. But no expense is directly tied to the brand recognition this produces, and therefore it does not get reported as goodwill. An exception exists when the company purchases another company and pays the price above what the company is valued at on its balance sheet. When this happens the premium paid is booked as goodwill. This treatment puts the investor at a disadvantage. It's difficult to make an apples-to-apples comparison when one company is permitted to show at least some of their goodwill on the balance sheet, and another is not. It can also be argued that when it comes to goodwill, too much is a bad thing. It's an indication that the company paid a premium for a name. And should the company ever be liquidated, there's nothing for them to actually sell. This is an asset that does not have a direct use. A good exercise is to compare companies as though they do not have any goodwill on the balance sheet. Simply subtract goodwill from owner's equity, make a comparison, and then ask yourself which company looks more attractive. This gets us closer to the apples-to-apples comparison that we are after.

Intangible Assets

Goodwill is not the only intangible asset on the balance sheet. The others will be appropriately grouped together as intangible assets. Companies often own patents, trademarks, and copyrights, and these intangible assets have value. Unlike goodwill, a company can sell copyright. But that does not mean we do not encounter valuation problems with these assets. A company must report its patents, trademarks, and copyrights at cost, not at what they are truly worth. So just like goodwill, it is difficult to make an apples-to-apples comparison with intangible assets. I suggested above that you subtract goodwill from owner's equity for the purposes of comparison. It is beneficial to make the same comparison with both goodwill and intangible assets excluded from owner's equity. This provides a figure that's referred to as net tangible assets.

Liabilities

Accounts Payable – Accounts payable is the complete opposite of accounts receivable. It's what the company owes for expenses incurred on a short-term line of credit. We know that it is desirable to accelerate the collection of accounts receivable, and there is always a concern that some accounts will not be collected. The same concern does not extend to accounts payable. So long as the company has the wherewithal to make good on their expenses, we would rather have them pay their bills as late as permissible per the vendor agreement. You can think of it as an interest-free loan (albeit it a very short one). By delaying their payments, a company basically obtains a cash float. The ultimate goal is to accelerate the collection of accounts receivable while postponing the remittance of accounts payable. A company that manages this well will have a financial advantage over a company that does not. Just like accounts receivable, we can use a ratio to compare accounts payable turnover between companies in the same industry: Cost of Revenue / Accounts Payable = Accounts Payable Turnover To express as a factor of days: 365 / Accounts Payable Turnover = Accounts Payable Turnover expressed in Days. Where a low ratio is desired for the accounts receivable turnover, we want to delay our accounts payable, so a high ratio is desired.

Debt

The perception that debt is bad is not always true. Just like personal debt, corporate debt can be used wisely, though it can also be a cause for concern. When an individual takes out a loan for their education or to buy a house, they are taking on debt that will pay them back. The house is expected to appreciate in value, and it provides the homeowner with free rent, no matter how long they live there. An education, while expensive, is intended to pay the individual back with a higher-paying job. These are both great uses of debt. A credit card balance, on the other hand, does nothing more than compound interest against the individual. The same rules apply to corporate debt. There is good debt, and there is bad debt. Is the company issuing bonds to fund new projects that will pay them back in the future? Or are they taking out loans to keep themselves afloat in light of poor sales? As dividend investors, we are particularly concerned with debt. If the amount is small, then there is really nothing left for the investor to consider. But large debt holdings should prompt further investigation to obtain a better understanding of what the debt is for. It is a great sign when debt levels are falling. Debt for new projects can be good, but it is still better to see debt going down and not up. It is an indication that previous projects are paying off. When reviewing companies from the same industry, a comparison of debt as a percent of either cash of total assets can be beneficial. It is also beneficial to compare debt as a percent of total equity. If two companies are comparable on other grounds, the company with the least amount of debt is preferred. To evaluate as a ratio, compute as follows: Debt / Equity = Debt-to-Equity Ratio. A low ratio is desired. But keep in mind there are many good uses of debt. In order to compare ratios under the proper context, an understanding of how the debt is used should be obtained.

Equity

In simple terms, equity is the book value of the company. It is the assets minus the liabilities, which equates to the net assets that remain and belong to the shareholders. If it is negative, it is a cause for concern. It means the company owes more than they have. Different methods can be used to calculate book value depending on the different classes of equity reported on the balance sheet. For our purposes, we will look at two of them: Assets − Liabilities = Book Value (owner's equity) (Assets − Goodwill − Intangible Assets) − Liabilities = Book Value (owner's equity)

We've already discussed how book value will differ from market value and that a stock with book value greater than market value should be a candidate for investment. The second approach, which focuses on tangible equity, is also important. Goodwill will become worthless during liquidation. Patents, trademarks, and copyrights could, in reality, fetch much less than their book value in the event that they can even be sold. The very fact that the company is being liquidated indicates a lack of profitable earnings, which implies that its patents, trademarks, and copyrights no longer hold value. If the company is thriving, it is a greater indication that its intangible assets hold value and could be sold at a profit. But such companies generally do not go through the liquidation process. Book value derived from net tangible assets provides a clearer, more conservative view of what the shareholder is likely to receive during liquidation. For this reason, it's the figure we'll use to compare market value to book value. A common ratio used to evaluate companies in the same industry is the return on equity: Net Income / Equity = Return on Equity

The higher the ratio, the better the company is thought to be putting its equity to use.

Retained Earnings

The retained earnings is part of equity. It is the sum of all net incomes that the company earns, less any dividends that it pays. As dividend investors, it is important to know that dividends are not an expense to the company. They do not get reported on the income statement, and they do not reduce net income. Dividends are what gets distributed to shareholders after net income has been calculated. And while they do not increase expenses, they are a cash outlay and, therefore, have an impact on the balance sheet. A cash dividend will decrease retained earnings. It also reduces the company's cash position. In order for a company to pay its dividend, they must have both positive retained earnings and the appropriate amount of cash. It is important to understand that a net loss will decrease retained earnings, and thus impact the funds available to distribute in the form of a dividend. This is one reason that we want to invest in companies where net income increases each year. The other reason is that rising net income combined with increased revenues is a sign of both growth and efficiency. While we do want to earn dividends, it makes sense that receiving them will affect the value of the company; what once belonged to "the company" now belongs to us. This is a tradeoff. But while a dividend payment will decrease retained earnings, positive net income will increase retained earnings. So what we really want is a company whose dividend distribution is less than its earnings, as this will sum to a positive impact on retained earnings. As we work our way through the following attributes, we will see exactly how to identify the type of company we want to invest in.

Attributes

Reviewing a company's financial statements is the first step to determine if a stock is worthy of investment. If you do not like what you see on the financial statements, then there is no reason to proceed further. It is time to move on to a different company and see if their stock fits your requirements. For companies that do show promise, in terms of increasing sales, managing efficiency, and maintaining a healthy balance sheet, there are further attributes that you will want to review. Some of them pertain specifically to the stock. It is important to understand that a company and its stock are not one and the same. A company can have beautiful financial statements, and the stock can still be overpriced. Sometimes, it pays to bide your time and wait for a correction. Other times, you are better off redirecting your efforts to a different company. While some of the attributes pertain solely to the stock, other attributes will incorporate figures from the financial statements and, thus, pertain to both the stock and the company.

Volume

It is important to know the average number of shares that trade each day. This will not tell you if a stock is fairly priced or even a good buy, but it will tell you how liquid the investment is. Some stocks might only average a couple of hundred trades each day, while others average in the millions. Keep your eyes open because low-volume stocks are present in all segments, from large-cap stocks, all the way down to microcap stocks. Low volume is an indication of a large bid-ask spread, meaning that to buy the stock, you have to pay more than what the seller on the other end of the trade is willing to accept. The difference between the bid (selling price) and the ask (buying price) goes to the market-maker as a commission, and if the market-maker is willing to handle low-volume security, they are going to want a larger commission for their effort. You can think of the bid-ask spread as an additional fee that you pay on every investment, and the lower the volume traded, the more likely it is that you will pay a higher fee. If the volume is too low, it's an indication that you might have difficulty selling the stock once it has been purchased. If you own more than the average daily volume or even a sizeable percent of the average daily volume, it will be difficult to unload the investment without driving down the price. So if you buy into a sock that only trades a couple hundred shares a day, watch it go up 15%, and then try to sell it all at once, you will probably drive the price down in the process and receive less than the 15% gain you were expecting. With some stocks, you might not be able to sell them at all, at least not until a prospective buyer eventually pops up, and that buyer might not be willing to pay anything close to where the stock last traded. The same applies to ETFs. An ETF that tracks the S&P 500 is likely to experience high trading volume, where a junk bond fund could conceivably trade in smaller increments, have a higher bid-ask spread, and be more difficult to unload. If your starting place for stock selections is the S&P 500 Dividend Aristocrats, then volume should not be a concern. These are heavily traded companies that garner a lot of attention. But if you decide to stray into other areas, keep your eyes open and make sure there is plenty of trading volume before you buy in.

Trailing P/E Ratio

A big mistake that new investors make is thinking that the cost of a share indicates whether or not the investment is expensive. A stock that sells for $25 is not half as expensive as a stock that sells for $50, precisely because each company has a different number of shares outstanding. What you are really buying is an ownership interest in the company, and if each company has a different number of shares outstanding, then comparing the cost of stock A to the cost of stock B is not an apples-to-apples comparison. The P/E ratio is used to form some even ground. We might not be able to compare the cost of stock A to the cost of stock B in any meaningful way, but we can compare the earnings of each company in a way that is exceptionally meaningful. What the P/E ratio does is it takes the price of a stock and divides it by the earnings per share.

P/E Ratio = Price Per Share / Earnings Per Share

For example, if a company sells for $10 per share and its earnings is $0.75 per share, then it has a P/E ratio of 13.33. If the investor were to actually receive that $0.75 in earnings each year as a distribution, it would take the investor 13.33 years to earn back the $10 that she invested in the company. Generally speaking, the lower the P/E ratio, the better. If the P/E ratio were to be 11 instead of 13.33, then it would only take 11 years to earn back the investment. The investor is not going to actually receive the earnings, and if the company is paying a dividend, we hope that the dividend is less than the earnings. If it is not, then the dividend is not sustainable. But the P/E ratio is still the most valuable tool we have for comparing the cost of one stock to another. If the P/E ratio is high, it is an indication that investors are expecting higher earnings growth relative to companies with a lower P/E ratio. Otherwise, they would not pay a higher price. And while expectations of future growth might seem attractive, I'm going to warn against buying stocks with high P/E ratios because what this really means is that you are paying for future earnings that are only expected to be higher than present earnings; they have not materialized yet. At the same time, if a P/E ratio is too low, it is an indication that market sentiment is bearish. The shareholders wouldn't part with their investment at such a low price if the outlook was promising. At the time of writing, the S&P 500 has a collective P/E ratio of 31.32, and this ratio is considered high (and viewed by many as exceptionally dangerous). If we look at historical averages, we see that the S&P 500 has a mean P/E ratio of 16.58 and a median P/E ratio of 15.68. These are considered much safer ratios, and a P/E ratio of 12 is considered attractive. The average P/E ratio will, of course, differ by sector, as some sectors are simply more expensive to invest in than others. The tech sector is a great example because there is potential for exponential growth based on some revolutionary new invention. Therefore, tech stocks on average have higher P/E ratios than the rest of the market. When looking at the lower end of the spectrum, a P/E ratio down around 9 is thought to be dangerous, and anything below this is considered bearish and an indication of short selling. It should also be noted that the trailing P/E ratio is the metric to focus on, as this ratio is based on historical earnings. They also publish a forward P/E ratio based on analyst estimates for future earnings. This ratio should be ignored due to the fact that the analysts are frequently wrong. The forward P/E ratio is both arbitrary and meaningless.

200-Day Moving Average

There's a saying amongst investors that asset prices will revert to the mean. This suggests that if the current selling price differs significantly from its historical average, the price will eventually move back in the direction of the historical average. A stock that has been moving up (or down) is expected to revert at some point. And while it cannot be guaranteed with certainty when this reversion will occur, it happens frequently enough that traders base their strategy on this attribute. Even though our focus is geared toward investing rather than trading, this attribute is still a valuable tool.

The 200-day moving average is a metric commonly used to measure a stock's current price in relation to its average price over the past 200 days. As the name implies, the average will change each day because it is a moving average, and this keeps the figure relevant. If a stock is priced too far above its 200-day moving average, we assume that the price will eventually drop. If a stock is priced too far below its 200-day moving average, we assume that the price will eventually rise. Our goal is not to make a quick profit off of this reversion. Rather, we're going to review a variety of attributes

for each stock we consider. If we find a good candidate for a long-term investment, we'll buy it. But all else being equal, it's better to invest in stock while it is priced below its 200-day moving average than to get in on a stock that's priced above its 200-day moving average. If two stocks are equally attractive, purchase the one that looks cheaper based on its current price in relation to its 200-day moving average.

Current Ratio

While our goal is to identify investments to hold for a minimum of five years, the current ratio is important in terms of analyzing a company's current sustainability. It is calculated as: Current Assets / Current Liabilities = Current Ratio

A current ratio above one is an indication of stability, where a current ratio below one is a cause for concern. In other words, you want the sum of the company's current assets to exceed the sum of the company's current liabilities. So long as current assets exceed current liabilities, the company is in a good position to carry forward with daily operations. If the ratio falls below one, then it's an indication that the company either needs to liquidate a long-term asset (which could disrupt future operations) or experience a disruption to its current operations. It's advisable to simply avoid investing in companies with a current ratio below one.

% Held by Insiders
To the extent possible, we want to invest in companies that are predominately owned by insiders. And if "predominately owned" is too ambitious, then we want insiders to at least own a sizeable holding in the company. Why? Because strong insider ownership aligns the interests of upper management with that of the shareholders. It prevents management from making decisions that improve their own financial well-being at the expense of the stock price. If they own shares in the company, then every decision they make will be geared toward increasing the value of the stock. There are, however, plenty of successful companies with a small percent of insider ownership.

Not every holding in your portfolio is going to have 20 % of the stock resting in the palms of upper management. And while that's fine, it's still better to invest in companies with high insider ownership, especially if the percentage of institutional ownership is low. Typically, insiders are awarded shares by the company, and once the shares have vested, they have the option of either holding or selling their stock. Some investors pay a lot of attention to actions of insiders. A good rule of thumb is that insider selling does not matter. Holding too much stock in the company you work for is poor diversification. If the company goes out of business, then you lose both your job and your investment. From that perspective, it makes sense for an insider to sell their stock as soon as it vests and then reinvest the proceeds in a different company. At the same time, they could be selling their shares simply because they want to spend the money. Investment decisions should not be based on insider selling. There are too many variables to consider when it comes to why an insider might sell, and attempting to analyze trends in insider selling reveals absolutely nothing about the company. Conversely, when an insider makes the decision to buy the company stock, it's an incredibly bullish signal. That is, they purchase shares with their own money, in addition to those that they are awarded for their work. It's a sign of extreme confidence when insiders want to hold more stock than what has been awarded to them by the company. When this situation arises, a conservative investment in the company, even when other attributes are less than ideal, is warranted.

% Held by Institutions

This attribute holds more importance than insider ownership. It can make or break your investment decision. It's the institutional investors who truly set the price of a stock, and they do this by buying and selling in large quantities. It's the buy/sell decisions made by these funds, along with hedge funds, private equity funds, and pension funds that truly determine the price of a stock. When the individual investor buys a few hundred shares of a stock, they do so at whatever price the market is offering. But when a big hedge fund acquires 0.01% of a company, which might be hundreds of thousands of shares, this act of buying pushes the price up. The same thing happens when they unload a hefty portion of their investment—they can't get rid of too many shares without driving the price down. So it makes sense to look at the percent held by institutional investors, and with this metric, we want small a percent as possible. If hardly any of the shares are held by institutional investors, it means that they haven't driven the price up yet. At the same time, a small holding by institutional investors means that there's not much they can unload onto the market. In order for there to be a big sell-off, they would have to buy it first. Be leery of any stock that is greater than 80 % owned by institutional investors. Granted, this attribute has no impact on the company's profits or their ability to continue paying a dividend, but it could be an indication that the company is overpriced. If high institutional ownership is coupled with a high P/E ratio, it is best to stay away. If you like the company but do not care to purchase them at too high a price, simply add them to your watch list and see if you can get in at a lower price after the institutional investors reduce their holdings.

Short % of Float

This is another attribute that gives us a glimpse into what other investors might already know. But before we delve into how this attribute can be used to our advantage, I want to recommend that you never take a short position in a stock. If you're unfamiliar with the term, then good! It's a tool that should only be used by skilled hedgers but is commonly used by gamblers. It has no place inside the typical retirement portfolio. But for the sake of thoroughness, I'll provide an explanation. Short selling is the practice of selling a stock before you buy it, and then later closing out the position by making a purchase of the stock. Basically, it's buying and selling in reverse, and in order to make a profit off of a short sale, the stock price needs to go down. So you're not investing in a company that you like, but, instead, are betting against a company's stock. The short seller, by his own will, is putting himself in a position where the upside potential is limited to the price of the stock, yet the downside potential is completely unlimited. The stock could triple in value, and somewhere along the line his broker is going to close the position and send him a bill. But just because we do not want to sell short does not mean that information on short positions is not useful. By reviewing the percent of a company's shares that are sold short, we can attempt to gauge what other investors think of the stock price. If less than 2 % of the shares are sold short, it tells us that other investors aren't concerned with the outlook (or they're at least not so concerned that they're going to bet against the stock). This, combined with other information, could persuade us to buy. But if we see that 10 % of the stock is being sold short, it means that others are betting against it, and we should proceed with extreme caution. It does not matter if we do not know why so much of the stock is being sold short; it's an indication that the other investors know something that we do not. As a general rule, if more than 3 % of the outstanding shares are being sold short, be cautious. If the short % of float gets up around 5 %, it's best to just stay away. If you like the company and believe that a recent influx of short-sellers is simply an indication that the stock is overpriced, add the company to your watch list and see if you can get in at a lower price after the short sellers close their positions.

I, however, do not recommend joining the short sellers in an effort to profit from a short-term drop in price. Just because a stock is expensive and overdue for correction does not mean that the correction is coming anytime soon. It's extremely difficult to predict when a justified change in price will actually occur. That's why the strategies discussed in this book focus on long-term goals rather than short-term movements.

Profile and News

Yahoo! Finance publishes a profile and links to news articles for just about every stock out there. The attributes we've discussed are all quantifiable, but your research needs to encompass so much more than this. The profile will tell you exactly what you would expect it to. It lists the sector and industry that the stock belongs to, what their specific services and products are, the brands they own, where the headquarters is located, and, of course, a link to their website. News articles are especially important.

Not everything that affects the price of a stock is going to make the front page, so it's important to get out there and find out what's being reported about the company. Yes, it's imperative to do quantifiable analysis like comparing P/E ratios and profit margins, but it's also important to understand that not all information that affects the stock price is found in the financial statements. Has the company announced a new product release? Is there pending litigation? Did they just get a patent approval? Or did a patent just expire? Will the next round of tariffs hurt them? Or will the tariff benefit them at the detriment of a different sector? These are things you need to know before making an investment. And you need to continue reading after you've bought the stock. This is the reason that I recommend limiting your individual holdings. Somewhere in the neighborhood of five investments should be sufficient. Otherwise, it becomes a tremendous amount of work.

Additional Attributes to Consider When Selecting Dividend Stocks

The attributes we've discussed are important when considering an investment in any stock. But the dividend investor has more work to do. The following attributes pertain directly to stocks that pay dividends.

Dividend Yield

This is the dividend payment measured as a percent of the stock price. If a stock sells for $5.00, and the company distributes quarterly dividends of $0.05, then the dividend yield is 4% (0.05 x 4 / 5 = 0.04). The yield is expressed in terms of total annual payments, but most companies distribute their dividends quarterly. As dividend investors, we are attracted to a high yield, but we know that it's dangerous to chase after the wrong investment just because we like the distribution. As discussed with the Dividend Aristocrats, a long-term investor should be attracted to a stock with a sustainable dividend that increases over time. The yield on the current stock price is only a consideration that new investors make. The yield on the price initially paid for the stock becomes increasingly more important as new investors evolve into long-term holders.

Payout Ratio

This is our primary gauge for a sustainable dividend. The payout ratio is the percent of net income that is being distributed. If net income is $2.00 per share and the company pays a $0.27 quarterly dividend, then the payout ratio is 54% (0.27 x 4 / 2). The lower the payout ratio, the better. If it only takes a small percent of the company's earnings to distribute the dividend, then the dividend is considered sustainable. I recommend only buying companies with a payout ratio of 75 % or less.

Once they exceed this amount, it becomes difficult for the company to keep increasing its dividend during economic downturns or any situation that causes net income to suffer. If you can find a payout ratio much smaller than 75 %, that's even better! A payout ratio of 30 %, for example, is considered attractive.

Cash Flow

While a healthy payout ratio is crucial, it's also important for the company to collect on their earnings. Just about every publicly traded company does its accounting on an accrual basis, meaning that earnings are recognized on sales, not on the receipt of cash. Some of those sales might be collected immediately, while others sit in accounts receivable and are aged over an extended period of time. So while the payout ratio is the most important measure, I recommend taking a look at the company's cash flow to ensure that enough money is coming in to sustain the dividend payment.

If cash flow is not keeping pace with sales, it could spell trouble. Generally, if the cash flow from operating activities is 125 % or more of the dividend payment, then the dividend is thought to be safe. We will not be dissecting the cash flow statement as we did with the income statement and balance sheet. While the entire statement should be reviewed before making an investment, for our purposes, we're going to hone in on a key figure. The cash flow from operating activities tells us how much money the company brought in from their core activities (as opposed to money that comes and goes through their investing and financing activities). The reason we evaluate the dividend based on operating activities is simple; we do not want to invest in a company that has to borrow to pay their dividends. We want a company that brings in real money through its core operations, and then distributes a portion of that money to shareholders. If cash flow from operating activities is at least 125 % of the dividend payment, it's an indication of sustainability, particularly if the company is increasing its retained earnings year after year.

Moving Forward

The attributes we've discussed aren't just important when selecting a stock but should also be used to monitor your stocks after they've been purchased. Companies change with time, and the shareholders should stay informed.

You need to know if earnings are increasing or decreasing if more of the stock is being sold short, or if the payout ratio has changed. If the company starts taking on more long-term debt, you need to determine if it's because they have promising new projects or if they're having cash flow problems. A successful stock picker keeps up on everything. And this is precisely why I recommend making index funds the bulk of the portfolio. If you're driven to do this work, do it with a small percentage of your portfolio in an effort to gain an edge over the market.

Chapter 3: Dividend Investing for Passive Income

For hundreds of years, long-term investors invested in dividend stocks. At the beginning of the 20th century, most of the money made in the stock market in the US came in the form of dividends that companies paid to their shareholders. It is one of the opportunities that an average investor can enjoy now, too. This age is dominated by speculation in various securities. People tend to believe that they can make a killing in the stock market by selecting the right stock that would rise by a thousand percent, and they will win a jackpot. Unfortunately, most speculators end up losing it all. They ignore long-term profits and tend to choose short-term strategies to invest in stocks. Very few investors now think about a company in terms of whether it pays dividends or not. Most are searching for growth stocks that start their existence in the market from $5 or something and, in a matter of a few years, skyrocket to $100 or even more. They search for future stocks of CISCO, Wal-Mart, Apple, or Google that are going to fly like rockets to the moon and will make them wealthy beyond their wildest dreams. Very few find these stocks. Some pick up some penny stocks and lose a substantial amount of their money investing in them. However, the facts speak for themselves. Some say that for the past 100 years or so, more than forty percent of the famous S&P500 returns came from dividends. The statistics should make one think whether or not it is better to leave short-term strategies and concentrate on the long-term ones. One of the best strategies is, of course, investing in dividend stocks. When you start delving into the subject, you will see how many advantages this kind of investing has over other most popular trading strategies. Let us look through some of the benefits of buying and holding dividend-paying stocks.

Benefits of Dividend Investing

You earn from dividends and from rising share prices. So, this shows that there is a possibility to make money in two ways. Firstly, you get dividends, and most are paid quarterly. Secondly, you can also make substantial amounts of money from a rise in your shares. As you know, stocks rise and fall, and since you are in these special dividend stocks for the long haul, you are surely going to benefit in these two ways: from steady dividends and from rising prices of your stocks.

- Steady income year after year

  Those who only expect to make money as shares rise will often have to sit out through bear markets when all stocks are falling, and they do not get the privilege of getting a steady income from the market in those times. However, those who own dividend stocks can enjoy never-ending streams of cash in good times and bad. Even if the price of your shares is falling, your dividends are still paid, and your steady stream of income never stops.

- The power of compounding when reinvesting your dividends

  Some investors talk about the power of compounding that they get when they reinvest the dividends. In a nutshell, compounding is getting current/future earning from previous earnings. So, if you get dividends and you use them to buy more shares of a company that pays them, next time, you will get more dividends (and consequently more cash). If you invest those, you will again get more shares and more dividends. These earning will keep growing tremendously if you continue doing this, year after year until you retire and have probably created yourself a nest egg. This type of investment protects your wealth from losing its value during inflation. We do know that during inflation, money starts losing its value. As prices grow, your money gets less and less power to buy things due to rising prices. For centuries, investors have tried to protect their hard-earned cash gold and in dividend stocks. Inflation often follows an overheated economy when everything is booming, and various new businesses spring up. That's when companies make bigger profits and, consequently, pay more significant dividends. Your price of shares rises, and so do the dividends. from depreciation by investing in

- Dividend stocks outperform those that do not pay dividends
Growth stocks may do very well during booms. However, as fast as they rise, they plummet when financial bubbles burst. Those who have held to those stocks often lose all of their profits and even more. Dividend stocks may not take you for such an extraordinary ride upward, but they will also not take you down hard when the economy heads south. So, those who follow long-term investment strategies and do not jump in and out of the market, trying to get a quick buck, will earn cash in good times and bad. Value stocks that they hold make them money even during very bad times because dividends do not stop coming. On the other hand, those who have been following short-term strategies have no streams of income from the market in bad times, and they need to wait for another boom in order to make

money from rising prices in stocks. These stocks provide you with financial safety and stability. As people grow older, they want less risk and more stability and security. That is precisely what investing in dividend stocks is all about. You protect yourself from falling markets by still keeping a steady stream of income. Prices of these stocks are often cheaper, but as dividends rise together with prices of shares, you earn more and more. In the same fashion as gold, dividend stocks have proven to be one of the safest ways to invest in the stock market. It relieves you from the pressure of where to enter and exit the market

Short-term investors are very concerned as to where they have to enter and exit the market. They intend to capitalize on fast stock price moves, and it is crucial to be right on time when the move starts. Long-term dividend investors do not have to worry about that. They simply select the best-paying dividend stocks and accumulate their wealth slowly but surely. They do not have psychological pressure regarding daily market fluctuations, as they know they are there for the long haul.

How to Pick Dividends
Similar to nearly everything else in life, there is no magic key to tell you exactly how to pick the winning dividend. That magic key would be almost as good as a lottery tracker that would tell you the exact number to choose. However, there are certain things that you can do to make

sure that you are picking the right dividends and that you are getting the right money from the ones you have chosen. It is a good idea to make sure that you are picking everything in the right way so that when the time comes, you can truly cash in on the dividends. Choosing the right ones will allow you to do so more quickly and will give you the chance to make even more money.

Profits in the Company

The profits of the company are the number one thing that you should look at when you are deciding whether or not to choose them for your dividend investment. A company needs to have high profits for you to choose them, and they need to show that they are going to have these profits for a long time in the future. It is a great way to ensure that the profits are going in the right direction and to make sure that you are going to be able to make money off of the investment that you make. A company that has good profits is a good company.

Size of Payouts

You can always check the size of the payouts that the company has made in the past to find out possible payments you can expect from the company. By simply looking at the trading profile of the company, you will be able to see how much they pay out, how often, and what it takes out of the profits that they have made. When you look at this amount, you need to consider all of the aspects of the payouts, and this also includes the initial investment amount. Compare that amount to what you are planning on investing in the company and see if the payouts will be worth what you are going to invest in the company.

It is vital to ensure that you are looking at all of this information in a way as if you were going to actually invest in the company.

The health of the Company

Just because a company has great profits and appears to be healthy does not mean that they are going to continue to be healthy. One of the most popular cases to look at is the case of Whole Foods Market. They are a huge company that has a lot of help from the people who shop there and the profits that they make. They did really well when the crunchy organic movement was happening, but since the recession hit, their health has failed drastically. They are no longer profiting in the way that they would have been. When you are considering an investment, consider the future health of the company. Just because it is profiting now, will it be profiting five years in the future? Generally, a company that is trendy or one that is relatively new will not be able to offer healthy profits in the future. The reason for this is due to the ways that things are being done with the company and the difficulty for the company to understand that they are not going to do as well as what they once thought they were going to be able to do.

History of Problems

No matter what you look at with the company, you need to always look at the history of the company.

Ask yourself some questions: Do they have any blemishes in their history? What have they done in the past? Do they do a lot of business on a regular basis? Are they affected by the seasons? Each of these questions will tell you what you need to know about the history of the company and the way they worked in the past. In investing, it is not uncommon for history to repeat itself, so if a company had issues in the past, there is a high chance that they will have problems in the future. Keep this in mind when you are investing in the company, and even when you are just researching the options that you have when it comes to investing in the company. By looking at the history portfolio of the company, you will be able to make sure that you are getting the most out of the experience. You are also going to see what is going on with the company so that you can make more critical decisions about the future.

Some Tips for Dividend Investing

What would a helpful book about dividend investing be without some quick tips on companies that are among the best to choose? While these are going to pay you only a small amount of dividend payments, they are the ones that are going to be steady and stable for an extended period of time. If you are hoping to make money from these companies, you can always invest more money into it so that you can get higher payments. The top companies to choose a dividend investment plan from are Wal-Mart, Target, Dr. Pepper, and Hershey. They are companies that have high profits and relatively high payouts. While it is impossible to tell you that you should choose a company to invest in (illegal in most areas), having an idea of what these companies are all about can help you decide on your own, whether or not you want to choose the company. Be sure that you choose a company that works with you because that is what you want. Do not decide to invest your money in a company because a book told you to or someone else told you to. Do your own research, learn about the companies, and figure out exactly what you want to get out of the investment opportunity.

Chapter 4: The Right Mindset

When you are investing in anything, it is all about what you think you can do and what you hope to achieve. These are two very different things, but they can both be used together to make sure that they are providing you with the best information that you need. It is always a good idea to keep a positive mind and outlook when you are investing and ensure that you have aspirations that you can reach. Doing each of these things will give you the chance to become better at investing and give you the best dividends possible.

Preparation and Planning

Getting ready to start investing requires a certain mindset. You need to make sure that you mentally prepare yourself to be able to invest and to choose the right dividend investment. For example, you cannot just go into it, thinking that you are going to make tons of money right from the start. You will not make a lot of money, and you may end up sorely disappointed because of the way that things are going. When you think about dividend investing, you may jump immediately to the passive income that you will eventually receive. You need to shift your way of thinking, though, to the months and years that it will take you to get to that point. If you do not think about the hard times that will come before you make the passive income, you will have a harder time getting to that point.

Outlook

Always have a positive outlook. The only way that you can lose money with this type of investment is if the company closes. As long as they are open, they should be profiting, and you will be able to take advantage of that from the dividend investment that you made. It is important to make sure that you know that things may not always be perfect. Even when you do not get a high payout for your periodic payment, you will still be getting a payment. It is important to just ensure that you are positive and that you know that higher payments are probably coming in the future. By making sure of this, you will be able to maintain a good outlook for the future with your passive income. It is always a good idea to make sure that you are getting the best outlook possible.

Goals

Have goals for your passive income and your dividend investment. Know what you want to make, how comfortable you want to be, and whether or not you want to make this a full-time career. If you set goals for yourself when it comes to dividend investing, you can then break those goals down and figure out exactly how much you need to invest in order to get to that point with your specific goals. Once you have made the goals for yourself, you need to stick with them.

That will sometimes mean that you need to invest more money into the company or the business to be able to reach the goals that you have; that amount of money will be completely worth it for you in the end. It is a good idea to keep in mind that you have goals. Knowing that you have a goal in mind will make it sting a little less when you have to put more money back into the company you have invested in so that you will be able to do more with what you have with the company.

Once you have hit all of the goals that you had intended, you should probably make more goals. While the passive income will be able to help you for quite some time, you should still have a plan for the future when it comes to investing. This is something that you need to do with every type of investing, but it is much easier to do with dividend investing. Make sure that you know what your goals are for after you hit your initial goals. Once you have hit your initial goals, you can always switch up your mindset. While you should still be looking forward to doing more with the money that you make, you can make plans to actually enjoy the passive income.

By making these plans, you will give yourself the best chance possible at doing better with it in the future. You can also consider reinvesting some of the passive income that you have already made so that you can make even more money. Your "after goals" are really where you can start to flourish with the money that you have made. It is the place that will allow you the chance to make more money. Your mindset, after you have reached your goals, should be the best mindset possible and should give you a chance to begin to profit from that money.

Continuing Success

Success is all about what you make it. If you want to make the most amount of money possible, you will see the chance to reinvest your money as an opportunity to do more. If you have a negative mindset, you may not want to invest your money back into the business—it's passive income, it should be working for you. The great thing about what you can do with the money is that you can literally do anything that you want. You can choose to just enjoy the money that you have made, or you can choose to make even more money when it comes to the way that you are doing things. Be sure to choose your mindset for your continued success wisely. There is a huge difference in someone who is retiring with passive income and someone who puts in a small amount of work to keep amassing a fortune. Do you want to be the person who makes more or the person who just collects the money?

Financial Risk Management

No matter what we do or the precautions we take, there will always be risks in our life. Some of the risks we run into, however, can be guarded through insurance. Defending against these risks is an essential part of creating a robust retirement plan. One thing that everyone should have is a form of auto and home insurance. If you have a relatively high net worth, it may be beneficial to add a form of umbrella policy on top of your existing insurance policies. Umbrella policies add an extra layer of insurance by allowing you to have additional liability protection. An example of an umbrella policy coming into play is shown in a scenario that happened to one couple, whom we shall refer to as Frank and Elsa. This couple decided to retire in their 60s and lived in a home with a pool. They were fond of hosting friends and often had parties in their homes. One unfortunate evening, one of their guests accidentally fell into the pool, landing in a manner that left her paralyzed, and the medical bills of the injured guest cost millions. Fortunately, the couple had added an umbrella policy that allowed them to protect their retirement assets from being consumed by the aftereffects of the unfortunate incident. Their umbrella policy covered one million dollars ($1,000,000) of the cost, in addition to the five hundred thousand ($500,000) paid out by their homeowner's policy. An insurance agent will be the one best equipped to assist you in choosing the right policy for you in order to protect your assets. Another hotly discussed issue is life insurance. Many often wonder if they still need life insurance, and if they do get it, what kind or what extent of coverage they should get.

Life insurance serves three purposes, each aligned to the different stages of our lives. The first one is when we are still young, as life insurance helps to ensure that our spouse and children will have some measure of protection if we pass away too early. The second purpose arrives in middle age, ensuring that our spouse or young children will have a comfortable financial situation if you pass away early in your retirement years. The third and last purpose is if we reach old age, and this type of insurance ensures that we can leave a financial legacy behind. The best time to decide on life insurance is before you retire. One way of determining the best option is to imagine the aftereffects of your passing, and what situation your spouse and other dependents will be left in. Once you pass, they will lose your salary or your social security benefits or your pension. Getting life insurance is a way to protect and remedy the income gap that will arise after you pass. Some life insurance policies are permanent and may evolve over time. You may initially get them as protection for your retirement, and they may eventually be turned into ensuring your financial legacy. It also goes without saying that the costs of such insurance should be accounted for in your budget.

There are many different kinds of insurance that one can get in order to ensure different levels of coverage—too many to be discussed here. It is best to discuss options with your financial advisor in order to find the best coverage for you to achieve these goals. You should also ensure that you minimize unnecessary coverage, as stopping payment of the premiums on these policies may allow for some extra funds during your retirement. One last thing that should be mentioned is disability insurance. This type of insurance is most crucial during your youth and middle age when you are actively working. After all, your best asset is your capability to earn, and you have to protect against anything happening to it. After you retire, this becomes of less importance, as there is much less income generation that has to be protected. In fact, most disability policies do not pay out if you are disabled when unemployed. This policy, therefore, is important while you are working, but it becomes useless once you retire. In summary, you should plan your insurance to shore up weaknesses in your retirement plan and mitigate risks. Talk to your insurance agent and financial planner to find the best form and amount of coverage that will serve the goals of your retirement plan.

Here are the action steps:
- To cover the areas of leaving a financial legacy and risk management, here are some tips.
- Compile all relevant data to ensure a clear assessment of strong points and weak areas.
- Ensure that the list of your beneficiaries is kept up-to-date.
- Make sure that the primary documents for managing your estate are kept updated.
- Prepare for worst-case scenarios; insurance coverage serves as a contingency plan
- Assess what type of life insurance would suit you and your goals for your retirement plan.

- Establish a good working relationship with your financial advisor and insurance agent in order to facilitate the development of a solid retirement plan.

Growing and Maintaining Your Income

Now that you have learned how to make the best dividend investment in your entire portfolio, you will need to learn how to manage all the wealth that you are going to have in the end. This may actually be the trickiest part of dividend investing and is often the part where everyone slips up and loses the money that they have made. It is best that you are prepared for your passive income and that you are doing what you can to make sure that you are getting what you need out of it.

Save It

The easiest thing that you can do with the income that you get is to save it. It is a good idea to try to save around 50 % of what you make from the passive income, and this is easy to do, especially if you have not taken on investing full-time. Save the money so that you will have it later on in case something happens or just for the sake of saving it. By doing this, you will give yourself a great start to retirement, vacation fund, or something else that will make your life better. It should be relatively easy to save the money that you have made with passive income. Since you do not have to worry about the problems that come with a traditional job, you will not need to worry about making money. You can also save a much larger amount of money if you are using the investment as supplemental income.

If you are using the investment as your main source of income, it may be more difficult to save 50 %, but there is still a chance that you will be able to do it.

High Interest

The best way to save your money is to find a high-interest savings account. This can be from your bank, online, or even on a CD that will make you more money. The best thing about high-interest savings accounts is that they are yet another form of passive income. You do not have to do anything other than put your money in the account, and it will experience growth during that time. This is a great way to make even more money than what you already made on the investment. The high-interest savings account will obviously not make you as much money as reinvesting it or even the initial investment, but it will help to keep it in your hands and grow a little bit more. The more money that you put into the account, the higher the interest will be because you will be able to make more money from what you were doing with it. It is a good idea to always find the highest rate possible and stick to it. You can always find out if the bank or institution where your money is at can raise the interest amount and, in fact, some banks do that automatically if you keep your savings account open for a long time.

Spend It

If you have a plan to spend your dividend investment income, you will be less likely to spend it on things that you do not need. Set aside what you are going to spend out of the money that you make and ensure that you only spend that much. If you give yourself a set amount of money, you will be less likely to spend recklessly and make purchases that you may regret later on, after you have run out of the dividend payment. It may seem counterintuitive, but you can even put aside money specifically that you can waste on things that you do not want. This is "blow" money that you can spend on anything, from new high heels to a gallon of ice cream at the grocery store. The money is yours to use in any way that you want, and it will help you to budget it. You will find that the more money you make, the harder it is to budget. Keep a 10 % rule for your "blow" money so that you can make sure you do not get out of hand with it and can keep it below your average spending amount. This will help to keep your spending in check.

Invest It

Investing the money that you have made from your initial investment is one of the easiest ways that you can grow the wealth that you have already made from dividend investing.

The investment that you make does not need to be perfect, and it is something that you can feel good about. Any type of investment is better than nothing, and putting your money back into investing is a great way to make even more money. When you are going to reinvest the money that you have already made, there are two different ways that you can do it. You can make money and put it back into the investment that you already did, with the dividends. Or, you can choose to try something different in the investment world. By making sure that you know how to do each of these things, you will have plenty of options when it comes time to make more money from what you have already.

Try New Things

If you have money that you want to use and invest, but you do not want to do anymore dividend investing, you can always try to do a different type of investment. There are many different options that you can try out, but the majority of these will be profitable if you know how to put your money in the right place. Trying out an index fund or something similar will be an excellent way for you to make the most amount of money on top of what you have already made. You may also consider something like a REIT. Switching it up and trying something different can change the portfolio that you have and give you the variety that you need to make sure that you are doing things the right way.

It can be hard to guarantee that you get that variety, especially if you are focusing on dividend investments. However, investing some of the money back into something else is the easiest way for you to make sure that you are making the most money possible. Your portfolio will thank you for the variety that you have added to it.

Put It Back In

Another option that you have when it comes to your investments is to put the money back into your dividend investment. You do not need to put all of your money back into the investment that you have already made, but it is a good idea to choose the right way to be able to invest if you are working toward doing more with what you have to offer. If you are going to invest money back into your dividend investment, you need to make sure that you do it the right way. Do not invest all of your money into the same venture. This is dangerous and could leave you with no income. If you are able to invest money, you should do around 50 % of the money that you have made. This is a good number because it will leave you feeling that you have made a good choice with keeping the money, as well as putting it back into the investment. You can also make a lot more money from investing 50 %, as opposed to 15 % or 25 %.

Chapter 5: Beginner Mistakes to Avoid

While we're on the subject of risk, let's discuss some common dividend investing mistakes that many beginning investors make. Even the most experienced investor, who has taken the time to study the markets really well, can make a terrible mistake. The bad thing about investment mistakes is that they are very costly. You might regret ever making them, and this can go on for a long while. It is good to be on the lookout for some of the common and costly mistakes that you could make, like any other investor, so that you can minimize the occurrence. This way, you might invest and enjoy your decisions thereafter. Many of these are avoidable, and I've made many of them myself! Hopefully, you can learn from my mistakes and the mistakes of others!

1. Focusing too much on yield. Many investors often focus too much on the dividend yield that they forget that yield and risks are directly related. The higher the dividend yield, the less likely the dividend is sustainable long-term, and the greater the risk for a dividend cut. That's why you want to shoot for the "Goldilocks" zone of 3–7 %. Dividend yields in that range can be sustained by strong and well-run companies. Shooting for the stars with a 10 % yield is just asking for trouble! Do not get too caught up in yield!

2. Going for high yields. This is a common mistake in investment, and it is a trap that almost all investors go for. The yields of a company can be really attractive, and an investor may overlook all other important factors just because a company registered good yields. The financial health of a company should matter more because you are not investing in the company for short-term benefits. Consider the sustainability of the dividend, as well as ensure that you will be getting something for the years that you invest in that company.
3. Cheap does not equal value. A lot of dividend growth investors like to focus on the numbers (especially me). Many investors salivate at the prospect of investing in a dividend company trading at a "cheap" valuation. However, stocks are sometimes cheap for a good reason. They're bad businesses! Would you be willing to pay 10x earnings for a business that pays a 7 % dividend but with earnings that are declining at 8 % a year? Probably not. Always be wary when a stock trades at a significant discount (25 % +) relative to peers or the stock market average. I've lost more money buying "cheap" stocks than I have bought companies at a fair price and at a slight discount to the market.
4. Ignoring possible future dividend growth. The importance of research before investing helps you to determine the trend at which the company is going so that you will know its possible performance years to come. This is very important. You do not want to get the same dividend payment you got this year, twenty years to come. You need to invest in a company that has a likelihood of increasing its dividends payout over the years.

Invest in the right company. Chances are, its share price will eventually go up, and its dividends will be high.

5. Failing to diversify. This has been discussed earlier in this book. Diversification helps an investor to spread the risk so that you will not lose everything in the case of a problem. Market conditions change, and they might affect your investment. If you have invested in just one or two sectors, the chances of losing your investments will be high if the two sectors are affected by the market conditions. Besides, you want to enjoy what other sectors are offering and, therefore, invest in more sectors.

Ignoring the outcomes. After investing, many investors do not pay attention to what will happen after that. Their main concerns become the dividends they are expecting at the end of a certain period of time, and this can lead to your failure if you are not careful. You need to classify your stocks to know which ones require more attention than the others. You need to keep checking what is happening in the market to determine if you have made the right decision. If there are stocks that will start to do better, you commit to them, and if there are those that are not doing so well, you give them your total attention to be able to make the right decisions when the time comes.

The Biggest Mistakes to Avoid When Growing Your Portfolio

A big reason that dividends are looking more and more attractive to investors these days is that the yields and bonds are stressfully low, and investors who are looking to plan for their eventual retirement are looking toward dividend-paying stocks for a more dependable income that builds efficiently over a longer period of time. Dividend investing has become a popular strategy during a time where fixed-income is falling into lows that haven't been hit before, and the baby boomer generation is preparing to enter the world of retirement. That is not to say there is not any sort of pitfalls, as with anything in the stock market during tough economic times. There are a number of catches in the face of all of the good things that dividend portfolios bring—a list of about seven according to San Francisco advising company, Forward Management, in a report entitled How Not to Invest in Dividend Stocks. Relying on Overly Mechanical Investment Plans. These kinds of strategies often ignore basic shifts, as well as dividend policy changes, which could build a problem for the investor's dividend profits flow. This has happened a few times in Europe where many of the telecommunication companies that paid via benefits had higher makes that had increased beyond completely, which, as mentioned previously, is a danger sign that things are planning to go down because what climbs up must come down.

Ignoring a Variety of Growth Factors

Profitable investors have to see and evaluate not only the dividend yields that every company has settled but also what the company's potential is made for both growth and appreciation—expansion allows every single child have more settlement over a longer period of time, which often can help them keep a livable income when they join the old-age community. For illustration, let's imagine that an investor has a portfolio with $1 million and would like to withdraw about $50,000 per year for expenses like home, food, and so forth. If the trader earns about 3 % in whole returns, less than 1/2 of the starting equilibrium will remain after two decades. Another 10 years later, that same trader earning only 3 % could well be close to jogging out. Now, if the same person was able to grow their returns to about 7 %, they would have savings of about $3 million after a 30-year period.

Showing Favoritism to the Home Market

There are many options overseas in other countries that have a booming economy, and these are paying dividends, which have higher averages; they are obviously more positive to investors, in addition to sometimes providing better options in the United States. Investing in the particular global market has developed into an important factor in the ability to diversify a portfolio by such industries in those fast-growing markets. By way of example, people are beginning to move cloud surgical procedures overseas to African countries since the demand is increasing there, such as Amazon, in addition to VMware. In 20 years, those markets had increased their shares in the world economy and are the cause of about 47 % in the world's gross home product.

Focused Toward Those Blue Chips

Investors sometimes claim there's more safety in having those larger dividend stocks, but they also cost more to buy shares and will not offer as much in return as they once did than the ones that are smaller in cap size.

Those larger companies usually offer a liquidity advantage but still do not offer a lot of opportunities to see increased dividend yield. Investor demand has risen so much that those blue-chip stocks are becoming too costly to even consider as options for a diverse and successful portfolio.

Giving Macro Factors More Weight

There is always plenty of risks with regard to any form of investing—it's inevitable as you will find emerging markets that supply some intriguing probable—especially involving troubled nations, along with possible booms in Europe, the Middle East, and Africa. Those regions may provide a large number of international revenue benefits and local operations, which might be less affected by macro trends. For example, the stocks from the European market aren't becoming valued as high as it should be due to the current crisis, which, in turn, causes doubt for buyers. But there is still a chance to find some stronger companies that offer dividend payments in that part of the world that might provide some potential gains that can help your portfolio.

Chapter 6: Examples of Success

The biggest reason anyone wants to get into the world of investing, especially in the dividend sector of the market, is usually so that they can make enough money to cover the expenses that come with retirement. So there is a lot that has to be done to prepare for that day you decide you do not want to do a full 40-hour workweek anymore, which starts with deciding which strategy to go with and then fine-tuning it as the market changes over time (because what works now may not work the same way in 20 years). How to reach those goals is focused on the type of dividend investing that generates good cash flow for multiple decades, and that's easily done by following these guidelines.

Always Contribute to Your Portfolio

The first rule is to continuously add money into your dividend profile, preferably some out of every paycheck or a higher amount every month. What happens is that investors are allowed to average the expense of their value over the course of several years. This provides the ability to build a dividend folder, which does not require the need to purchase all of your current stock in one single lump sum; it often is not always the best option for those looking forward to retirement. If people ignore it, then the benefits are limited as they are only building what is already there. Even though you will find there is a reinvestment option, you will stand to make more money faster with the help of adding more into your investments. Think about that when you get that third cup of coffee brew that you have every morning.

Seek a Dependable Dividend

The second rule is to maintain a focus on dividend growth stocks, which come from companies that usually offer a consistent increase in rates in distribution to the shareholders. If you want to have your dividend payouts cover your expenses while you are relaxing on the beaches of Maui, then you will want to have a dependable company to invest in for those long periods. That is why investors attempt to find ways to avoid the risk of inflation and put their money in stocks that they can afford to increase their payouts on if they ever need to.

Focus on the Quality, Not Necessarily the Quantity

This task is bringing the savings into a brokerage account pertaining to additional investments. It means that a good investor should build a collection of standard screening criteria so that you can have a report on dividend leaders, as well as achieves; this is long unless you can trim the list to a more manageable amount. In case a company offers a lot more than 25 %, dividends that have been observed rises at least 10 years in a row and trading under 20 times already in the market. While some may be (pun intended, the larger payout ratios) indicative that the company is benefiting from a boost in market value that will not last for a longer time, you would not much like the dip on this roller coaster. This could change with respect to the industry that the company you happen to be potentially investing in. Quality can become determined after careful research from the details for each stock. This helps the investor figure out whether the stock options offer enough to provide a rising revenue rate and correlating dividend obligations in the decades to come. A properly diversified portfolio will provide good success for the different income stocks that you carefully picked.

Create a Diversified Portfolio

This is done so that you do not only lessen the risk of loss, but you also shield the investor by purchasing as many stocks from numerous different companies as you can for a far steadier income that will come in handy during retirement. You do not want to keep all your eggs in one basket, as the old saying goes. Some experts suggest that an investor's stock portfolio should include almost 30 individual companies across many industries. Think of a retail center and the number of stores one usually has. They do not just have restaurants or department stores. There are specialty stores for gaming fans, photography folks, craftsmen, sports supporters, baby clothes, toys, and almost everything in between. Would a mall with 20 or 35 Starbucks stores sound extremely fun? It likely wouldn't be extremely successful.

Reinvest Wisely

When it comes to putting your money back into your dividend portfolio, do not do it too soon, and let your dividends build up. This is where the power of compounding interest comes into play, where you are gaining more money in a shorter time. Not everyone uses that strategy and will most likely hold their money for safer reinvestments and keep them with the steady growths.

As with almost everything in this world, the earlier you begin, the more options and knowledge you tend to have. Similarly, when it comes to your retirement funds, the longer that you have had them invested, the higher your return on investment, and your options will become better. Having money stay in the annuity longer will mean that you may not have to invest as much in the FIA, especially if you compare it to only investing in the latter part of your career. It also allows you to fund your FIA much earlier and end up with a more substantial, stable income. There are many financial tools you can make use of in order to fund your FIA, including but not limited to, non-qualified assets, such as brokerage or savings accounts, property sales, or even inheritances. For the average Joe, however, most of their nest egg is placed in their workplace pension plan. There are ways, however, for people to manage their funds in order to enable them to shift their investments from low and moderate risks to principal-protected funds that guarantee a steady income for life. If you are over the age of fifty-nine (59) years old, and you regularly contribute to your work's 401(k), 403(b), or TSP, you are most likely eligible to take the option to move the balance into an IRA while you remain to contribute to your pension plan. This is known as an "in-service withdrawal," and while it is not a commonly known fact, most employer plans permit their beneficiaries to do this. You can simply give your human resource department a call in order to check whether or not this option is available to you.

Why is this option a good one in the first place? Having an IRA opens up your options, allowing you to diversify your portfolio. It also allows you to get more specialized advice, and maybe even allow for better investment opportunities. This may also serve as a risk reduction for possible market loss the closer you get to actually retiring. Remember that even if you do avail of this option in your company plan, you should still be able to give a portion of your salary to your regular pension, and your employer should continue to match these contributions. Many people move a large portion of their account balances, hoping to ensure the largest return on investment and moving it into the principal protected bucket to maximize the stable return on investment. No matter how you want your funds to be distributed among the various risk types, you should take at least a cursory look at some advantages and disadvantages of the various types of investment tools. If you choose to look at the surface of the IRA and a 401(k), you would most likely come to the conclusion that they are practically the same.

After all, they are both designed around providing you with options after retirement; they both assist you in reducing your taxes and are even both referred to by the Internal Revenue Service as "qualified plans." However, remember that tax-deferral simply means that you are postponing your tax payments, and the most likely outcome is that you will not save on taxes in the long run, but rather just shift the tax calculation and expense to a later date. There is even a possibility that the tax rates would have changed to your disadvantage, or the tax bracketing has been redesigned and may force you to pay more than you would have.

Tax-qualified plans are often actually liabilities that must eventually be paid—a type of balloon mortgage. Though they do have all these things in common, there are certain significant nuances between a 401(k) and an IRA. While there are small differences here and there, we will examine seven things that an IRA would allow you to do, where you wouldn't have the option with a 401(k).

1. With an IRA, you will not be limited when it comes to options for investing. Your regular 401(k) has a few dozen funds that you may select from, and if you're lucky, it may even reach a hundred or more options. However, IRAs have tens of

thousands of options available to them, with the financial tools, including stocks, mutual funds, bonds, annuities, and even more.

2. An IRA allows you to feel secure in your income after retirement. This concern is growing more and more, especially after the market crashes in the 2000s, first in the years 2000-2002, and the bubble burst in 2007-2009. These recessions have made people wary, especially since they are no longer confident that the market will continue to have stable growth. 401(k)s do not generally afford you the option of an assured income for either the employee in question or their spouse. In fact, the only investment tool that guarantees that kind of security is an annuity, available to those with IRAs. This income will be stable, regardless of what happens in the market.

3. An IRA also affords you the capability to access some of your retirement plan's finances before your actual retirement. While this sounds like a minor advantage to have, considering that the funds are there to be used after you retire, sometimes, things come up, and we need to dip into our nest egg in order to take care of certain situations. 401(k)s do not have this freedom afforded to those who avail of it, as the company's regulations govern the use of these plans.

Therefore, 401(k)s tend to be less accessible and may even shut you out from your funds entirely until you retire. There are cases, however, where you can loan from your fund, but this option is not available to everyone and still depends on your company's policies. When this option is available to you, you are still limited to only fifty percent (50 %) of what your account is worth, and even then, it is capped to fifty thousand dollars ($50,000). IRAs have no such limitation but do keep in mind that when you access your IRA, you will have to pay income tax on it, as well as pay a 10 % fine on what you withdrew. However, if there is an emergency, those penalties may just be worth having in order to access your funds.

4. As the prior statement explained, taking distributions earlier than retirement age will lead to it being taxed, as well as having a ten percent (10 %) penalty. There are certain exceptions to this rule, however. One such exception is taking funds from the IRA in order to finance educational expenses, such as tuition, school supplies, or other relevant matters for yourself or your immediate family. Taking distributions for this purpose exempts you from the penalties. There is no such freedom for 401(k) plans.

5. All qualified accounts, IRAs, and 401(k)s included, are tax-deferred, meaning that no matter what, you will eventually pay taxes on these funds. However, when you take funds from your IRA, you may choose not to have anything withheld. 401(k)s do not have the option to eliminate withholding and are subject to the standard twenty percent (20 %) withholding tax.

6. IRAs also allow you the option to merge multiple RMDs between different accounts. Some people, due to their varied work history, may have multiple 401(k)s and other retirement

plans due to multiple employers in their work history. However, there is a crucial difference between having multiple 401(k) plans and multiple IRA accounts. If you have more than one 401(k), you have to calculate your RMD for each and every plan individually and avail of them separately. IRAs also require you to calculate the RMD for each, but they allow you to combine them and access them from an individual IRA or any mixture of IRA accounts that you wish. If you want to do this with your 401(k), you will be incurring a massive fifty percent (50 %) penalty, cutting your available access in half.

7. IRAs allow you to directly contribute to a charity of your choice. This may qualify as a fringe benefit, however, as it only counts as an advantage for those who do not need the stable income from the IRA account and consistently make charitable donations.

The IRA provides an option called qualified charitable distribution, allowing those who wish to avail of it to donate any amount up to a cap of one hundred thousand dollars ($100,000) to the charity of their choice, with that donation not being listed on their IRS taxes. Taking the option of a qualified charitable distribution does not allow you to apply a deduction due to charity, but the income that you used to donate will not show up on your tax return. It means that at the end of the day, you may end up paying less taxes in total, as compared to taking the money, listing it as income, then donating it, and availing of the charitable donation deduction. A qualified charitable distribution can also make up for your required minimum distribution. These are some of the major benefits of using an IRA over a standard 401(k).

Remember, you may have the option to shift your funds from your current 401(k) into an IRA, using the aforementioned in-service withdrawal, as long as you are still employed at the company concerned. However, while there are many advantages to having an IRA over a 401(k), this does not mean that they are better across the board. 401(k)s also have their advantages; one of them is that they tend to have less related costs than an IRA.

Day Trading for Beginners

How to Day Trade for a Living: Proven Strategies, Tactics and Psychology to Create a Passive Income from Home with Trading Investing in Stocks, Options and Forex

Table of Contents

Introduction..**192**

Chapter 1: Introduction to Day Trading............................**195**

   How Day Trading Works

      How to Start

      Consider Constraints and Goals

      Choose a Broker

      Capital Needed to Start Day Trading

   Day Trading Basics

      Lack of Risk Management

      Improperly Tested or Untested Trading Strategies

      Broker

      Technology

      Order Types

      Trader Personality and Tendencies

   Volume, Price, Technical Indicators

   Introduction to Investing in Stocks, Options, and Forex

      Day Trading Stocks

      Day Trading Futures

      Day Trading Forex

   Social Trading

Chapter 2: Risk Management and Account Management..**213**

   Hire a Stockbroker

Develop a Trading Plan
Maintain Simplicity
Establish a Stop-Loss Level
Determine Your Position Size
Curb Your Emotions

Chapter 3: How to Find Stocks for Trade..........................222
Conduct Repeated Day Trading on the Same Stock
Conduct Generalized Daily Searches for Favorable Stock
Execute A Stock Screener Based on Preferential Criteria

Chapter 4: Day Trading Tools and Platforms...................227
Day Trading Tools and Services
Features of the Best Day Trading Platforms
Day Trading Charts
  Technical Indicators
  Types of Charts Used in Day Trading
Introduction to Candlesticks
  Bullish Candlesticks
  Bearish Candlesticks
  Indecision Candle

Chapter 5: Trade Management and Price Action for Day Trading..240
Day Trading Risk Management
Price Action in Day Trading

Chapter 6: Day Trading Strategies..253
Breakout Trading
Scalping
News Releases Trading
Range Trading

    High-Frequency Trading (HFT)

Chapter 7: Technical Analysis..262
    Trendline Analysis
    Volume Analysis
    Candlestick Charting

Chapter 8: Psychology and Mindset.......................267
    Do Not Rationalize Your Trading Errors
    Beware of Your Trading Decisions
    Keep Your Emotions in Check
    Be Patient When Trading

Chapter 9: Day Trading Rules...275
    7 Rules of Day Trading
        How to Enter and Exit A Market
        Trading Rush Hours
        Be Cautious of Margin Trading
        Be Realistic
        Be Knowledgeable
        Cut Your Losses
        Risk Management Plan
    Other General Day Trading rules
        Keep A Trading Journal
        Tax Rules
        Manage Number of Trades
        Have A Trading Plan
        Don't Chase Trades
        Emotions
        A Positive Mindset
        Be Patient

Always Use A Stop Loss Order

Embracing Technology

Follow The 80/20 Rule

Use Limit Orders, Not Market Orders

Avoid Penny Stocks

Number of Stocks

Importance of Leverage in Day Trading

How the Securities and Exchange Commission Works

History

Chapter 10: Successful Trade..................................289

Making A Successful Trade Step-By-Step

Making a Watchlist

Choosing and Purchasing Stocks

Understanding Entry and Exit

Knowing How to Stop Loss

Knowing When to Sell

Examples of Day Trades

Trading Breakouts

Trading Ranges

Flag Trading

Triangle Trading

Chapter 11: Success Tips for Beginner Day Traders..................................303

Advice and Methods for Beginners

Mistakes That Beginners Make

Why and How Most Traders Fail

Chapter 12: Taking Profits, ROI and Passive Income..................................315

ROI
Conclusion..324

Introduction

Congratulations on purchasing *Day Trading for Beginners* and thank you for doing so. The following chapters will discuss everything a beginner would need to know concerning Day Trading and making a substantial passive income from home.

The first chapter is an introduction to Day Trading. The chapter begins with an explanation into the workings of Day Trading, it offers a breakdown into its basics and describes the meanings and importance of Volume, Price, and Technical Indicators to a Day Trader. The chapter concludes with an explanation of social trading and then a comparative mention of investments in Stocks, Options, and Forex trading.

The second chapter is a dive into the intricacies of risk management in Day Trading as well as the best Account Management strategies for traders in this line of business. The third chapter is a teaching on the strategies a beginner to Day Trading can begin his or her quest for stocks. The chapter covers the importance of conducting repeated Day Trading on the same stock, the process of conducting daily searches, and the process of executing a stock screener based on preferential criteria.

The fourth chapter is an in-depth study of the Day Trading tools and strategies. This chapter covers the tools and services available for Day Traders and then offers an explanation into the features of the Best Day

Trading Platforms. The chapter concludes with a study of the charts available for Day Trading and an introduction to candlesticks. The fifth chapter is an explanation of the proper Day Trading risk management strategies and the meaning of Price Action in Day Trading.

The sixth chapter is an introduction and comprehensive study of some of the leading Day Trading strategies. Some of these include Scalping, breakout trading, range trading, and High-frequency trading, among others. A beginner will need to be familiar with these for he or she to start Day Trading in the best possible way.

The seventh chapter is about technical analysis, or in other words, the study of the price changes and trends of a stock or security. The chapter begins with a study of trendline analysis, and it continues to explain everything involved in volume analysis, and concludes with candlestick charting. Chapter eighth is about the mindset or psychology a day trader should have whenever he or she is trading. The chapter goes into detail to explain making trading decisions, keeping emotions at check, and exercising patience on every trade.

Every line of business has rules that all the players have to abide by, and people need to follow them to ensure a level playing field for everyone. The ninth chapter covers the various rules and regulations governing Day Trading, and it begins with the seven rules of Day Trading, other general rules, and concludes with an explanation of the workings of the Securities and Exchange Commission.

The tenth chapter begins with a step-by-step guide to making a successful trade, and then it provides a few examples of day trades. The eleventh chapter continues with the theme of success, since it begins with advice and methods that beginners should heed to, and concludes with the most common mistakes day traders make and a list of reasons people fail in Day Trading. The last chapter explains how an individual should expect an ROI and make a substantial passive income through Day Trading.

There are plenty of books on this subject on the market, thanks again for choosing this one! Every effort was made to ensure it is full of as much useful information as possible, please enjoy!

Chapter 1: Introduction to Day Trading

In order to understand Day Trading, it is important to know what it is not. Day Trading is not investing, which, in simple words, is the process of purchasing a stake in an asset with the hope of building a profit over time. Time, in this case, is subjective; however, investors can hold on to an asset for years or even decades.

Investors usually invest in organizations that pay off debts, make good profits, and have a good range of popular products and/or services. On the other hand, Day Trading is the process of purchasing and selling assets within the same day, often using borrowed funds to take advantage of small price shifts in highly liquid indexes or stocks.

How Day Trading Works

There was a time when the only people able to trade in financial markets were those working for trading houses, brokerages, and financial institutions. The rise of the internet, however, made things easier for individual traders to get in on the action. Day Trading, in particular, can be a very profitable career, as long as one goes about it in the right way.

However, it can be quite challenging for new traders, especially those who lack a good strategy. Furthermore, even the most experienced day traders hit rough patches occasionally. As stated earlier, Day Trading is the purchase and sale of an asset within a single trading day. It can happen in any marketplace, but it is more common in the stock and forex markets.

Day traders use short-term trading strategies and a high level of leverage to take advantage of small price movements in highly liquid currencies or stocks. Experienced day traders have their finger on events that lead to short-term price movements, such as the news, corporate earnings, economic statistics, and interest rates, which are subject to market psychology and market expectations.

When the market exceeds or fails to meet those expectations, it causes unexpected, significant moves that can benefit attuned day traders. However, venturing into this line of business is not a decision prospective day trader should take lightly. It is possible for day traders to make a comfortable living trading for a few hours each day.

However, for new traders, this kind of success takes time. Think like several months or more than a year. For most day traders, the first year is quite tough. It is full of numerous wins and losses, which can stretch anyone's nerves to the limit. Therefore, a day trader's first realistic goal should be to hold on to his/her trading capital.

Volatility is the name of the game when it comes to Day Trading. Traders rely on a market or stock's fluctuations to make money. They prefer stocks that bounce around several times a day, but do not care about the reason for those price fluctuations. Day traders will also go for stocks with high liquidity, which will allow them to enter and exit positions without affecting the price of the stock.

Day traders might short sell a stock if its price is decreasing or purchase if it is increasing. Actually, they might trade it several times in a day, purchasing it and short-selling it a number of times, based on the changing market sentiment. In spite of the trading strategy used, their wish is for the stock price to move.

Day Trading, however, is tricky for two main reasons. Firstly, day traders often compete with professionals, and secondly, they tend to have psychological biases that complicate the trading process.

Professional day traders understand the traps and tricks of this form of trading. In addition, they leverage personal connections, trading data subscriptions, and state-of-the-art technology to succeed. However, they still make losing trades. Some of these professionals are high-frequency traders whose aim is to skim pennies off every trade.

The Day Trading field is a crowded playground, which is why professional day traders love the participation of inexperienced traders. Essentially, it helps them make more money. In addition, retail traders tend to hold on to losing trades too long and sell winning trades too early.

Due to the urge to close a profitable trade to make some money, retail investors sort of pick the flowers and water the weeds. In other words, they have a strong aversion to making even a small loss. This tends to tie their hands behind their backs when it comes to purchasing a declining asset. This is due to the fear that it might decline further.

How to Start

People who want to start Day Trading should do several things to put themselves on the right path. Firstly, they need to step back and ask themselves whether this form of trading is really for them. Day Trading is not for the faint of heart. It requires a high level of focus and is not something people should risk their retirement plan to do.

Actually, beginners should consider opening a practice account before committing their hard-earned money. Reputable brokerage firms provide such accounts or stock market simulators to aspiring traders, through which they can make hypothetical trades and see the results.

In addition, aspiring day traders need to have a suitable brokerage account before they begin trading. Some brokers charge high transaction costs, which can erode the gains from winning trades. In addition, good brokers provide research resources that are invaluable to traders.

Aspiring traders who discover that Day Trading is not for them should do what smart investors do, which is engaging in long-term investing in a diversified fund or stock portfolio. They should regularly add more funds to their accounts and let the magic of growth expand their investment portfolio. This may not be as thrilling as Day Trading, but it is better than doing something that will clean out one's savings.

Consider Constraints and Goals

Before investing the time, energy, and effort in learning or creating and then practicing Day Trading, prospective day traders should consider their constraints and goals. For example:

1. Traders need to determine whether they have enough capital to engage in Day Trading. If they lack the capital, they should wait until they have it while they are learning about and practicing different trading strategies.
2. They should understand that achieving consistent gains takes several months to a year, even when practicing several hours each day. For those who practice intermittently, it will take longer to achieve success; therefore, prospective traders should put in the time and effort required to achieve their goals.
3. Once they start trading, they need to commit to trading for at least two hours a day, depending on their commitments.
4. Until their trading profits match or surpass their income, new day traders should not quit their day jobs. They also need to determine the ideal time of day to trade based on their other commitments. In addition, they should ensure that their trading strategy fits that time of day. Essentially, their trading strategy needs to fit their life.
5. People who want to venture into Day Trading need to determine whether they want to do it with the aim of quitting their regular jobs. To get to the point where they can replace their day jobs by Day Trading, prospective traders need to understand that they

will probably need to practice and trade for a year or more, depending on their dedication.

Aspiring day traders should consider the factors above before investing their time and money in learning this line of trade.

Choose a Broker

While new traders are practicing and developing their trading strategies, they should set aside some time to choose a good and reputable broker. It may be the same broker they opened a demo or practice account with, or it may be another broker. Actually, choosing the right broker is one of the most important transactions day traders will make because they will entrust the broker with all of their capital.

Capital Needed to Start Day Trading

How much capital people need to start Day Trading depends on the market they trade, where they trade, and the style of trading they wish to do. There is a legal minimum capital requirement set by the stock market to day trade; however, based on the individual trading style, there is also a recommended minimum.

A day trader needs to have enough capital to have the flexibility to make a variety of trades and withstand a losing streak, which will inevitably happen. Traders also need to determine the amount of money they need, which requires them to address risk management. In addition, they should not risk more than 2% of their account on a single trade.

Capital is the most important component when it comes to Day Trading. By risking only 1% or 2%, even a long losing streak will keep most of the capital intact. For day traders in the United States, the legal minimum balance needed to day trade stocks is $25,000. Traders whose balance drops below this amount cannot engage in Day Trading until they make a deposit that brings their balance above $25,000.

To have a buffer, U.S. day traders should have at least $30,000 in their trading accounts. Stocks usually move in $0.01 increments and trade in lots of 100 shares; therefore, with at least $30,000 in their accounts, day traders will have some flexibility.

Day traders can usually get leverage up to four times the amount of their capital. A trader with $30,000 in his/her account, for example, can trade up to $120,000 worth of stock at any given time. Essentially, the trade price multiplied by the position size can equal more than the trader's account balance.

Day traders can trade fewer volatile stocks, which often require a bigger position size and a smaller stop loss, or stocks that are more volatile, with often require a smaller position size and a larger stop loss. Either way, the total risk on each trade should not be more than 2% of the trading account balance.

Day Trading Basics

Day Trading, on the surface, looks like it should be relatively easy. New day traders think it is all about making several simple trades as the price moves, making a little money, and repeating the whole process tomorrow. However, many dangers lurk in the Day Trading markets; unfortunately, a large percentage of new day traders are not aware of these dangers.

Some of the pitfalls for day traders include:

Lack of Risk Management

Often new day traders often lack risk management protocols, which is a huge danger. Sometimes, they have an incomplete strategy for managing risk. Nevertheless, they are usually optimistic about their Day Trading abilities, which often causes them to overlook critical risk management steps. Establishing a basic risk management strategy involves the following steps:

- **A Stop Loss**

Traders should place a stop-loss order in each trade they make to control their risk. People who are starting out on Day Trading should limit their risk on each trade to 1% of their trading account balance. The difference between their entry price and stop-loss price, multiplied by their position size, is their risk.

- **A Daily Limit**

A daily-stop loss limit can help day traders by limiting how much money they can lose in a day. If day traders suffer multiple losing trades each day, they may still find themselves down more than 10% in a single day. A typical daily-stop loss limit should not be more than about 3% of a trader's account.

Therefore, if the trader loses 3% on any given day, he/she will stop trading for that day. As day traders develop a profitable trading record and gain experience, they can adjust their daily-stop loss limit to be equal to their average profitable trading day. By placing this limit, a typical winning day will recoup the losses from a single day.

Improperly Tested or Untested Trading Strategies

New day traders are often so eager to start trading and make money that they start using untested or improperly tested trading strategies with real money. Others, however, try out their strategies on demo accounts, and if they make a few successful trades, they immediately start trading with real money. Unfortunately, both of these approaches will probably lead to future disappointment.

Successful day traders, on the other hand, test their strategies on many different market conditions through demo trading to learn the pros and cons of their strategies before using them with real money. They demo trade for several months until they are comfortable with their Day Trading strategies before risking real capital with their strategies.

Broker

Choosing the right broker is one of the most important trades for a day trader. Day traders deposit their capital with their brokers, and yet some of them do not take the time to research their broker until a problem arises. Scam brokers, for example, can pop up anywhere.

Traders who find themselves working with such a broker will find it very difficult or even impossible to withdraw their money and any profits. Fortunately, scam brokers usually do not last long thanks to forum complaints. Therefore, a careful online search will reveal any problems with a broker.

A more subtle broker problem is constantly slow quotes. Day traders need direct and uninterrupted access to their broker, who then sends their orders to the appropriate exchange. They should test their broker's trading software because poor software will make it hard to execute trades in a timely manner.

Technology

No one is immune to technology problems. For example, computers can crash, power can go out, the internet can go down, and much more. Day traders cannot get out of a losing trade quickly if technology fails; therefore, they need to place a stop-loss order on every trade.

In addition, they need to program their broker's phone number into their cell phone and landline phone, so they can call them quickly in case of a problem. It is a good idea to have a mobile version of their trading platform on their internet-enabled mobile devices, which might still be operational if their computer crashes.

Order Types

The profits and losses day traders make come from the orders they place. Day traders should know their order types for getting in and out of a market order or a limit order. They also need to know how to set profit targets and stop-loss orders, both for going short and long.

For professional day traders, placing orders is automatic, like switching on a car's turn signal, when about to change lanes. Day traders who do not know their order types will have slow and clumsy trading or even place the wrong order type, which will cost them money.

It is normal for some trading mistakes to happen; however, compounding such mistakes with order-related trading mistakes is a recipe for disaster. Before they start trading, new day traders should know their order types.

Trader Personality and Tendencies

Another hidden danger for a new day trader is his/her personality and tendencies. In the beginning, Day Trading will be confusing, infuriating, and stressful in a way a new trader never thought it could. There are endless possibilities in the markets, and no one cares what anyone else is doing.

This freedom, however, can be unnerving and dangerous for many traders, which is why many of them lose money. When people are starting out, they do not know how they will react under different stresses and pressures. Some choose to quit, others to overtrade, and others still are too afraid to trade.

Many distractions keep people from staying focused and trading effectively. Traders should take a critical look at their personality to identify their shortcomings and then work to develop these six important Day Trading traits.

Volume, Price, Technical Indicators

Day traders can use technical indicators to provide trading signals and assess the current trade. Keltner Channels, a popular technical indicator, use average prices and volatility to plot lower, middle, and upper lines. These three lines move with the price to create the appearance of a channel.

Chester Keltner introduced these channels in the 1960s, but Linda Bradford Raschke updated them in the 1980s. Today, traders use the later version of the indicator, which is a combination of two different indicators, which are the average true range and the exponential moving average.

Created by J. Welles Wilder Jr. and introduced in 1978, the average true range is a measure of volatility. The moving average, on the other hand, is the average price for specific periods, with the exponential variation giving more weight to recent prices and less weight to less recent prices.

Keltner Channels are useful to day traders because they make trends more visible. When a certain asset or stock is trending higher, its price will frequently come close, touch, or even move past the upper band. In addition, the price will stay above the lower band and middle band, although it might occasionally barely dip below the middle band.

When an asset or stock is trending lower, on the other hand, its price will regularly come close to the lower band or reach it; however, sometimes it will move past the lower band. The price will stay below the upper band and often below the middle band.

Day traders should set up their indicators so that these guidelines hold true, at least most of the time. If the price of a stock is moving constantly higher but not reaching the upper band, the channel may be too wide, and the trader will need to decrease the multiplier. However, an asset that is trending higher but constantly touching the lower band shows that the channel is too tight, requiring an increase of the multiplier.

For their indicator to help them analyze the market, day traders need to adjust it correctly. If they fail to do this, then the guidelines for trading will not hold true, and the indicator will not serve its intended purpose. Once they set up the indicator correctly, day traders should purchase during an uptrend when the price of the asset pulls back to the middle band.

They should place a target price somewhere near the upper band and a stop-loss order halfway between the lower and middle bands. On the other hand, if the price of the asset is hitting the stop-loss too often, and the trader has already made the necessary adjustments, he/she should move the stop-loss a bit closer to the lower band.

This will give the trade more wiggle room and reduce the number of losing trades the trader has. During a downtrend, when the price of the asset rallies to the middle band, day traders should short sell, which means selling the asset with the hope of buying it back at a lower price.

It is also important to place a target near the lower band and a stop-loss order about halfway between the upper and middle bands. This trading strategy leverages the trending tendency and provides trades with a 0.5 risk to reward ratio. This is because the stop-loss point is approximately half the length of that of the target price.

However, traders should not trade all pullbacks to the middle line. If a trend is not present, this strategy will not work effectively. Sometimes, the price of the asset moves back and forth between hitting the lower and upper bands. This method will not be effective in such situations.

Therefore, day traders should ensure the market's pattern is following the trending guidelines. If it is not doing so, they should use a different strategy. The Keltner Channel strategy tries to capture big moves that may evade the trend-pullback strategy. Day traders should use it near the opening of a major market when big movements happen.

The typical trading strategy is to purchase when the price breaks the upper band or sell short when it drops below the lower band within the first 30 minutes of the market opening. The middle band, however, acts as the exit point. This type of trade does not have a profit target. Traders simply exit the trade whenever the price touches the middle band, whether the trade is a winner or a loser.

Introduction to Investing in Stocks, Options, and Forex

When most people hear the term Day Trading, they think of the stock market. However, day traders also participate in the forex and futures markets. Some day traders, for example, trade options, but most traders who do so are more likely swing traders who can hold positions for weeks or days, but not fractions of a trading day.

People who want to be successful day traders should initially focus on a single market, such as the stock market. Once they master that market, they can try to learn and practice trading other markets if they choose.

Day Trading Stocks

Those who are thinking of Day Trading stocks should consider a few important factors. These are:

1. Under U.S. law, the minimum starting capital for Day Trading stocks is $25,000. However, they need to add a buffer above this amount and start with a capital of at least $30,000.
2. Market hours for Day Trading are from 9:30 am to 4 pm Eastern time. However, traders can still place trades one hour before the market opens.
3. The ideal periods to day trade stocks are from 8.30 to 10.30 am and 3 to 4 pm ET, when volatility and volume are high.

4. Day traders can trade a wide variety of stocks. They can also trade the same stock or a small number of stocks every day, or find new stocks to trade each week or even each day.

Based on these factors, prospective day traders will determine whether the stock market is a good option for their Day Trading. If they do not have the initial capital required, for example, they should consider the futures or forex markets, which require less starting capital.

In addition, if they cannot trade during the most ideal trading hours, their efforts will not produce as much fruit as they would have if they were available during those optimal hours.

Day Trading Futures

Some of the important things to consider about Day Trading futures include

1. There is no legal minimum starting capital required to begin Day Trading futures. Experts, however, recommend starting with $2,500 to $7,000 if one is trading the popular futures contract. The more money one starts with, the more flexible one will be when it comes to making trading decisions.
2. The official market hours for trading the S&P 500 and E-mini are from 9.30 am to 4 pm ET.
3. The optimal time to day trade ES futures is from 6.30 to 1030am and 3 to 4p Eastern time.
4. Commodities futures contracts also provide reliable Day Trading opportunities.

5. Most day traders who deal with futures often focus on one futures contract; however, others choose futures contracts seeing significant volume or movements on a particular day.

Day Trading Forex

Things to know about Day Trading forex include:

1. The minimum starting capital required is $500; however, experts recommend starting with $5,000 if one wants a decent monthly income stream.
2. Forex trades 24 hours a day; however, certain times are ideal for Day Trading than others.
3. Day traders can trade any different currency pairs, but beginners should stick to the GBP/USD or EUR/USD. These two currency pairs offer more than enough price movement and volume to generate a good income.

Based on these three factors, day traders will likely determine whether this market is appropriate for them to day trade. Those with limited capital should consider Day Trading the forex market, which is more flexible than other markets.

Social Trading

Social trading works somewhat like a social network. However, there is a big difference, which is that instead of sharing pet photos, dinner photos, and selfies, people use social trading networks to share trading ideas. Essentially, traders use this platform to interact, brainstorm and watch the trading results of other professionals in real-time.

Some of the benefits of social trading include:

1. Access to reliable and helpful trading information
2. Ability to earn while learning
3. Quick understanding of the trading market
4. Ability to build a trading community of investors

Since social trading networks cater for both professionals and beginners, they create a reliable trading community, which allows day traders and other types of market traders to generate an income as they learn.

The allure of this form of financial trading is undeniable. It is more exciting for a trader to earn a living working from the comfort of his/her home, rather than working a regular 9 am to 5 pm gig. However, inexperienced or careless day traders can destroy their portfolios within a few days.

Chapter 2: Risk Management and Account Management

Both account and risk management exercises are activities that coincide as you go through the Day Trading investment cycle. It is very important for you to ensure that you achieve your aims of making significant profits, while at the same time, mitigating losses from the capital in which you invested.

Managing your account and the risks associated with Day Trading involves the responsible handling of the available equity in your brokerage account. You can perform account management through further investment in profitable stocks, ingenious trade maneuverability, or exiting from trade deals that stagnate.

On the other hand, your risk management strategies involve responding appropriately to alleviate prospective losses in an uncertain future and limiting the degree of your exposure to financial risks. The following are some of the primary strategies that you can apply to your Day Trading to ensure active risk and account management:

Hire a Stockbroker

As a beginner or a new investor participating in Day Trading, it could turn challenging if you went at it alone. You need advice on the right stock opportunities in which to invest, guidelines on how to handle probable financial risk exposures, and knowledge of technical analysis to keep track of your capital progress.

A qualified and registered stockbroker typically offers these financial services at a commission or flat fee. You need to seek the assistance of such stockbrokers to tap into their experience and expertise in Day Trading. Besides, the chances of attaining your profitable goals increase when you employ the services of a stockbroker.

Account management and risk management are strategies that are innate to a stockbroker, especially when given access to the account. Therefore, you need to open a brokerage account from which all your Day Trading activities take place. Maintaining liquidity in this account is as essential as making the right trade deals.

Since you may not interact with the stock market all the time, running the trading account becomes the responsibility of your stockbroker. You need to give him or her freedom to make informed choices on long and short trades, however risky they might seem at first. Trust your broker to understand what he or she is doing with the account and hence the need to hire an honest stockbroker, preferably from a well-known brokerage firm.

In addition, it is usual for your stockbroker to have extensive experience with managing financial risks. Most of the strategies meant to combat potential financial threats such as spreads are somewhat complex to understand, let alone apply them effectively. The same levels of complications and fair sophistication apply to the tools used for technical analyses.

You need to follow these analytic tools to make informed choices based on their data. A stockbroker comes in handy at this point to assist in data interpretation. You also get to learn about the various management strategies of which you had no idea previously. Generally, account and risk management in Day Trading is often all about making the correct decisions from technical analysis.

Develop a Trading Plan

This document is a crucial tool for you as a new investor in Day Trading. If you do not possess such a program, then it may be time to develop one that tailors to your specific trading. Creating a trading plan is an activity that you need to perform with the help of your stockbroker. The broker typically has experience in the Day Trading sector, and so he or she can offer you pointers on the trading opportunities that have the potential of being productive. Based on this vital tip, you can create a comprehensive trading plan that contains an overall objective that is set out. Besides, the program should have tactical or short-term goals set at regular intervals during the cycle. The primary purpose of these operational targets is to enable you to keep track of the progress of your Day Trading activities.

Once you complete the creation of a trading plan, you must stick to its guidelines at all times. You and your broker need to have a chance at Day Trading's success. Hence, you both have to adhere to the rules of the trading plan. It sets out instructions on how you should react and what measures to take with your capital under different situations. Since the future of Day Trading is often uncertain, it is essential for your plan to cover emergency financial responses. If you diligently adhere to your trading plan, your likelihood of attaining profitable returns eventually increases significantly. In addition, you will have a policy of intervention to potentially risky financial exposures.

Maintain Simplicity

In Day Trading, you may falsely believe that you need to overextend yourself on high-risk investments to make substantial amounts of return. This belief is a dangerous position for you to adopt when getting into Day Trading. Keep in mind the notion that the underlying stocks are often a more volatile type of security than other investments. Fluctuations in the value of the traded stock are frequent and typically occur over a relatively short period.

You must learn how to make small trade deals on the stock from the low-risk end of the trading spectrum. Beware of succumbing to the desire to stick your neck out for the riskier stocks. Greed and emotional influence are the leading causes of such irresponsible trading practices. In the case of a specific trade deal turning awful, you need to exercise restraint from the urge to make illogical trading decisions to try to cover your previous loss.

Besides, keep an eye out for volatile stocks and avoid trading in them as much as possible. If you can, distance yourself and your portfolio from such stocks. Ask your broker to let go of highly fluctuating stocks entirely due to their corresponding high levels of financial risk. All these missteps are easily avoidable when you stick to the simple trading practices laid out in your trading plan.

As a result, you will evade massive losses associated with complicated, high-risk trading that is subject to a high level of emotional influence. Proper and responsible account management demands that you avoid rash decisions that may lead to prospective losses and missing out on potential profits. Risk management also takes care of itself by minimizing your exposure to the high-risk end of the trading spectrum and keeping clear of volatile stocks.

Establish a Stop-Loss Level

To manage the amount of risk to which you are willing to expose your trading portfolio, you can issue orders that reverse potentially hurtful financial positions. A stop-loss order limits the amount of stock price that you can tolerate without taking a significant financial hit.

This order enables your stockbroker to cease all the Day Trading activities immediately. It allows him or her to instantly stop either buying or selling any further stocks based on the unfavorable prices. The order indicates the specific stock price beyond which you cannot risk either purchasing or offloading, respectively, because doing so would expose you to an apparent financial loss.

Getting into an apparent losing situation is an irresponsible practice on your part. Eventually, you will end up with a depleted brokerage account due to the mismanagement of the available capital that you previously had. Stop-loss orders are especially useful when conducting Day Trading on volatile stocks. It is advisable to set the stop-loss order to an amount that is as close as possible to your trading entry point.

Besides, close monitoring of the fluctuating price of your particular stock is a must to ensure the successful execution of the order when required. As you can realize, when used in this manner on the volatile stocks, such stop-loss orders act as risk management tools that mitigate the financial downside associated with rapidly fluctuating stocks.

Determine Your Position Size

Position sizing involves making decisions on the amount of capital with which you intend to take part in particular day trade. The size of your investment is directly proportional to the level of risk exposure. A high-volume trade will invariably expose you to more financial risks than a small number of trade deals.

Your brokerage account will often get caught in the crosshairs of high-risk transactions and Day Trading practices. Exhaustion of the amount of available capital in your trading account becomes even more likely. Therefore, an early determination of your trading position is essential before engaging in any form of transaction. Your position size divides into an account and trade risk based on the number of shares of stock that you acquire on a particular trade.

For you to minimize any potential financial downfall resulting from the degree of your account risk, you must set a limit on the amount of capital to trade in each deal or transaction. A fixed ratio or small percentage is often the recommended format for this account limit. Maintaining consistency is vital in setting these account restrictions.

Do not keep altering the allocated portion for different trading deals. You should pick one value and apply it to all of your transactions during the Day Trading. A preferable limit should be one percent of your available capital balance or less. Make sure to adhere to the strategy of simplicity by making only small amounts of capital allocations to the low-risk stocks.

In addition to the risks to your trading account, the other financial exposure from position sizing concerns the trade risk. The best strategy to counteract trade risk involves the use of stop-loss orders. The gap between the entry point to your Day Trading and the specific numerical amount set as the limit on the order constitutes your trade risk. As earlier mentioned, this order enables you or your stockbroker to exit from a trade deal upon reaching the set limit of loss. This action results in capping further loss of capital; hence, it contributes to managing financial risk in this manner.

Consequently, you should execute stop-loss orders close to your trading entry point to minimize the likelihood of potential losses spiraling out of control. Be careful not to set it excessively tight to inhibit your ability to carry out any trading. Position sizing is responsible for both account and risk management. The evasive maneuvers described usually contribute towards minimizing risk.

Remember to allow for some flexibility when setting the restriction value on a stop-loss order. You need this leeway to give your stocks a chance to increase in value without encountering an obstacle in the form of the stop-loss order. Such moves enable you to maintain a healthy trading account. As previously mentioned, the number of shares needed for a potentially profitable trade relates to your ideal position size, as shown below.

The ideal number of shares required (Position Size) = Account risk / Trade risk.

Curb Your Emotions

Emotional influence on Day Trading practices can turn counterproductive very fast if you are not careful. The primary emotions to look out for are self-confidence and fear. Excessive confidence can cause you to have a false sense of self-belief in your trading abilities. As a result, you may end up making illogical trading choices and decisions based on your cockiness.

You should understand that you become more prone to develop a false sense of overconfidence whenever you are on a winning streak. The successive trade deals that end up panning out give you an air of self-belief that could be subject to abuse. You get to trust your super abilities in trading and dare to engage in more risky transactions. It is at this point that you will experience a massive financial catastrophe, especially if you overextend yourself financially. Beware of situations that seem too good to be accurate as well.

The other emotional input of concern is the fear of experiencing losses. Overcoming this fear is possible as long as you trade in amounts of money that you can afford to lose in case the transaction goes wrong. In Day Trading, you are bound to have trouble due to market fluctuations, especially when dealing with volatile stocks.

Losses are part and parcel of Day Trading, and you must learn how to bounce back after a particularly nasty run of successive losses. You may experience crippling fear that could render you unable to continue trading if you do not have a coping mechanism for potential losses. In addition, the fear of further losses may discourage you from taking risks resulting in missing potentially profitable opportunities.

Fear is responsible for holding onto a stock position for too long, as well. Instead of selling your shares at a reasonable profit, you may decide to wait on much higher prices leading to a loss if the trend in stock price undergoes a reversal. Another critical factor to consider in risk and account management is the tendency to chase after quick profits to cover for a recent run of bad trade deals and accompanying losses.

You must adhere to your trading plan guidelines and instructions even during such tough times. Do not modify or alter your response and come up with stupid decisions that you usually would not make. Remember that for you to ensure responsible management of your capital, you need to start making choices based on logic. Emotional corruption can hamper your ability to make significant profits and expose you to unnecessary risks.

Chapter 3: How to Find Stocks for Trade

In Day Trading, you will need to deal in stocks and their fluctuations in prices. Buying and selling stocks depend on the number of shares of a particular stock that you have. When you conduct profitable trade deals, the chances are that you will have a healthy trading account. The available capital in your account is vital to enable you to continue investing in the Day Trading opportunities.

However, if you experience a run of losses and bad transactions, you are likely to run out of capital eventually. A series of successive losses tend to cause an emotional reaction from most traders. Beware of trying to recoup your losses by chasing profits based on rash decisions. It is also essential to trade only with an amount of capital that you can afford to lose. Remember to adhere to your trading plan for guidance and instructions on how to respond to financial losses.

You can also apply the strategies laid out for risk management. Stock markets tend to vary in their trends over time, and hence, you are bound to go through a couple of difficulties. The most crucial aspect of this emotional roller coaster is how you react to both returns and losses. Besides, in case you want to increase your profit margin, you should know how you would acquire more stock for your trade deals.

Since the availability of securities for Day Trading may not be an issue, you should try to focus and narrow down your stock selections. Identification of potentially profitable stocks can be a challenging affair. However, there are tactics, skills, and techniques that you can apply to ensure that you invest in the most productive kind of stock.

Conduct Repeated Day Trading on the Same Stock

This tactic involves carrying out your Day Trading under the same condition's multiple times. You need to identify your most profitable stocks and focus all your trading expertise and time on only these particular stocks. This move ensures that you always get some form of returns from your investment since you already know how it usually performs. Avoid trading in many different types of securities or stocks. The selection of a few stocks whose market trends are easily understandable should be your next step. You can narrow your possibilities to around three or four stocks in which you can become an expert.

Once you have identified the relevant stocks, you must dedicate your full attention and monitoring to their market trends. When choosing your preferred stocks, make sure to select those with sufficient volume in the market. This strategy allows for the adjustment of your calculated position size. When dealing with volatile stock, this flexibility enables you to apply for stop-loss orders with big margins to your corresponding small trading positions.

The opposite move is correct for a calm stock market. You will have the freedom to take an expansive trading position coupled with tight margined stop-loss orders. In addition, using this information, you will get to know the best periods to buy or sell specific stocks that would maximize your returns. The more you trade, the more you will be in a position to acquire more stock at a favorable market price. Eventually, you will end up with a lot of stock held as assets within your Day Trading portfolio.

Conduct Generalized Daily Searches for Favorable Stock

You can decide to perform your Day Trading activities in the old fashion way by looking for the volatile stocks that trend attractively. Volatile stocks are more likely to make significant movements in the course of your Day Trading. This technique requires a high degree of self-discipline to keep searching for productive stocks even during tough periods.

It is different from the repeated trading explained above. This trading exercise does not impose a recommended limit on the number of shares you can seek and does not involve Day Trading on the same stock repeatedly. As a result, you end up actively looking for favorable stocks from the vast online stock market to trade daily.

Ideally, you need to spend your time monitoring the market for the presence of stocks that are big movers and trending well. Consider researching the day before. You need to find out information about the stock availability and potential for returns. This research may include looking into the institution or company. Besides, you can find out how the product performs with market consumers.

For you to maximize your likelihood of acquiring more stock, pay attention to relevant breaking news affecting the stock. Also, be on the lookout for the stocks that earnings are due and any new stocks flooding the market on the following day. All this information should give you an upper hand in your quest to purchase and hold more trading stocks.

Execute A Stock Screener Based on Preferential Criteria

This tool is a computer software program that looks for any available stocks upon its execution. You can search for stocks based on your customizable criteria. Ideally, you should seek a limited number of stock types that show excellent levels of volatility and raw volume. Restrict your search criteria to about three or four stocks as well. Such limitations will enable you to focus all your attention on the effective management of selected stocks and their trading accounts. A weekly stock screener search can occur for you to spend ample time trading on the stocks that meet your search criteria.

Beware of distractions from other commodities that are not on your search results. Succumbing to temptations from a seemingly attractive stock will result in a spiraling fall into your potential financial ruin. Also, note that if a particular stock maintains a regular rate of returns, do not switch stock types. You have to keep profitable returns, as well.

When run correctly with the relevant criteria, a stock screener can supply you with a range of various profitable stocks from which you can choose. Depending on the filtration criteria, the following are some examples of online stock screeners:

1. StockFetcher.com
2. ChartMill.com
3. StockRover.com
4. Finviz.com

To avoid wasting time on endless searches for the biggest movers and the best stocks, try limiting your searches to a handful of stocks. This search should ideally take place once a week, preferably over a weekend. Once you have identified your small group of favorable stocks, spend the rest of the time involved in actual Day Trading. Focus your attention on only these listed stocks for at least the whole week until your next search is due. By following this technique, you will end up accumulating and Day Trading in the kinds of stock that you deeply understand and are customizable to you too.

Chapter 4: Day Trading Tools and Platforms

People develop and adopt various tools and platforms to enhance a trader's experience while trading. Initially, a beginner may view the whole process of a transaction as being too difficult due to how complex some markets appear to be. However, with the right information, a person can receive proper guidelines that will introduce him or her to the business and gradually propel him or her into expert traders. The knowledge will enable him or her to develop his or her technical and fundamental analysis that will inform his or her successful trading strategies.

Below is information that introduces a person to the tools and platforms that various traders utilize in their businesses. Moreover, there is also an introduction to some trading aspects like Day Trading, technical indicators, chart types, and candlesticks. Read on to learn more.

Day Trading Tools and Services

Day Trading or intraDay Trading takes place when a trader enters a trade and holds a particular market position for a short time before exiting. A day trader opens and closes that position in a single day. A trader undertakes Day Trading to avoid losses associated with overnight risks and, instead, aims to use volatility to his or her advantage. A trader needs to have some tools and services that are essential to accessing and succeeding in Day Trading. They include:

1. **Electronics** – A day trader needs a computer and a phone where the laptop or desktop has enough memory to run the trading software without crashing or lagging. Additionally, he or she needs a phone to make relevant communications to appropriate people, such as calling brokers.
2. **Direct Access Trading Brokerage** – An intraday trader should obtain the services of a suitable broker who fit his or her requirements in Day Trading. He or she needs to hire one who offers a low commission and allows for the use of customized Day Trading software.
3. **Software** – A trader needs to carry out research and find the Day Trading software that matches his or her needs and strategies well. He or she also should ensure that the computer is compatible with the software and that his or her broker can access it.
4. **Trading Platform** – The intraday trader must learn about various Day Trading platforms and their features and select to use the one that will fulfill his or her trading objectives. Besides, he or she should ensure that the platform matches his or her skills and knowledge concerning trading tools and analysis.
5. **Internet Connection** – A trader must ensure to have an excellent and stable internet connection to help him or her to avoid the errors that take place due to poor accessibility. He or

she views old data rather than the current prices on the market since the unstable connectivity results in lagging and misinformation. Additionally, he or she can create backup internet access, such as having different internet providers for his or her mobile phone. In doing so, if one internet provider has issues, the trader can still access the other connection.

6. **Knowledge and Skills** – An intraday trader should continually learn and practice trading to improve his or her skills. He or she can learn individually and practice via online tutorials or use an expert as a guide to perfect his or her trading skills.

7. **Features of the Best** Day Trading Platforms

A Day Trading platform is essential because it helps a trader to transact efficiently and ensure to minimize risks and make profits. The following are some of the best Day Trading platforms and their features:

1. **Charles Schwab** – Provides the best premium features that are critical to a trader's success in the market and is the easiest to learn. It offers competitive rates and has a balance since it provides vital trading and functionality tools while lacking certain customization features.

2. **Tradespoon** – Has flexible rates and suits traders of all levels as it provides professional and widespread trading tools. It has a rich library of studies and historical information that a trader can use to gain further knowledge or customize his or her trading strategies.

3. **TD Ameritrade** – Offers a trader excellent trading tools and guidance to help both beginners and experienced traders to grow in the market. It also provides retirement resources for traders. It has expensive rates, as it is the most resourceful platform that also provides traders with the chance to develop and undertake real-time stock scans and other advanced analysis.
4. **Interactive Brokers** – It provides the best rates and best suits the high-volume traders due to its professional features like programmable order types like algorithmic types. It does not allow for research, but its tools suit the hyperactive and active traders.
5. **E-Option** – Offers the best features for advanced traders as it enables them to access sophisticated and customized tools that they can use to undertake in-depth technical analysis and trade moves.
6. **Fidelity** – Contains several tools that enable a trader to transact efficiently, such as customized profiles, automatic identification of general patterns, chart trading, and drawing tools, among others. It also offers competitive rates due to its practicality.

Day Trading Charts

Day Trading refers to a trader entering and exiting a market position in a single day while charts use historical data to provide a trader with feedback regarding the conditions of a market. A trader using trading charts in his or her trades receives significant additional information that helps him or her to make appropriate decisions in Day Trading. They enable him or her to study the past price movements and patterns that assist him or her to understand the current market and even make some predictions on particular trades.

A day trader needs to understand the various aspects of Day Trading charts, which are technical indicators and the different chart types. Knowledge of these two features enables him or her to possess a comprehension of vital tools that help him or her to make a profit from the trading day's volatility.

Technical Indicators

An intraday trader utilizes technical indicators to carry out technical analysis of the market. They enable him or her to look at and understand the various meanings of chart patterns. The patterns provide him or her with a visual representation of the price movements and trends in the market that allow the trader to make sound and profitable decisions in the trade. Some of the commonly utilized indicators in Day Trading include:

1. Simple Moving Average (SMA)

An SMA indicator uses an average that consists of the total amount of the closing prices in a given period and dividing the sum by the number of days in that period. A day trader can make profits if he or she uses a fast-moving average since the slower ones can cause losses if there is a reversal or end of a trend. Many traders frequently use a 10-day moving average because it does not lag and indicates the direction and considerable moves of prices in the market.

2. Oscillators

These refer to indicators such as the Relative Strength Index (RSI) and the Moving Average Convergence Divergent (MACD) that reflect unclear price trends. The signals move between the upper bounds and lower ones, and the subsequent readings provide the day trader with feedback regarding the market conditions.

3. Volume Indicators

A volume indicator will signal to a day trader changes concerning the number of trades taking place. The trader will know when there is a considerable amount of transactions and indicate the area in the market where they occur. He or she can then quickly take up an appropriate position and make profitable moves in the Day Trading market.

4. Average True Range (ATR)

These indicators enable a day trader to evaluate the trades before entering it. As a result, he or she makes accurate and well-informed decisions because the ATR indicator utilizes the actual price of securities to provide a precise representation of volatility.

Types of Charts Used in Day Trading

Many traders use different charts to maneuver the Day Trading markets. Each trading chart contains various features that work to provide diverse and useful information to a trader. A trader looks at the graphs and utilizes those that best suit his or her trading aim and strategies. The following are some popular types of charts that a trader can use to interpret and understand the market conditions.

1. Candlestick Charts

Candlestick charts are easy to understand and use, and they provide a trader with the most feedback by signaling where a price travels in a given period. They also enable him or her to incorporate information concerning frames of time. In this case, he or she can identify the highest and lowest price points, along with the last closing price that takes place in that particular period.

Candlesticks assist a trader in getting precise visual readings of the market by presenting only relevant information, such as the Heikin-Ashi chart that shows trends and reversals. Different candlestick charts also show various aspects of the market, such as time, volume, and price movements.

Some candlestick charts only use the movements of the price to help a day trader to identify the resistance and support levels. The resistance levels indicate the highest highs of trade, whereas the support levels show the lowest lows. Renko is an example of such a candlestick chart that employs colored bricks to reflect the trends of a trade.

When there is a downward trend, the blocks visible will be black, while white ones will be visible when an upward trend takes place. The bricks also move in terms of the price movement whereby a new white or black block appears in the following column if the price respectively moves above or below the previous one.

Other candlestick charts help a day trader to find points of reversals and sets of swing highs and lows. These charts enable him or her to determine areas and conditions of bias in the market, which assist him or her in making appropriate moves that give him or her gains. An example here is a Kagi chart that uses changes in price directions to signal reversals.

The intraday trader sets a particular reversal amount, and the price direction will shift to the opposite side once it reaches that predetermined percentage. It also indicates swings concerning high and low line signals, in that, the lines become thinner as the market drops below the previous swing. Conversely, the line gets thicker as the stock increases above the prior swing.

2. Bar Charts

Bar charts provide a day trader with signals that are easy to read and interpret as they use color, horizontal, and vertical lines to reflect range or price in a given period. The horizontal lines show the closing and opening prices, whereas the vertical lines indicate the price range of a particular duration. Additionally, traders use them along with candlestick charts to reflect the trading actions in the market.

A bar with candlesticks uses the variation between the low and high to show the trading range. The top of the candle or wick represents the high state while the bottom of the candle signals the low one. Moreover, the chart uses different colors on the candlestick to indicate the opening and closing prices within a period of interest. A red candle could represent the closing price at the low end of a candle and have the opening price at the high end. Meanwhile, a green candle reflects its prices in reverse of the red candle.

3. Line Charts

Line charts indicate to an intraday trader the history of prices by showing a track of the closing prices in the market. The trader forms the lines when he or she links several closing costs in a given frame of time. He or she uses line charts along with other kinds of trading charts to get essential information for a successful Day Trading experience.

4. Charts Based on Time Frames

All the trading charts that a day trader utilizes contain frames of time that he or she set according to his or her aim or trading strategies. The trader can use intraday charts breaking down into 2-minute, 5-minute, 15-minute, and hourly charts. Each time interval indicates the price actions of trade of interest, and he or she can use the information represented to make relevant trading decisions and moves.

5. Free Charts

An intraday trader can use free charts that are available online and offer the trader not only with tools for technical analysis but also with advice, demonstrations, and guidelines about chart analysis. Different free charts provide various features such as delayed futures data, real-time data, and selection of frames of time and indicator accessibility. Furthermore, these charts enable a trader to participate in various markets like the forex, futures, stock exchanges, and equity markets.

FreeStockCharts and the Technician are examples of free charts that an intraday can access and utilize without spending anything.

Introduction to Candlesticks

The Japanese merchants developed candlesticks to monitor daily momentum and prices in the rice market in the 18th Century. A candlestick is a kind of chart that shows the opening, closing, high, and low prices in a particular period. As a result, it helps a trader to identify the entry or exit points of a market since it signals how the investor's feelings influence the trades.

The broad section of a candlestick is the real body, which a trader uses to determine if the closing price of trade was lower or higher than the opening price. Additionally, they also employ colors to help him or her to identify the state of the closing price more quickly.

The real body of a candlestick is green or white when the stock closes higher and red or black when the stock closes lower. Hence, the colors assist the trader to quickly interpret the market conditions at a glance and make appropriate decisions without wasting time.

The candlesticks' different colors also represent the sentiments of the market by indicating the outlooks of the traders. They signal if the traders have a bearish, bullish, or indecisive approach to the market. A trader then makes a judgment and takes up relevant positions in the market that provide him or her with gains.

Bullish Candlesticks

A bullish sentiment takes place when traders do a lot of purchasing because they expect the price of an asset will increase in a given period. As a result, the bullish outlook will form an intense buying pressure in the market. The bullish candlesticks will have a long green or white real body to show that the stock prices closed at a higher place than the opening price. Furthermore, it helps a trader to determine significant price actions at a particular area and time if a long white candle appears at an appropriate support level of price.

If the price initially moves significantly lower after the open and then shifts to close in the high vicinity, the bullish candlestick forms a reversal pattern called a hammer. The sellers lower the prices in a trading session, and it results in an intense buying pressure, which leads to the trading session ending on a higher close.

Thus, a hammer creates an uptrend, and its real body is short with a lower and longer shadow since sellers are reducing the prices. An inverted hammer indicates a reverse of the hammer candlestick since it develops in a downtrend. Other bullish candlesticks that a trader can utilize in the market include the morning star, the piercing line, bullish engulfing pattern, and the three white soldiers.

Bearish Candlesticks

A bearish outlook refers to the situation where there is an intense pressure of selling in the trading markets. It occurs when traders carry out a lot of selling trades in a particular duration. The bearish candlesticks have a long red or black body that signifies that the stock prices closed at a lower position than the opening price. Therefore, as the day goes on, the stock price falls leading to the opening price is higher than the close of the previous day. It leads to the formation of a long black candlestick that does not have an upper shadow but only possesses a short lower shadow.

Traders also refer to the bearish candlesticks as the hanging man, and they utilize them to try to select a bottom or top in the market. Moreover, the patterns of a bearish candlestick tend to indicate a switch in the attitude of investors. The sentiment changes from bullish to bearish after a length of time. Examples of bearish candlesticks include the bearish harami and bearish engulfing candlesticks.

Indecision Candle

This candlestick differs from the bullish and bearish types in terms of its body shape. While the bullish and bearish candlesticks are long, the indecision candle has a small real body, in that, the open price and the close price are near each other. Additionally, there are long wicks that attach to each side of the body and are equal in their lengths. The candlestick's body also lies between the low and the high, resulting in it being at the center of the entire candle range.

This candle occurs at a trend's top and bottom and can indicate to a trader about price or trend reversals if it develops at significant places on the chart after undergoing long moves. The name of this candlestick comes from the indecisive conduct that it shows since it signals both bullish and bearish activities. The stock closes at around the same place as the opening price because the bears and bulls were both very active in the market.

This double price action leads to there being two long wicks on either side of the candle's body. Their presence and lengths indicate that the price attempted to shift both upwards and downwards in the trading session. Consequently, it signals that no one won in the market and that it failed to maintain higher and lower prices. The Doji candlestick is an example of an indecisive candle.

These features mentioned above provide descriptions and information concerning the various tools and platforms used in trading. A person needs to understand them to allow him or her to gain vital knowledge that will help him or her to trade in the markets successfully.

Chapter 5: Trade Management and Price Action for Day Trading

Day Trading Risk Management

In all forms of trading, traders have a specific level of risk that they may be willing to take. Since the ultimate aim of participating in any particular trade is to gain profits, your exposure to risk should be as minimal as possible. In Day Trading, the incidence of risk may not be as damaging to small-scale low-risk traders. However, failure to enforce risk management strategies may be financially catastrophic for large investors and companies. The following risk management strategies could be of use to new investors in Day Trading:

a. Employ stop-loss orders
b. Take favorable positions
c. Stick to your trading plan
d. Make low-risk trades
e. Seek expert assistance

1. Stop-Loss Orders

These orders provide a mechanism for you to minimize the extent of any potential losses. The stop-loss order mandates the trader or your stockbroker to cease a particular type of trade instantly upon meeting specific conditions. Ideally, these orders indicate the range of values beyond which a given trading action begins to become significantly unprofitable. It applies to both short and long trading positions. Falling prices are not ideal for stock sellers, and stock buyers frown on expensive costs.

For instance, you could set a particular limit for the range of losses that you may be willing to tolerate adequately. Beyond this limit, your damages would start affecting your bottom line significantly, hence the need for an immediate halt to the trade deal. For them to act as a risk management tool, you need to have your stop-loss orders in place long before taking part in Day Trading. In this manner, you will be covering a potential loss that is yet to occur as opposed to reacting to real-time unfavorable stock prices.

2. Position Sizing

Taking a favorable trading position is the essence of position sizing. Before jumping into any trade opportunity, you should acquire relevant information about that trade. This data should enable you to make the appropriate selection when choosing to take a position. Ideally, rising stock prices with the expectation of a corresponding upward trend in the price chart favor buying stocks. Hence, this Day Trading scenario warrants you to take a long position. Short positions are beneficial when the prices drop or when the trading chart shows a sustained downward trend in the stock price. Position sizing is more of an account management strategy but also applies to risk evasion techniques. If you grow accustomed to taking productive positions, your risk index decreases, and vice versa. Therefore, you should seek assistance with position sizing and how to take up profitable positions if the need arises.

3. Trading Plan

You need to keep track of the progress of your Day Trading investments. In this regard, you must stick to the guidelines set out in your trading plan. This plan provides you with instructions on how to react or respond to specific scenarios in the course of your Day Trading. These directives usually offer the best course of action in the event of most adverse financial situations. In addition, if you strictly stick to your plan from the beginning, you will have no risk to manage later. Besides, you could seek the help of your stockbroker when drawing up a new trading plan. Make sure to capture every probable adverse eventuality and how to mitigate the risks associated with it. Trading plans often discourage you from making decisions based on emotions, which would likely happen in the absence of a trading plan.

Simple Trades

Day Trading often has small margins for either profits or losses. Therefore, you must learn to conduct small but assured trade deals in this strategy. It is advisable to refrain from lusting over the promises of impractically significant returns. The greed resulting from chasing quick profits over short time intervals is counterproductive to your ultimate aim. When you conduct illogical trades using large amounts of money, you are likely to run out of your available capital sooner than you expect. A simple trade has to be low in its risk index, small in amount, and a value that you can afford to lose. Volatility and trade volume are factors that affect your type of trade, but if you stick to logic, your profits will outnumber your losses. Most financial risk exposures are the consequences of rash decisions and poor Day Trading habits. If you have challenges in trying to identify the viable trading opportunities, you could seek the help of other seasoned traders or a stockbroker.

4. Expert Assistance

Whenever you engage in an unfamiliar trading practice, it is advisable to know what you are doing. The same advice applies to investors who are new to Day Trading. Heeding to this counsel will spare you from financial ruin down the line. One way you could make use of available Day Trading expertise is by hiring a stockbroker. Trading blindly without any idea of the expectations is a risky proposition. Stockbrokers are often highly experienced traders in their own right. They know about all the potentially profitable trading opportunities and doomed trades that are bound to go bust.

Therefore, when you have a qualified and registered stockbroker by your side, you are less likely to get yourself into financially risky situations. It is essential that you can predict a wrong trade deal from a mile away, but since you cannot, a stockbroker may be the next best option. In addition to spotting potentially wacky trade deals, your stockbroker is typically responsible for managing your brokerage account. He or she participates in the different trading commitments and takes favorable trading positions on your behalf. As a result, the chances of making a fruitless trade decision are minimal.

Price Action in Day Trading

Price action is one of the strategies used by traders who take part in Day Trading. It relies on the movements in the price of the security under trade. Plotting the raw stock prices against the trading period on a chart is necessary, thereby showing the behavior of your stock value over a specified time. Indicators that are common to other strategies play an insignificant role when using price action.

As a price action trader, you will not bother to find out the conditions affecting particular price movements in either direction. You will take the pattern at its face value because you put more credence to the trends in the stock prices than their contributing factors. As per this reasoning, it could be an excellent time to sell your stock when the prices start rising due to its corresponding increase in value. A downward trend is suggestive of falling prices; hence, buying the stock at favorable prices is possible.

As an investor or trader, your point of entry into Day Trading is dependent on potential profitability and minimal risk exposure. Buying at the least reasonable price and selling at the highest stock price are the two main objectives in price action Day Trading. Besides, technical analysis comes from the price action of a particular stock over a specified period. Price action mainly deals with the ongoing, real-time stock price fluctuations. It is an instant form of Day Trading strategy without the lagging period or delays experienced in waiting for the relevant indicators.

You can modify your stock price chart to show distinct price movements in different colors. This color transition alerts you to a trading opportunity due to the obvious and easy to spot a change in price direction. Once again, you will only concentrate on the upward or downward trend in the price and if that particular pattern will hold. The following concepts describe some everyday experiences attributed to price action Day Trading:

a. Price Breakouts
b. Candlestick Charts
c. Optional Indicators
d. Support and Resistance
e. Technical Analysis

1. Price Breakouts

A primary concept for you to understand is the Day Trading event of a breakout. It is common in almost all cases of price action trading. A breakout is a sudden jump in stock value in either direction from an extended hovering position. This spike in your stock price is readily visible on a price action chart. A breakout is an indicator that alerts you to a possible trading opportunity. However, it could also be a false breakout, in which case, the prices would soon rebound in the opposite direction.

For instance, if the price of a particular stock keeps fluctuating between $25 and $27 for about a month, you would not think much of the security. Yet, if the stock price goes up to $29 in one day after the month, your curiosity and alertness would peak. This sudden upward spike in the stock price is the breakout. Ideally, you would assume that the price is about to keep rising and continue on this trajectory for the foreseeable future. Therefore, as a price action trader, you would take a long position on the same stock hoping for a significant profit from the increasing value. However, the breakout could turn out to be false, and the spike to $29 was only a one-day occurrence.

In this case, the rebound effect would cause the stock value to start dropping. A possible explanation could be that the upward spike caused many other price action traders to buy the stock, which in turn led to more investors who previously held shares to sell. Based on the mechanism of economies of scale, this influx of stock security into the market causes its price to start falling. The price could decrease by a considerable margin past the initial low of $25 to the horror of the traders who took an initial buy position. If you bought plenty of shares based on the initial upswing in the breakout ($27 to $29), you would experience a massive loss afterward.

This uncertainty is part of the characteristics of price action trading, i.e., you can only know the previous behavior of a particular stock, but you cannot predict its future action. Learn to accept the possibility of losing some capital in such price action trades that do not go according to your expectations. Price action trading is akin to speculative trading. Hence, the best mentality you can have is to try to increase your profit margins on the good days more than your losing margins.

2. Candlestick Charts

Another mechanism that is useful in price action trading is the use of candlestick charts. These charts provide more information about the stock price that may assist you in making a more informed decision. The candlestick chart contains details such as the opening and closing prices of a specific stock; hence, you get to know the range of this value within a day. In addition, the candlestick charts show both the maximum and minimum amount of the stock in a single day of trading.

In this case, you can estimate the real value of the stock by averaging these particular values.

Due to this additional data, more accomplished day traders often use a combination of candlestick charts and breakouts in their price action strategies for a detailed source of information. They both eliminate the confusion caused by multiple interpretations of the same price action chart. You may see a downward trend and think that the stock value is decreasing, while another person might conclude that a turnaround or price reversal may be imminent. In the end, you both take contrasting positions on a single trade that are equally justifiable. This need for an overall complete picture enables you as a trader to come up with a trading resolution based on the whole trading status of a given stock price. For instance, a particular stock may show multiple drops in its intraday price while keeping with an overall upward trend on a week over week basis. As a result, such dreaded incidents as the rebounds associated with the stand-alone price action breakouts will not catch you off guard again.

3. Optional Indicators

In addition to candlestick charts, you may incorporate a group of specific indicators depending on your objective. However, due to lag delay, trade indicators are not essential to price action trading. In case you need them, trade indicators can easily fit on a price action chart. Examples of such commonly applied indexes include:

- **Moving average**

This indicator enables you to pick out the mean price movement of your particular stock over a specified time frame. In its purest form, this indicator centers on the average value of your security or commodity under trade based on the most recent behavior of that particular stock.

- **MACD indicator**

The acronym for this indicator stands for Moving Average Convergence Divergence. It depicts momentum by relating the previously mentioned moving average to a specific point on the price chart. This point indicates the price level at which you may decide to purchase stock, thereby making it subjective. Taking a particular position depends on this interaction. A possibly long trading position is considerable if the MACD indicator goes above your level or price point.

- **Stochastic Oscillator**

Just like the MACD, this indicator is descriptive of momentum, as well. First, based on your trading hunch, you decide on an appropriate trend that your stock price will take. This hopeful trend will enable you to estimate the expected value in the stock price at a particular time in the future. Next, sit back and wait for the trading to reach your estimated time. Finally, use the stochastic oscillator to verify whether the current stock price and pattern at this new time match with your earlier speculated expectation.

- **RSI indicator**

This indicator is suggestive of a market that is either overbought or oversold on a particular security or stock. This description is a measure of the strength of that specific stock within the stock market. Hence, the acronym for this indicator stands for Relative Strength Indicator. It enables you to make an informed judgment on the viability or risks of trading in a certain way and on a particular stock.

- **Fibonacci Retracement**

This indicator is useful for testing the level of support or resistance when subjected to the trends in the price action chart. You can obtain a detailed perspective of the stock market based on the patterns formed by this indicator. This information guides you on when and how to trade as well as on which particular stocks to trade.

- **Bollinger Bands**

Whenever you want to find out the usual trading price range of a particular stock, you should use this indicator. Bollinger bands typically show you the stock price limits beyond which breakouts occur. A brief consolidation of the stock price typically occurs within such Bollinger bands. A breached Bollinger band is usually indicative of a breakout, thereby requiring you to alter your taken position.

4. Support and Resistance

These terms describe the behavior of the price action trend. Ideally, you often encounter an oscillating pattern in an ordinary stock trading session. Some uptrends typically alternate with their corresponding downtrends. The highest point or level of the stock price that the stock can reach, as depicted by the price action chart, is the resistance. All trends past this point either hold position or reverse their direction downwards. A rise in the price of a particular stock often means that buying securities is the predominant trade activity.

At first, the buyers in the stock market outnumber the available security in circulation, leading to an increase in the price. The price chart, therefore, registers the uptrend. With high stock prices, investors who hold a lot of stock will take up short positions. More stockholders follow suit resulting in a stock market overflowing with that same stock. This time, the particular security outnumbers the buyers, and its price stabilizes, but if this imbalance continues, the stock prices will begin to drop. Therefore, the point at which the stock prices stop their upward trend is the resistance.

Support, on the other hand, is the exact opposite of resistance. It is the lowest price that a given stock reaches beyond which the only further direction becomes upwards. In the above scenario, the high stock prices begin to fall in a saturated market. The fall is due to the concept of economies of scale. More buyers purchase increased amounts of stock at progressively cheaper costs hence the downtrend on the price action chart. This downward direction in the price of commodities would scare any more stockholders away from selling.

Therefore, the market soon runs into a deficiency of available stock. At this stage, once again, the stock buyers outnumber the insufficient stock in circulation. The trend holds steady for a while as per the price action chart. A prolonged state of a low volume of securities in circulation triggers an increase in its price. This outcome is valid because of the more demand from buyers outnumbering the circulating stock supply. This change in the trend of the stock price signals the point of support.

5. Technical Analysis

In the case of technical analysis, data from price action trading charts are essential for such indicators as the patterns of ascending triangles. These triangles are useful in predicting an imminent major breakout. This prediction is due to previous attempts at a series of multiple minor breakouts by periods of a rising price trend. The pattern caused by the efforts of these bull trends is typically indicative of a gain of momentum with each attempt. From this informative data analysis, you can expect an overall breakout shortly.

Along with the technical analysis, trend and swing traders use price action as a source of data for their indicators or tools as well. Concurrently, they can obtain information on the levels of resistance and support for the specific trade deals in which they participate. For this data to become productive to them, the swing traders need to have the skills required for price action interpretation. Of more use to such external traders, is the ability to derive relevant predictions of the corresponding breakouts or consolidation from the price action charts. Beware of applying technical analysis to raw price action data. For technical analysis to make sense, you need additional information such as the trading volume, market factors, and investor influence.

In the absence of accompanying technical analysis, the psychological and emotional weight might creep into your decisions. As a result, your mental faculties experience clouded judgment, thereby rendering your incapable of making logical choices. Price action trading is beneficial to small traders looking for low-risk opportunities to invest their small amounts of capital. They are usually in search of a quick profit over a brief period so that a single breakout event may suffice. Complex and in-depth analysis is probably more applicable in large-scale settings, for example, corporations, companies, financial institutions, and wealthy private investors. This category of investors is typically long-term and is often on the hook for massive capital loans over an extended period.

Chapter 6: Day Trading Strategies

Day Trading is the buying or selling of an asset or security, within the course of a single trading day. A trading day refers to the span of time when a particular forex or stock exchange is open. Trading days are usually seven to eight hours long, from Mondays to Fridays.

Day Trading uses various techniques and strategies to make a profit from price changes for a specific asset. It involves adjusting to events that bring about short-term market fluctuations.

News releases and announcements such as corporate earnings, interest rates, and other economic statistics give information about what the forex or stock market can expect. Day traders can then benefit from the market by attuning to the significant moves the market makes.

Day Trading, therefore, uses several intraday strategies, including breakout trading, scalping, news releases trading, range trading, and high-frequency trading (HFT).

Breakout Trading

A breakout happens when the price of a stock moves beyond the Support or resistance level. The Support or resistance level is the point at which the increase in the price of security stops because of an increase in the number of sellers who want to sell at that price. Day traders use breakout trading to take a position within the early stages of a trend.

A day trader buys an asset when the price of the asset breaks above the resistance level, or the trader sells an asset when the price of the asset goes below the resistance level.

Day Trading uses breakouts because breakout set-ups mark the begging point for significant price trends, significant price swings, and an increase in the unpredictability of the market or volatility. Such breakout set-ups include pullback-consolidation Breakout, reversal-consolidation breakout, reversal at support or resistance level, strong area breakout, and finally, false breakouts or fake-outs.

Pullback-consolidation breakout takes place within the first five to at most twenty minutes as soon as the forex or the stock market opens. The term pullback refers to the price drops that are comparatively short before the prices go back up.

A pullback is usually a few consecutive sessions. Consolidation refers to the case when there is a longer pause before the prices go back up. Pullbacks provide entry points for day traders who want to enter a position when there is a significant upward price movement of a commodity.

Reversal-consolidation breakout happens when a significant move in one direction is followed immediately by a more substantial step in the opposite direction. That is then followed by a long pause or consolidation. After the consolidation, day traders push the price in the reverse direction, assuming that the initial trend was wrong.

Reversal at Support or resistance level is a stage where the stock price has reversed frequently before. When this happens, day traders are not able to push the price of a security in a specific direction.

Strong Breakout happens when a breakout was so strong that it brought about a price gap. Day traders use strong breakouts to buy assets while avoiding selling any commodities in the market. That is to avoid making losses when the price continues to move upwards, following the Breakout. Traders place stop-loss orders when buying assets at this point, to reduce loss.

False Breakouts or fake-outs take place when a price breaks past the Support or resistance level but does not continue moving upward in that direction. When this happens, traders plan their exit by canceling out orders to reduce potential losses. Alternatively, traders avoid taking the first Breakout they see.

Generally, day traders wait until the price moves back to the original breakout level before they trade breakouts. The traders expect to see whether the price will move back to generate either an upward or a downward trend, depending on the direction the traders are trading.

Scalping

Scalping is a Day Trading strategy that day traders use to try to generate small profits on small price changes throughout the day. When scalping, day traders assume that most assets or stocks will complete the initial stage of a movement. However, traders do not know the direction the stock prices will move. That is because, after that first movement, some stocks may stop advancing, while others may continue to develop.

As a result, day traders aim to take as many small profits as they can, while maintaining a higher ratio of winning trades compared to the losing trades. That strategy helps the traders to keep benefits that are equal or somewhat more significant than losses.

Day traders use three types of scalping. The first type is market-making. In market making, the trader attempts to make profits on the gap between the bid and the asking price of a security. The traders achieve this by issuing out a request and an offer for a particular stock. However, a trader makes extremely small profits because he or she must compete with the other market makers for the shares on both bids and offers.

The second type is more traditional, where traders buy large numbers of shares, which they later sell for a profit when there are small price movements. In this case, traders enter into positions for a couple of thousand shares and wait for small price movements measured in cents.

The third type is much closer to the old method of trading. In this type of scalping, a trader puts up a certain number of shares on any set-up from his or her system and exits the position as soon as the first exit signal develops near the 1:1 risk-reward ratio.

News Releases Trading

Day traders trade news events that are worth trading because news events have the capacity to increase volatility in the short-term. Therefore, traders look for financial information that will cause price movements in the currency market. The currency market mostly responds to economic news from the United States (U.S), and to other financial news from around the world.

Traders mostly follow economic news from the eight major currencies. Such currencies include the U.S. dollar (USD), the British pound (GBP), the Euro (EUR), the Swiss franc (CHF), the Japanese yen (JPY), the Australian dollar (AUD), the New Zealand dollar (NZD), and finally the Canadian dollar (CAD).

Generally, the most significant news releases from any country include information on inflation, trade balance, manufacturing industries surveys, interest rate decisions, retail sales, business sentiment surveys, consumer confidence surveys, industrial production, natural disasters, political unrest, and unemployment. Therefore, because the relevance of these releases may change, traders keep an eye on the focus of the market at all times.

Traders trade news releases by looking for consolidation periods ahead of big numbers and trade the breakouts that are on the back of the numbers.

Range Trading

In range trading, day traders employ support and resistant levels to make their trade decisions. In other words, traders take note of overbought (resistance), oversold (support) areas, buy at the oversold area, and sell at the overbought area.

Day traders use this strategy in markets that are constantly fluctuating, with no visible long-term trend. The goal of a trader is to identify points at which stock prices have gone above or below the regular prices but will likely move back to the original value, or points where support or resistance has formed and is expected to hold again.

As such, range trading uses the Support and resistance strategy, and the breakouts and breakdowns strategy. In using the

Support and resistance strategy, traders buy when the price is close to the support level, and sell when the price reaches resistance. Traders use technical indicators such as the relative strength index (RSI), the stochastic oscillator, and the commodity channel index (CCI). Traders use the indicators to confirm the oversold and overbought situations when the price oscillates or fluctuates within a trading range.

For example, a trader can buy a stock when the stock price is trading at Support, and the RSI showing an oversold reading below 20, and sell when the RSI gives an overbought reading above 60. To reduce the chances of making losses, a trader can place a stop-loss order outside the trading range.

In using the breakouts and breakdowns strategy, traders enter in the direction of a breakout or a breakdown from a trading range. Traders make use of indicators such as price action and volume, to check whether a price movement is in force.

High-Frequency Trading (HFT)

The high-frequency trading strategy makes use of algorithms to capitalize on short-term market inadequacies.

HFT uses dynamic computer programs to manage a large number of orders within seconds. High-frequency traders achieve this by making use of complex algorithms to analyze various markets and to complete market orders depending on market conditions. Therefore, traders with fast delivery speed profit more than those with slower delivery speeds are.

HFT brings in liquidity to the markets and does away with small bid-ask spreads. The liquidity that HFT produces disappears within seconds, and therefore only traders with quick execution speeds can benefit from it. Additionally, HFT removes small bid-ask spreads, which bring in minimal profits.

Major investment banks, hedge funds, and institutional traders or investors use HFT to handle a significant number of orders at super high speeds. The HFT platforms allow traders to manage millions or orders and evaluate multiple markets and trades within seconds, thus giving the traders a considerable advantage in the open market.

HFT has become popular in the open market following the introduction of incentives that high-frequency trading offers so that institutions can add liquidity to the open market. By giving small incentives, trades acquire more liquidity, and the institutions involved reap benefits from every trade they make, in addition to their high execution speeds.

Day Trading is, therefore, a career that requires traders to understand the basics of the marketplace. Individuals who try to take part in Day Trading without any knowledge and experience often lose their investments. A day trader should, therefore, be skilled in technical analysis and chart reading, to understand the ins and outs of the products or services that he or she trades.

Additionally, day traders should only invest capital, which they can afford to lose. That will help the traders leave out their emotions when trading while protecting them from financial devastation. In addition, a trader needs to have an execution plan in order to have an edge over the rest of the market.

Various strategies that a day trader can capitalize on include swing trading, trading news, and exploiting price differences of identical financial instruments on different forms. These strategies will help the trader to make consistent profits with minimal losses.

However, a profit-making strategy is ineffective without discipline. Lack of discipline can make traders make huge losses because they fail to initiate trades that meet their own standards.

Day traders mostly depend on volatility in the market to make profits. That is to say, a commodity may get the attention of the trader when the price of the commodity continually fluctuates during the day.

In addition, day traders rely on securities that are profoundly liquid because the liquidity gives the traders the opportunity to change their positions without interfering with the price of the security. When the cost of the underlying security moves up, a trader may enter a long position or a buy position, and sell the security when the price moves down so that he or she can profit when the price falls.

Day Trading consequently requires access to some of the most sophisticated financial services and instruments in the open market. Hence, day traders need access to various news sources and competent analytical software. In addition to these instruments, the traders will need to have a competitive edge in the market that will help them to acquire more profits than losses.

A trader can become more competent by taking time to understand how the market works, coming up with an execution strategy, having enough capital to start, and finally, by taking on trading opportunities that are within his or her trading limits. Day Trading requires sound methods that will give a person a statistical edge in every trade he or she makes.

Chapter 7: Technical Analysis

Technical analysis is the study of the price changes and trends of a stock or security. The study involves traders inspecting a stock's trading history through technical indicators and charts in order to determine the future direction of the stock price.

Statistical trends, such as price movement and volume identified from the past, determine future trading opportunities. Technical analysts, therefore, focus on price fluctuations, trading signals, and analytical charting tools to examine the strength or weakness of a specific security.

Technical analysis is more dominant in forex and stock markets where traders limit their attention to short-term price movements. Technical analysts aim to comprehend the market emotion behind the price patterns by looking for trends rather than evaluating the basic qualities of a stock.

Technical analysts assume that markets are resourceful with values representing influences that impact the price of a stock or security. However, the analysts acknowledge that price fluctuations are not entirely haphazard but move in recognizable trends that have a tendency to reoccur in the course of time.

There are two different approaches to technical analysis: the top-down approach and the bottom-up approach. The top-down approach involves evaluating securities that fit into a certain standard. For example, a trader may want securities that moved away from their 50-day moving average as a buying prospect.

The bottom-up approach deals with assessing stocks that appear primarily interesting for potential entry and exit points. For example, a trader may discover undervalued security in a downward trend and use technical analysis to find a particular entry point when the security price stops decreasing.

Different types of traders use different types of technical analysis. While position traders may use analytical charts and technical indicators, day trades may use simple trend lines and volume indicators to arrive at trade decisions. Similarly, traders coming up with computerized algorithms may use a combination of technical and volume indicators in their decision-making processes.

Trendline Analysis

Day traders study trends to forecast the future price changes of stock. Historical trends in the price movement give day traders an idea of what the price movements will be in the future.

Day traders carry out trend analysis on short-term, medium, and long-term time frames. In that way, the traders can determine when the price of a security will rise or fall. Along with that, traders can also predict when the market will rise or fall.

By being able to determine price movements, traders aim to time the market so that the traders can enter long positions or buy when the stock prices are at their lowest and sell when the shares are at their highest buying price.

As such, day traders pay attention to an economic institution's financial information and general economic conditions in order to forecast accurately, the future trend of an investment in the marketplace.

For instance, a trader's trend analysis shows that company X's security is at a low price, and according to past price action, the security's price tends to rise once it hits that low price. Consequently, the trader may take that as an indication that he or she should buy the company's security in order to make a profit when the security price moves up.

However, when the trader miss's information that the company laid off 30 percent of its workforce, in an effort to refinance its debt due to payment problems, then the trader may be setting himself or herself up for a loss.

Therefore, although technical analysts may use large amounts of data to carry out an analysis, there is no guarantee that the analysts' predictions will be accurate.

Volume Analysis

Volume analysis involves the evaluation of the number of shares or contracts that a particular stock or security has traded within a specified period.

Day traders use volume analysis to examine patterns in volumes in relation to price movements. As a result, the traders are able to know the importance of changes in the price of an asset or security.

Like any other technical indicator in the market place, the volume presents buy and sell signals to traders. Traders can know which signal to take by studying the pattern of the price movement. Are the trends strong in one direction? In addition, the traders can look at the moving average at the point of a breakout to determine whether the price movement captures the sentiments of significant investors.

When the demand for an underlying stock is high, it means that many traders have an interest in the underlying stock and are therefore prepared to pay more for it. The volume gives an indication to day traders of how many investors want certain security.

Day traders use two types of volume indicators; the positive volume index (PVI) and the negative volume index (NVI). Both indicators operate based on the previous day's trading volume and the market price of a commodity. Consequently, when the trading volume goes up from the previous day, the traders fine-tune the PVI. When the trading volume goes down from the previous day, the traders adjust the NVI accordingly.

Traders use the PVI and the NVI to evaluate how volume affects price movement. An increase or a decrease in the PVI implies that the volume drives the price movement. Contrariwise, an increase or a reduction in the NVI suggests that the volume has a minimal effect on the price changes.

Candlestick Charting

Day traders use candlestick charting to trace price fluctuations. The traders utilize the candlestick charts to show the price changes during a single time period for any time frame. For instance, each candlestick on a 4-hour chart shows the price movement within four hours.

The peak point of a candlestick displays the highest price a stock traded during the set period, whereas the lowermost position indicates the lowest prices of the stock during that time period. The part in between the highest and the weakest points in the candlestick shows the opening and closing stock prices for that period.

Traders choose the colors to use in the candlestick charts as a way to follow the price movements at a glance. As a result, traders get more visual cues and trends as they carry out technical analysis.

Chapter 8: Psychology and Mindset

Day Trading, like any other form of investment, is subject to influence from human emotion and psychological impact. Whenever money or capital is in play, people tend to take matters rather personally because of the inevitable consequence of the hope that comes along with the promise of significant returns. People will strive to make money while at the same time, avoid circumstances that may cause them to lose their capital. It is from this zero-sum mentality that the influence of psychology or emotions may creep into a sensible mindset. Such control takes over every aspect of the Day Trading instincts that you learned over time.

Your knowledge goes out of the window when a situation that triggers your psychological response arises. A high degree of counter-productivity thus ensues. It, eventually, leads to the dismissal of logical decisions in favor of hunches as well as the need to chase after fleeting profits and cover your previous losses. For you to manage your Day Trading expertise through challenging scenarios, you need to look out for emotions that alter your reasoning capability adversely. Try to improve and nurture a productive mindset, while at the same time, avoid promoting a mental culture that justifies negativity falsely. The following few behaviors and traits are central to your particular mindset whenever you decide to participate in Day Trading:

Do Not Rationalize Your Trading Errors

This mindset t is one of the leading obstacles to the progress and eventual success of your Day Trading endeavors. You are often prone to justify any trading mistakes that you make to the detriment of moving forward. For instance, you get an entry into a particularly promising trade deal later than necessary in spite of your much earlier knowledge of its potential for profitability. The delay causes you to miss an excellent opportunity at the previous entry point. However, you decide to justify this misstep by convincing yourself of your preference for trading late over missing the same deal entirely.

The downside to such delays is often a faulty sense of size estimation in taking your trading position. Hence, the resulting increased exposure to financial risk you become disadvantaged by. Beware of your procrastination when it comes to productive openings that are currently available in Day Trading. If you possess this tendency, consider getting rid of it as soon as possible before it costs you a lot more capital in the long run. In case you are not prone to the frequent postponement of your responsibilities to a later date, be alert for the development of this mentality with the trading company that you keep. You can quickly become influenced by the kind of traders from whom you seek advice on more complex trading strategies. When present, stockbrokers affect your trading ethos, as well.

Poor trading etiquette from these external sources will rub off on you and vice versa. Try to keep the company of well-known responsible trading partners and stockbrokers when the need arises. Another rationalization scenario involves a run of profitable results. Based on a series of trade deals that made you successive returns, you begin to convince your brain of your seemingly high intelligence. This false belief in your skills may lead you to overestimate your trading expertise. Before long, you may start engaging in Day Trading on a hunch rather than apply logic to your decisions. You stop referring to your trusted trading plan and jump into many trading opportunities haphazardly. After a while, these instances of carelessness and trading arrogance will catch up with you because they always inevitably do. Your chances of plunging into a financial disaster go up.

With your eventual financial ruin come the cases of psychological meltdown leading to a negative feedback loop. A wrong decision from your misplaced sense of conceitedness will invariably lead to high-risk exposure. As a result, you suffer significant losses eventually, and consequently, your emotional health suffers, causing you to spiral into a state of depression. This loop is often self-propagating, meaning that it feeds onto itself. Bad decisions lead to adverse outcomes and a fragile mindset, which, in turn, is prone to make more bad decisions, and the loop goes on and on. Keep in mind that in Day Trading, such a feedback loop is often disastrous. All these adverse effects arise from your initial false sense of justification for a wrong deed.

Beware of Your Trading Decisions

This advice is so apparent that it sounds redundant when mentioned. However, decisions are typically the product of your reasoning and judgment at a particular moment. When it comes to decisions on Day Trading, psychological influence is often a determining factor in the process. Keeping your wits about you is very crucial, especially when everything seems to be out of control. You need to realize that every trade has its ups and downs and how you deal with the challenging times is often more consequential. Try to maintain a logical mindset when making Day Trading choices from a variety of bad options. When it seems that an imminent financial downturn is inevitable, the extent of your loss becomes essential. In this case, you will need to make a sensible decision on the degree of losing margins that you can tolerate adequately.

At this point, you are probably in a state of so many overwhelming emotions that your foggy mental faculties become clouded. An expected human response is to run away from danger, naturally, but in certain situations, fleeing may not be an option. A reflex in a trading scenario often leads to an impulsive decision. Such a choice is, in turn, typically not well thought or deliberative. You should confront your unfavorable circumstances head-on and attempt to fix the situation, however hopeless. This sense of perseverance is usually the essence of most trading excursions, especially when the times become financially rough. Going through the loss of some capital and other Day Trading challenges is often a painful experience that can lead to illogical decisions.

Always remember to uphold vigilance and adhere strictly to the guidelines in your trading plan when confronted with obstacles during your trades. The trading plan usually has instructions on how to handle these seemingly desperate situations. In addition, the prior preparation of any trading guide is generally free of emotional or psychological influence; hence, you can rely on it to maintain neutrality. Also, beware of making trading resolutions when going through a phase with a foul mood. Such conclusions are bound to lead you into a financial catastrophe, especially if you are not careful. Learn to put off the verdict to a time when you can resume logical thinking. When you make any rash decision, it can only result in your further exposure to even more risk.

Keep Your Emotions in Check

Learn to stick to a Day Trading system and method that you trust. Such a strategy may be one that has a history of always making significant returns. Once you master and fully grasp how to apply a specific approach to your trading deals, try to fine-tune it to your preference based on your ultimate objectives. Afterward, stick to this tried, practiced, and tested system in all your searches for valid trade deals. On some days, the stock market may be slow with a low volume of trade. The volatility in such a case is often negligible. However, due to an unchecked emotional influence, you develop a sense of greed or lust for profits.

The desire for benefits on a slow day is common. It leads to the urge to trade on anything to make a small profit. In this situation, you will move from Day Trading into gambling. Trading requires a logical mindset on your part with a lack of psychological attachment whatsoever. Gambling is a consequence of emotional and mental factors running amok in your Day Trading system. If a particular trading style worked on multiple times in the past, teach your brain to consider it. Your trusted trading system will indicate a lack of valid trade opportunities on a specific slow market day. In this case, curb your emotions, desires, and urges to chase a quick profit; however strong they seem.

You should never allow yourself to resort to gambling under any circumstances. Gambling is detrimental to healthy and responsible Day Trading behavior. The risk exposure exponentially rises when you grow accustomed to the desire for profits. If a given day of trading is unfavorable, you should not take part in invalid and unworthy deals. In addition, you should only trade on verifiable opportunities. At certain times, you may experience a series of successive returns in a relatively short period. Learn to know when to stop and how to curb your lust for wanting more returns. Trust your system to trade only on valid deals; however, multiple opportunities are available. An emotion that goes unmonitored in such situations is the greed for more profit.

You convince yourself psychologically that the various deals could be a sign of your lucky day. This mentality in a false belief is wrong, and you need to be aware of it. Your psychology can play deceitful tricks on your logical mind leading to high-risk trading deals. You must realize that in Day Trading, it is almost impossible to get more returns out of a system than what the stock market offers. Emotional corruption also comes into play in a scenario where you bite off more than you can chew.

The greed for substantial amounts of returns may cause you to take high-risk trading positions for a chance at quick profits. However, you must remember that profits and losses are both possible outcomes from a Day Trading session. Therefore, you need to learn to trade in amounts that you can afford to lose. After all, Day Trading involves taking a chance based on a speculative position. You should practice trading in small amounts of money within the confines of low-risk deals. In this case, a potential loss may not be as damaging as the earlier high-risk trading position driven by greed. Eliminate the role of emotions in Day Trading and learn to accept the uncertainty of an unknown future outcome.

Be Patient When Trading

Patience is a crucial trait to have when you take part in Day Trading due to the upswings and downward trends in stock prices. It can become challenging to identify the right entry or exit point for a particular trading opportunity, given the fluctuating nature of a volatile market. However, when you master the art of being patient and studying the trade intently, you can come up with a winning strategy. Having a planned approach is essential, and you should prepare one before engaging in any Day Trading. Often, most seasoned traders include trading strategies for different market conditions in their trading plans. Hence, when making your trading plan, consider incorporating a trading strategy within it.

If unsure of how to proceed, you can always seek the assistance of qualified stockbrokers. They have the experience of encountering various Day Trading scenarios in the real world. If trustworthy, they could provide you with invaluable insights on coming up with a proper strategy. Now it is up to you to stick to the plan in every session in which you participate. Patience demands that you pay attention to the planned strategy and ignore any attractive distractions when trading. For instance, a brief upswing from a potential price action breakout may be misleading. It might cause you to falsely believe that the stock price is about to pick momentum and keep rising on the chart.

However, as attractive as this scenario might be, a sense of diligent patience demands that you ignore it and refer to your strategy. Upon referral to your trading plan strategy, you may encounter the concept of false breakouts. You also learn that these false upswings in trend usually follow a prolonged period of price consolidated. As a result, your patience allows you to evade a potentially wrong entry point to a trading position. You are also able to pick the right exit point from a particular trading session based on strategic patience. The price action chart acts merely as a guide for your trading actions and not the determining factor.

Chapter 9: Day Trading Rules

Day Trading is the ability to buy and sell financial instruments within the same trading day. There is a group of day traders called the pattern day traders (PDT) these are just traders who make more than four trades within five days and who use a margin account to trade. Day Trading has rules, and failure to adhere to certain rules can be costly. Rules also vary depending on location and the volume you trade.

7 Rules of Day Trading

The following rules of Day Trading, if used correctly, can help traders make profits and avoid huge losses.

How to Enter and Exit A Market

Day traders should have a predetermined plan in place of when to enter and exit a market. A trader can quickly find yourself out of the game as soon as you press the enter key if they do not have a plan. As a day trader, you have to accept the fact that you do not control the market. Therefore, one of the key factors to succeeding in Day Trading is usually determined by your ability to enter and exit your trading positions. Knowing the prices at which you wish to enter and exit can help make profits or save you from losing out on more.

When making the plan:
- Use indicators
- Set a target price before you enter the market.
- Know how much stock you plan to trade
- Plan for when to exit the market - when the market is going against your expectations, do you exit your position to avoid bigger losses?

Trading Rush Hours

Another important Day Trading rule is to avoid the first hour after the market opens and the last hour before it closes. It is wise to wait and observe during those times. Do not be eager to jump in as soon as the market opens. The first and last hours are the most volatile times in the market. This is because the stock is likely reacting to some overnight news releases, and this is when the big investors and trading experts compete. In the last hour, traders are also rushing to close out their positions.

Be Cautious of Margin Trading

Another important rule is to trade with the money you have, not borrowed money. It is important to be cautious of margin trading. Trading on margin means that you are borrowing money from a brokerage firm to trade; Money you will have to pay back. A margin account increases your purchasing power and allows you to use borrowed money to increase financial leverage; however, not all trades are profitable. Therefore, you risk losing the small bit of your capital as well as the borrowed money. Margin trading should be used in trades that you are sure will be profitable.

Be Realistic

Another important Day Trading rule is to avoid greed. It is very easy to be carried away by greed when trading, do not lose out on small profits because you think you can make more. It is very important to remain realistic about profits. The market is always changing; sometimes, it is better to settle on a small profit than to make big losses.

Be Knowledgeable

Do not day trade if you do have no sufficient knowledge of what is happening in the markets. Not everyone can trade in the market. Most traders start with paper trading and intense training. You need to be aware of information about the stocks you plan to trade, basic trading procedures, and always be on the lookout for anything that can affect your stocks. You can start by practicing using a demo account; this is a trial and error account, where you do not use real money. This account enables traders to experiment with trading before they can set up a real funded account.

Cut Your Losses

This is the number one rule in trading; cut your losses. Placing a trade is taking a risk; every trader, even the best in the world, has had bad trading days. Losing is part of trading. Traders need to accept their losses when the market starts going against them instead of hoping for a turnaround. This can be a lethal mistake. Have an exit strategy and react accordingly. Accepting your loss reduces the chance of it happening again. By cutting your losses, you learn from it and make the necessary changes to avoid a repetition.

Risk Management Plan

Risk management plans help cut down losses. The idea is to avoid risking more than you can afford to lose. With a risk management plan, even when a trade goes wrong, they still have money to trade tomorrow. Traders follow the 1% rule, which allows them to trade only 1% of their capital on any single trade. This ensures that only 1% of their money is at risk on any single trade.

Other General Day Trading rules

These rules are not binding but can be helpful when making trading decisions:

Keep A Trading Journal

The process of Day Trading can be nerve-wracking, and in most cases, traders do not remember with clarity and context all the moves they made at the end of the day, so as a rule, it is important to journal while you are trading. It does not have to be detailed, and you can write in bullet points and edit later. Journaling gives you the ability to track your trades, gains, and losses. You can also use the information to analyze your overall market performance and tweak your strategies.

Tax Rules

There is no one size fits all when it comes to tax rules. Taxes depend on the country where you are trading. Each country has different tax obligations, and the consequences of not meeting them can be extremely costly. It is important to research on taxes before you start trading.

Manage Number of Trades

A good rule of thumb is to avoid making more than three trades a week. It is more difficult to keep an eye on multiple trades at once, especially if you luck experience. If a trader makes four or more-day trades within five days, the account moves from cash account to a pattern day trade account, also known as a margin account, which has certain limitations like:

- **Minimum Account Balance**

Day traders who use margin accounts must maintain a minimum balance of $25,000. This does not apply to day traders who use cash brokerage accounts. If the account balance falls below this amount, the owner loses any buying power. This minimum balance can be maintained in the form of cash and securities. Pattern day traders are not allowed to cross guarantee to meet the minimum balance.

- **When the minimum capital is not reached**

When a pattern day trader account goes below $25,000, they are issued with an equity call. The balance must be restored using cash or other marginal equities. Traders should deposit the funds within five business days, and they are not allowed to make a withdrawal on the amount for at least two working days.

- **Increased leverage**

Pattern day trade accounts have increased access to margin and, therefore, leverage. They may have access to twice the standard margin amount when trading stocks. The amount is usually decided every morning.

Have A Trading Plan

Another important trading rule is to always have a trading plan and stick to it when trading. One of the worst habits' traders have is trading impulsively without any guidelines. Traders should assess their success or failure on a trade based on how they stuck to their trading plan and not whether they made a profit or a loss. Ensure that your trading plan works for you and stick to it.

Don't Chase Trades

Another rule is to avoid is chasing trades. Sometimes traders decide to chase fast-moving stocks when the market makes large and quick moves in prices instead of focusing on their trading plan. Even though the move can lead to more profits, sometimes trading decisions made in a rash can be costly. Most traders learn the importance of this rule when their poor trading decisions cost them.

Emotions

Another rule of Day Trading is not to let your emotions affect your trading decisions. Emotions have a way of influencing a trader's performance. The two common ones are fear and greed. These emotions can make a trader miss desirable gains or miss opportunities. This is why traders have to follow the rules and stick to the trading plans they made when their mind was rational. Traders should learn to be self-aware of moments when emotions are taking over and counter the response.

A Positive Mindset

A trader should always start his or her trades with a positive mindset. Avoid letting any negative thoughts or situations hinder your judgment abilities. In trading, it is important to focus on your actions, your strategies, and tools to be a success; all this requires a positive mindset.

Be Patient

Day Trading takes years of experience to master. It takes time to develop successful strategies; therefore, patience is key. You might experience losses after losses, which can make you lose hope, but with time, it gets better. Part of being patient is to plan when to buy stock and wait for the best time to sell

Always Use A Stop Loss Order

A stop-loss order is issued when a trader places an order with a broker to buy or sell the stock once it reaches a certain price. Stop-loss orders are ideally used to limit loss. When you have a stop-loss order, you do not have to monitor stock all the time. Sometimes, frequent fluctuations can activate the stop-loss order; therefore, it is advisable to select a stock-loss percentage that allows for such fluctuations.

Embracing Technology

Technology has proven to be very successful in helping day traders view and analyze the market. Technology has made it possible for more and more people to access trading, traders can practice light-speed trading, have a virtual trading platform for 24 hours a day. Traders need to embrace technology while trading, gone are the day one had limited time to trade, now, when one market closes, another opens.

Follow The 80/20 Rule

The 80/20 rules suggest that 80% of your profits should be generated by 20% of your trades. 20% of your work should generate 80% success. This rule can be used to analyze four key areas when trading

- **Trading performance**

This rule can be used to improve trading performance and analyze relationships like which tools, indicators, and strategies are causing the most wins and losses. What day of the month do you make wins and losses?

- **Individual performance**

This rule can also be used to improve efficiency. How much time do you spend on a task, and why? What do you do that reduces or increases your focus on trading? By analyzing such questions, you can know what areas need improvement

- **Market Understanding**

80/20 rule can help one improve their understanding of the market. For example, the market usually does not trend 80% of the time and trends 20% of the time.

- **Strategy performance**

The rule is useful in analyzing the efficiency a trader's strategy is. Are the majority of the wins the result of a specific strategy? Do the tools and indicators influence the strategies positively or negatively?

Use Limit Orders, Not Market Orders

Market orders are used to inform brokers to buy and sell an asset at the best available price at the time of execution. However, the best is not always profitable. Instead, traders should use limit orders. Limited orders have a controlled minimum price and maximum price for buying and selling, and therefore traders can ensure they remain profitable.

Avoid Penny Stocks

Penny stocks are small capital company stocks that are purchased cheaply per share. As the name suggests, these were stocks that traded for less than $1 per share. However, nowadays, penny stock is stocking that trade for $5 per share. So, why should we avoid penny stock?

- They are not traded on public exchanges like regular stocks. Therefore, there is not enough financial information about them to determine if they are good investments. Companies that sell this penny stock are also not subject to certain disclosures, and therefore can mismanage their financials.
- Companies offering the penny stocks are usually new in the market, and therefore it is hard to predict their performance
- Penny stocks are not as liquid as most people would think; people buy and sell them over the counter, and do not trade

them on a public exchange. Therefore, it becomes hard to find a buyer if you wish to sell.
- Since penny stocks have low asset value, they have high risk. The company can go bankrupt, making you lose money.

You are better off buying reputable stocks from solid companies.

Number of Stocks

If you are a beginner, as a rule, only buy one or two stocks during a Day Trading session. You can increase the number as you learn the game, but as a newbie, it is advisable to focus on one or two stocks to be able to track and find opportunities. You can easily miss good opportunities if you have too much going on.

Importance of Leverage in Day Trading

Leveraging in trading is the ability to use borrowed funds from brokerage firms to increase one's trading position. It is considered high risk because it increases the amount of profit or loss a trader makes. Leverage is usually given a fixed amount that varies depending on the brokerage firm. Forex trading offers very high leverage ratios. Ratios can be as high a 400:1, and this means a trader with $1,000 in their account can trade up to $400,000 in value. This is because if the accounts are managed properly, the risk becomes manageable.

Leverage is important in Day Trading because:

- It reduces the amount of capital a trader needs to trade, which gives them room to take on other trades
- It allows traders to get greater returns for small up-front investment
- Leverage does not affect any profit or loss that a trader makes.
- Leverage can reduce the risk of certain types of trades.
- Leverage makes the market exciting.
- When you use leverage and make a profit, you can pay back the borrowed amount and still have more money left than if you had just invested your capital
- In some countries, it offers favorable tax treatment.

Generally, a trader should not use their entire available margin. Leverage should only be used when the advantage is on one's side. Most experienced traders usually trade with very low leverage to protect their capital against any trading mistakes they make. Experienced traders should not be afraid of leverage, especially when they learn how to manage it.

How the Securities and Exchange Commission Works

The security and exchange commission (SEC) is a government agency in charge of overseeing the security markets. It also protects investors and facilitates capital formation. The SEC maintains efficient, transparent, and effective markets.

History

Before SEC was formed, the blue-sky laws were enacted and enforced at the state level to protect the public against fraudsters. Although the laws varied across states, all companies offering securities to the public as well as stockbrokers and brokerage firms had to register themselves. These blue-sky laws were found to be ineffective as companies like the Investment Bankers Association ignored them. The congress then created the SEC through the Security Exchange Act of 1934, which was passed after the stock market crashed in 1929. It was created to restore the public's confidence in financial markets.

SEC was to address two notions:

- Companies that sell securities to the public should be honest and release any information to the public that may affect their securities.
- Investors should be treated fairly.

The SEC is made up of three organizational structures:

1. The Commission Members

The commission is made up of five commissioners carefully selected by the president, who all belong to different political parties. They retain their seats for five years, and one is designated as chairperson. They may serve for an extended 18 months past their five-year term if there is no immediate replacement.

2. Divisions

SEC consists of five divisions:

- Trading and Markets- this division monitors how the industry operates, interprets any proposed changes, and oversees self-regulatory organizations like all broker-dealer firms, investment houses, the Financial Industry Regulatory Authority (FINRA). The SEC has delegated the tasks of making rules and enforcing them to FINRA.

- Corporation Finance - this division oversees public companies' disclosures and ensures investors get relevant information so that they can make informed investment decisions for the companies.

- Enforcement-together with three other divisions, enforcement investigates privately any SEC law violations and takes action on violators. The SEC only prosecutes civil suits; the justice department handles criminal cases.

- Investment Management-this division supervises registered investment companies as well as registered investment advisors. The division also administers various federal security laws. Other responsibilities include

    - Interpreting laws and regulations for the public
    - Responding to no-action requests
    - Enforce any matters involving investment firms.

- Economic and Risk Analysis- this division integrates economics and data analytics into the core mission of the SEC. The division uses a variety of academic work and market knowledge to help commissions solve complex matters.

When handling civil suits, the SEC can only perform two actions:
- Injunction-this an authoritative warning or order, any violations can lead to fines or imprisonment
- Issue civil money penalties and the disgorgement of illegal profits

3. **Regional Offices**

US SEC has 11 regional offices throughout the country. The regional offices have the following offices:

- The Office of General Counsel-which gives legal advice to the commission as well as represent the agency in court
- The Office of Compliance, Inspection, and Examinations- this office is in charge of inspecting stock exchanges, broker-dealers, mutual funds, and credit rating agencies.
- The Office of the Chief Accountant- ensure any auditing and accounting policies set by the SEC are enforced
- The Office of Information Technology-oversees the IT department
- The Office of internal Affairs-represent the SEC abroad
- The Inspector General
- The SEC Office of the Whistleblower-this office rewards individuals who voluntarily share information that leads to successful law enforcement actions.

Chapter 10: Successful Trade

Trading can only be productive when traders take the exercise seriously and conduct thorough market research.

A successful trade is one that effectively puts a trading plan into action, among other factors. The trading plan helps to ensure that a trader has a more focused trading strategy and that he or she does not take trades outside of the trading plan. Other factors include trading discipline, technology, and developing a trading style.

Consequently, successful traders take their time to understand how the investment market works and thereby improve their strategy.

Making A Successful Trade Step-By-Step

Executing trades successfully is a process that requires a trader to follow the steps below to have an effective plan.

Making a Watchlist

A watchlist is a record of stocks or securities that a trader looks at to see whether the shares or securities suit his or her trading plan. There are many stocks in the marketplace to keep an eye on, without a watchlist.

Watchlists give the trader an idea of what investments he or she may want to add to his or her collection. A watchlist should be simple and based on current information of the biggest gainers, for example. The best stocks are those whose prices keep moving in a favorable direction.

Therefore, in every single day's watchlist, a trader should try to find the winning stocks from the previous day, especially if the shares have positive news and the right chart breakout. That is because the stocks will continue trading in the market the following day.

Besides, a trader should begin with a wide range of stock selections, and then narrow down stocks according to what he or she is looking for, as he or she observes the trend. When the trader knows what he or she is looking for, he or she will eliminate stocks that do not suit his or her trading strategy.

In addition, it is wise for a trader to list the most popular stocks and to check why the stocks are popular picks for other traders. The factors that make the stock popular will most likely be issues that other traders hold in a high volume. Such considerations should then be the trading standards for the trader.

Moreover, a trader should understand how the fluctuation in stock prices directly affects the way that driving forces react to different commodities in the market. In that way, the trader will develop his or her trading style and have an easy time assessing the patterns of the stocks on his or her watchlist.

There are certain things that a trader should avoid having in his or her watchlist. First, a trader should not have too many stocks on the list. A good number would be anywhere from five to ten stocks. That will help the trader to have a better chance to understand how the trade works.

Secondly, a trader should not focus on big trades. When a trader aims small, he or she misses little, thereby cutting losses quickly. Big trades run the risk of having huge losses. The idea is to win more and get better profit on the wins than the amount one loses because losing is part of the trade.

Choosing and Purchasing Stocks

When buying a company's stock, a trader becomes a stakeholder or a part-owner of that company. The value of the trader's investment, therefore, depends on the general well-being of the business.

Therefore, when buying a stock, a trader should start with a company that he or she knows. In so doing, a trader gets a place to start and avoids buying stocks without understanding how the company intends to make money.

Additionally, a trader should take into account the stock price and valuation. More experienced investors tend to look for securities that are cheap or undervalued to reap benefits when the stock price goes up.

However, a trader should know the kind of stock he or she wants, and he or she should understand that cheap is not always right and expensive is not still bad. A commodity may be cheap because its business is slowing down, and a commodity may be costly because investors expect their earnings to increase rapidly in a few years.

In addition, a trader should evaluate the financial stability of the company before buying the company's stocks. The trader can assess the revenue growth, check the bottom line, check the company's balance sheet to know how much debt the company has, and then finally find a dividend.

After choosing a stock, a trader can buy the stock first by opening a brokerage account. When opening the brokerage account, the trader should find out the brokerage fee.

A broker that charges low or does not charge at all will be an ideal choice. Along with that, a trader should check whether the broker offers educational tools, guidance on trading, stock market research, and easy access to help centers.

Secondly, the trader should identify the stocks that he or she wants to buy by researching companies that he or she already knows from past trading experiences.

Thirdly, the trader should decide how many shares he or she wants to buy. It is advisable to start by purchasing a single stock, to get a feel of what the trade is like and the trader deciding whether he or she would want to continue in the business.

Afterward, the trader can select his or her stock order type. Most investors buy stocks either with market orders or with limit orders.

With a market order, the trader is signifying that he or she will buy or sell the security at best available current market prices. A limit order gives the trader more control over the price at which he or she will buy or sell.

Finally, the trader can then improve his or her stock selection to begin the journey of carrying out successful trades officially.

Understanding Entry and Exit

An entry point is the price at which a trader buys or sells a stock. A good entry point marks the beginning of a successful trade. A trader can find a proper entry point by doing market research and maximize profits in each business.

To find valid entry points, a trader should research, study, and learn the relevant parallels and factors that are influencing the market. For example, a trader can study and find an attractive stock but feels that the price of the stock is very high. In that case, the trader will buy if the price reduces to a certain level. That level will be the trader's entry point.

Consequently, the process of finding an entry point requires a trader to practice patience and wait for the appropriate time to buy, to get returns on his or her investment.

After evaluating the market, a trader should then decide whether to enter a long position (buy) or a short position (short). Concerning that, the trader should avoid risking too much. That is, the trader should invest what he or she can afford to lose.

Additionally, a trader should utilize limit orders to buy or sell a currency pair at a particular price or a better price. The use of technical indicators will come in handy when creating trading signals. Technical indicators will give the trader essential information about the market and currency pairs.

Accordingly, a trader should make his or her transactions occasionally, because market conditions can change due to technical influences and financial news releases.

An exit point is the price at which a trader closes the position. A trader may, therefore, sell at an exit point, or buy to close the position if he or she anticipates selling it later at a higher price.

A trader can exit either through take-profit orders or through stop-loss orders. A take-profit order is a limit order that stipulates the exact price of a commodity or the exact profit level in which a trader wants his or her broker to close the trader's position. A stop-loss order, tells the broker to close the trader's position when the stock suffers losses.

When coming up with an entry-exit plan, the trader needs to decide how long he or she intends to be in the trade. In addition, the trader needs to know how much risk he or she is willing to take.

Knowing How to Stop Loss

A broker places a stop-loss order once the stock reaches a particular level. A stop-loss helps to limit a trader's loss on a stock position.

For example, when a trader buys a share at $10 per share, he or she can place a stop-loss order for $8. Therefore, is the security's price falls beyond $8, the broker will sell the trader's shares at the prevailing market price.

A trader can know where to place his or her stop-losses by using the percentage method, the support method, or the moving average method. Many traders use the percentage method.

The percentage method involves calculating the percentage of stock a trader is willing to risk before he or she closes his or her position on the trade.

For instance, if a trader is willing to lose 10 percent of the value of security before he or she exits and the trader owns securities that are trading at $40 per share, the trader would place his or her stop-loss order at $36. That will be 10 percent below the market price of the security.

The support method also allows the trader to tailor his or her stop-loss level to the commodity that he or she is trading. As such, the trader needs to find the most recent level of support and place his or her stop-loss slightly below that level.

For example, if the trader owns a share that is currently trading at $30 per share, and he or she finds $25 as the most recent support level.

Therefore, the trader should place his or her stop-loss slightly below $25. Placing the stop-loss slightly below the support level gives the commodity's price space to come down and bounce back up before the trader closes his or her position.

The moving average method requires the trader to apply a moving average to his or her security chart. A moving average is a technical indicator that analyzes the price changes of stocks while reducing the impact of random price fluctuations.

A trader may want to use a long-term moving average as compared to a short-term moving average to avoid placing his or her stop-loss too close to the stock price and getting closed out of his or her trade too soon.

As soon as the trader puts the moving average, he or she should set his or her stop-loss immediately below the level of the moving average. For instance, if the trader's share is currently trading at $30 and the moving average is at $26, he or she should place the stop-loss below $26, to allow the stock price space for movement.

Knowing When to Sell

A trader should start selling his or her stock when he or she miscalculated the decision to buy the stock, when the stock price shoots up dramatically, and when the stock has reached an unsustainable amount.

A trader will know whether he or she made a profit or loss the minute he or she sells the stock. While the buying price may help the trader to know how much advantage he or she has gained, the selling price guarantees the profit, if any.

While selling a stock should not be a common occurrence because trading in and out of positions could be detrimental to a trader's investment, postponing the decision to sell the stock when it is the right time to do so may also yield unfavorable outcomes.

For example, a trader may buy a stock at $20 to sell it at $25. The stock price reaches $25, and the trader decides to hold out for a couple of more points. The stock hits $27, and the trader still holds out to maximize on profit should the stock price move further up. Suddenly, the price drops back to $24. The trader waits until the price hits $25 again, but this does not happen. The trader then gives in to frustration and sells the stock at a loss when the stock price hits $18.

Consequently, if a trader sells at the opportune time, he or she will experience the benefits of buying the stock. However, the trader should not try to time the market because timely selling does not necessarily require accurate market timing. The focus should be on buying at one price and selling at a higher price, even when the higher price is not the absolute top.

When a trader discovers that he or she made an analytical error in buying a stock, the trader should sell the stock even if it means that he or she will make a loss.

If a trade does not meet the trader's short-term earnings predictions and the price of the shares takes a fall, he or she should not sell the stock if the business is not losing market shares to competitors. If the company loses market shares to competitors, then that may be a good reason for the trader to sell the stock.

Alternatively, a trader can sell his or her stock when the stock price rises dramatically in a short period for particular reasons. The trader should take his or her gains and move on.

Additionally, a trader could sell when the company's valuation is becoming higher than its competitors are, or when the company's price-to-earnings ratio goes beyond its average price-to-earnings within five or ten years.

However, when a company's earnings decline when the demand is low, and the company starts cutting costs. That would be a chance to exit the position before any further decline in the value of the company's stock.

In addition, a trader could sell his or her stock for financial needs. That may not be a good reason from an analytical point, but securities are assets, and traders have the freedom to cash in their assets when the need arises.

Examples of Day Trades

Trading Breakouts

Given that traders always want to cut losses quickly, trading breakouts is ideal for scanning potential losses because a trader can see when he or she is making a wrong decision.

The trader first needs to identify a price level that represents his or her breakout trading level. Afterward, the trader enters the market once he or she sees that a security price goes beyond the defined range. The trader can then close the stock above the resistance level.

That means, when the price of a stock moves out of a defined price range, a trader can move to a new high or low. For example, a trader can buy when the market price breaks higher, or goes beyond a failed resistance level, and sell when the market breaks lower, or goes below a failed support level.

However, a trader should only buy when the price pulls back to the original breakout point to avoid the likelihood of being trapped in a false breakout.

Trading Ranges

When a trader trades ranges, he or she aims to take advantage of the fraction of the market that is not trending. For example, if the market only trends 40 percent of the time, that leaves the trader with 60 percent to explore.

Trading ranges take into account the support and resistance levels, which develop when the stock price oscillates. The trader first needs to make sure that the stock price does not break above or below any level in between the highs and lows, assuming that two similar highs and lows have already happened in that price fluctuation.

For example, a trader may notice that a particular stock was starting to form a price during a specified period. After the stock price forms the initial peaks, the trader may start placing long or short trades based on the stock's trendlines, along with the resistance and support levels. Trading ranges ends when the stock does not show a breakout from either trendline.

Flag Trading

Flag trading is about a trader identifying flag shapes on a price chart. Flag patterns are easy to spot. The direction in which the flag blows shows the path of the primary trend and indicates that a stock is going through a steady upward trend.

The shape of the flag forms when a stock makes a strong move upward, on high volume, and then consolidates at the top of the pole, on low volume. The trend continues when the stock breaks out of the consolidation pattern on high volume.

Flag patterns can trend either upwards or downwards while following the same volume and breakout patterns. For example, in an upward-trending flag pattern, the price action moves up during the first trend and then declines through the consolidation area. That is an indication that traders have entered the market in a new wave of enthusiasm.

In a downward-trending flag pattern, the price action does not always decline during the consolidation. That is because of fear and anxiety over the falling prices that make traders avoid taking action.

Triangle Trading

Triangle trading has three types of triangle chart formations: symmetrical, ascending, and descending triangles.

The symmetrical triangle forms when the slant of the price's highs and the slant of a price's lows meet at an apex to form the shape of a triangle. What this means is that the market is making lesser highs and lows that are more significant. Neither the buyers nor the sellers are moving the price far enough to create a clear trend.

The ascending triangle forms when there are a resistance level and a slant of higher lows. That is an indication that there is a certain level that the buyers cannot seem to go beyond. However, the traders put pressure on the resistance level for a breakout to happen. While the breakout may not occur quickly, the traders are at least able to push the price up by a margin.

The descending triangle is just like the ascending triangle only that it is inverted, and traders consider it a breakout pattern. The breakout happens when the stock price falls through the bottom horizontal trendline support while a downtrend begins again. The bottom trendline or the support, in this case, becomes resistance.

Chapter 11: Success Tips for Beginner Day Traders

Traders undertake Day Trading because it offers them the chance to take advantage of small movements of the price while avoiding the losses linked with overnight risks. An intraday day trader uses various trading strategies and analytical skills to make appropriate decisions that give him or her money. The more experienced a trader is, the more prepared the trader is to succeed in the market.

On the other hand, a beginner in Day Trading does not have the training and experience that will add additional protection against losses. Thus, he or she uses caution, technical and psychological strategies, and strict discipline to allow him or her to make money and manage the associated risks. Here is information concerning advice for profit achievement, and the dos and don'ts that provide tips for success in Day Trading for a beginner.

Advice and Methods for Beginners

A beginner starts Day Trading with the hope and belief of achieving success in the market. The trader feels that he or she is ready to undertake the trade with the knowledge and skills that he or she possesses. Nonetheless, there are some tips that he or she can follow that will enhance his or her trading experience and increase the chances of success. Some of the advice and methods that can assist a beginner in Day Trading are:

1. **Carry out Research Continuously** – Continually researching enriches a trader's knowledge and skills, which help him or her to create and apply better and profitable strategies and decisions.
2. **Prepare and Follow a Trading Strategy** – Always have a trading plan before undertaking trade and adhere to its guidelines. It helps a trader to know which position to take and the entry and exit strategy.
3. **Control of Emotions** – A trader is a human who experiences emotions as he or she trades. Day Trading is a fast-moving market with high risks involved. A trader may be in a profitable position at a time, but swings in the market can change quickly, and he or she starts experiencing losses. The fear of losing in the market can make a trader think and react to trade emotionally, which can lead to further losses. He or she should manage his or her feelings and use only the factual data to make decisions in the market.
4. **Reserve Time for Trading** – Day Trading needs a trader to commit time to the business, as he or she needs to track price movements, make trading strategies, and make appropriate judgments of the trade. It is a full-time job, and the trader needs to take it seriously by fully concentrating on the trading tasks.
5. **Prepare Funds for the Investment** – A trader must set aside some amount of money specifically for trading. Moreover,

within that amount, he or she should decide on a trading formula that will determine the money to risk for each trade. In so doing, he or she will manage risks whereby he or she will still have money in the first account even if a deal fails. He or she will only lose that small percentage in that particular investment.

6. **Having a Risk Management Strategy** – Day Trading requires risk management strategies that will help a trader to avoid or minimize any losses in a trade. Besides money management, a trader also needs to prepare exit strategies in case of unfavorable changes in the market, such as developing a stop loss.

7. **Properly Time the Trades** – Day Trading involves fast movements of prices and sudden changes in market conditions. A trader needs to get his or her timing right to ensure the entry and exit of trade results in success. It also helps him or her not to miss trading opportunities.

8. **Know When to Quit** – A trader should know when to exit a trade and abandon a particular trading strategy. If a plan or deal is not working, he or she should know when to stop to prevent further losses.

9. **Stop Focusing on the Money** – The trader should concentrate on the trading strategies to ensure that they will help him or her trade successfully. Focusing on the money will make the trader become anxious or impatient with the market and end up making rash decisions that are detrimental to the business.

10. **Realistic Expectations about Profits** – Being realistic about Day Trading will help a person to trade better and

eventually succeed in the business. He or she will know the realistic chances of success and will work within those realities. He or she will not make rash decisions in an attempt to make impossible profits.

11. **Use Appropriate Type of Orders** – Day Trading incorporates the use of orders to manage risks and minimize the losses in the market. A trader should utilize the right order according to his or her trading condition. He or she can choose to use limit orders or market orders to enable precise trading and making profits.

12. **Avoid the Penny Stocks** – They say cheap is expensive, and the same applies in Day Trading. A trader should avoid penny stocks because they have low chances of success and are mostly illiquid.

13. **Begin with Small Trades** – A trader should take small steps as he or she starts in Day Trading. He or she begins with few trades and uses them to enhance his or her skills and experience before slowly advancing and using more share in the trade.

14. **Take Full Advantage of the Technology** – Technological advancement provides a trader with access to various education, tools, and software that can help him or her to succeed in Day Trading. He or she should take advantage of these features to continually learn and practice, which will build his or her expertise and confidence in the trades. They will also help him or her to enhance his or her technical, analytical skills.

15. **Keep a Record of the Trades** – A trader needs to take notes about all the trades that he or she undertakes. He or she writes about the trading experience where he or she includes details

about the planning, entry, and exit of the trade. These records will help him or her to keep track of historical data regarding a particular market. They will also provide him or her with a reference that he or she can use to make predictions about specific trades.

16. **Learning from Losses** – The trader should learn from the trading experiences that he or she goes through in the market. He or she needs to take the losses as lessons that guide him or her on how to avoid failure.
17. **Take Responsibility of the Trade** – A trader should bear the responsibility for all outcomes in his or her trade because he or she made the decisions concerned. He or she should not blame the market for any losses or failures that he or she experiences.
18. **Maintain discipline in the Trade** – The trader should always maintain control in all aspects of Day Trading. He or she should strictly follow the guidelines of the trading strategies to ensure successful trade.

Mistakes That Beginners Make

Day Trading requires a trader to spend a lot of time and effort to achieve success. An expert trader knows to follow specific trading rules and procedures to ensure that he or she will make profits and avoid experiencing losses. However, beginners lack the experience and end up making mistakes that make their trades unsuccessful. Below are some of the errors that lead to failed trading:

1. **Timing Poorly in Trade** – Day Trading is all about timing, and failure in getting it right can lead to considerable losses. The trader uses his or her timing wrong and loses trading opportunities since the price already moved to an unfavorable direction.
2. **Trading Without a Plan** – A trader starts trading without any plan or strategy regarding the trade. Hence, he or she does not know how to deal with a crisis or a sudden change in price action. It leads to an overall failure of the trade.
3. **Changing the Trading Strategy Frequently** – A trader should use a strategy that he or she understands and suits the trade. However, he or she may change the plan so much that none of them works successfully. A strategy that suits one deal may not suit another, and likewise, the trader cannot use too many plans on the same trade.
4. **Chasing Trades** – A trader becomes impatient and anxious about market conditions and decides to pursue the market in an attempt to make profits quickly. However, the market is a shadow, and he or she will not succeed in catching and controlling it. Rather than waiting for the trade to present an opportunity, his or her impatience leads to failure since he or she exposes himself or herself to more risks.
5. **Averaging Down** – A trader continues to hold on and add to a losing position in the market in the hope that the price trend will reverse and start giving him or her gains. He or she loses a lot more when the reversal does not take place.
6. **Taking a Position before the news is out** – A trader decides to take a particular trade in the market in an attempt to

anticipate the news release. The unknown risk here can lead to considerable losses since the price may move against his or her expectations after the announcement of the report.

7. **Trading immediately after the News** – A trader can place himself or herself in a losing position when he or she starts trading soon after the release of the news. The price initially moves quickly and sharply after the announcement but may change direction once the volatility reduces. It can result in a trader experiencing loses as the price moves in the opposite direction.

8. **Trading Without a Stop Loss** – Trading without a stop loss exposes a trader to experience potentially unlimited losses. A stop-loss helps him or her to manage the risks by moderating losses since the trader can exit the trade when the price shifts against him or her.

9. **Risking Excessive Capital** – A trader who does not have proper money management risks the amount of money for investment. He or she uses all or a significant percentage of his or her capital on one trade instead of utilizing a smaller portion and breaking it down. Thus, he or she ends up losing his or her entire budget if the business fails to lead to reckless utilization of funds. The trader risks more money that causes him or her to lose sleep.

10. **Psychological Weaknesses** – The trader here lets his emotions decide the actions that he or she takes when Day Trading. The fear, greed, and impatience lead to him or her making rash judgments and exposing himself or herself to

higher risks in the market. He or she also underestimates the market and makes hasty decisions that lead to failed trades.

11. **Trading Correlated Pairs** – A trader increases the risks when he or she transacts using correlated pairs in the market. He or she loses the double if they move against him or her since they link to each other. Hence, he or she doubles his or her losses when trading correlated pairs.

12. **Going All In** – The trader risks everything and takes a more significant trade than usual due to the temptations of doubling profits. However, he or she loses significantly if the business fails.

13. **Following the Crowd** – A trader follows the decisions and actions of other traders in the market. Rather than thinking and making his or her judgments, the trader follows the crowd. He or she does not stick to the guidelines of his or her trading strategy and instead makes moves that might ultimately lead to a losing position in the market.

14. **Having Unrealistic Expectations** – The trader has an impractical view of the market and has high expectations of profits. He or she makes highly risky decisions to try to obtain that gain. Nonetheless, the risks he or she faces leads to foreseen and unexpected losses from the trades of interest. Additionally, he or she does not accept losses since he or she sees profits as the only results in the market.

15. **Leaving Out the Margins** – A trader forgets about margins and ends up trading with money that he borrowed from a broker. Margin can help a trader to increase gains when he or

she applies it appropriately. Hence, a trader leaving it out leads to the collapse and failure of a trade.

16. **Utilizing the Wrong Brokers** – A trader can use a broker who manages his or her trades poorly. The broker may lack knowledge or access to specific essential trading software and may have poor communication skills. These features cause the trader to have a wrong broker who will create financial trouble that can escalate to trading failures.

17. **Lack of Knowledge and Training** – A trader rushes into Day Trading without having the necessary skills and experience for ensuring success. He or she ends up taking more on his or her plate and ends up failing miserably in the markets.

18. **Lack of Post Trade Analysis** – Trading without recording the trade and its aftermath can lead to a trader repeating mistakes that previously caused losses. The post-trade analysis provides him or her with an account of the trade's history, which can inform future trading strategies. However, the absence of such a report can make a trader lose the chance of identifying critical decisions and learning from them.

19. **Trading Using Fundamental Data** – A trader using fundamental data to undertake Day Trading fails because intraDay Trading uses technical analysis to make trades. Day Trading involves price movements in the short-term and a trader gambles when he or she ignores the trading strategies and starts utilizing economic data.

20. **Poor Discipline while Trading** – A trader fails to stick to his or her trading plan and becomes messy in the market. Disorganization leads to him or her, making unclear

decisions that can cause losses. He or she may want to undertake different positions at a sensitive time since the lack of discipline causes panic and confusion.

Why and How Most Traders Fail

Trading in the stock market requires a combination of skills and experience to ensure that a trader can make profits. An intraday trader also applies them to enable him or her to gain in a single day while simultaneously try to avoid losses in the market. However, many traders seem to experience more losses than gains while trading in the short amount of time of intraday markets. These traders fail because they have weaknesses regarding their knowledge, skills, mindset, and expectations of a trade. Here are how these factors affect a trader and lead to his or her failure in the market.

1. Inadequate Knowledge

Knowledge is an essential tool to possess in any aspect of life. It is especially vital to a trader as it provides him or her with the expertise that develops and improves his or her trading skills. Thus, when a trader does not have adequate and proper education concerning trading, he or she sets himself or herself up for a disastrous trading experience. He or she does not understand the trading tools and lacks analytical thinking that forms the essence of trade. Consequently, he or she cannot make trading strategies nor implement risk management rules, leading to losses and failure in the stock market.

2. Poor Skills

Some traders fail in the markets because they know but not the skills needed to achieve success. A trader who does not continually practice his or her trading will result in having poor skills. Day Trading is a business that requires a person to learn and train continuously for several years before he or she can identify as a proper trader. However, many traders have little training, experience in the markets, and view themselves as qualified. It leads to the traders taking on more than they can handle, which ultimately leads to failure.

3. Mindset

The psychology of a trader can determine whether he or she succeeds in the trade. Most traders may fail in trading despite having adequate skills and experience due to psychological weaknesses. They approach the trades with the wrong emotions and attitudes that lead to unsuccessful ventures.

- **a) Emotions** – A trader lets his or her feelings influence his or her decisions and actions in the market. He or she allows his or her fear of losing money to control him or her. The trader ends up panicking and rushing into risky decisions that cause losses.
- **b) Attitude** – A trader has a flawed approach where he or she lets greed and overconfidence dictate his or her judgments. The trader thinks he or she is invincible and views the market as a playground. He or she takes risky positions that eventually lead to failure.

4. Unrealistic Expectations

Most traders think that they will succeed and leave no room for losses. Such a trader believes that his or her trading strategies are perfect, and he or she takes trades with higher risks. He or she trades assuming in luck rather than the actual conditions of the market. As a result, he or she risks too much and applies poor trading strategies that backfire and lead to significant losses. Additionally, a trader's unrealistic expectation of profits leads to him or her being impatient and enters a trade with little training and planning. These factors combine to ensure the failure of a trader in the market.

Day Trading involves certain risks, especially since it takes place in a short amount of time. A person needs to know the conduct and attitude to have, and the mistakes to avoid when trading. Learning and understanding these tips for Day Trading will help a beginner to start and continue the trade successfully.

Chapter 12: Taking Profits, ROI and Passive Income

The primary objective for you to engage in Day Trading is to attain significant returns on your capital. For this aim to be attainable, you must apply productive strategies to your Day Trading involvement. In Day Trading, patterns in the stock price are bound to recur, and if you are keen, you can spot these trend repetitions. You can have a particular trend that matches a similar one that you encountered previously. The recurrence may not match the actual price values, but the overall uptrends and downtrends may be identical. The time frame between the similar trends may vary between days and weeks, but the resemblance is noticeable when you sharpen your focus.

Based on these recurrences, you can take advantage of this knowledge to make profits from Day Trading. If you know how the stock price behaved last time, you can accurately predict its future movement. This assumption is valid as long as the circumstances and price patterns match. Using a price action chart, you can put your newfound strategy into action. A majority of these approaches involve looking out for an event called a breakout. The following scenarios describe various setups in which the breakouts favor entry into a particular trading position:

1. **IPC Breakout**

This breakout acronym stands for Impulse, Pullback, and Consolidation. This phrase describes the behavior of the stock price on the price action chart. You need to look for a pattern characterized by these movements in the value of its stock. Usually, within the first few minutes, a cycle in Day Trading will start with a significant move in a specific direction in the form of an impulse wave. A pullback reaction typically follows this impulse wave.

A pullback is akin to applying instant brakes on the sharp initial impulse movement. From the pullback section, you will notice that the price hovers over a small range for a while. This period is the consolidation phase, where the stock price experiences a sideways movement. Note that the consolidation phase confines itself within the margins of the first impulse wave.

In the case of a fall in stock price beyond the open end, a different outcome may ensue. In this scenario, you will have both hovering and pullback happening at a value much lower than the opening stock price. At this point, your patience comes into play. You need to stand by for a potential breakout in the direction of the earlier impulse wave. Pay attention not to perform any trade in the event of a breakout in the reverse direction. The activation of a buying position is dependent on the stock price, breaking at a value that is greater than the consolidation level. For instance, in case the earlier scenario ensued, and the stock price pulled back after an initial drop, trading is valid only when the breakout occurs over the consolidation.

When buying, it is advisable to take a long position on a small bid above the highest point of the consolidation phase. Taking a long trading position allows you to make a profit from a later increase in the price of the stock. In case you become interested in taking a short trading position, you can make an equally tiny bid below the lowest point of the consolidation.

A short trading position enables you to make a profit from a later drop in price. In both trading positions, you will determine your entry point based on a potentially favorable future outcome. This particular pattern setup is typical of the beginning of a trading session. Movements that take place close to the opening time are usually significant and potentially profitable. Always remember to discern the price action trends carefully before trading since any setup that lacks the distinctive sections is probably wrong.

2. RC Breakout

A Reversal and Consolidation breakout lacks the smaller pullback section found in, the earlier setup. In this case, you will have the usual significant impulse section, followed by a much higher reversal. Note that the reversal occurs in a direction that is opposite to the impulse wave. The reversal section is immediate to the impulse without any signs of a previous pullback. Due to the slight difference between RC and IPC breakouts, you need to pay special attention to the reversal trend. You should ignore any movement that occurs before the reversal. Wait for an imminent pullback from the reversal spike that ought to be smaller than your first or preceding impulse. The reversal wave now acts as your point of reference with which comparisons of the pullback and later consolidation take place.

Once you achieve a level of price consolidation, follow the guidelines as before in the earlier setup. If the breakout occurs either above or beneath the extreme points of consolation, you can take a relevant trading position. Always bid small amounts of your capital in Day Trading since the margins are rather low, as well. An example of an RC setup involves an initial drop in the stock price of about 50 cents followed instantly by a reversal of, say 70 cents.

In this case, you need to concentrate your focus on the reversal rally of 70 cents that puts you back in the money anyway. The initial fall in price is the impulse wave, and it causes a distraction of which you should be wary. The more significant reversal should be your reference point, especially since you currently have an overall net trend of going upward. A pullback and consolidation phase should come after the reversal phase and finally accompanied by the awaited breakout.

3. Check for Reversal at Support and Resistance points

These two points signify the general pricing regions of a price action chart as opposed to real stock values. Support occurs when the falling trend of a particular stock price reaches its minimum point for that same trading cycle. The stock price cannot continue dropping beyond the support level. At support, the trend undergoes a period of consolidation before a reversal takes place. Upon reversing its direction, the price trend keeps rising to a point beyond which any further price increase becomes impossible.

This maximum level of the stock price is the resistance. Both support and resistance are typically indicative of how the various trading positions affect the movements of the stock market price. The economies of scale with the supply and demand forces are applicable here as well. In the context of Day Trading, excessive buyers lead to resistance, while support is the result of too many sellers. Once you identify the support and resistance regions, look out for the presence of consolidations at these levels.

A positive trading signal occurs in case of a breakout over the consolidation section at a support point. The same is valid for a breakout that happens beneath the consolidation at the resistance level. Beware of the market behaving unexpectedly. In rare circumstances, the stock price may breakout above the consolidation phase at the resistance level. In addition, the same might happen at the support region, and you encounter a breakout below the price consolidation. Although highly unlikely, these kinds of unusual breakouts are still possible. In such cases, you need to exit from your trading position immediately. You could use the breakout as your exit point. Therefore, your level of concentration has to be sharp to stay alert to such improbable eventualities.

4. Strong Area Breakout

This strategy enables you to participate in Day Trading above and below the resistance and support levels, respectively. These trending patterns are rare but still possible; hence, you need to develop and have a proper approach in place in case they arise. These regions located beyond the support and resistance points are the so-called Strong Areas. It is within these areas that you need to search for the relevant breakouts for you to conduct your trading.

First, you should take note of a trend that reached up to identical values at the resistance or support level multiple times. This pattern shows that the restrictive level is about to break. Based on the volume of trade in the stock market, such a trend is predictable. It is bound to break either its resistance or support. Trading on such values is often challenging because the margin beyond which the pattern exceeds the limit is usually small. You can decide to take a long position on a breakout trend that breaches the resistance.

However, beware of the lack of a sustaining rally beyond that level. Therefore, you should continue bidding only smaller amounts of capital on any breakout above the resistance level. The same reasoning applies to traders taking short positions on those breakouts that breach the support level. The amount of profit from such Strong Area breakouts is often insignificant compared to the larger margins experienced with the standard price action trading.

5. False Breakout

This type of breakout is useful as a confirmatory tool for other trading strategies. A false breakout is indicative of a price that attempts a particular movement, but fails and eventually goes in the opposite direction. For instance, consider an RC breakout setup where the reversal was higher than the initial impulse. After the reversal section, you would experience a brief pullback followed by a consolidation. Your expectation from the consolidation phase would likely be that the price takes an upward trend. This assumption is per the direction of the much higher reversal pattern.

However, due to the market forces, there is usually a small breakout downward for a brief moment straight after the consolidation phase. This breakout is false since the price would once again reverse and continue on its new upward trajectory. Knowing how to interpret and utilize false breakouts is essential in confirming the validity of your taken trading position. Using false breakouts in this manner is akin to proving a negative.

ROI

When you take part in Day Trading, you should expect a return on investment that corresponds to your input capital. Large amounts of capital outlay are typically disadvantageous due to the low rate of return. Investing in small amounts of money regularly usually results in a more productive rate of returns. Success at Day Trading is often a prerequisite for you to attain a significant return on your investment. The following factors affect your capital's margins of profits directly:

1. Risk on Each Trade

This risk refers to the amount of your capital that is in danger of losing its value whenever you trade. It also refers to the trading position that you take every time you participate in Day Trading. For you to maximize your returns, you should have this risk under control. Risk management is achievable by setting a maximum limit on the amount of capital with which you can trade. For instance, you can set a limit of one percent of your available equity for commitment to a particular trade.

Also, use stop-loss orders to enforce this resolution. You need to adhere to these conditions strictly, every time you engage in any Day Trading transaction. It often becomes more comfortable to estimate your position size once you have both the stop-loss and entry point values. You need to realize that risk is a potential loss, and therefore, your aim must be to gain more money than you lose. You should learn to risk as little as possible while maintaining a higher margin for any probable profits.

2. Reward to Risk Ratio

As mentioned earlier, you should strive to be in a position where your profit surpasses the amount of capital that you lose. This ratio shows you this relative association between the two outcomes. For you to get on the right track towards gaining profits, your reward to risk ratio has to be higher than one. Whenever you minimize your risk to one percent of your capital, you are in an excellent position to gain from any particular trade. This position is reinforce-able by the fact that your denominator in the ratio would become the one percent. For maximum returns, the preferable reward to risk ratio is 1.5 to 1. A reversal in the price trend or your premature exit from the trade is the only limitation to your returns. Beware of your stop-loss level whenever you seek a higher reward to risk ratio.

3. Win Rate

As the name implies, this rate describes the percentage of your trade deals that turned out profitable. This rate has a close relation to the reward to risk ratio and is often in use simultaneously. To maintain an excellent ratio that is acceptable for your level of returns, you need a win rate above fifty percent. For instance, with a rate of 1.5 to 1 and a win rate of fifty percent, you will gain an overall return of twenty-five percent on the trade. Your profits are calculated as follows: (50% of 1.5) minus (50% of 1). As you can see, win rates below the recommended fifty percent would result in a loss of your capital.

4. Number of Trades

Since your specific aims concern the win rate, and the reward to risk ratio, the number of trades in which you can trade is limitless. You can take part in trading as many times as it takes you to maintain your statistics at the recommended values. The more trades you take part in, the more your overall margin of returns. However, the trick is to keep to the fifty percent profitability rate. As a result, if you want to engage in more trades, make sure not to lose a significant number of them. With all these factors in place, you can now control your returns on investment.

Conclusion

Thank you for making it through to the end of *Day Trading for Beginners: How to Day Trade for a Living, Proven Strategies, Tactics, and Psychology to Create a Passive Income from Home with Trading Investing in Stocks, Options and Forex*. Let us hope it was informative and able to provide you with all of the tools you need to achieve your goals, whatever they may be.

Now you are aware that Day Trading is the process of purchasing and selling assets within the same day, often using borrowed funds to take advantage of small price shifts in highly liquid indexes or stocks.

Day traders use short-term trading strategies and a high level of leverage to take advantage of small price movements in highly liquid currencies or stocks. Experienced day traders have their finger on events that lead to short-term price movements, such as the news, corporate earnings, economic statistics, and interest rates, which are subject to market psychology and market expectations.

Day traders can use technical indicators to provide trading signals and assess the current trade. Keltner Channels, a popular technical indicator, use average prices and volatility to plot lower, middle, and upper lines. These three lines move with the price to create the appearance of a channel. Chester Keltner introduced these channels in the 1960s, but Linda Bradford Raschke updated them in the 1980s. Today, traders use the later version of the indicator, which is a combination of two different indicators, which are the average true range and the exponential moving average.

Created by J. Welles Wilder Jr. and introduced in 1978, the average true range is a measure of volatility. The moving average, on the other hand, is the average price for specific periods, with the exponential variation giving more weight to recent prices and less weight to less recent prices. A trader using trading charts in his or her trades receives significant additional information that helps him or her to make appropriate decisions in Day Trading.

Managing your account and the risks associated with Day Trading involves the responsible handling of the available equity in your brokerage account. You can perform account management through further investment in profitable stocks, ingenious trade maneuverability, or exiting from trade deals that stagnate. On the other hand, your risk management strategies involve responding appropriately to alleviate prospective losses in an uncertain future and limiting the degree of your exposure to financial risks.

Technical analysis is the study of the price changes and trends of a stock or security. The study involves traders inspecting a stock's trading history through technical indicators and charts in order to determine the future direction of the stock price.

Statistical trends, such as price movement and volume identified from the past, determine future trading opportunities. Technical analysts, therefore, focus on price fluctuations, trading signals, and analytical charting tools to examine the strength or weakness of a specific security.

Day Trading, like any other form of investment, is subject to influence from human emotion and psychological impact. Whenever money or capital is in play, people tend to take matters rather personally because of the inevitable consequence of the hope that comes along with the promise of significant returns.

After reading this book, your next step should be to practice what you have learned by signing up and becoming a Day trader. When you apply these tips, you will become an expert day trader much faster.

Finally, if you found this book useful in any way, a review on Amazon is always appreciated!

Forex Trading for Beginners

Simple Strategies to Make Money with Forex Trading: The Best Guide with Basics, Secrets Tactics, and Psychology to Big Profit and Income from the Financial Market

Table of Contents

Introduction...**332**

Chapter 1: An Introduction to Forex Trading.................**335**

    What Is Forex Trading

    Principles of Forex Trading

    Different Types of Forex Traders

    Advantage of Forex Trading

    Why Forex

Chapter 2: Basics of Forex Trading.................................**351**

    Important Terminology and Trades

    Forex Markets

    Currency Pairs and Their Prices

    Quote Currency

Chapter 3: How to Get Started in Forex Trading............**361**

    Who Is A Foreign Exchange Broker?

    What Is the Account Balance, and Why Does a Broker Need It?

    What Are Platforms and Tools?

Chapter 4: Technical and Fundamental Analysis in Forex Trading..**373**

    Technical Analysis

    Fundamental Analysis

Chapter 5: Psychology and Mindset of A Forex Trader..**382**

    Attitude Approach

    Personality Types of Traders

Chapter 6: Forex Strategies and Strategies for Beginners 396
Forex Trading Strategies
Forex Strategies for Beginners

Chapter 7: Forex Trading Signals 413
What Are Forex Trading Signals?
Types of Forex Trading Signals and How They Work
- Manual Forex Trading Signals
- Automated Forex Trading Signals

How to Choose the Best Trading Signals
Should Forex Traders Use Free Forex Signals or Paid Forex Signals

Chapter 8: Tips to Winning in Forex Trading 427
Tips and Secrets for Success in Forex Trading
Risk Management in Forex Trading

Chapter 9: Cryptocurrency in Forex Trading 445

Chapter 10: Examples of Trade 455
Example 1
Example 2
Example 3

Chapter 11: Mistake That Beginners Make in Forex Trading 460

Chapter 12: How to Make Money with Forex Trading to Create Passive Income 468
Forex Signals
Forex Robots
Social Trading

Conclusion 473

Introduction

Congratulations on purchasing *Forex Trading for Beginners* and thank you for doing so. The following chapters will discuss the important steps and information a beginner should take and heed to if he or she wants to succeed in Forex Trading.

The first chapter is an introduction to Forex Trading, and it goes into the definition of Forex, and lists down the principles of forex trading. Furthermore, the chapter goes into detail to explain the different types of forex traders, the advantages an individual would enjoy by becoming a forex trader, and reasons an individual should choose forex trading over other forms of trading.

The second chapter dives into the basics of forex trading, and it begins with the definition of important terminologies and trades. The chapter provides an in-depth explanation of forex markets, currency pair basics, and concludes with quote currency. The third chapter is a guide for beginners on the things they need to do to become forex traders. The chapter begins with an explanation of the role of a foreign exchange broker, the importance of a considerable account balance, and the various tools and platforms a forex trader should make use of.

The fourth chapter is an in-depth study of Forex Trading technical analysis and fundamental analysis, and in addition to the value, they offer a forex trader. The fifth chapter is about the mindset a forex trader needs to develop, since such an individual must develop a form of discipline and way of thinking that the direction of the markets will not influence easily. The chapter discusses the attitude approach and the personality types traders have.

The sixth chapter is a study of the different strategies forex traders can implement in their business to become successful. The chapter begins with an explanation of the most popular and effective strategies traders use and then concludes with the most appropriate strategies for beginners.

The seventh chapter is about the various Forex Trading signals, and it begins with an explanation of the signals. The chapter continues to explain the most popular signals traders use out there and how they work, both the manual and automated forex trading signals. The chapter concludes with a guide to choosing the best signals and evaluating the free forex signals option.

The eighth chapter is a valuable resource on the tips an individual would need to follow to start winning in Forex Trading. The chapter explains the different tips and best kept secrets, and it concludes with the strategies a trader can implement to manage risks. The ninth chapter is about cryptocurrencies and the value they can have on a forex trader's business strategies.

The tenth chapter offers three forex trading examples that a beginner would look at to have even more insights into this business. The eleventh chapter is an explanation into the mistakes Forex Traders make, and the preventive measures, as well as solutions a new trader should look into to have better chances of success.

The final chapter is about making money as a forex trader. The chapter explains how forex signals, forex robots, and social trading can help a beginner to make the most out of every trade.

There are plenty of books on this subject on the market, thanks again for choosing this one! Every effort was made to ensure it is full of as much useful information as possible, please enjoy!

Chapter 1: An Introduction to Forex Trading

If you have been to a foreign country, you know that you cannot buy your favorite food and drinks in the country you are visiting with your home country's currency. To avoid such a predicament, individuals have the option to convert their money into the currency of the country they are visiting at the airport.

In addition, you may have received some payment for services in a foreign currency, and you needed to exchange the money into your country's currency for you to use it. Regardless of the situations you had interacting with foreign currency. It is likely highly you have participated in forex in one way or another. A person can participate in Forex Trading whether he or she is traveling to a foreign country, or doing business in his or her country.

What Is Forex Trading

The word 'forex' is short for 'foreign exchange.' It involves the process of converting one currency into another currency for reasons including tourism, trading, and business.

Although a person can participate in foreign exchange by traveling to a different country and exchanging his or her currency for the foreign country's currency, the foreign exchange market is more significant than that. The foreign exchange market is a global forum for exchanging substantial national currencies against each other.

Due to the international spread of finance and trade, the forex markets experience high demands for foreign currencies, which makes the market the most significant money market in the world.

When multinational companies intend to buy goods from other countries, companies need to find the local currency first. That exchange will involve vast amounts of currency exchange. As a result, the local currency value will move up as the demand for that currency increases. With that exchanging going on around the world, the exchange rate always changes.

When global traders exchange currencies, currencies have a specific exchange rate, the price of currency changes according to the law of supply and demand; the higher the demand, the higher the supply and the higher the exchange rate.

The foreign trading market has no centralized marketplace for foreign exchange. Foreign exchange bureaus operate electronically through computer networks between traders all over the world.

Therefore, foreign trading goes on for 24 hours a day, six days a week in leading financial centers of major capital cities around the world. Investment and commercial banks carry out most of the Forex Trading in the international marketplaces in place of clients and investors.

Principles of Forex Trading

1. Learn the Market's Trends

It is essential for one to be able to predict the changing nature of the foreign exchange market in order to be successful in Forex Trading.

Accordingly, a person should understand the general direction of the marketplace. Trends can be uptrend, downtrend, or sideways trend. Identifying a pattern can profit a person in that he or she will be able to trade with the trend.

Uptrends are trends that move upwards, indicating an appreciation in currency value. Downtrends move downwards as an indication of depreciation in currency value. Sideways trends show that the currencies are neither appreciating nor depreciating.

2. Stay Focused and Control Your Emotions

Forex Trading is a challenging marketplace that can cause a person to lose confidence and to give up in the toughest of times. That is understandable given that traders put in their hard-earned money.

As a result, when a person experiences loss, he or she can lose focus when negative emotions become overwhelming. Some of the negative emotions a person may experience include panic, frustration, depression, and desperation.

It is, therefore, essential for one to become aware of the negative emotions that result from Forex Trading so that he or she may minimize the emotional effects of loss and remain focused.

3. Learn Risk Mitigation Tactics

In order to achieve the profits that a person anticipates, the person needs to minimize the likelihood of financial loss.

Since the forex market keeps on changing, the risks, therefore, keep on changing. The most crucial risk management rule is that a person should not risk more than he or she can afford to lose. Traders who are willing to invest more than they make, become very susceptible to Forex Trading risks.

Consequently, a person can mitigate potential losses by placing stop-loss orders, exchanging more than one currency pair, using software programs for help, and limiting the use of financial leverage.

4. Establish Personal Forex Trading Limits

A person should know when to stop Forex Trading. One can stop Forex Trading when he or she has an unproductive trading plan, or when he or she is continually experiencing losses.

An ineffective Forex Trading plan may not bring trade to an end, but it will not function as well as a trader may expect. In that case, the trader can consider stopping the trade, constantly changing markets, and the decreasing volatility within a particular foreign trading tool may also cause a trader to take a break from Forex Trading.

In addition, when a person is not in a good physical or emotional state, he or she may want to think about taking a break to deal with personal issues.

5. Use Technology to Your Benefit

Being up-to-date with existing technological developments can be gratifying in Forex Trading.

Given that forex markets utilize the online forum, high-speed internet connections can increase Forex Trading performance significantly. In order to make the most of Forex Trading, a person must take it as a full-time occupation, and he or she must embrace new technologies. Similarly, receiving forex market current information with smartphones makes it possible for forex traders to track trades anywhere.

Forex Trading is an aggressive enterprise that needs a trader to have an equally competitive edge. Therefore, a forex trader needs to maximize his or her business's potential by taking full advantage of the available technology.

6. Make Use of a Forex Trading Plan

A Forex Trading plan comprises of rules and guidelines that stipulate a forex trader's entry, exit, and money management principles.

A trading plan provides the opportunity for a forex trader to try out a Forex Trading idea before the trader risks real money. In so doing, a trader can access historical information that helps to know whether a Forex Trading plan is feasible and what outcomes he or she can expect.

When a forex trader comes up with a Forex Trading plan that shows potentially favorable outcomes, he or she can use the trading plan in real Forex Trading situations. The idea is for the forex trader to adhere to the trading plan.

Buying or selling currencies outside of the Forex Trading plans, even if a trader makes a profit, is poor trading, which can end any expectation the plan may have had.

Different Types of Forex Traders

Because foreign markets become flooded with the constant demand for currency exchange, four types of currency traders facilitate the smooth operation of forex markets.

1. Scalpers

Forex scalpers are dealers who buy or sell currencies, hold on to the exchanged currencies, and then wait for them to have higher and favorable exchange rates before the dealers can change their new currencies back to their original versions.

The scalpers hold deals for seconds to minutes and open and close several positions within a single day. In other words, scalpers go in and out of positions several times each day.

Scalpers trade currencies based on real-time analysis. Scalpers aim to make a profit by selling or buying currencies and holding on to them for a short time before buying or selling the currencies back to the forex market for small gains.

Therefore, that means that scalpers should love sitting in front of their laptops or computers for the entire forex session without taking their eyes off the screen.

Scalping is widespread moments after essential data releases and interest rate announcements. That is because high-impact reports generate significant price moves within a short period.

However, while profits can accrue rapidly with profitable trades, huge losses can also accumulate if the scalper is using a faulty system or if the trader does not understand what he or she is doing.

2. Day Traders

Forex day traders control trading positions during each trading day. Day traders close the trading positions at the end of the trading day and ensure that there are no positions that remain open during the night.

Forex day traders use currency day trading systems that regulate whether to buy or sell a currency pair in the foreign exchange market. A currency pair is the quotation of two different currencies where the trader quotes the value of one currency in comparison to the other.

Day traders target day currencies that are very liquid to leverage their capital as soon as investment prices change in favorable directions. The traders pick a price position at the start of the day, act on their assessments, and finish the trading day with either a profit or a loss.

Forex day traders avoid holding positions overnight because that may result in stock price gaps, a consequence, which can be very costly.

3. Swing Traders

Swing traders take hold of a position over a few days to several weeks. They hold places for more than one trading session, although not longer than several weeks or a couple of months.

Swing traders aim to capture huge potential price moves. Some swing traders may look for volatile stocks with constant movements, whereas others prefer stock prices that are more predictable.

Swing traders have exposure to overnight and weekend risks, where prices could rift and open the following forex session with markedly different rates. However, swing traders can generate profit by using established risk or reward strategies that will help them to determine where they will enter assets, where they will place stop-loss orders, and to know where they can make profits. Stop-loss orders help to limit the loss when stock prices fall.

Swing traders come up with plans and strategies that will give them an advantage over may trades. The traders do that by looking for trade arrangements that facilitate predictable price movements in the price of the asset. However, no trade arrangement works every time.

4. Position Traders

Position traders hold on to investment positions for long periods, anticipating the investments to appreciate. The periods can extend from weeks to months. In that regard, position traders are less concerned with short-term changes in price movements.

Position traders follow trends, believing that once a pattern starts, it is likely to continue. As such, position traders incline toward obtaining the bulk of a trend's move, which would generate profit in their investment capital.

Position traders use both fundamental and technical analysis to help in making trading decisions. They also depend on macroeconomic influences, old trends, and overall market movements to get to their anticipated end.

For a trader to have success in position trading, the trader has to know the entry or exit points and have a strategy to mitigate risk mainly by placing stop-loss orders.

Advantage of Forex Trading

1. Easy to Modify

Forex Trading markets put no restrictions on how much money a forex trader can use. Forex traders can trade a variety of goods and services.

In addition, the forex market does not have many rules and regulations for the forex trader to follow. The regulations that exist guide forex traders on when to enter and when to exit a trade.

2. Individual Control

Nobody controls the foreign market. Therefore, a forex trader has complete autonomy concerning making a trade. The forex market regulates itself and levels the playing field.

There are no intermediaries involved – a forex trader trades directly in the open forex market, and a retail forex broker eases that process.

3. Lucidity of Information

The Forex Trading market gives information straightforwardly to the public about the rates and price movement forecasts. The forex market traders have free and equal access to the market's information, and that makes it easy for the traders to make calculated and risk-free trading decisions.

Forex traders also have access to past information that helps in analyzing the market tendencies and forecasting the direction, which the market will take.

4. Widespread Options

The forex market provides a variety of options to forex investors. As a result, forex investors can take advantage of the available options to trade in different currencies in pairs.

An investor has the option of getting into foreign exchange spot trade or trading in currency futures to make the most of his or her investment.

5. High Liquidity and Volume

The forex market trades in large amounts of currencies at any given time because of how active the foreign exchange is. Therefore, there are high chances for forex traders to trade currency pairs on demand.

Under normal market conditions, a forex trader can buy and sell quickly with the anticipation that there will be another forex trader on the other end who is willing to trade back.

6. Money-Making Gains

The forex market provides Forex Trading measures that guard against financial loss. To ensure that a forex trader maximizes of gaining profits, the forex market has provisions for minimizing loss through making stop-loss orders.

Stop-loss orders enable forex traders to determine the closing price of their trade and thereby avoiding unforeseen losses

7. 24-Hour Market

Foreign exchange markets remain open for 24-hours a day and 6 days a week. That means that the market stays open most of the time, and it is not subject to external factors that may affect it.

Consequently, forex traders are flexible to work during the hours that suit them best.

8. Low Operation Costs

Operation costs in the forex currency markets are competent in trading in the forex market. The cost of operation in the currency market is in the form of spreads measured in pips. A pip is the fourth place after the decimal point of a percent.

For example, is the selling price was 2.5887, and the buying price was 2.5889, then the transaction cost is 2pips. Brokers may charge commissions on a fraction of the amount of the trade.

9. Chief Financial Market

The forex market is the biggest financial market in the world. That is because global corporations and big financial institutions participate dynamically in the foreign exchange market.

The foreign exchange market empowers major financial institutions to retail stockholders to seek out profits from currency variations connected to the global economy.

10. One Can Use the Leverage

The forex markets allow forex traders to capitalize on the advantage. Leveraging enables forex traders to be able to open positions for thousands of dollars while investing small amounts of money.

For example, when a forex trader trades at 40:1 leverage, he or she can trade $40 for every $1 that was in his or her account. That means that the forex trader can manage a trade of $40,000 for every $1,000 of investment.

Why Forex

The foreign exchange market is open to all types of traders, and it is more accessible than any other online trading platform in the world. Similarly, one can start trading with as little as $100. Therefore, foreign exchange markets have lower exchange capital prerequisites compared to other financial markets. A person can quickly sign up to open their trading account online, where most forex retail brokers operate.

Forex Trading is easy to learn, although it may be challenging to master. However, once an investor understands how the forex market works, he or she will be open to a world of vast opportunities that include becoming a foreign exchange account manager. A foreign exchange account manager can accumulate profits from trading as well as earning commissions for managing the Forex Trading accounts.

Foreign exchange markets make provisions for forex brokers to develop considerable trading volumes because of the leverage that the forex markets offer. That explains why forex traded get rewards like deposit bonuses when creating a Forex Trading account. Likewise, forex brokers give several incentives and promotions to financial institutions that enter Forex Trading. As a result, the forex market becomes a stimulating marketplace for Forex Trading.

Forex traders form international social communities as more people sign up every day. The social networks help forex investors to encounter an entire community of foreign exchange traders, thus making the forex market an interactive market to trade. In addition, forex traders can find many international forex experts, contributors, critics, and educators, among other members, in every conceivable language.

Moreover, forex traders can buy and sell risk-free, using a demonstration trading account. The account prevents traders from putting their investment at risk, and the traders can, therefore, move to the live forex markets whenever they please. The trading accounts enable forex traders to have access to real-time market information and the latest trading wisdom from foreign experts.

The forex market infrastructure is sophisticated, causing the performance of traders to be even more level. The forex market also has low spreads and commissions, thus making the transaction costs relatively small as a result. Besides, the foreign exchange market educates forex traders on global events, as the traders continue to trade online. Favorable trading conditions are crucial for foreign exchange traders.

Heavy security measures guard the foreign exchange markets, and several authorities control every forex broker. The bodies exist to make sure that forex traders have a safe space to carry out Forex Trading activities. However, forex traders are only with regulated brokers. Therefore, one must conduct a background check on available brokers in order to ensure that he or she works with the regulated brokers.

Online Forex Trading makes use of advanced trading software that generates regular updates that help forex investors to make real-time Forex Trading decisions. Consequently, Forex Trading becomes a rewarding way to buy and sell online, also due to third-party software developers who provide add-ons and plugins for popular trading platforms.

Finally, the forex markets allow traders to buy low and sell high. What's more, forex traders can trade assets without owning them, a practice that is called short selling. Furthermore, the use of leverage enables

Forex traders to buy or sell more substantial amounts than what they have in their deposits.

Chapter 2: Basics of Forex Trading

The term Forex Trading stands for foreign exchange trading, which is the purchasing or selling of one type of currency in exchange for another one. Also known as FX, it is a global over-the-counter market where investors, traders, banks, and institutions speculate on, purchase, and sell world currencies.

Forex Trading happens over the interbank market, which is a channel through which currency trading happens 5 days a week, 24 hours a day. It is one of the biggest trading markets in the world, with a worldwide daily turnover estimated to be more than $5 trillion. This is because countries, businesses, and individuals all participate in Forex Trading.

Actually, when people visit another country and convert their currency to the local currency, they are participating in the FX market. The demand for a particular currency at any given time will either push its value up or down in relation to other currencies. Therefore, people who want to venture into Forex Trading should understand a few important things before making their first trade, including:

1. Learning about currency pairs and what they mean
2. Market pricing

Forex transactions involve the simultaneous buying and selling of two different currencies known as currency pairs, which include a quote currency and a base currency. One of the most popular currency pairs on the forex market is the Euro/US Dollar. Also called the counter currency, the quote currency is the second currency in a forex pair.

Forex prices often have four decimal places due to their very small spread differences. However, they can also have any number of decimal places. Trades on the forex market are often worth millions of dollars; therefore, even tiny price differences can add up to a significant profit.

However, such massive trading volumes mean that a small spread can also lead to significant losses. Therefore, forex traders should consider the risks involved and trade carefully.

Important Terminology and Trades

A position, in terms of Forex Trading, describes a trade in progress. A long position, for instance, means that a forex trader purchased currency expecting its value to go up. Once he/she sells it back to the market at a higher price, the trade is complete, and his/her long position closes.

A short position, on the other hand, refers to a situation where a trader sells a certain currency with the expectation that its value will decrease, with the aim of buying it back at a lower price. The short position will close once the trader buys back the currency, ideally at a lower price.

If the currency pair of EUR/USD, which refers to Euro/US Dollar, was trading at 1.0914/1.0916, for example, investors planning to open a long position on the Euro would purchase one Euro for 1.0916 US dollars. They will then hold on to the currency and hope that its value will increase, and then sell it back to the market once it appreciates.

On the other hand, investors looking to open a short position on the Euro will sell one Euro for 1.0914 US dollars, with the expectation that its value will depreciate. If their expectations come true, they will buy it back at the lower rate and make a profit.

Forex Markets

With central banks, retail forex brokers, commercial corporations, commercial banks, hedge funds, individual investors, and investment management firms participating in the forex market, it is easy to see why this market is larger than equity and futures markets combined.

Placing a trade in the forex market is quite simple. The basics of Forex Trading are very similar to the mechanics of other financial markets, such as the stock market. Therefore, traders with prior experience in any type of financial market should be able to understand Forex Trading quite quickly.

1. Basics of the Forex Market

The FX market is a global network of brokers and computers from around the world; therefore, no single market exchange dominates this market. These brokers are also market makers and often post bid and ask prices for currency pairs, which are often different from the most competitive bid in the FX market.

On a more basic level, the foreign exchange market consists of two levels, i.e., the over-the-counter market and the interbank market. The OTC market is where individual traders execute trades through brokers and online platforms. The interbank market, on the other hand, is where large banking institutions trade currencies on behalf of clients or for purposes of balance sheet adjustments and hedging.

2. Hours of Operation

The FX market is a 24-hour market, from Monday morning to Friday afternoon in Asia and New York, respectively. Essentially, unlike markets such as commodities, bonds, and equities that close for a while, the forex market does not close even at night. However, there are exceptions. Some currencies for emerging markets, for example, close for a short while during the trading day.

3. The Currency Giants

By far, the US dollar is the biggest player in Forex Trading, making up approximately 85% of all forex trades. The second most traded currency is the euro, which makes up close to 39% of all currency trades, while the Japanese yen comes in at third place with 19% of all currency trades.

The reason that these figures do not total 100% is that every forex transaction involves two currencies. Citigroup and JPMorgan Chase and Co. were the biggest participants in the FX market in 2018, according to a study conducted by Greenwich Associates. Actually, these two banks commanded more than 30% of the global forex market share.

Goldman Sachs, Deutsche Bank, and UBS made up the remaining top five places. According to a settlement and processing group known as CLS, the daily trading volume in January last year was more than $1.8 trillion. This is a testament to just how popular, and massive Forex Trading is around the world.

4. Origins of the Forex Market

Up until the First World War, countries based their currencies on precious metals like silver and gold. This system, however, collapsed, and the Bretton Woods agreement became the basis of currencies after the Second World War. This agreement led to the creation of three international organizations to oversee economic activities across the world.

These organizations were the General Agreement on Tariffs and Trade, the International Monetary Fund, and the International Bank for Reconstruction and Development. In addition to creating these international organizations, the agreement adopted the US dollar as the peg for international currencies, instead of gold.

In return, the US government had to back up dollar supplies with an equivalent amount or value of gold reserves. This system, however, ended in 1971 when Richard Nixon, the US president at the time, suspended the US dollar's convertibility into gold. Nowadays, currencies can pick their own peg, and the forces of demand and supply determine their value.

Currency Pairs and Their Prices

These are quotations of two different currencies, such as EUR/USD. They quote the value of the first currency, which is the base currency, against the second one, which is the quote currency. Essentially, a currency pair compares the value of the first currency against the second one, showing how much of the first/quote currency can but one unit of the second/base currency.

An ISO currency code identifies currencies. This is the 3-letter alphabetic code, such as EUR for the euro, associated with a particular currency on the international market. When traders place an order for a currency pair, it means that they are purchasing the base currency and selling the quote currency. According to FX trading statistics, the most liquid currency pair in the world is the EUR/USD, followed by the USD/JPY.

1. Currency Pair Basics

Forex Trading happens in the foreign exchange market, which is the most liquid and largest market in the financial arena. Although it involves the simultaneous sale of one currency and purchase of another, forex traders should think of a currency pair as a single unit to purchase or sell.

Essentially, when a forex trader purchases a currency pair, he/she buys the base currency and, in effect, sells the second/quoted currency. The buy/bid price represents how much of the quote currency he/she will need to purchase one unit of the base currency.

On the other hand, when the trader sells a currency pair, he/she is selling the base currency and implicitly getting the quote currency. In this case, the sell/ask price for the currency pair will represent how much he/she will receive in terms of the quote currency for selling a single unit of the base currency.

2. Major Currency Pairs

There are numerous currencies in the world, which means that there are just as many currency pairs. Currencies come and go; therefore, the total number of currency pairs tends to change. However, investors categorize currency pairs based on their daily trading volume. Those that trade the most against the USD are the major currencies, and these include:

1. EUR/USD
2. USD/CHF
3. USD/JPY
4. USD/CAD
5. GBP/USD
6. AUD/USD

These major currency pairs account for almost 80% of the global Forex trading volume. They usually have high liquidity and low volatility and are indicative of well-managed and stable economies. In addition, they have narrower spreads than other currency pairs and are less susceptible to currency manipulation strategies.

3. Cross Currency Pairs

Also called crosses, these currency pairs do not include the US dollar. A few years ago, investors looking to trade crosses first had to convert them into the US dollar and then into the currency they desired. However, nowadays, investors can make direct cross currency pairs exchanges.

The most popular crosses feature minor currency pairs, such as GBP/JPY, EUR/JPY, and EUR/GBP. Cross-currency pairs are usually more volatile and less liquid than major currency pairs.

4. Exotic Pairs

These consist of currencies from smaller or emerging economies, paired with a major currency. Compared to two types of currency pairs discussed above, trading in exotics involves higher risk because they are significantly volatile and less liquid, which means they are more susceptible to currency manipulation.

Exotics also have wider spreads and are extremely sensitive to certain financial developments and unexpected changes in the political climate.

Quote Currency

Commonly referred to as the counter currency, the quote currency is the second one in both an indirect and direct currency pair. The quote currency determines the value of the base currency. In an indirect quote, the domestic currency is the quote currency, while the foreign currency is the quote currency in a direct quote.

The value of the quote currency falls as the rate in the currency pair goes up. This is the case irrespective of whether the pair is indirect or direct. It is important for forex traders to understand the pricing structure and quotation of currencies in the FX market. Forex brokers tend to trade certain currency pairs in specific ways.

Therefore, understanding the fundamentals of the quote currency is an important step towards finding success in Forex Trading. The exchange rate of a currency pair shows how much of the quote currency traders need to buy or sell to sell or buy one unit of the base currency. The value of the quote currency will be decreasing as the currency pair's rate increases, whether it is indirect or direct.

USD/CAD, for example, is a direct quote that denotes the cross-rate between the US dollar and the Canadian dollar, which is the quote currency in this case, while the US dollar is the base currency. Therefore, investors will use the Canadian dollar as a reference to determine the US dollar's value. From a US perspective, the Canadian dollar is a foreign currency.

The EUR/USD currency pair, on the other hand, describes the cross-rate between the euro and the US dollar; however, it is an indirect quote. In other words, the US dollar is the quote currency, and the euro is the base currency. In this case, the US dollar is the domestic currency that determines the value of a single unit of the euro.

The investment market can easily relieve investors of their money if they fail to prepare themselves well or adhere to the fundamental principles of trading. In any investment market, trading can be exceedingly tricky and difficult. However, success comes with adequate practice and education, and anyone with the right mindset can succeed at Forex Trading.

Learning about foreign exchange trading is the first thing that prospective forex traders should focus on. There are tons of learning materials and tools available to both experienced and new forex traders. It is also important to work with a regulated broker with several years of experience.

Chapter 3: How to Get Started in Forex Trading

Who Is A Foreign Exchange Broker?

Brokers are the intermediaries who link investors with their capital. Some traders may choose to invest in the forex trade, and therefore they will invariably become in need of a foreign exchange broker. Forex is a shortened version of the term Foreign Exchange. This phrase represents the financial market site within which various trading processes, deals, and transactions in foreign currency take place. Based on this description, a foreign exchange broker is, therefore, a registered and more qualified expert in currency trading.

Such forex brokers offer their services to prospective investors in foreign exchange and other currency traders who may require specific complex services. They identify opportunities, execute complicated trading strategies, and manage financial risk exposure on your behalf. Hence, a foreign exchange broker will assist you in achieving your aims of making a significant profit and mitigate potential losses. He or she is responsible for guiding you on how to manage your investment capital in the currency market.

Those brokers who deal in foreign exchange services typically know when and how to react or respond to volatility within the financial market. They provide the support mechanism that enables you to navigate through the uncertainty associated with currency trading successfully. In addition, such forex brokers often have extensive experience as previous traders in the forex markets. Therefore, you should always heed their advice and pay attention to their guidance or occasional recommendations.

Most forex brokers, upon hiring, will come with various trading platforms and accompanying tools to assist you in proper forex investment. Management of your available capital and exposure to risk may be your responsibility, but the advice of a forex broker is equally essential. The currency trading tools and relevant software platforms vary in their specific applications and features. Forex brokers will also make sure to teach you about the extensive range of traders and expertise required to master each of the separate platforms.

For you to understand the data and information contained in Forex Trading tools, you need to learn particular skills in technical analysis. This analytical expertise is transferable from the forex brokers to prospective traders and new investors through learning. You can grasp some knowledge of how to perform and correctly interpret the various forms of foreign exchange technical analyses. The associated foreign exchange terminology is relevant to know, as well. The foreign exchange broker can bring your attention to any other currency investment opportunities that may be available in the financial market.

Besides, the forex broker can distinguish the productive and probably profitable currency deals from the doomed ones. Due to the lax regulations in the currency market, you should beware of fraudulent brokers. You need to be highly suspicious of those brokers who claim to specialize in foreign exchange per se. whenever you encounter such seemingly dedicated brokers, you should sever ties with them instantly. You should engage a general stockbroker who has an additional registration in Forex Trading. Besides, it is rare to find phony stockbrokers due to the stringent regulation of the stock markets and stock exchanges. Select a well-known brokerage firm to have a chance of success in trading currencies.

The foreign exchange is the largest financial market in the world currently, and it is the most liquid kind of all the available markets too. Daily, it can experience currency exchanges to the tune of trillions. You will need the guidance of a foreign exchange broker to participate in this market, especially if you are new to the concept of currency trading. With the advent of the World Wide Web, this market has had an exclusive electronic presence online.

The internet connects the various stakeholders involved in Forex Trading, such as financial institutions, private investors, retail traders, and foreign exchange brokers. Since it is an online entity, the forex market is always active throughout the day. Whenever you want to participate in the currency trade, you need to interact with the other currency queries in the market. This interaction is possible by posting relevant orders online for you to engage in either buying or selling currencies or even conduct both.

When you are new to foreign exchange, you can begin investing in retail trading. Here, profits and losses are simply the difference between your buying and selling prices of the relevant currencies. When buying currency, you will hope for a rise in its value over the allocated trading time frame. The opposite is exact of a situation involving selling money, and therefore, these two scenarios are the distinct routes to making a profit in cases of simple retail trading. You may experience motivation for a change in the currency price. Hence, you are more likely to roll over your positions on most days. Rollover positions attract a commission or fees depending on the kind of forex broker that you use. However, this charge and other brokerage costs get an automatic credit or debit to your forex account.

Spot transactions describe the types of trade deals that ensure immediate resolution without the need for a rollover. Such trades are especially useful for people who are sensitive to nagging costs, charges, and fees. Only the presence of holidays can render spot trade deals impossible and hence the need for its postponement. Another way to interact in foreign exchange involves speculating on the future value of a particular currency relative to a different one.

This activity needs your correct predictive skills in the future exchange rate between a pair of specific currencies. Speculation is a tactic that is relevant to futures and forwards in the forex market. These two types of Forex Trading differ in their customizability after the expiry of a specified trading period. It is possible to customize the forwards with the currency under trade. The possibility maintains even after the lapse of the trading time interval. The futures, however, are not as customizable as forwards, and in fact, they do not permit it. Therefore, a foreign exchange broker would advise you on how to proceed with these situations.

As earlier mentioned, spot transactions are usual in retail trading, while currency forwards and futures involve trading with some degree of speculation. You will need to deal in futures contracts when making predictions in the currency market. Its principle is similar to options trading whereby you begin by purchasing a currency futures contract.

Next, you should take a particular position on the future behavior of a specific currency relative to another different type of currency. Your contract becomes due for settlement upon the expiry of your allocated trading period. However, currency futures do not allow for any further negotiations past the expiry period. This strictness is unlike the situation with bespoke forward contracts that would enable settlement at any time. Besides, you should close your futures contract trading position before the expiration date to avoid additional settlement costs. Just like options trading, taking multiple trading positions on the future values of various currencies is possible, as well.

What Is the Account Balance, and Why Does a Broker Need It?

The account balance is the amount of equity or capital available in your brokerage account due to investment in the currency market. It is essential to have such an account to enable the foreign exchange broker to carry out the buying and selling executions on your behalf. Since your investment is in the currency market, this brokerage account is your forex account, as well. Opening a forex account for a new investor is a simple exercise that is akin to opening a personal bank account. After setting up a forex account, you should seek the services of an accomplished and registered forex broker. All foreign exchange trade deals and transactions should go through your forex broker. Therefore, he or she needs to gain access to this forex account and have permission to transact in the currency market on your behalf.

An investor's limited involvement in the daily running of the account necessitates that the forex broker takes over these duties. In addition, other financial liabilities charged to this account include the commissions and brokerage fees. You should check on the forex account regularly to keep track of the progress of your investments.

It also allows you to carry out responsible financial management based on the difference between your finances and risk liabilities. Productive risk management strategies become possible based on the available capital balance in the account at a particular moment. Since the currency market tends to turn volatile without warning, your forex account must maintain its liquidity status. The available balance provides your forex broker with the necessary leeway to take immediate corrective measures when a specific currency trade deal begins to go wrong. The best way to ensure that the brokerage account retains activity is to make regular deposits into it.

A standing order is a useful way of guaranteeing the liquidity status of the forex account. Your order will execute the transfer of a certain sum of money from your private account at regular intervals of your choosing. This automatic process eliminates the downsides associated with forgetfulness on your part. In the case of currency trading that involves derivatives, the forex broker can easily buy and sell futures contracts based on their speculation at a particular time.

Currency fluctuations require your forex broker to take a specific position promptly to take advantage of the time factor in currency trading. Financial delays from an inactive or overdrawn brokerage account are often responsible for some of your indirect losses. As a result, your forex broker will miss out on potentially profitable opportunities in the currency market.

Another importance attributed to the forex account is the possibility of a quick integration with the trading platform and technical analysis tools. Your forex broker will have access to both the forex account and the trading platform in a single place. Hence, making informed decisions becomes an instantaneous activity. The forex broker reacts to data and information from technical analyses with the appropriate monetary input.

This activity may involve either more investment in a promising opportunity or a straightforward exit from a non-productive trade deal. You can easily relate the comparison between any technical analyses performed and the balance available in your forex account. Your forex broker has the freedom to make long-term decisions and speculation only if he or she is sure of the availability of capital. Because of taking such high risks, your forex broker is more likely to make higher profits for you.

In the case of taking long positions on forwards and futures contracts, the forex broker should feel confident in his or her level of liquidity. Confidence breeds more self-belief, and eventually, the forex broker ends up conducting sensible transactions. Emotional reactions to trading positions are typical of forex brokers who are always wary of taking risks due to the fear of losing the scanty balance available. Insufficient capital and account mismanagement typically result in forex brokers who continuously engage in illogical trade deals to cover recent losses. You will find such forex brokers participating in the short-term local currency trading more frequently with your capital.

Further investigation of your forex broker may reveal the underlying cause as the fear of losing your money and, in turn, his or her commission. Always make sure that you are abreast of the condition of your forex account. You can offer appropriate instructions and proper orders on the level of risks that you may tolerate. Such instructions are only possible if you keep track of the activities in the account. In addition, you and your forex broker can plan risk management strategies together to limit your exposure to unnecessary financial risks. The forex broker will grow accustomed to your mannerisms gradually, and soon he or she will understand your objectives. At this point, the forex broker becomes comfortable enough to exert the full range of his or her trading expertise towards the attainment of your financial goals.

What Are Platforms and Tools?

A trading platform is the graphical user interface provided by computer application software, and it enables the trader or investor to interact with the aspects of his or her trading transactions. A Forex Trading platform is a standard provision from most forex brokers to their clients, investors, or other retail traders. It also acts as a source of commission for the forex brokers by charging an access fee to use it.

After seeking a foreign exchange broker, most traders will get a couple of trading platform recommendations from these same brokers.

Forex brokers are often adept at their jobs, and hence these recommendations are typically advisable. When you decide to participate in foreign currency trading, you will need to familiarize yourself with the skills of taking profitable market positions. Therefore, you will have to purchase, download, and install the software on your computer and learn to navigate around the online platform.

In case you are new to online Forex Trading, it may become somewhat challenging to make your way around the platform. For you to understand and succeed in this particular endeavor, you will need the assistance of an online foreign exchange broker.

Due to the competition among different foreign exchange brokers, some of the online trading platforms may be available at a discount or even free of charge. It is essential that you know which one will work best for you based on their simplicity of use, precision, and online forex broker support. Most of your investment and capital management decisions depend on your understanding of the forex market. A robust and versatile platform should make it easier for you to come up with informed choices. In addition, an excellent online platform should have an online forex broker standing by for technical analysis and support.

Another aspect concerning Forex Trading platforms is the range of the available versions. They vary from the low end of the trading spectrum to the high end of trading end users. You can have the primary platforms consisting of rudimentary trading user interfaces for the beginners and new investors. Besides, there are sophisticated platforms that contain multiple analytical tools with enhanced graphics and live streaming capability for seasoned traders.

When choosing a relevant platform, you should keep in mind the amount of capital you intend to invest and the level of risk exposure that you can tolerate. The initial cost and the presence of subscription fees are other vital deliberations to make during the selection process as well. All the essential features needed for Forex Trading are common to most platforms; hence, the availability of multiple and excessive aspects is not such a significant consideration when buying one. You can narrow down your choice to the platforms that have the features that you will require only. As an investor, you should make decisions concerning the kind of platforms based on your forex broker's reputation.

Meta Trader is the most famous Forex Trading platform in the market currently. Its development resulted from the use of a versatile programming language that employs scripting as an execution method, i.e., the MQL program. Meta Trader can support multiple types of order executions, allows for simultaneous editing while trading, and can conduct hedging operations. In addition, the platform has an embedded email system, technical indicators, analytical, graphical objects, and the ability to chat online with fellow traders.

Currently, the Meta Trader platform is in its fifth version. Other platforms' primary purposes differ from foreign currency exchanges. However, they often have some level of forex capacity inbuilt within their structure. Examples of these different platforms include the IG group, CMC Markets, X-Trade Brokers, Pepper Stone, Forex.Com, Robin Hood, Trade Station, TDA merit trade, and Interactive Brokers.

On the other hand, foreign exchange trading tools are the indicators that show you how the market and your capital are performing. They are mainly the outcomes of technical analysis conducted on the various trading positions taken in your Forex Trading deals. The presentation of the results of such studies occurs via a graphical user interface that provides relatable information that is easily understandable. Most trading platforms have embedded tools within their structure to provide all the necessary data at one point. This platform flexibility eliminates the need to acquire separate stand-alone tools for each analytical process. The kinds of information derived from currency trading tools are in the form of graphical objects such as tables and charts for reports and analysis, respectively.

Line graphs are specifically standard in trend and pattern analysis. Monitoring currency fluctuations is better using such a graphical representation. Hence, most, if not all, trading tools are akin to the technical, analytical tools that are exclusive to foreign exchange trades. The only slight difference is that they are currently presentable online via computers as opposed to the previous use of paperwork.

The tools that are within the Meta Trader platform provide information on daily market analysis as well as Forex Trading signals on market trends and fluctuations. Consistent capital and risk management strategies are essential deliverables credited to the use of Forex Trading tools. You can adjust your trading position based on the data from these tools. The adjustments may involve reinforcing your stance on a forex position due to the use of a more valuable currency in a favorable market. In addition, you can consider exiting a trade deal altogether when the currency values become too volatile to sustain investor confidence.

Currency converters, economic calendars, financial news streams, and various types of calculators are additional tools available on most Forex Trading platforms. Computation of potential profits and losses within the Meta Trader platform is possible using tools such as profit, pip, margin, and invest-profit calculators. Your financial risk increases with the rise in the volatility of the currency market.

In such a situation, the margin calculator is also responsible for conducting your probable risk assessment. Forex Trading applications that are customizable to your smartphones are another form of tools available to you during trading. These so-called apps are beneficial in that they are portable and enable you to keep track of your financial progress at any time, as well as in real-time. Examples of such mobile forex tools include Coin Trader, FX Trader, Trade Interceptor, Forex Hours, and XE Currency.

Chapter 4: Technical and Fundamental Analysis in Forex Trading

Forex Trading involves a market of an electronic network of brokers, individual traders, institutions, and banks, which trade a variety of national currencies. Excluding a holiday, a forex market opens throughout for five days a week, and it is the liquid and most prominent financial market worldwide. Forex Trading is essential to traders and financial institutions as it offers them profits from the movements of the currency. Technical and fundamental analyses are the two primary methods that a trader can use to study and assess the forex market.

A trader needs to learn and understand how the two forms of analysis work. He or she also should be able to tell the difference that takes place in the application of each analysis type. This knowledge will help him or her to read the market better and even make fitting speculations regarding the direction of specific currency movements. As a result, the trader can take up appropriate positions in the market that will enable him or her to receive gains from the trades.

Below is information that provides a breakdown of how technical and fundamental analysis functions in Forex Trading.

Technical Analysis

Technical analysis is a methodology that a trader uses to study and make predictions concerning currency or price movements in the forex market. He or she observes the patterns of the price like flags, double bottoms, and triangles on a chart and interprets the actions of the cost to find out the market conditions. As a result, he or she should have excellent analytical skills to evaluate the technical charts correctly. A trader that utilizes technical analysis has a short, medium, or long-term view of the trade he or she undertakes.

Technical analysis bases its operation on historical information about price movements since traders believe that history will repeat itself. They think that the price on the market will move in the same way as in the past if they find any similar historical patterns. A trader would be keen on a particular price level and build his or her trades on it if it provided a necessary price action in the past. Thus, he or she studies past movements of price and use that information to find out the current market conditions and possible price movements.

Technical analysis provides the visual representation of past movements of the price that inform a trader of the situation in the market. The price patterns and statistical trends in the analysis assist him or her to know the best time to enter or exit the market. Additionally, the technical signals also show him or her significant trading opportunities. Hence, technical analysis understanding can help a trader to make decisions that bring him or her gains. Simultaneously, it will also assist him or her to avoid trades or making unnecessary moves in the market that may result in considerable losses.

A trader uses various technical indicators to analyze the Forex Trading market, technically. Understanding how the indicators function can help him or her to comprehend the market conditions. Subsequently, he or she can then choose and apply the most appropriate trading strategy that will place him or her in the most profitable position in the market. The essential indicators that technical analysts employ in the forex market include:

1. Relative Strength Index Indicator (RSI)

The Relative Strength Index is an oscillator that provides a trader with signals to help him, or her sell high and buy low. It indicates to a trader the status of a currency, whereby it shows the overbought or oversold levels. The readings of an RSI indicator range from zero to 100, and they signal the speed and shift in price movements. The currency has overbought status when the value is above 70. Similarly, when the number on the oscillator is below 30, it indicates the oversold levels of that the currency.

Moreover, the RSI places the bullish and bearish price momentums against the price's graph and compares them. Bullish dynamics of the cost can cause overbought levels, while the bearish ones can produce oversold levels. As the forex market trends, a trader enters the trade in the trend's direction as the indicator recovers from the extremes. He or she finds the RSI going through a reversal from oversold levels or readings below 30 if there is an uptrend in the market. He or she then enters in the direction of that trend.

2. Slow Stochastic Indicator

The slow stochastic is an oscillator that helps a trader to identify profitable trade points in the forex market. It also assists him or her in determining the oversold and overbought levels in the trade. Its readings interpret the same as those of the RSI. It also uses the percentageK and the percentageD lines to indicate to the trader an entry point of a deal. The movements of these two lines on the oscillator will signal to the trader about a strong buying position that is in the direction of the price trend. A trader can take up such a place if the percentageK line crosses over the percentageD line through reading at the 20-level.

3. Moving Average Indicator

The moving average indicator helps a trader to determine trends, identify trade areas, and evaluate the forex markets. It assists him or her to establish the resistance and support levels as well as the patterns that indicate great buying or selling positions in the trade. A moving average indicator is also a lagging one because it also determines the current price direction, albeit with a lag. This delay stems from the signal utilizing historical data to establish the moving averages.

A trader can use the simple moving average (SMA) or the exponential moving average (EMA) to carry out the analysis. The SMA gives the simple mean of an asset in a given amount of time by adding all the closing prices and dividing the sum by the given number of days. If a trader uses a 20-day SMA, then he or she finds the total amount of the closing prices of the last 20 days and divides the total by 20.

An EMA provides the averages of the latest prices, unlike the SMA, which focuses on a long sequence of data points. A trader uses a particular formula to calculate the EMA, that is, Current EMA = [(Current closing price - (previous day EMA) × multiplier) + previous day EMA]. The formula for the multiplier or smoothing constant in the above equation is 2/ (1+N), where N= the number of days.

A forex trader uses the momentum to determine the entry and exit points in the market. He or she enters the trade when the currency pair moves in the moving average's direction and exits when it runs in the opposite direction.

4. Moving Average Convergence Divergence Indicator (MACD)

This MACD indicator uses crossovers, divergences, and rapid rise and falls to show the link between moving averages of prices. In turn, it indicates the variations in momentum through a visual display, which helps a trader in recognizing a ranging or trending forex market. The calculation of the MACD involves the trader subtracting the 26-EMA period from the 12-EMA period, which provides him or her with the MACD line. A 9-day EMA of the MACD gives a trader the signal line in this indicator.

The trader can trade according to the movements of the MACD line concerning the signal line. He or she can buy when this line crosses beyond the signal line or sell when this line crosses beneath the signal line in the forex market. Moreover, the trader can determine a downward or upward bias of the currency pair by identifying the lines with regard to the zero lines.

He or she also can combine the MACD with a ranging or trending market to increase efficiency and minimize loss. The trader can place stops below the latest price extreme that is before the crossover. In doing so, he or she establishes a limit on the trade at the double the amount of his or her investment. The MACD provides the trader with suitable conditions when he or she uses crossovers of the MACD line in the trend's direction.

Fundamental Analysis

This methodology is the second type of analysis that a trader can use in the forex market. Unlike the technical analysis, this type concerns itself with the intrinsic value of an asset or currency. It evaluates the political, social, and economic factors that create a target price or establish value in the market. It uses information from features like interest rates, Gross Domestic Product (GDP), inflation, and others to analyze the trading conditions. A trader using fundamental analysis needs to have excellent analytical skills regarding statistical and economic data.

A fundamental trader in the forex market will assess a country's economic health by evaluating the trends of various data points and generally determine the strength and movements of the currency. He or she looks at various economic indicators and interprets them to find out the value of money. The essential economic signals that a trader can analyze the situation of the economy include:

1. Inflation

Inflation is the increase in the quantity of money in circulation due to the growth of a country's economy. The more the money there is available, the more expensive the goods and services are in a country. When the economy of a state experiences too much inflation for an extended period, the associated currency becomes less valuable. The deprecation comes about because of there being too much supply of the money.

Conversely, the currency increases in value if an economy goes through deflation. Deflation takes place when there is little money in circulation. It leads to the country providing services and goods at lower prices. However, the value of the currency also drops when deflation carries on for a long time because there will be little money to support the economy. A country should balance the supply and demand aspects of its economy to ensure neither extreme devalues its currency.

2. Interest Rates

Interest rates are important indicators for fundamental analysis as they level the economy and can help a trader to discover trading opportunities. A common type of interest rate traders analyze is the nominal kind. The central banks create this nominal interest rate by referring to the principle that private banks pay to borrow currencies from them.

The central banks stimulate the individuals and private banks to borrow currency by lowering the interest rate as needed by the economy. It results in more valuable currency and improved performances in productivity, economics, and consumption. However, low-interest rates for extended periods can lead to there being too much money and form economic bubbles. Thus, the central bank balances the scale by cutting the prices of borrowing and providing less money for use by businesses, individuals, and banks.

3. Gross Domestic Product (GDP)

The gross domestic product provides the best indicator of a country's economic health by measuring all the services and goods that the state produces and supplies in a given period. Typically, a trader looks at the products and services in an economy in terms of supply and demand. However, the GDP focuses on the supply side of the analysis. The indicator assumes that the state made dependable and exact approximations based on a significant understanding of both supply and demand.

Hence, the increase in GDP should have a corresponding increase in gross domestic product demand. If the supply does not grow along with a rising GDP, it indicates that the economy is unhealthy. This indicator comes about because the economy in such a state shows that the goods and services provided are unaffordable.

Technical and fundamental analyses are critical in the evaluation and understanding of the forex market. The indicators provide visual information that helps a trader to comprehend and react quickly to the trade. The factors that influence a country's currency, such as economic indicators enable fundamental analysts to determine the cause for an increase of decrease in currency value. Therefore, learning elements that make up technical and fundamental analysis can assist a trader in achieving considerable success in Forex Trading.

Chapter 5: Psychology and Mindset of a Forex Trader

Human beings can be complicated and fascinating creatures. Many factors may influence how they think and behave in a given situation. However, at the base of every decision and reaction lie two essential features that ultimately determine a person's conduct. They are the attitude and personality of an individual. How a person sees things and the personality that he or she possesses will define his or her reaction to an event.

Similarly, the attitude and personality type of a forex trader will determine if he or she will succeed or fail in trading. These elements define his or her mindset as he or she enters and participates in the market. Thus, appropriately applying them can ensure a forex trader transacts successfully while simultaneously maintaining his or her psychological wellbeing. Here, we look at the mental mindset of a forex trader from two perspectives. The first angle is the attitude approach, and the second one is personality types.

Attitude Approach

The attitude of a forex trader determines how he or she views and interprets the market and its conditions. Having the right outlook is vital as it helps a trader to control his or her emotions and handle the vicissitudes of Forex Trading. Managing feelings and maintaining objectivity while trading will ensure success for a forex trader. The following are some of the attitudes that can help a trader to improve his or her mindset and achieve success in Forex Trading:

1. Organization

An organized trader makes relevant preparations before and during a trade that enhances his or her chances of success. A person should have an organization in all the steps involved in the trading, including decisions before entering a forex trade:

- **Create a Trading Plan** – A trading plan provides a trader with a sequence of what is taking place in the market and some expectations. It helps him or her to keep track of the market conditions in a systematic way that facilitates effective decision-making.
- **Think Before Entering a Trade** – A trader should carry out extensive research regarding the trade and weigh all possible options before starting. He or she should be as objective and logical as possible when deciding to enter the market.
- **Maintain a Record of the Trades** – A trading journal is essential in Forex Trading as it provides the trader with relevant feedback concerning his or her situation on the market.

2. Confidence

Having confidence in the market is booster as it helps a trader to avoid making rash decisions or switching back and forth.

- **Have Full Confidence in the Decisions** – Having belief and full confidence in the decision a trader makes is vital as it signifies that he or she does not fear the trade. He or she analyzed everything in detail and logically came to that particular decision. Hence, he or she does not worry, even if he or she does lose in the end.
- **Following the Map of Price Action** – A trader should trust the information that price action provides. It indicates the market conditions and offers a useful guideline that can help a trader to make decisions without the influence of emotions.
- **Avoid Gambling** – A confident attitude helps a trader to avoid gambling in the market because he or she does not panic. Instead, he or she takes time to evaluate the situation before making a move.

3. Patience

Patience is a virtue that also applies to a forex trader. Keeping calm despite the profits and losses in the markets can help a trader to avoid the dangers of reacting emotionally in the markets.

- **Value Quality Over Quantity** – Being patient enables a trader to make profits consistently for an extended period. He or she will receive small benefits but will last for a much longer time, rather than rushing for huge gains and losing trade quickly.
- **Use the Daily Charts to Learn** – Learning using the daily charts enable a trader to develop an outlook of looking at the bigger picture of the market. It will also allow him or her to

practice some trading strategies and make appropriate corrections before entering the forex market.

4. Realistic Expectation

Understanding the trade and having realistic expectations will go a long way into helping a trader to succeed in Forex Trading. It helps him or her to make the right plans, use appropriate strategies and decisions in the market. It also helps to keep his or her emotions in check.

- **Understand the Independence of Each Trade** – Regardless of previous experiences, a trader must understand and identify each trade as a different transaction. It helps the trader know that the next trade's success or failure is absolute.
- **Trade Using Disposable Capital** – A trader should trade using only disposable capital. He or she should risk the money that he or she does not need; otherwise, he or she should not enter the trade.
- **Avoid Sleepless Nights** – A trader should not continue with a trade that he or she doubts. He or she should drop it if he or she loses sleep due to worrying about the risks involving his or her investment.
- **Do Not Take Trades Personally** – A trader should not have an emotional attachment to the trade. Doing so assists him or her to avoid taking the trades personally and view the forex market as a fluctuating trading environment.

5. Learning from Each Experience

Lastly, a person needs to take every experience from the market as a learning lesson. He or she needs to take into account the aspects and decisions that led to the success of failure of a particular transaction. This lesson is even more important in Forex Trading because recognizing the errors made can enable a trader to convert a loss into a profit. He or she looks at the mistakes involved, analyzes every decision, and the subsequent reactions in the market.

The failed trades will provide a trader with relevant information such as clues for what the mistake is and the reasons for the loss. Failures tend to offer a trader relevant information that can enable a forex trader to succeed in the future by avoiding repeating mistakes.

Personality Types of Traders

A person can also look at the psychological mindset of a forex trader from the perspective of the personality. Each individual has his or her personality trait that defines who he or she is. Every personality type consists of different strengths and weaknesses. Forex Trading, as is with other similar transactions, can produce a considerable profit at the moment but cause significant losses at another.

A trader experiences various emotion when it comes to dealing with money matters. He or she invests and trades his or her money to receive profits. He or she also wants to minimize risks and avoid losses as much as possible. Hence, whenever the trader experiences significant gains or losses, he or she goes through strong emotions that bring out his or her personality. The type of character that a trader has is essential because it determines how he or she will behave in the trading market. The trader's personality will define how he or she thinks, the decisions he or she makes, and the subsequent actions.

Therefore, a person needs to understand the various types of personality that a trader can possess. This knowledge will help him or her to comprehend why some traders make individual decisions in particular periods. Additionally, it will enable the individual to study his or her behavior and identify the personality kind that describes him or her. As a result, the person can recognize his or her strengths and weaknesses. It will enable him or her to know the area to improve.

Learning and understanding these types of personalities can help a person to determine the ones that suit Forex Trading the best. He or she will be able to identify and adopt the personality kind that brings about consistent gains in the trading processes. A beginner in Forex Trading can have a chance to prepare himself or herself better before entering the trade. An experienced trader can get more knowledge that will assist him or her to make appropriate enhancements that eventually lead to improved profits and overall success. The following are some of the essential types of personalities and the characteristics that describe them.

1. The Detailed Type

As the name suggests, a detailed trader pays attention to the details of the trade. He or she takes his or her time to look carefully before leaping into a transaction. The trader uses rationality to evaluate the entire situation and everything relating to the market before trading. He or she logically and systematically carry out relevant researches, take detailed notes, and combine all the information received to inform his or her decision.

Furthermore, the trader with this personality also writes trading notes regarding his or her situation in the market. He or she inputs the reasons for writing the points that he or she has and utilizes them to determine the next moves in the market. The attention to detail helps a trader to make decisions that have minimal risks. Conversely, he or she can waste time analyzing before entering a market and end up losing on potentially profitable trades.

2. The Innovative Type

A trader with an innovative personality is instinctive and thinks on his or her feet. He or she uses his or her intuitive skills to read people and events, think and make judgments when trading. Trading involves making the right moves at the correct time to ensure one does not incur losses and, instead, receive profits. An innovative trader carefully analyzes the information available and makes appropriate decisions to form or improve a trade. He or she uses creativity to assess and interpret the information at hand.

Additionally, the creative thinking that a trader with this personality possesses enables him or her to reach relevant conclusions quickly. He or she observes and interprets the significant meanings from large amounts of feedback and information. The trader then swiftly takes immediate action that helps to take advantage or solve issues arising from the market conditions. The innovative traders are keen, quick thinkers, and decisive. This personality provides them with features that can make good leaders.

3. The Playful Type

A trader possessing a playful personality kind has a fun-loving nature. He or she enters and carries out a trade with a playful attitude. This trader is optimistic, in that, he or she sees the bright side of things. He or she views the business as one that will succeed, even if a current transaction is causing losses. He or she also has a lot of positivity that makes him or her have a playful approach to the trade.

Moreover, a trader with this personality involves a certain level of social interaction as he or she trades. He or she communicates and includes other people in his or her thoughts regarding a trade. He or she may even take some advice from other traders about a particular problem. Nevertheless, the weakness of a playful trader type is that he or she is emotional due to his or her positive and optimistic characteristics. Sometimes he or she lets his or her sentiments cloud his or her rationality in the thought and decision-making processes.

4. The Spontaneous Type

A trader with a spontaneous personality does not spend time evaluating and making detailed trading strategies in a trade. He or she has a hard time concentrating on such details. Instead, he or she thinks about a situation as it occurs in the market and makes a decision quickly. The lack of concrete strategies and analysis may expose him or her to avoidable risks that he or she may not expect.

5. The Values-Driven Type

A trader with a values-driven personality is independent in his or her approach to the market. He or she does not follow the crowd and, instead, weighs up the situation, thinks carefully, and makes the relevant trading decisions. Additionally, a value-driven trader concerns himself or herself with certain aspects regarding the trade. He or she emphasizes factors such as relationships, ideas, and the substantial returns of a transaction. Independence enables this trader to look at the bigger picture of the market and make reliable decisions.

However, his or her weakness lies in the emotions that he or she experiences while trading. The trader puts significance that is more considerable on his or her values, which can lead to missed opportunities. Emotions can also make him or her less logical when analyzing the markets.

6. The Administrative Type

An administrative trader adapts to changes and makes effective decisions accordingly. He or she is realistic and practical about the trades and makes sensible moves in the market. He or she can lead other traders or delegate when necessary.

7. The Accurate Type

An accurate trader is attentive to details. He or she applies a detailed evaluation of the situation and notes down every detail concerning the trade. He or she uses a Forex Trading journal to record every assessment and market condition. He or she refers to these details to help him or her to analyze or solve a particular problem.

8. The Independent Type

A trader with an independent personality type does not follow other people's decisions. The trading market is always moving, and it can easily lead to traders making judgments according to the crowd. Emotions can cause someone to allow the decisions and actions of others to determine his or her moves in the market. However, the independent trader thinks for himself or herself.

This trader observes the situation, studies it, and even tries to look at it from different points of view. Once he or she assesses the state of the market, he or she makes the most suitable decision for his or her trades. An independent trader uses creativity and innovatively to come up with strategies and solutions to any issues that arise in his or her transactions. Consequently, the trader's independence causes him or her to be a weak team player because he or she does not have strong social skills.

9. The Facilitative Type

A trader with a facilitative personality trades in a precise and systematic manner. He or she regards trading as a serious business and uses a sober attitude when dealing in the market. He or she meaningfully think about the appropriate moves to make in the transaction and makes the final choices in an organized manner. He or she looks at not only his or her trades but also the entire market. It forms a bigger picture that informs his or her judgments.

Besides, a facilitative trader likes to engage with other traders in the market. Unlike the independent type, this trader enjoys trading in a social setting where he or she gets to work while sharing ideas with others. As a result, the facilitative trader can succeed when cooperating with others, such as in trading partnerships or teams.

10. The Socially Responsible Type

A trader with a socially responsible personality places great importance on the values he or she holds dear. Accordingly, he or she makes strategies and decisions that are in line with these values. He or she also only takes up new chances or makes moves in the market that are in consonance with his or her social ideologies. Aside from respecting and upholding the values of interest, the trader also takes delight in social life. Thus, he or she enjoys a social life while being responsible for maintaining significant social ideology.

11. The Artistic Type

A trader with an artistic personality type uses creativity and intuition while trading. He or she employs his or her artistry and uses creative and original thinking processes to make relevant moves in the market. An artistic trader is more creative and intuitive when compared to other traders in the business.

Likewise, he or she possesses flexibility in the personality that allows him or her to change and adapt to different conditions in trading. Despite this, he or she must take care not to let his or her emotions cloud his or her judgment. He or she should be wary of too much emotional connection with the trades.

12. The Supportive Type

A supportive trader owns portions of the qualities that make up complete and successful traders. The characteristics that he or she possesses enable him or her to provide support to others in the trading world. A trader with this type of personality is conscious, with a lot of insight into the factors associated with the market. He or she also approaches transactions with a somber attitude that helps him or her to make sound decisions in the trade. These qualities attract other traders; in that, they make the supportive trader dependable.

13. The Adventurous Type

A trader with an adventurous personality experiences great success while trading. The success comes from the fact that he or she utilizes factual data to make any judgments regarding the market. He or she uses data to evaluate the situation of the trade rationally before making appropriate decisions. As a result, he or she applies a systematic thought process and makes the most sensible choices that lead to success. Furthermore, an adventurous trader tends to take more risks in the market.

The more the risk there is in a trade, the higher the returns a trader will receive. Thus, he or she utilizes his or her flexible mind to assess a market critically and decide whether he is open to a particular trade. Consequently, the adventurous trader is decisive in trading as he or she uses facts, logic, and analysis to make productive and profitable decisions. Nonetheless, he or she must take care not to push his or her sense of adventure too far. The trader should be mindful of taking too many risks as the strategy may backfire and lead to considerable losses.

Ultimately, the main factors that significantly determine and influence the psychological mindset of a forex trader are emotions and the types of personality. The hope of receiving profits and the fear of losing money can drive a person to make decisions that can make trading success or complete failure. An individual need to understand the characteristics, personality, and attitude that an individual has. Understanding these elements of a person can enable a trader to know how to improve his or her approach to Forex Trading. He or she can also learn the dos and don'ts when dealing with the pressures of Forex Trading. In all, the knowledge from such comprehension will help a trader to enhance his or her mindset to ensure Forex Trading success.

Chapter 6: Forex Strategies and Strategies for Beginners

Forex Trading strategy is what forex traders do to buy or sell financial instruments at a given time to generate profits. Forex Trading strategies are nowadays done, either manually or automatically. A trader is using manual strategies when he or she interprets the trading signals and as a result, decides to buy or sell. The automated method is where a trader comes up with an algorithm that studies the trading signals and executes trades on its own.

Before choosing a Forex Trading strategy, it is important to identify which of these four trading styles fits your personality:

1. Day Trading

Day trading is a short-term trading style designed to buy and sell financial securities within the same trading day. That is closing all positions by the end of the trading day. In Day Trading, you can hold your trades for minutes or even hours. Day traders deal with financial instruments like options, stock, currencies, and contracts for difference. Many day traders are investment firms and banks. Day traders use technical analysis to make trading decisions.

Pros

- Day traders are not affected by unmanageable risks and negative price gaps because all positions are closed by the end of the trading day.
- There are a substantial number of trading opportunities
- Traders can be extremely profitable due to the rapid returns

Cons

- Traders can be extremely unprofitable due to the rapid returns
- You don't have to be concerned with the economy or long-term trends
- Huge opportunity cost
- Day traders have to exit a losing position very quickly, to prevent a greater loss.

2. Swing Trading

Swing trading is where a trader holds an asset between one and several days in an attempt to capture gains in the financial market. This type of traders doesn't monitor the screens all day, and they do it a few hours a day. Swing traders usually rely on technical analysis to look for trading opportunities. Swing trading position is held longer than day trading position but shorter than buy and hold investments. They have larger profit targets than day traders.

Pros

- Swing traders can rely solely on technical analysis, which simplifies the process
- Requires less time to trade compared to day-trading

Cons

- Swing traders are exposed to overnight and weekend risks
- Generally, swing trading risks are as a result of market speculation
- It is difficult to know when to enter and exit a trade when swing trading

3. Scalping Trading

Scalping is the fastest trading style where traders hold positions for a very short time frame. Traders here gain profits due to small price changes. The scalpers hold a position for a short period to gain profits. Traders with large amounts of capital or bid-offers spread narrowly prefer scalping. Scalping follows four principles:

- Small moves are more frequent - even when the market is quiet, scalpers can make hundreds or thousands of trades
- Small moves are easier to obtain - small moves happen all the time compared to large ones
- Less risky than larger moves - scalpers only hold positions for short periods therefore because they have less exposure the risk is also lower
- Spreads can be both bonuses and costs. Spread is the numerical difference between the bid and ask prices. Various parties and different strategies view spread as either trading bonuses or costs.

Pros

- Positions can be liquidated quickly, usually within minutes or seconds
- Very profitable when used as a primary strategy
- It's a low-risk strategy
- Scalpers are not exposed to overnight risks

Cons

- Requires an exit strategy especially during large losses
- Not the best strategy for beginners; it involves quick decision-making abilities.

4. Position Trading

Position trading involves holding a position open for a long period expecting it to appreciate. Traders here can hold positions for weeks, months, or even years. Position traders are not concerned with short-term fluctuations; they are keener on long-term views that affect their positions. Position trading is not done actively. Most traders place an average of 10 trades a year.

This strategy seeks to capture full gains of long-term trading, which would result in an appreciation of their investment capital. Position traders use fundamental analysis, technical analysis, or a combination of both to make trading decisions. To succeed position, traders need plans in place to control risk as well as identify the entry and exit levels.

Pros

- Traders have a longer period to reap fruits.
- Trader's time is not on demand. Once the trade has been initiated, all they can do is wait for the desired outcome

Cons

- Traders may fall victim to opportunity costs because capital is usually tied up for longer periods.
- Position traders tend to ignore minor fluctuations, which can turn to trend reversals, a change in the price direction of a position.

Forex Trading Strategies

There are several types of forex strategies; however, it is important to choose the right one based preferred trading style to trade successfully. Some strategies work on short-term trades as well as long-term trades. The type of Forex strategies you choose depends on a few factors like:

- Entry points - traders need to determine the appropriate time to enter the market
- Exit point-trader need to develop rules on when to exit the market as well as how to get out of a losing position
- Time availability

If you have a full-time job, then you cannot use day trading or scalping styles

- Personal choices

People who prefer lower winning rates but larger gains should go for position trading while those who prefer higher winning rate but smaller gains can choose the swing trading

Common Forex Trading strategies include:

1. Range trading strategy

Range trading is one of the many viable trading strategies. This strategy is where a trader identifies the support and resistance levels and buys at the support level and sells at the resistance level. This strategy works when there is a lack of market direction or the absence of a trend. Range trading strategies can be broken down into three steps:

- **Finding the Range**

Finding the range uses the support and resistance zones. The support zone is the buying price of the security while the resistance zone price is the selling price of a security. A breakout happens in the event that the price goes beyond the trading range, whereas a breakdown occurs in the event that the price goes below the trading range.

- **Time Your Entry**

Traders use a variety of indicators like price action and volume to enter and exit the trading range. They can also use oscillators like CCI, RSI, and stochastics to time their entry. The oscillators track prices using mathematical calculations. Then the traders wait for the prices to reach the support or resistance zones. They often strike when the momentum turns price in the opposing direction.

- **Managing Risk**

The last step is risk management. When the level of support or resistance breaks, traders will want to exit any range-based positions. They can either use a stop loss above the previous high or invert the process with a stop below the current low.

Pros

- There are ranges that can last even for years producing multiple winning trades.

Cons

- Long-lasting ranges are not easy to come by, and when they do, every range trader wants to use it.
- Not all ranges are worth trading

2. Trend Trading Strategy

Another popular and common Forex Trading strategy is the trend trading strategy. This strategy attempts to make profits by analyzing trends. The process involves identifying an upward or downward trend in a currency price movement and choosing trade entry and exit points based on the currency price within the trend.

Trend traders use these four common indicators to evaluate trends; moving averages, relative strength index (RSI), On-Balance-Volume (OBV), and Moving Average Convergence Divergence (MACD). These indicators provide trend trade signals, warn of reversals, and simplify price information. A trader can combine several indicators to trade.

Pros

- Offers a better risk to reward
- Can be used across any markets

Cons

- Learning to trade on indicators can be challenging.

3. Pairs Trade

This is a neutral trading strategy, which allows pair traders to gain profits in any market conditions. This strategy uses two key strategies:

- Convergence trading - this strategy focuses on two historically correlated securities, where the trader buys one asset forward and sells a similar asset forward for a higher price anticipating that prices will become equal. Profits are made when the underperforming position gains value, and the outperforming position's price deflates
- Statistical trading - this is a short-term strategy that uses the mean reversion models involving broadly diversified Security

Portfolios. This strategy uses data mining and statistical methods.

Pros

- If pair trades go as expected investors can make profits

Cons

- This strategy relies on a high statistical correlation between two securities, which can be a challenge.
- Pairs trade relies a lot on historical trends, which do not depict future trends accurately.

4. Price Action Trading

This Forex Trading strategy involves analyzing the historical prices of securities to come up with a trading strategy. Price action trading can be used in short, medium, and long periods. The most commonly used price action indicator is the price bar, which shows detailed information like high and low-price levels during a specific period. However, most traders use more than one strategy to recognize trading patterns, stop-losses, and entry, and exit levels. Technical analysis tools also help price action traders make decisions.

Pros

- No two traders will interpret certain price action the same way

Cons

- Past price history cannot predict future prices accurately

5. Carry Trade Strategy

Carry trade strategy involves borrowing a low-interest currency to buy a currency that has a high rate; the goal is to make a profit with the interest rate difference. For example, one can buy currency pairs like the Japanese yen (low interest) and the Australian dollar (high interest) because the interest rate spreads are very high. Initially, carry trade was used as a one-way trade that moved upwards without reversals, but carry traders soon discovered that everything went downhill once the trade collapsed.

With the carry trade strategy:

1. You need to first identify which currencies offer high rates and which ones have low rates.
2. Then match two currencies with a high-interest differential
3. Check whether the pair has been in an upward tendency favoring the higher-interest rate currency

Pros

- The strategy works in a low volatility environment.
- Suitable for a long-term strategy
- **Cons**
- Currency rates can change anytime
- Ricky because they are highly leveraged
- Used by many traders therefore overcrowded

6. Momentum Trading

This strategy involves buying and selling assets according to the strength of recent price trends. The basis for this strategy is that an asset price that is moving strongly in a given direction will continue to move in the same direction until the trend loses strength. When assets reach a higher price, they tend to attract many investors and traders who push the market price even higher. This continues until large pools of sellers enter the market and force the asset price down. Momentum traders identify how strong trends are in a given direction. They open positions to take advantage of the expected price change and close positions when the prices go down.

There are two kinds of momentum:

- Relative momentum - different securities within the same class are compared against each other, and then traders and investors buy strong performing ones and sell the weak ones.
- Absolute momentum - an asset's price is compared against its previous performance.

Pros

- Traders can capitalize on volatile market trends
- Traders can gain high profit over a short period
- This strategy can take advantage of changes in stock prices caused by emotional investors.

Cons

- A momentum investor is always at a risk of timing a buy incorrectly.
- This strategy works best in a bull market; therefore, it is market sensitive
- This strategy is time-intensive; investors need to keep monitoring the market daily.
- Prices can shift in a different direction anytime

7. Pivot Points

This strategy determines resistance and support levels using the average of the previous trading sessions, which predict the next prices. They take the average of the high, low, and closing prices. A pivot point is a price level used to indicate market movements. Bullish sentiment occurs when one trades above the pivot point while bearish sentiment occurs when one trades below the pivot point.

Pros

- Traders can use the levels to plan out their trading in advance because prices remain the same throughout the day
- Works well with other strategies

Cons

- Some traders do not find pivot points useful
- There is no guarantee that price will stop or reverse at the levels created on the chart

8. Fundamental Analysis

This strategy involves analyzing the economic, social, and political forces that may affect the supply and demand of an asset. Usually, people use supply and demand to gauge which direction the price is headed to. The Fundamental analysis strategy then analyzes any factors that may affect supply and demand. By assessing these factors, traders can determine markets with a good economy and those with a bad one.

Forex Strategies for Beginners

When starting on Forex Trading, it important to keep things simple. As a beginner, avoid thinking about money too much and focus on one or two strategies at a time. The following three strategies are easy to understand and perfect for beginners.

1. Inside Bar Trading Strategy

This highly effective strategy is a two-bar price action strategy with an inside bar and a prior/mother bar. The inside bar is usually smaller and within the high and low range of the prior bar. There are many variations of the inside bar, but what remains constant is that the prior bar always fully engulfs the inside bar. Although very profitable, the inside bar setup does not occur often.

There are two main ways you can trade using inside bars:

- As a continuation move - This is the easiest way to trade inside bars. The inside bars are traded in trending markets following the direction of the trend.

- As a reversal pattern - the inside bars are traded counter-trend

When using this strategy, it is important to look for these characteristics when evaluating the pattern:

- Time frame matters - avoid any time frame less than the daily.
- Focus on the breakout - best inside bar trades happen after a break of consolidation where the preceding trend is set to resume.
- The trend Is your friend - trading with the trend is the only way to trade an inside bar
- A favorable risk to reward ratio is needed when trading an inside bar
- The size of the inside bar in comparison to the prior bar is extremely important

2. Pin Bar Trading Strategy

This strategy is highly recommended for beginners because it is easy to learn due to a better visual representation of price action on a chart. It is one of the easiest strategies to trade. Pin bars show a reversal in the market and, therefore, can be useful in predicting the direction of the price. Pin bars consist of one price bar, known as a candlestick price bar, which represents a sharp reversal and rejection of price. Candlestick charts are the clearest at showing price action.

There are various ways traders trading with pin bars can enter the market:

- At the current market price

- Using an on-stop entry
- At limit entry, which is at the 50% retrace of the pin bar

To improve your odds when using the pin bar strategy:

- Trade with the trend
- Wait for a break of structure
- Trade from an area of value

Some of the mistakes pin bar traders should avoid include the following:

- Assuming the market will reverse because of a pin bar
- Focus too much on the pin bars and miss out on other trading opportunities
- All pin bars are not the same and should not be treated as such

3. Forex Breakout Strategy

A breakout strategy is where investors find stocks that have built strong support or resistance level, wait for a breakout, and enter the market when momentum is in their favor. This strategy is important because it can offer expansions in volatility, major price moves, and limited risk. A breakout occurs when the price moves beyond the support or resistance level. The breakout strategy is good for beginners because they can catch every trend in the market. Breakouts occur in all types of market environments.

Traders establish a bullish position when prices are set to close above a resistance level and a bearish position when prices close below a support level. Sometimes traders can be caught on a false breakout, and the only way to determine if it is a false breakout is to wait for confirmation. False breakout prices usually go beyond the support and resistance level; however, they return to a prior trading range by the end of the day.

Good investors plan how they will exit the markets before establishing a position. With breakouts, there are two exit plans:

- Where to exit with profit-traders can assess the stock recent behaviors to determine reasonable objectives. When traders meet their goals, they can exit the position. They can either raise a stop-loss to lock in profits or exit a portion of the position to let the rest run
- Where to exit with a loss - breakout trading show traders clearly when a trade has failed, and therefore they can determine where to set stop-loss order. Traders can use the old support or resistance level to close a losing trade

Pros

- You can catch every trend in the market
- ·Prices can quickly move in your favor

Cons

- Traders can get caught in a false breakout
- It can be difficult to enter a trade

Tips for trading breakouts:

- Never sell on breakdown or buy on breakout both carry extreme risks
- Trade with the trend
- Wait for higher volume to confirm a breakout
- Take advantage of volatility cycles
- Enter on the retest of support or resistance
- Have a predetermined exit plan

Note

Beginners are more likely to be successful in trade than their experienced counterparts are because they have not yet cultivated any bad habits. Experienced traders have to break bad habits and put aside any emotions built over the years.

Chapter 7: Forex Trading Signals

How can a forex trader find out which Forex pair and time frame is best to buy or sell? For starters, the forex trader can move from one chart to another to identify the forex market trend. However, in view of the fact that markets change from time to time, switching through charts can be a tedious exercise. Additionally, some patterns may be erratic and unpredictable, and therefore fail to make a profit.

Nevertheless, if a forex trader could find a way to examine all the currency pairs swiftly and time frames to find the best trend, he or she can expect a dramatic increase in profitability in any method he or she trades. Forex Trading signals can help forex traders make such critical decisions about profiting from their investments.

What Are Forex Trading Signals?

Put simply, Forex Trading signals are guidelines and recommendations that help inexperienced forex traders to open Forex Trading positions. The signals are a type of system that forex traders use to make crucial decisions about their trade. In that regard, Forex Trading signals provide details about how to open a new Forex Trade.

Examples of such details include details about which currency pair to trade, when to open the trade (open date), whether to buy or sell (position), and information on the opening price. In addition, they provide details on the stop-loss level to set if the forex market starts to experience loses, and the target profit level, that is, the point at which the trade should close so that forex traders can secure their profits.

Accurate and timely signals help forex traders to have success in their trade, whereas wrong signals reduce the opportunity for forex traders to earn and to make profits from their investments.

Forex Trading signals send email alerts that show trading arrangements for the next 24-hours. Various Forex Trading signals providers give free trial services that allow currency traders to become familiar with signal illustrations to calculate the values of the currencies. In that way, currency traders are able to evaluate the quality and the reliability of the Forex Trading signals before traders can pay subscription money.

When looking through Forex signals services, the forex trader must ensure that the Forex Trading signal provider offers the type of signals the forex trader needs.

Types of Forex Trading Signals and How They Work

Each signal is different from the other, and every forex trader needs to have a basic idea of the operation of the two types of Forex Trading signals. A forex trader can choose the type of signal to use, depending on his or her needs and depending on the signal's function.

Manual Forex Trading Signals

Manual forex signals require human traders to analyze the market before Forex signal providers distribute the signals. The human traders comprise of a team of financial analysts and experienced forex traders who carry out Forex market analysis and open the trading signals.

When the traders receive signals, they log into their Forex account and key in the trades. That means that the trader will need to be available at all times to key in the trades.

What are the benefits of Manual Forex Trading Signals?

Higher Profit Targets: The profit targets in manual trading signals are typically more significant than in the automated trading signals unless the signal provider uses a scalping tactic. Profit targets help forex traders to reduce risk by establishing a target price when the forex trader wants to take profits on a trade.

Consequently, manual signals that large financial institutions offer their clients target hundreds of pips when the high-frequency signals target fractions of a pip. A pip is short for 'point in percentage,' and it is a significantly small measure of variation in a currency pair in the Forex market.

For example, if a currency sells at 3.6997, and buys at 3.6999, then the pip is 2.

Useful Trading Tools: Manual trading signals are indicators that highlight excellent trading prospects. A forex trader can conduct his or her own forex market analysis, come up with his or her own plan and strategy, and use the manual signals to crosscheck his or her evaluation.

The use of manual signals also enables the forex trader to sort out risk levels depending on the conditions of the forex market. A forex trader is in charge of all the trading functions. Therefore, when the forex market is volatile, the forex trader can reduce the number of currency units that he or she will buy, and increase the size once the market stabilizes.

Profitable Risk-Reward Ratios: Risk – reward ratios measure how much a forex trader's potential reward is, for every amount of money that he or she risks. For example, if a forex trader has a risk-reward ratio of 1:5, it means that the forex trader is risking $1 to make $5 theoretically. It is, however, not definite that the trader will earn $5.

Consequently, manual signals often provide risk-reward ratios of 1:1 or better, compared to the automated signals, which give a minimum of 1:2 risk-reward ratio. Even with a risk-reward ratio of 1:0.5, a forex trader stands to gain $0.5 for every dollar he or she trades over the long term.

Trading News Releases: Trading news is an approach to buy or sell equities, currencies, and other financial instruments in the forex markets. Manual forex traders issue out outcomes of the news releases in ways that offer significant winning potential.

Manual forex traders or financial analysts examine news reports and identify the causes that will cause the forex market to move in a specific direction. Therefore, the forex signal providers issue out manual signals from the financial analysts, which predict what numbers, will be released.

With such expectation, forex investors start trading before the release of the actual numbers. That is unlike using trading robots, which are not always able to trade the outcomes of the news releases.

Flexibility: Manual Forex Trading signals have the capacity to adjust to market changes and fluctuations. Forex investors make profits by buying or selling as many currencies as they can.

Consequently, when a forex investor receives a manual trading signal for a trade, which appears to be heading in a profitable direction, the forex signal provider may extend that take profit level and increase the profit productively. Thus, manual Forex Trading signals provide forex investors with suck kind of flexibility in the forex market.

Human Experience: One of the most positive aspects of manual Forex Trading signals is human intelligence and expertise, which cannot compare to that of computers. Many skilled forex traders have a good feel of the forex market and can, therefore, tell the best time for buying or selling to gain profitable trades. Robots do not often perceive such upward or downward trends.

Because crowd psychology drives the forex market, human reasoning ingrains manual trading signals. As a result, the manual signals can manipulate the market trends for maximum profitability.

What are the shortcomings of Manual Forex Trading Signals?

Manual trading signals are suitable for extending profit targets, but the process of issuing out signals can be time-consuming. Even though manual signal providers may not need to conduct all the forex market analysis, they still have to open the Forex Trading platform and carry on with the trading business.

Additionally, manual signal providers are not able to follow the manual signals distributed during nighttime or work hours. In addition, manual trading signal providers do not have extensive coverage of a variety of other currency pairs. That is because many signal providers focus their attention on significant currency pairs, thus leaving out other financial instruments that include cryptocurrencies, stock indices, and commodities.

Automated Forex Trading Signals

Automated Forex signals have robotic programs, which analyze the market before the forex signal providers issue out the signals.

Due to the impracticality of trading forex on a part-time basis, many forex investors, brokers, and independent financial institutions have created trading systems that distribute forex signals that tell the user when to trade.

With automated Forex Trading, buying or selling can be as simple as pushing a button or making a telephone call to the signal provider.

What are the benefits of Automated Forex Trading Signals?

It Does Not Involve Any Paperwork: Signal providers do not go through any complex processes involving paperwork, in order for them to get started on distribution signals.

It Saves Time: A person does not have to remain transfixed on their computer monitors or screens all day long to buy or sell. The automated trading robot takes care of all the tasks 24-hours a day.

Similarly, one does not have to spend time coming up with his or her own trading plan. Instead, a person can choose to follow a forex trader who has a similar Forex Trading strategy and risk profile as his or her own. In that way, the person will have more time to set trades and to keep an eye on different forex markets.

In addition, forex traders and signal providers do not have to worry about missing trades because automated trading performs trades much faster than any human being.

Passive Trading: Automated Forex Trading signals are not subject to any human emotions, and therefore, are a clear-cut set of rules to follow.

Easily Accessible to Beginners: Precise automated forex signals help beginner forex traders to learn how experienced traders buy or sell. Beginners can achieve this by replicating the trades of the more experienced traders who have shared their successful strategies.

Similarly, beginners do not need to have minimum balances in their Forex Trading accounts to begin trading. Furthermore, automated signals can boost the confidence of beginner traders concerning the forex market. Beginner traders can relate their analysis to that of their signal's provider and thereby learn more about Forex Trading while accumulating profits.

Independent Control of Trading Account: Only the forex traders and signal providers can access their accounts. What's more, traders sign in the account in their name, and they do not have to give a power of attorney to any other person.

Back-Testing Trading Strategies: Trading robots have the ability to use historical data to evaluate the viability of a trading strategy and thus finding out how the plan will play out in the forex market.

Forex traders can fine-tune such strategies to yield outcomes that are more positive. When the trading robot performs the back-testing, signal providers can confidently open their trade because the providers will have a better idea of how the trading robots will perform in the future.

What are the disadvantages of Automated Forex Trading Signals?

Automated Forex Trading signals are not flexible. There are times when a forex investor may need to manipulate a trade or to forego a deal when the market goes in the opposite direction.

For example, when news breaks out about a hurricane hitting the investor's country, the investor will know that the trading platform will not remain stable. As a result, the investor may end up making losses following the effects the hurricane will have on assets sold on the trading platform.

Additionally, an automated Forex Trading account can breakdown potentially creating significant issues. A computerized trading account can stop endorsing trades, thus leaving trades to linger or cause the system to crash entirely. Alternatively, the automated account can have a technical error or a virus in the software where forex traders can lose all the money in their accounts at once.

How to Choose the Best Trading Signals

How can one know how to choose the best trading signals? Below are the factors a person should consider in making that decision.

The Regularity of Trading Signals: In the search for the best trading signals in the forex market, a trader should look for signal providers who issue favorable trading signals and alerts recurrently. That is because signals will not take too long to appear even if a person misses one or two signals. In that way, a trader can become consistent with his or her trading.

Variety of Financial Instruments: Signal providers who offer signals on diverse financial tools make it possible for a forex trader to choose investments from a wide range of options. Outstanding trading signals on commodities, currency pairs, stock indices, and cryptocurrencies give forex traders access to various financial instruments across different asset classifications.

Negligible Drawdowns: Choose signal providers who have minimal and negligible consecutive losing trades, but have solid equity growth curves. That will help in producing excellent performance in terms of investment profitability.

Constant Profits: It is essential to identify trading signals with excellent and consistent trading outcomes. A forex trader can accomplish this by choosing signal providers who are experts at analyzing the forex market and are therefore able to adapt to the continually changing market conditions.

Experienced signal providers demonstrate a focused effort in providing regular forex signals of the highest quality.

Therefore, how can a person know how to choose the best Forex Trading signal providers?

Credible Profitability History: Is there evidence of unrealistic profits? A forex trader should smell a rat when a signal provider issues out signals with five or more pips profit from a trade. That level of profit would be unrealistic and not trustworthy.

Consequently, a forex trader should search for signal providers who have authenticated track records. The best option would be to verify the track records through third-party online verification facilities.

The Timing of the Signal: It is wise for a forex trader to outline the schedule of the signals. That is because the trader may not have a lot of time to spend in front of his or her computer waiting for the signal provider to issue out a signal.

In order not to miss out on signals, a forex trader should check the signal provider's time zone and master the times during which the signal provider sends out signals. That is an important consideration to think about before signing up for a Forex Trading signal service.

Trial periods can help a forex trader to know the times the signal providers distribute signals.

Free Trial Period: It would be wise for a person to choose a signal provider who gives a free trial period. That will prevent the person from getting into the market without knowing how the signals work and possibly risking all of his or her investment.

Knowing whether a signal provider is right or not helps a person to develop trust with the provider. Trial periods provide opportunities for a person to test the signals and to confirm whether the set-up of the signals conforms to his or her trading style.

Random Signals: Some Forex Trading signal providers distribute random signals that seem to have no apparent strategy. Robots could generate such signals, which may lack thorough analysis.

Consequently, a forex trader should evaluate the trading positions of the signals – are they long-term or short-term? In addition, the trader should check to see whether the signals are founded on technical analysis, or fundamental analysis, or a mix of both. Therefore, a person should evaluate signals to know whether they will be suitable for his or her trading style.

Details About the Signal Performance: Are the details short and simple? Aspects such as entry point, stop loss, and take profits should be easily understandable so that a forex trader can visualize all the factors to decide whether a signal is lucrative and appropriate.

The best Forex Trading signals, therefore, take into account definitions and forex market assessments that associate with the Forex Trading signals. Forex traders may not feel confident to use signals that do not explain why a forex trader should open a particular trade.

Are the Signals Easy to Follow? Forex Trading signals that are easy to follow are those that are in a well-organized format. The structure will, therefore, have definite entry and exit prices and stop loss figures. These will help in financial management and the steady growth of a forex trader's trading account.

Additionally, the signal provider should post Forex Trading videos, webinars, and watch lists for additional customer support. Similarly, Forex Trading signal providers should be willing to answer all questions that pertain to trade formats and signals.

Should Forex Traders Use Free Forex Signals or Paid Forex Signals

Free forex signals and paid forex signals differ in terms of quality. Individuals who sell other products tend to issue out free forex signals. Therefore, although the individuals' free forex signals may work in getting a person interested in investing in Forex Trading training, the individuals have absolutely no interest in the quality of the signals themselves.

Additionally, free forex signal providers offer free trials that give beginners limited information that leaves the beginners wanting to learn more. Learning Forex Trading requires a lot of effort, which can yield positive outcomes. Consequently, even the best free Forex Trading signals do not teach beginners how to trade, because they cause the beginners to depend on other forex traders.

With paid forex signals, a person gets the experience he or she paid for. Paid forex signals give beginner traders access to support. For instance, when paid forex signals act unreliably, signal providers will provide the beginners with direction unlike using free forex signals where beginner traders will have no forthcoming support.

Therefore, a forex trader should not trust providers that guarantee results without proof. Genuine signal providers should be willing to share their performance history. Paid services provide helpful information for beginners to help them to become knowledgeable in forex money matters and the management of risks. Such data can be valuable to beginner traders who would like to control their investment directly in the future.

Forex Trading signals are instrumental in helping forex traders conduct market analysis within a short period. Similarly, forex signals mean that a trader will not have to sit down for extended hours waiting to get his or her outcomes. Moreover, forex traders can build their career within the first few months of their trading experience.

Chapter 8: Tips to Winning in Forex Trading

To the uninitiated, navigating the forex market successfully can seem like a difficult task. However, success is possible if one takes the right steps and trains properly. Just like training for a marathon, training is essential to winning in Forex Trading. Success requires targeted effort, practice, patience, and time.

Forex traders need to have specific goals in mind. With the right direction, training, and guidance, mastering the foreign exchange market is within anyone's reach. Winning at Forex Trading has little to do with hot picks, which are often fallacies created by people masquerading as experts in this field.

On the contrary, success stems from the ability to learn from both right and wrong trading choices to determine the patterns and strategies that work best for one's personality and goals. People are different; therefore, no single trading strategy will work for everyone.

Fortunately, there are several tips for winning in Forex Trading that can help beginners master the complexities of the largest market in the world. Actually, in terms of the value of average daily trading volume, the FX market dwarfs the bond and stock markets. Forex traders, therefore, have several inherent advantages over traders who engage in other forms of financial trading.

Small investors with modest capital can find success and trade their way to a fortune. The forex market is one of the few markets that can make this a reality. Trading the forex market is relatively easy. Doing it well and generating a consistent income, however, is not so easy. Therefore, it is important to learn the secrets and tips for success.

Tips and Secrets for Success in Forex Trading

1. Pay Attention to Daily Pivot Points

Forex traders should watch daily pivot points closely. This is especially important for day traders. However, it is also important for swing traders, position traders, and even traders who focus on long-term positions. It is important to do so because tons of other forex traders do the same.

In a certain way, pivot trading is like a self-fulfilling prophecy. Essentially, markets often find resistance or support at pivot points since thousands of pivot traders place orders at those points. Consequently, when a large volume of trading moves happens at these points or levels, there is no other reason for the move except that many traders placed orders expecting such a move.

However, pivot points should not be the only basis of a Forex Trading strategy. Rather, regardless of one's strategy, one should watch these points for signs of either potential market or continuation of a trend. Forex traders should look at pivot levels and the trading activities that take place around them as a confirming indicator to use in conjunction with their chosen strategy.

2. Define Trading Style and Goals

Before setting out on any journey, travelers need to have a clear idea of where they are going and how to get to their destination. In the same way, forex traders need to have clear goals, in addition to ensuring that their trading strategies will help them achieve those goals.

Each Forex Trading style or strategy comes with a different risk profile. Therefore, traders who want to win in Forex Trading need to find and adopt the right approach and attitude to trade profitably. Those who cannot imagine going to sleep with an open market position, for example, should consider focusing on day trading.

Forex traders with funds they believe will benefit from a trade appreciation over several months; on the other hand, they should think about position trading. Essentially, it is important for a forex trader to determine whether his/her personality will fit any particular trading strategy. Any mismatch will probably lead to certain losses and stress.

3. Trade with an Edge

Successful forex traders only risk their hard-earned money when a market opportunity provides them with an edge. In other words, they do so when the opportunity presents them with something that will boost the chances of their trades being successful. This edge can be various things, even a simple thing, such as selling at a price level that one identifies as strong resistance.

Forex traders can also increase their probability of success and their edge by having several technical factors in their favor. If the 100-period, 50-period, and 10-period moving averages all meet at the same price level, for example, it will likely offer significant resistance or support for a market because many traders will be acting together by trading off any of those averages.

Converging technical indicators also provide a similar edge. This happens when different indicators on many periods converge to provide resistance or support. Having the price hit an identified resistance or support level, in addition to having price movement at that level, is an indication of a potential market reversal.

4. The Trading Platform and Broker

Forex traders should spend adequate time researching a suitable trading platform and a reputable broker. It is important to identify and understand the difference between brokers and determine how each of them goes about making a market, as well as their policies. Trading the exchange-driven market, for example, is different from trading in the spot market or OTC market.

Traders should also choose the trading platform that fits the analysis they want to do. Traders who want to use Fibonacci numbers to trade, for example, should ensure the trading platform they choose has the ability to draw Fibonacci lives. A good platform with a bad broker is just as bad as a poor trading platform with a good broker. Therefore, forex traders need to find the best of both.

5. Preserve Capital

It is more important for traders to avoid huge losses than to make huge profits. For people who are new to Forex Trading, this concept may not sound quite right. However, it is important to understand that winning in Forex Trading means knowing how to preserve or protect one's capital.

According to the founder of Tudor Corporation, Paul Tudor Jones, playing great defense is the most important rule of trading. Actually, he is a great trader to learn from and study. In addition to building a hugely successful hedge fund, Tudor Jones has an excellent record of profitable trading.

He also played an important role in creating the ethics-training program needed to gain membership in all futures exchanges in the United States. Protecting the trading capital, or playing great defense, is very important in Forex Trading because many people who venture into Forex Trading are unable to continue trading as a result of running out of money.

Many forex traders drain their accounts soon after they make a few trades. Having strict risk management practices is important for people who want to win in Forex Trading. Traders who manage to preserve their trading capital are able to continue trading for as long as they want to, and might eventually become huge winners.

One great trade can fall into a trader's lap and significantly increase his/her profits and account size. One does not need to be the smartest trader in the world to make money in the forex market. If nothing else, the luck of the draw can have traders who manage to protect their capital stumble into trades that generate enough profits to make their trading careers a huge success.

6. Small Losses and Focus

After forex traders fund their trading accounts, they need to understand that their capital is at risk. Therefore, they should not depend on that money for their daily living expenses. Actually, it is better to think of those funds as vacation funds. Once their vacation is over, their money is gone.

Having this trading attitude will help prepare them to accept and learn from small losses, which will also help them manage their risk better. Forex traders should focus on their trades and accept small losses, which are normal in any type of business, rather than constantly and obsessively focusing on their equity.

7. Simple Technical Analysis

Consider this example of two forex traders in extremely different situations. The first trader has a specially designed trading computer with several monitors, a large office, swanky furnishings, trading charts, and market news feeds. He also has several moving averages, technical indicators, momentum indicators, and much more.

The other trader, on the other hand, works from a relatively simple office space and uses a regular desktop or laptop computer. His charts reveal just one or two technical indicators on the price action of the market.

Most people would consider the first trader to be more professional and extremely successful, and they would probably be wrong in their assumption. Actually, the second trader is closer to the image of a forex trader who wins consistently. Traders can apply numerous forms of technical analysis to a chart. Having more, however, does not necessarily mean having better.

Using a huge number of indicators might actually make things more complicated and confusing for a forex trader. They amplify indecision and doubt, causing him/her to miss many potentially profitable trades. Therefore, it is better to have a simple trading strategy with just a few rules, as well as a minimum of indicators to consider.

A few very successful forex traders make money from the forex market almost every day without using any technical indicators overlaid on their charts. They achieve this impressive feat without taking advantage of a relative strength indicator, trend lines, trading robots, moving averages, or expert advisors. Their market analysis involves a simple candlestick chart.

8. Weekend Analysis

The forex market ceases operation on the weekend. Therefore, forex traders should use this time to study their weekly charts to identify news or patterns that could affect their trades in either a positive or a negative way. This will give the objectivity, which will help them make smarter trading plans.

9. Placing Stop-Loss Orders at the Right Price Levels

In addition to protecting one's capital in case of a losing trade, this strategy is also an important aspect of smart Forex Trading. Many newcomers to the forex market assume that risk management simply means placing stop-loss orders close to the entry point of their trades. This is partly accurate; however, habitually placing stop-loss orders too close to their trade entry points is something that might contribute to their lack of success.

Sometimes, stop-loss orders can stop a trade, only to see the market make a reversal in favor of the trade. It is common for novice traders to endure watching this happen. Sometimes, this reversal proceeds to a level that would have seen them gain a sizable profit if the stop-loss order had not terminated the trade.

Obviously, traders should enter trades that allow them to place stop-loss orders close enough to their trade entry points to avoid making huge losses. However, they should place them at a reasonable price level, based on their analysis of the market. When it comes to reasonable placement of stop-loss orders, the general rule of thumb is to place them a bit further than the price the market should not trade at, based on market analysis.

10. Use a Consistent Methodology

Before a prospective trader enters the forex market, he/she needs to have a good idea of how he/she will make trading decisions. Essentially, forex traders should know the information they will need to make smart decisions on entering a trade or exiting one. Some traders choose to analyze a chart and the fundamental of the economy to decide the best time to trade.

Others, however, prefer to perform technical analysis to determine the ideal time to execute a trade. Whichever methodology or strategy a trader chooses to employ, he/she needs to be consistent and ensure the chosen methodology is adequately adaptive. In other words, it should be flexible enough to handle the forex market's changing dynamics.

11. Choosing the Right Entry and Exit Points

Most inexperienced forex traders do not know how to judge conflicting information that often presents when analyzing charts in various timeframes. Certain information, for example, might indicate a sell signal on a weekly chart, but show up as a purchasing opportunity in an intraday chart.

Therefore, if a trader is using a weekly chart to determine his/her basic trading direction and a daily chart to tie his/her entry, then he/she should try to synchronize the two charts. If the weekly chart is providing a buy signal, for example, he/she should wait for the daily chart to confirm this signal. In other words, keeping signal timing in sync is a good tip for winning in Forex Trading.

12. Calculating Expectancy

The formula to use to determine the reliability of a trading system is expectancy. Forex traders should analyze and compare past winning trades against losing trades, which will help them determine the profitability of their winning trades versus how much money they lost in their losing trades.

A simple way to do this is by looking at their last 10 trades. New forex traders who have not yet made any trades should study their chart to identify points where their trading system suggests an entry and/or exit point. In other words, new forex traders need to determine whether their system is profitable.

Having done this, they should write down their observations, total their winning trades, and divide the amount by the number of successful trades they made. For example, if a trader made 10 trades, four of which flopped, and six of which were successful, his/her win ratio would be 60% or 6/10. If the six winning trades made $4,800, then his/her average win would be $4,800/6 = $800.

If the trader's losses amounted to $2,400, then his/her average loss would be $2,400/4 = $600. By applying these results to the formula for calculating the reliability of a system, the trader will get E = [1 + (800/600) x 0.6 − 1 = 0.4, which is equivalent to 40%. A positive expectancy of 40% means that the trader's trading system will likely generate 40 cents to the dollar over the long term.

13. Positive Feedback Loops

Forex traders create a positive feedback loop following a well-planned and executed trade. When they plan a trade and execute it as expected, traders tend to create a pattern of positive feedback. In other words, success tends to breed success, which, in turn, builds confidence. This is especially true if the trade generates significant profits.

Even if a trader suffers a small loss following a well-planned trade, he/she will still build a positive feedback loop.

14. Keeping Printed Records

Printed records serve as a good learning tool for forex traders. Therefore, traders, especially new ones, should print their charts create a list of reasons for any particular trade, including the things that sway their trading decisions. They should mark the entry and exit points on the chart and make any relevant comments, such as emotional reasons for taking specific actions.

Forex traders need to objectify their trades to develop the discipline and mental control needed to execute trades according to their systems, instead of their emotions, greed, or habits.

15. Stress Less

This is an obvious Forex Trading tip. Trading the forex market under stress tends to lead to irrational decisions, which can end up costing a trader a lot of money. Therefore, forex traders should identify the source of their stress and try to get rid of it, or at least limit its influence on their actions.

When stress threatens to take control, a trader should take deep breaths and try to focus on other things for a few minutes. People have different ways of overcoming stress. Some exercise, while others listen to classical music. Traders should learn what works best for them.

Risk Management in Forex Trading

One of the most debated topics in financial trading is forex risk management. On one hand, forex traders want to get the most out of every trade, but on the other hand, they want to limit the size of a potential loss. Sometimes, traders need to take greater risks to gain the best returns. This is where the issue of risk management in Forex Trading arises.

Forex traders are in the business of making money. To do this, however, they need to learn how to limit potential losses. Unfortunately, many novice traders are just anxious to start trading without giving much thought to their total account size. They do not think of ways to minimize their potential losses before hitting the 'trade' button.

This type of investing is more akin to gambling. When forex traders make trades without following the rules of risk management, they are, in fact, gambling. They are hoping to land that jackpot, instead of focusing on the long-term returns on their investment. Risk management rules do not offer 100% protection; however, they can make traders very profitable in the end.

Consider this; people go to Las Vegas every day to gamble in hopes of winning a jackpot. Some do win; however, casinos still make tons of money. If people are winning big jackpots, how are casinos making so much money in the end? The answer is that they are still profitable because they earn more money from losing gamblers.

Casinos are excellent statisticians. They know that numerous gamblers will lose, and their money will be more than enough to pay for the jackpots won by the few successful gamblers. This is a good example of how casinos know how to control their losses. In the same way, forex traders need to know how to control their losses to improve their chances of being profitable.

Forex Trading, in the end, is a numbers game, which means that traders have to tilt every factor in their favor. Essentially, they need to be the statistician and not the gambler. Everyone knows that it takes money to make money. The money one needs to start trading largely depends on one's approach to a new trading business.

Losses are a reality of business, and traders will suffer some losses at some point in their career. This is the reason why it is important to have some risk management rules. Forex traders should only risk a small percentage of their accounts on each trade so that they can survive losses and avoid large drawdowns in their accounts.

New forex traders tend to assume that making money through Forex Trading is easy and fast. To find success in this business, however, traders need patience, commitment, dedication, and time. Traders should not just open trading positions without considering the currency risk, trading conditions, and risks that can affect their invested capital.

They need to use techniques and tools to manage their investments and risks. Those who fail to do this will be gambling instead of trading. Some of the best ways to manage risks in Forex Trading include:

1. Only Investing Money, one Does not Need

The first rule in any form of trading, including Forex Trading, is to invest the money one can afford to lose. Most beginners tend to skip or ignore this rule since they assume that it will not happen to them. Even gamblers do not take all their money to the casino to bet on black. Forex traders should not take unnecessary risks by investing the money they need.

Trading with money they need for their daily living expenses will only add emotional stress and extra pressure on their trading, which will affect their decision-making abilities and increase the likelihood of making costly mistakes. In addition, there is a chance they could lose all their trading capital.

The FX market is an unpredictable and volatile market; therefore, it is safer to trade conservative amounts from one's disposable income.

2. Think About Risk Tolerance

Before traders start trading, they need to identify and understand their risk tolerance, which will depend on the following:

1. Investment goals
2. Their age
3. How much they are willing to lose
4. Their experience
5. Their knowledge of the foreign exchange market

By determining their risk tolerance, forex traders will know they are in control of any situation because they are risking the right amount of money in terms of their financial objectives in relation to their personal financial situation.

3. Set Risk to Reward Ratio (RRR) to a Minimum of 1:3

Having a good understanding of the RR ratio will improve a trader's chances of being profitable, in addition to setting limit orders to protect his/her trading capital. The RR ratio compares and measures the distance between a trader's entry point and his/her take-profit and stop-loss orders.

For example, suppose that a trader is investing in the EUR/USD currency pair. If 50 pips is the distance between his/her entry point and stop-loss point, and 150 pips between the entry point and take-profit point, then he/she would be using a risk/reward ratio of 50:150, which is 1:3 because he/she is risking 50 pips to gain 150 pips.

The risk to reward ratio is an important tool to help traders set their take-profit and stop-loss orders, depending on their risk tolerance. Smart forex traders should control their downside risk. Although the RRR depends on a trader's risk tolerance, most traders use a ratio of 1:3, which means that they hope to earn 3 times what they are willing to lose.

4. Control the Risk per Trade

When thinking about their trading risks, forex traders should consider their trading capital. A smart risk management strategy would be to invest a small percentage of their trading capital in each trade. For example, 1% to 2% of their available capital per trade is a good starting point.

If a forex trader has $10,000 in his/her trading account, for example, the maximum loss allowable would be 2% of the available capital, which will amount to $200 per trade. Controlling the risk per trade is very helpful, especially if a trader goes through a losing streak. It helps forex traders to avoid huge drawdowns in their trading accounts and protect their trading capital.

5. Keep the Risk Consistent

As soon as they make their first profits, some forex traders, especially beginners, increase the size of their positions, which is a good way to wipe out their trading accounts. Forex traders should understand the importance of keeping their trading risk consistent. Just because a trader is on a winning streak does not mean that the next trade will make a profit.

Traders should avoid becoming risk-averse and over-confident since it can lead to them to change their risk and money management rules without good reasons. When they were working on their trading strategies, they probably set up rules to guide their trading positions. This is a necessary step towards setting up a winning trading strategy; however, they also need to stick to their rules to achieve long-term success.

6. Understand and Control Leverage

Due to its high volatility, the FX market is a leveraged market. In this case, leverage refers to the ability to invest more than the initial deposit through margin trading. Forex brokers will only ash traders to set aside a small amount of the total value of their positions as collateral.

By using leverage, traders can increase their profits quickly; however, they need to understand that this also applies to their losses. Therefore, they need to understand how margin trading and leverage work, in addition to how they affect their overall trading and performance.

However, using high leverage to generate huge profits, as some inexperienced traders do, is not a good idea. This is because a small change in the market can easily wipe out their trading accounts. In fact, the European Securities and Market Authority set limitations on the leverage brokers offer in August 2018.

7. Consider Currency Correlations

Since forex traders trade currency pairs, such as EUR/USD, it is important to understand the correlation between currencies linked to each other. Having a good understanding of currency correlations will help them control their trading portfolios more effectively by reducing the overall risk.

Correlation describes how one currency behaves in relation to another currency. When two currencies have a positive correlation, it means that they usually move in the same direction. Those with a negative correlation, on the other hand, will move in opposite directions.

To use currency correlations to their advantage, traders need to understand a few important things:

a) They should avoid opening several trading positions that conflict or cancel out each other

b) They should have a good understanding of commodity currencies
c) They should avoid opening trading positions with the same quote currency or base currency

No matter how unrealistic it may sound, many people going into Forex Trading expect to get rich overnight. The world of FX trading can be complicated and overwhelming, especially for beginners who do not know the rules. Before people go any deeper, they need to dip their toes into the forex pool.

Chapter 9: Cryptocurrency in Forex Trading

A cryptocurrency is a digital currency that acts as a medium of exchange. Currencies have gone through a series of changes since the barter system in the Stone Age period, to the paper currency in later years.

The term 'crypto' in cryptocurrency comes from the word 'cryptography.' Cryptography is a technique of using encryption and decryption as a means to safeguard communication in the company of third parties with ill motives. In order to work, cryptography requires a computational algorithm, a public key that the trader shares with everybody, and a private key, which acts like the trader's digital signature, which the trader keeps secret.

In Forex Trading, forex traders use cryptocurrencies as modes of payments and as trading instruments, forming currency pairs with other cryptocurrencies and currencies.

At this point, the future of currency could be cryptocurrencies. There are two major cryptocurrencies in the market: the bitcoin and ether. The bitcoin is a type of digital currency that is independent of a central authority. That is, the central bank does not regulate the distribution of bitcoins in the market. Instead, bitcoin uses a blockchain to carry out transactions on a peer-to-peer network.

Bitcoins started circulating in 2009, and its success has generated several competing cryptocurrencies called 'altcoins' or alternative coins. Altcoins include Litecoin (LTC), Namecoin, Peercoin (PPCoin), Ripple, EOS, and Cardano, among thousands of other cryptocurrencies currently in existence.

Ether is a type of currency that the Ethereum network acknowledges. Ethereum runs on blockchain technology to establish an open-source platform to create and redistribute applications that are decentralized, or independent of central authority.

Bitcoin and ether are the most significant and most valuable cryptocurrencies in the international market. While bitcoins transactions are manual, ether transactions can be both manual and automatic. A trader can use bitcoins for transactions involving goods and services, whereas ether uses blockchain to create ledgers that activate operations once a trader meets the required conditions.

Litecoin is similar to bitcoin in that Litecoin relies on an open-source global payment network that is not under any central authority's regulation. However, Litecoin has a more rapid block generation rate compared to bitcoin, since Litecoin uses a different algorithm.

Namecoin is more of an experimental open-source technology that boosts security, independence from a central regulating authority, censorship resistance, speed of internet infrastructure such as the Domain Name System (DNS), and privacy. Traders can use Namecoin to record and transfer random keys or names in a safeguarded manner.

It also has the ability to attach data to the random names. In that regard, Namecoin offers advanced privacy competences.

Peercoin (PPCoin) is one of the leading forms of cryptocurrencies with regard to market capitalization. It is the first digital currency that employs a combination of proof-of-work and proof-of-stake. The proof-of-stake algorithm formulates from the coins that individual traders hold. A trader holding 2% of the currency should receive a reward of 2% of all proof-of-stake coin blocks.

The proof-of-work blocks are less rewarding because the portion of the proof-of-work algorithm requires intensive energy for generating blocks compared to the minimal energy the proof-of-stake algorithm uses to create blocks. Consequently, the Peercoin network will become more energy-efficient as proof-of-stake rewards do not need a lot of processing power.

Ripple is both a cryptocurrency and a payment system. With regard to Ripple's cryptocurrency aspect, it follows an algorithm like every other cryptocurrency. Ripple's payment system makes it possible for users to transfer money in any currency to another user on the Ripple network in a matter of seconds. That means that Ripple transactions are much faster than other crypto coins, including bitcoin.

EOS is a robust infrastructure for decentralized applications that is blockchain-based and facilitates the development hosting and performance of economic-scale decentralized applications (dApps) on its platform. EOS uses the proof-of-stake idea to make instant high-level decisions among designated stakeholders.

Cardano is both a cryptocurrency and a decentralized platform that authorizes transactions without high-energy costs. Cardano seeks to safeguard the privacy of traders while being regulator-friendly. The platform uses the Ouroboros Pos algorithm to authenticate transactions.

Why use cryptocurrencies?

Little to No Operation Costs: When traders use traditional ways of carrying out transactions using paper currencies, they lose some amount of money when transferring currencies to or from bank accounts.

Cryptocurrencies have the lowest transaction fees, which amount to only about $2. An individual may encounter only three transaction fees. The charges include the exchange fees, the network fees, and the digital wallet fees when a person wants to store his or her crypto coins in the digital wallet.

24/7 Access to Money: Unlike using banks, individuals can access cryptocurrencies anytime, any day. Given that cryptocurrencies are not subject to any central authority, an individual can have access to the crypto coins any time of the day, even in the middle of the night.

Similarly, an individual can make unlimited purchases and withdrawals. That is contrary to using bank services where the bank places limits on the amount of money an individual can spend within 24-hours.

Available for Anyone: Billions of people around the world do not have access to bank accounts. However, many people have access to mobile phones and can use cryptocurrencies and blockchain technology to execute financial transactions through biometric, thus promoting prosperity.

Additionally, the process of signing up to use cryptocurrencies is brief and requires no paperwork.

Fast International Transactions: Unlike in banks, where transferring money from one place to another can take hours, transferring cryptocurrencies is a matter of seconds. That is because when moving cryptocurrency from one place to another, transactions do not need to go through all of the same checks and balances processes that banks follow before depositing funds.

Cryptocurrency transfers, whether within a country or outside the country, are quick and instant and do not require any transaction costs. Additionally, individuals can track their transactions in the blockchain.

High Privacy Levels: With cryptocurrencies, an individual does not have to provide personal information. That is contrary to banks, where individuals have to provide extensive personal data.

Moreover, individuals can carry out safe transactions because of the encryptions that go into the code of cryptocurrencies. Therefore, traders can have confidence in the cryptocurrencies security guarantee as more people use the specific blockchain.

People Have Control Over Their Own Money: Cryptocurrencies are not subject to the rules and regulations that the banks and other financial institutions enforce. If an individual remembers the password or the passphrase of his or her digital wallet, the cryptocurrencies are entirely under the control of the individual, and no one else can have access to the crypto coins.

Cryptocurrencies allow individuals to carry out trade with other people independently, without the presence of a third party or bank interference. That is because transactions with cryptocurrencies are peer-to-peer, meaning from people to people.

Reliable Alternative to Unstable Currencies: Cryptocurrencies does not bring about inflation and economic instability that individuals often experience from using traditional paper currencies. While not all individuals are subject to the incredible rates of inflation, other individuals can benefit greatly from shifting to use cryptocurrencies.

Many countries around the world allow the use of cryptocurrency, which is not affected by forex rates and interest rates. In fact, cryptocurrency offers more solidity and assurance to people living in economically unstable countries.

Accountability of Individuals and Companies: Regrettably, there are several business entities and big industries out in the business world, which allow corrupt and illegal business tendencies. Individuals want to ensure that they carry out their trades with honesty and integrity, upholding the trading rights and following the rules of conduct. However, trusting that a company or an individual has integrity based on the information they provide about themselves is not a reliable way to know the morals of their real practices.

Luckily, cryptocurrency introduces the blockchain technology that will change the way individuals and companies practice a trade — blockchain technology, which is not subject to change, unlike the traditional paper currency. Cryptocurrencies and blockchain technologies make companies and individuals answerable to clients. Moreover, traders get the opportunity to know more about the companies they trade with.

Strengthen E-Commerce: Given that many people like to carry out most of their transactions online nowadays, cryptocurrencies provide a safe option for shoppers to buy as many things as they would want, without concerns for fraud.

Cryptocurrencies not only reduce the risk of fraud for online shoppers, but they also protect the business vendors and merchandisers. Cryptocurrency transactions are permanent. That is because the cryptocurrency's electronic network ledger records the transactions. As a result, the transactions become irreversible and unchangeable, thus mitigating risk.

Additionally, using cryptocurrency creates endless opportunities for global commerce.

Secure Handling of Smart Contracts: Blockchain technology enables individuals to computerize practically every physical object or service in the blockchain. For example, when selling property, an individual can enter the value of the property into the blockchain and sell the property through automatic or smart contracts.

Consequently, banks, notaries, and financial advisors will no longer be necessary because individuals are able to carry out trades in faster and inexpensive ways. Additionally, an individual can securely manage his or her personal information in the blockchain and use it for taking loans, insurances, or even purchasing travel tickets.

Governments can also use automatic or smart contracts when giving out permits, when holding elections, and when collecting taxes, among other government tasks. Blockchain technology will also ensure transparency in government operations.

What are the disadvantages of using cryptocurrencies?

To begin with, cryptocurrency is a concept that is difficult to understand. People who are not tech-savvy may not understand how the blockchains work, or how blockchains store cryptocurrencies. In that regard, individuals are cautious of taking advantage of the benefits that cryptocurrency can offer.

As such, most people do not know the benefits of using cryptocurrency. However, it appears that, that more and more people are acquiring information about the digital currency. The response, therefore, is slow because people are not yet ready to make the switch from using banks to using cryptocurrency.

As more individuals enter into the cryptocurrency domain by acquiring their crypto every day, there is still a long way to go and a lot of work to do with regard to the teaching people how cryptocurrencies work. Consequently, a cryptocurrency needs to circulate the money market more, so that people can have exposure to it and they can begin to accept to use it

The other significant drawback that cryptocurrencies have is the challenge of constant fluctuations in their market prices. As a result, traders find it challenging to use the crypto because traders can never be entirely sure what the value of the crypto will be in the upcoming days.

Additionally, most traders do not accept digital money. That is because the concept of digital money is still new, and many traders do not trust digital money yet. What's more, many companies have not embraced the use of digital funds, even though cryptocurrency is a growing trend. The reason for that could be that companies are not willing to take a risk with the constantly changing prices. In addition, companies may not be aware of how cryptocurrency can generate profits.

Lastly, most people may not know where to get cryptocurrencies, how to store, and how to use the cryptos. Although people can search for information on cryptos online, the idea is that no person, young and old, should have any challenges when it comes to dealing with cryptocurrencies. Instead, the trade should become an organic or natural part of people's lives, the same way that paper currency is.

In conclusion, the rate at which the world is becoming technologically interconnected calls for a complete transformation in the process of buying and selling products and services. Cryptocurrencies are one of the ground-breaking innovations in the context of technological interconnectedness that will revolutionize global forex trade.

Consequently, more traders will accept cryptocurrencies, and more people will switch to using cryptos. In that way, cryptocurrencies have a huge potential to become the most widely used medium of exchange in the future.

Chapter 10: Examples of Trade

Forex trade involves a trader going long for the first currency and short for the second one. He or she purchases the first currency using money and then waits before selling it to make a profit. The trade takes place utilizing the current rates of exchange at the time of the transaction. Thus, the fluctuations in the exchange rates determine if the value of a particular currency is high or low. It helps a trader decide when to enter or exit a trade, or when to buy or sell a currency.

For example, a trader followed the prevailing GBP/USD exchange rates and paid USD 24,200 to purchase GBP 20,000 in mid-January 2017. The value of the British pound increased over the following months against the dollar. The trader then decided to sell the £20,000 that he has for approximately $27,000. He or she closed out his or her position and received USD 27,000. Thus, he or she made a profit of USD 2,800 because initially, he or she started with USD 24,200 and closed out with USD 27,000.

A trader can utilize various strategies and means to ensure that he or she achieves success in Forex Trading. He or she can use trading instruments such as disposable risks, leveraged features, spread bets, and CDF contracts. A CDF contract is a deal between two sides to trade the difference between the closing price and opening price of a contract. It stands for 'Contract for difference' and is a complicated, advanced, and high-risk instrument as a trader can experience a rapid loss due to leveraged features.

The following are some examples of forex trade and the outcomes that indicate a winning or losing trade:

Example 1

A trader can calculate his or her profits and losses when he or she closes out a forex trade. He or she finds the difference between the price of buying and selling the currency and multiplies it by the transaction size. The difference will determine whether he or she experiences a winning or a losing trade. For instance, a trader purchases Euros (EUR/USD) at 1.2166 and later sells them at 1.2156. The transaction size of that trade is 100,000 Euros. He or she will calculate the profit using the formula: ($1.2166 - $1.2156) × 100,000. This will lead to $0.001 × 100,000 = $100. Hence, his or her profit from that forex trade will be $100.

Likewise, the forex trader will calculate a loss if he or she sold the Euros (EUR/USD) at 1.2060 and buy them at 1.2070. He or she will use the formula ($1.2060 - $1.2070) × 100,000. This will give -$0.001 × 100,000 = -$100. Thus, he or she will have a loss of $100 from that trade.

Moreover, the trader can use the current bid to find out his or her unrealized losses and profits on open positions. He or she substitutes that bid accordingly in the formula to calculate the unrealized profit or loss. For example, if he or she purchased Euros at 1.2166, and the current rate of a bid is 1.2116, then his or her unrealized loss is $50. The calculation is ($1.2161 - $1.2166) × 100,000= -$0.0005 × 100,000 = $50. If he or she sold the Euros at 1.2060 and the current bid rate is 1.2055, the unrealized profit here is $50: ($1.2060 - $1.2055) × 100,000= $0.0005 × 100,000= $50.

The trader subtracts any extra charges in the transactions like commissions, to find out his or her exact profits and losses.

Example 2

A trader can transact in the forex market in terms of the amount of money he or she is willing to risk. He or she takes a certain amount from his or her investments fund account and uses it to trade. He or she can win and double the initial risked amount or not succeed and end up losing the money. For instance, a trader has $10,000 in his or her account as the money available as a disposable risk. During an investment, he or she decides to use $2,000 and ventures that amount in the forex trade.

The trader researches and finds out that the chances of achieving a profit goal of interest are 70%. He or she can then choose to invest that amount in the trade in two ways. First, he or she can risk the entire $2,000 and form a profit goal of $2,000 while going long at the opening. Additionally, he or she can also set a stop loss of $2,000 in the trade. If the deal succeeds, he or she wins an additional $2,000 in profits. Nonetheless, he or she may also lose the business, and the entire invested amount since the risk of failing, in this case, is at 30%.

The second way that the trader can invest the money is to split it and risk only $200 per trade. He or she also modifies the profit goal to $200. Thus, he or she can make ten trades and significantly reduce the chances of losing the entire $2,000 since the risk associated here is less than 1%.

Example 3

A forex trader can also use a leveraged instrument to trade, which provides him or her with a trading margin. He or she makes a profit if the trade moves in his or her direction margin. Conversely, he or she loses the deal if it pushes against the trader. For instance, a trader with an investment amount of $6,000 trades on a margin of 1:50. This margin means that he or she can practically manage a capital of $300,000.

A beginning trader utilizes a smaller margin of 1:20 to minimize the risks associated with contrasting trade moves that can result in a 100% loss of capital. Thus, he or she uses a margin of 1:20 with the initial money of $6,000, which enables him or her to control $120,000. He or she decides to bet that the USD will fall against the Euro and then enters a trade on a long side to transact the EUR/USD. The current exchange rate of the EUR/USD is 1.405, while he or she will practically be trading $120,000 to Euros. He or she calculates it by the 120,000/1.405 = 71,174 Euros.

Forex Trading involves several strategies that a trader can employ in the market. He or she can study the various ways of Forex Trading and select the ones that best suit his or her profit goal and trading tactics.

Chapter 11: Mistake That Beginners Make in Forex Trading

All traders have passed through the beginners' phase, and they have made their share of newbie mistakes. Most traders continue to make mistakes as they venture deep into trading, but smart ones view these mistakes as learning opportunities rather than sulk over then. People can be very emotional where their money is concerned, but it is important for traders to detach themselves from this mindset so that they can make rational decisions.

The occasional lapse is forgivable, but at the end of it all, the trader's money is at stake, so he or she should work hard to protect it and grow it. If you are new to trading, you can learn from those who have gone ahead of you and avoid some of the common mistakes that they have made which include:

1. Trading Without Much Knowledge

The first mistake that people make when they decide to try Forex Trading is getting into the forex market without proper knowledge of how to maneuver and make money. Forex Trading is something that takes years to master. In addition to trading knowledge, experts in trading have vast experience in trading. Although newbies might have the former and not the latter, they can still succeed in trading but with proper planning and guidance.

Investing in the forex market is similar to investing in a business. People hardly invest in sectors or businesses that they have little knowledge. They usually take their time to study how to conduct business in a particular area. People interested in Forex Trading should also treat trading as a business that they are interested in investing in. They should not forget that they need to protect their capital just as they would if they were putting it in a business venture by stocking up on information.

New traders can gather information from trading books, articles, and any other material available that touches on the subject. There are also people who offer classes in the form of webinars and seminars. Beginners can also practice with demo accounts. Successful traders are well informed; they know the markets they operate in as well as indicators and strategies for investing in the stock market.

2. Trading Without a Plan

Trading plans are very crucial in investing in the financial markets. They offer a trader with a guideline of how they will invest their money in the forex market. More specifically, they detail the amount of money a trader is willing to put in a trade, the market conditions that are favorable for a person to trade, the duration of stay in the market and the exact time to get out of the market either after experiencing a loss or even after making a profit. Without such guidelines, traders conduct their business blindly with no focus.

Many new beginners in Forex Trading are guilty of this mistake. They enter the forex market without any plan and wonder why they keep failing in the trade. New beginners can formulate trading plans then test them in a demo account. They can keep adjusting their plans as they see fit until they are ready to test in the real market.

Once a trader begins to use his plan, he should ensure that he follows it. This way, he is able to remain rational when trading and keep his emotions at bay. The stop loss and stop profit serve to guide the trader on when to exit the market to avoid losing money and when a trade has been exhausted. More importantly, as traders write down their plans, they should focus on the right goals. If chasing after huge profits are all a trader wants, then he or she is bound to get disappointed. Setting realistic goals is crucial, even if it means making a little consistent profit.

3. Lack of Money Management

New traders are at free will to decide how much they are willing to invest in a trade. However, a number of beginners overleverage their capital. They put money that they cannot afford to lose in a single trade and risk a huge percentage of their portfolio or investment in the trade. Since making profits is never guaranteed, there is always the risk of losing money or the entire investment if one is not careful about how they manage their money.

New traders should calculate how much money they are willing to risk in a single trade according to their risk appetite. They should not make some decisions on a whim. The best way is to have a guideline from the beginning, in the form of a trading plan. A trader should know how many trades he or she should enter at any one single time. Without understanding, his or her risk/reward ratio, or win/loss ratio, a trader can end up investing his or her capital in the wrong way and lose the entire investment.

Therefore, it is crucial that traders and especially the new ones to learn a few money management skills before they join the market; otherwise, they may not survive in trading.

4. Overtrading

Some new traders are very fond of overtrading. This can mean that they either trade with money that they do not have or risk a big portion of their investment in a single trade. Insufficient capitalization is dangerous and is ill-advised. Traders should only trade with money that they have and not money that does not exist or money they have borrowed.

It is always devastating for a trader to lose money that they did not have. This often leads to them borrowing money elsewhere to compensate for their loss, or they have to struggle to get back above the margins. Even when a trader begins to make money, they should have a guideline of how much of their profit they should reinvest back in the market and how much of their capital they should put back.

Another mistake new beginner is fond of making is trading when the markets are not favorable as stipulated in their trading plan. When traders deviate from their plans and get into markets that they should not, then it means that they are overtrading. New traders should not assume that their strategies are faulty when the markets do not favor even if it is for a long while. Instead of getting into shaky water, new traders should always choose to save their money over spending it then losing some of it.

5. Trading Without a Stop Loss

A stop loss is very important as it acts as a warning sign to a trader and tells him or her when to stop trading because of the risk of losing further amounts with an investment. Due to possibly a lack of experience, some beginners never know when to cut their losses and move on to the next trade. When they start losing money, they always think that they can recover their money, so they continue trading despite their margins running out.

Other traders may have stop losses, but they do not have the discipline to stick to them. This group is no different from the one without a stop loss. Another set of traders may be tempted to move their stop loss in the negatives or readjust it to accommodate more losses when they trade, but this is also ill-advised. Traders should always move stop losses upwards and in the direction of a win rather than down and to an even larger loss position.

6. Ignoring News and Market Trends

New traders should also stick to their plans when they venture or approach trading markets. However, their plans should be flexible to accommodate market conditions as well as any news or events that might affect the movement of the market. For example, a trader might spot a good USD to EUR exchange. However, something might happen in Europe that might blow up the deal without the trader's knowledge. Without this information, from let us say the balance trade report from Europe, a trader cannot make an informed decision. Traders are supposed to make event calendars as they catch up with their daily news, this way, they are able to monitor and keep in mind what could affect their future trading decisions as well as any curveballs that they might encounter. Various tools can assist traders to check on prevailing ranges and trends. Understanding the history of a certain market can also help a trader know what the future market might look like.

7. Trading with Emotions

Trading with emotions or gut feelings is very common with all traders, not just new ones. Rather than use hunches, traders should study markets and read the statistics in order to make rational decisions. When the market seems to be favorable, it is very easy for a trader to put in more money or stay for a bit longer.

This is risky because trading markets can sometimes be volatile; they can change in an instant or overnight, leaving a trader in regret. It is important for beginners to stick to their trading plan. They should know when to collect their profit bags and leave. Similarly, when a new trader encounters a loss, they also take a break from the market but not a long one. Refraining from trading or sulking over previous losses is emotional trading. Even expert traders make losses and mistakes, but they always choose to pick up the pieces and move on to another trader rather than seat down and sulk.

If a trader is also too cautious, they can miss great deals that are within their trading plans. This fear can also make a trader deviate from his or her plan and try out trades that are not within the plan. This decision has the potential to lead to even further losses. In most cases, a good trading plan can recover losses. If this does not happen, then the trader can pull away from the forex market, assess their plan, or look for the problem in their plan, then adjust accordingly and get back into the game.

8. Adding to a Losing Trade

Sometimes beginners in trading are tempted to continue adding to an unprofitable trade, but eventually, even they can attest that this is a wrong move. No matter how sure a trader is about the next move in the market, multiplying losses is never a good idea. In most cases, it leaves the trader in a deeper loss position. Most traders in this situation are also incapable of making unbiased decisions that are within their trading plans. It is always better for the trader to close with a negative position than to increase their loss. It is okay to step back and regroup. The trader can also try another trade or wait for the market to be favorable again.

As earlier deduced, it is never a good idea to move the stop loss in an effort to avoid closing at a loss. New traders must learn the discipline of sticking to their plans and observing any guidelines that they had set before entering the market. Traders should also refrain from revenging on the market. Revenge trades can even make a trader double or triple the current loss that they have.

9. Choosing the Wrong Broker

The first and probably the most critical decision for a new trader is choosing a good broker. Giving money to another person is the first and biggest gamble that a trader will ever make. Whichever company the trader decides to give his or her trading capital should be legit. There have been incidents of people giving away their money to scammers.

A good broker should allow a trader to trade freely with his or her money and withdraw it whenever he or she wishes to do so. The first step in choosing the right broker is to look for one that matches your needs. If you have a small amount of capital, you should look at brokers who allow trading in micro-lots. The broker should also be regulated in the country they operate in and have a stable financial system.

It is important to carry a background check on the broker by researching on reviews about the broker. A trader should also check whether a broker allows them to deal directly with the market, or they normally redirect them to a dealing desk. He should also look at the willingness of the broker to address his concerns. Once the trader is okay with the above, he can open a demo account to test whether the broker offers what they say they offer. Smart traders do not deposit their entire trading capital with a broker; instead, they test the water first to assess the broker's availability, support, and accessibility to their money. If a broker proves worthy, a trader can go ahead and deposit the rest of his money.

Chapter 12: How to Make Money with Forex Trading to Create Passive Income

According to experts in the field of Forex Trading, it is possible to create a passive income through this form of financial trading. However, before jumping headlong into this type of financial trading, prospective traders need to ask themselves whether it is suitable for them, in addition to learning as much as possible about this line of business.

A passive income is the income stream traders or investors get at regular intervals and require little or no effort on their part to maintain it. Some of the common types of passive income include dividends from stock owned in a listed corporation, rental income, and interest income from bonds.

Other less common forms of passive income include royalties from a music record or publishing a book, or dividends from a non-listed company run by a family member or friend. Passive income may also arise from a new business model or income from a multi-level marketing network, where the income originates from other people's activities.

Some internet marketers, such as affiliate marketers, also receive passive income from internet traffic that continues to stream in from blogs they posted a long time ago. Nowadays, traders can make a passive income through the forex market.

In fact, one does not have to participate directly in the trading process or have tons of experience in this field of business. Forex traders can earn a passive income from this form of financial trading in several ways, with some requiring more work or input from the trader. Some of these include:

Forex Signals

These are short messages new traders can use to determine the best currency to trade and the right time to trade. Traders can receive important trading information through email, text messages, or any other type of communication, including social media platforms such as TX forums, Twitter, and other leading financial trading platforms.

These signals or messages are usually brief snippets of information, which instruct users to take specific actions, such as purchasing EUR/USD at a certain price. Sometimes, these signals feature various types of orders, such as a market order, pending order, or limit order. There are tons of sites that teach traders how to read and understand forex signals.

These signals can also be premium or free, with the former leading to better trades. Many providers of forex signals freely send important trading information to investors to boost their reputation in the financial trading industry. Forex signals are also great for people who want to earn a passive income trading options but do not have the time or opportunity to learn much about Forex Trading.

However, it is important to perform adequate research into providers of forex signals to avoid losing money. Forex traders, however, should approach these signals with utmost caution to make a good passive income.

Forex Robots

One of the best ways to make a passive income from the forex market is using a tool known as a forex robot, which performs automated trades on a trader's behalf. Once traders set up these forex robots, they do not have to do much else; however, they should keep an eye on the trades the forex robots are making for them.

To get started, traders need to perform adequate research into the software available for forex robots. They need to choose software that will meet their needs, in addition to being reliable when it comes to executing the right forex trades. After setting up this software, it will make forex trades based on preset signals.

In addition, it will use its acquired knowledge to purchase or sell at specific times, earning users a passive income in the process. However, it is important to understand that not all forex robots make passive income for investors as claimed. In the same way that a human can make a losing trade, a forex robot can also make the same mistake.

It is also important to understand that many so-called forex robots are frauds, which is why respected news platforms such as the Wall Street Journal and Forbes refuse to promote or advertise them. Unfortunately, this is particularly true when it comes to free forex robots. Therefore, new forex traders should analyze testimonials and reviews carefully before entrusting their investment to a forex robot.

Fortunately, several leading sites focus on reviewing different trading platforms. These sites try to give an honest opinion of different investment platforms and outline all the benefits and limitations of each platform. They also offer a detailed analysis of how these platforms work and how traders can get started on them, which is especially helpful to new traders.

Social Trading

The social trading network works in the same way as a social networking platform. Instead of sharing selfies or pictures of pets playing the piano, however, social traders share important information about forex or financial trades. This allows others to copy them and make passive income as well.

New forex traders simply need experienced traders they trust and copy their trading strategies to make money. In addition to making a passive income, they will also learn when, why, and how successful traders make their trading moves, which will give them more insight and understanding into the forex industry.

However, finding traders, they can trust and emulate is not as easy as it may sound. New traders need to set aside adequate time to perform thorough research into different social trading platforms, in addition to learning more about forex traders they want to work with and copy.

In certain situations, they might need to spend some money on the trader whose trading strategies they copy. However, this commission is negligible and not a big concern for new traders who want to make a passive income. Forex Trading is something that most people looking for ways to make some extra cash look into.

However, most of them do not know where to start. This discussion provides three great ideas for Forex Trading beginners to consider. Each of the options above requires a different investment in terms of time and effort. The most important thing to remember is that beginners should perform adequate research before picking a trading platform or strategy to use.

Nowadays, Forex Trading is one of the best ways for people to make a passive income working online. Millions of traders are earning a passive or active income every day through Forex Trading. This line of business is just like any other online money-making concept, but its profit potential is unrivaled. With modern technological advances and the availability of detailed information, anyone can make a passive income through Forex Trading.

Conclusion

Thank you for making it through to the end of *Forex Trading for Beginners: Simple Strategies to Make Money with Forex Trading: The Best Guide with Basics, Secrets Tactics, and Psychology to Big Profit and Income from the Financial Market.* Let us hope it was informative and able to provide you with all of the tools you need to achieve your goals, whatever they may be.

Now you know that the word 'forex' is short for 'foreign exchange,' and it involves converting one currency into another for reasons including tourism, trading, and business. The foreign exchange market is a global forum for exchanging substantial national currencies against each other.

The foreign exchange market is open to all types of traders, and it is more accessible than any other online trading platform in the world. An individual can start trading with as little as $100. Therefore, foreign exchange markets have lower exchange capital prerequisites compared to other financial markets.

Forex Trading happens over the interbank market, which is a channel through which currency trading happens 5 days a week, 24 hours a day. It is one of the biggest trading markets in the world, with a worldwide daily turnover estimated to be more than $5 trillion.

If the currency pair of EUR/USD, which refers to Euro/US Dollar, was trading at 1.0914/1.0916, for example, investors planning to open a long position on the Euro would purchase one Euro for 1.0916 US dollars. They will then hold on to the currency and hope that its value will increase, and then sell it back to the market once it appreciates. On the other hand, investors looking to open a short position on the Euro will sell one Euro for 1.0914 US dollars, with the expectation that its value will depreciate. If their expectations come true, they will buy it back at the lower rate and make a profit.

Brokers are the intermediaries who link investors with their capital. Some traders may choose to invest in the forex trade, and therefore they will invariably become in need of a foreign exchange broker.

The account balance is the amount of equity or capital available in your brokerage account due to investment in the currency market. It is essential to have such an account to enable the foreign exchange broker to carry out the buying and selling executions on your behalf.

A Forex Trading platform is a standard provision from most forex brokers to their clients, investors, or other retail traders. It also acts as a source of commission for the forex brokers by charging an access fee to use it. After seeking a foreign exchange broker, most traders will get a couple of trading platform recommendations from these same brokers.

Forex Trading signals are guidelines and recommendations that help inexperienced forex traders to open Forex Trading positions. The signals are a type of system that forex traders use to make crucial decisions about their trade. In that regard, Forex Trading signals provide details about how to open a new Forex Trade.

To the uninitiated, navigating the forex market successfully can seem like a difficult task. However, success is possible if one takes the right steps and trains properly. Just like training for a marathon, training is essential to winning in Forex Trading. Success requires targeted effort, practice, patience, and time.

Your next step should be to get a Forex Trading account, implement the strategies within the pages of this book, and start smiling all the way to the bank.

Finally, if you found this book useful in any way, a review on Amazon is always appreciated!

Options Trading Crash Course

The Beginner's Guide to Make Money with Options Trading: Best Strategies for Make a Living from Passive Income and Quick Start to Your Financial Freedom

Table of Contents

Introduction..**482**
Chapter 1: An Introduction to Options Trading..................**484**
   What Is an Option?
   Options on Stocks
   Put options
   Selling Options and Options Strategies
Chapter 2: Options Basic Definitions...............................**494**
   Strike Price
   Expiration Date
   Time Decay
   Options Chain
   How Options Are Priced
   In the Money
   At the Money
   Out of the Money
   Open Interest
   Volume
   Options Exchanges
   The Market Maker
Chapter 3: The Greeks...**510**
   Delta
   Theta
   Gamma
   Vega
   Rho

Minor Greeks

Chapter 4: Swing Trading with Options..................523

    What is Swing Trading?

    Support and Resistance

    Trade with the Trend

    Swing Trading Options

    Going Long on a Stock

    Shorting Stock Using Put options

    Tools to Spot Trend Reversals

    Chart Patterns That Indicate Trend Reversals

    Candlestick Charts

    Moving Averages

    Relative Strength Indicator

    Bollinger Bands

Chapter 5: The Iron Condor and Iron Butterfly..................555

    Removing Direction from the Trade

    Central Goal of the Iron Condor

    Iron Condors are Income Strategies

    The Lower Legs

    The Other Legs

    The Complete Iron Condor as a Single Trade

    The Iron Condor Relies on Time Decay

    The Iron Butterfly

    The Buyback Strategy

    Maximum Losses

    Summary

Chapter 6: Strangles and Straddles..................566

    Strangle Options Strategy

How to Implement the Strategy
Straddle
Tips and Things to Watch Out For

Chapter 7: Call and Put Spreads (Vertical Spreads)............582
Debit Spreads
Put Debit Spreads
Put Credit Spreads
Call Credit Spreads
Time Decay and Buy Backs

Chapter 8: Selling Options..594
Covered Calls
Cash Protected Puts
Naked Put Options

Chapter 9: Tips for Successful Trading..............................599
Set Stops on Your Trades
Letting Options Expire
Consider Rolling Out Trades That Aren't Working
Avoid Options With Low Volume
Attempting to Make up for Past Failures

Conclusion...601

Introduction

Congratulations on purchasing the *Options Trading Crash Course,* and thank you for doing so.

The concept of options trading strikes most investors as obscure and even dangerous and risky. However, as we are going to learn in these pages, investing and trading in options is actually a smart and effective way to make money and build wealth. We'll begin the book by explaining what options are and how they work. There are different types of options and multiple strategies used to trade options, and we'll learn about the most popular that are available. You'll learn how to go about trading options and how to work with your broker.

The goal of this book is to demystify options trading. When you learn what they are and why they exist, the shroud of mystery that surrounds these supposedly exotic financial instruments will vanish. You'll find out that options trading, when done with care, is actually a straightforward way to engage with the financial markets. By the end of this book, you'll be able to clearly define a call and a put, an iron condor, a spread, and even the so-called "Greeks".

We'll also learn about the psychology and mindset that are necessary for successful options trading. You'll come to understand how options trading differs from stock trading and investment, both in mindset and goals and techniques. You'll also learn about the most serious mistakes that beginners make when trading options and how to avoid them. You'll also learn how to use options in order to generate regular income.

Until recently, options trading has only been available to financial insiders. The development of technology associated with the markets has changed all that, and now anyone can trade options, and you only need a few hundred dollars to get started. With all the user-friendly trading platforms that are now available through the internet and on mobile, the only obstacle is that most investors don't understand options. This book will help to remove that obstacle so that you can join those earning profits and income from options trading.

So, thank you for choosing this book. There are a number of various titles on this topic out there. So, your choice of this book is certainly motivating. We hope that you will get the most out of this book as great care has been taken in making sure that it is both useful and informative.

Chapter 1: An Introduction to Options Trading

The first step to consider when engaging in options trading is to have a clear and accurate understanding of what an option actually is. Unfortunately, one of the things that is lacking in our society is a good financial education. Most people barely understand what the stock market is and how it operates, and options are a level above even that. In this chapter, we are going to lay a foundation for the rest of the book by helping you to understand what options are, why they exist, and what the different types and characteristics of options are. Then we will go into detail in the rest of the book so that you'll learn everything you need to learn in order to actually be able to trade options with success. Remember that all forms of investing and trading carry financial risk, and not everyone who invests or trades on the markets is going to succeed.

What Is an Option?

Options are not restricted to the stock market. The name option gives us a clue as to what these financial instruments are, however. An options contract is one which enables the buyer to have the *option* to do something. Options contracts can exist in any context where you are interested in buying something. The proverbial example that is used is the option to buy a new home.

Let's say that Jane is moving to her new job in Houston, Texas. She is interested in buying a new home in a good neighborhood that is reasonably close to her job. She has two kids, so she's also interested in buying a home in an area with a low crime rate and good schools.

She finds out that there is a new housing development near her job. She also finds out that it will take about 4 months to have a home ready for her to move in. Because of the high demand in the area, home prices are changing rapidly. She'd like to lock in a price for a home but wants to look around in the meantime. How can she do that? The answer is she can enter into an options contract with the developer.

The type of homes that Jane is interested in are currently going for $350,000. Jane tells the developer she is willing to buy a house at this price, but she needs 120 days to decide. The developer knows that prices are rapidly increasing, but to make a deal. He offers the possibility for Jane to lock in a lot and home for $360,000. She must buy the home on or before the date the contract expires 120 days from the date, she signs it. If she fails to close by that time, the contract expires, and the developer is free to sell the lot to someone else at market prices.

Jane is not taking too much risk because she is not forced to buy the home; she has the option. If prices end up dropping, she can simply let the option contract expire. If prices stay about the same or keep rising, and she doesn't find another home she is interested in, Jane can go ahead and exercise her rights under the contract and buy the house for $360,000. This is true even if the price of new homes in the area has jumped to $400,000 at the time the contract expires. So, by locking in a price, Jane may have put herself in a position where she could save a significant amount of money yet get the home (investment) that she wanted.

While laws may vary based upon the given specific contract type, though generally speaking, the contracts themselves can be bought and sold. The contract itself becomes valuable because of the *underlying* asset (in this case, the home), and the ability to buy that asset at the fixed price. In an environment of rising prices, this can provide a big advantage to buyers. In many cases, the buyers won't go through with the contract. Actually, executing the contract is called *exercising* the contract. Of course, if home prices in the area were to rise to $400,000, it would be worth it to exercise this options contract.

Jane may not want to do so. Maybe she found a different home more to her liking. However, since the contract has obvious value, she could sell it to someone else. Ever since financial instruments were invented, secondary markets were created soon afterward, where people traded them. Options are no exception.

Since an option derives its value from an underlying asset that is not directly traded or even owned by the person who buys the option, it is called a *derivative*. The media often talks about derivatives as if they are extremely exotic and complex, but it is really nothing more than that. A derivative is a financial instrument or contract that derives its value from an underlying asset.

Options on Stocks

The basic concepts of options that we described above apply to options on stocks. Since we now understand those basic concepts, let's define the specifics when it comes to options contracts on stocks. It turns out that options contracts on stocks are slightly more complicated than what we've described so far, but it's not horribly complicated if you take it step-by-step.

The first thing to note is the underlying. As far as options on stocks are concerned, its corresponding asset is 10 shares of a specific stock. That stock is a stock of a publicly-traded company on a major stock exchange. Options on stocks also include index funds. So, you can trade options on Apple, Facebook, or Boeing. You can also trade options on SPY, DIA, and QQQ, which are exchange-traded funds for the most significant stock markets such as the Dow Jones Industrial Average, the Standard & Poors 500, and NASDAQ 100, respectively.

For example, using a home purchase, we only talked about the option for someone to buy the home – we never considered having the option to sell a home. But with stocks, both concepts are equally important. The most basic concept is imagining having an option that would give you the possibility of purchasing those 10 shares of a given stock at a pre-determined sale point on or prior to the expiration date of the contract. This kind of deal is known as a *call option*.

You can see that in a market of rising prices, a call option favors the buyer. The potential buyer can lock in a price, and if they choose to do so, if the price per share actually rises by a significant amount (and by significant we mean significant enough to earn a profit if you turned around and sold the shares on the market), the buyer can buy shares at a discount.

In an environment of rising prices, since the option contract would give buyers such an advantage, that means the contract itself becomes more valuable. So, with everything else remaining equal, the price of said contact will be going up in a market of rising prices. People will be bidding up the price as more investors excitedly want to get their hands on the option.

There are going to be two types of buyers in the marketplace. Some buyers are really interested in getting a hold of the stock at a discount price. Others are simply hoping or anticipating that prices are going to continue rising, and so they anticipate that the price of the option is going to be higher in the future. In other words, they want to buy the option, and then turn around and sell it for a higher price a few days or weeks later at a higher price, so they can make a profit *from the option contract itself*.

When we are talking about anticipating making a profit from future changes in price, this is called speculating. The term speculating is associated with *trading*, which can be defined as short term purchase and sale of a financial asset with the sole intent of generating profits. It is important to keep this concept distinct from *investing*. The first difference between trading and investing in the time frame. Trading is generally done on short-term time frames of one year or less. In contrast, investing generally means five years or more. Investing is a long-term commitment to something you believe in.

Of course, investors hope that their assets are going to increase in value as well. Otherwise, they wouldn't invest. But they are in it for the long haul and are not going to be getting rid of their assets soon after they acquire them. The reasons for investing often go beyond simple profit. Investors may be passionate about the companies they invest in and the products they offer or believe that the companies they invest in represent the future of the economy. They may also take a broad view, and invest in index funds, based on the idea that the economy will grow with time.

It is crucial to have a clear understanding of the difference that lies between trading and investing, and understanding what "speculating" is, as an options trader. As we'll see later, you might have to express the fact that you understand the difference as an options trader to satisfy regulators.

Put options

Now let's turn our attention to the other major type of option on the equities market. The option we are going to be discussing is known as a "put option". This kind of contract entitles the buyer to acquire a set quantity of stock at a pre-determined sale point. That might appear to you as somewhat bizarre at first, so why would anyone want to do that? The answer is that put options are valuable to buyers in a market of declining prices. If the stock is dropping significantly below the fixed price agreed upon in the options contract, then it makes sense to either do one of the following. If you already own the shares, maybe you purchased them at a much higher price, and you want to limit your losses. In that case, a put option allows you to cut your losses at a given price point that may be significantly above the market valuation. You don't have to worry if the market price keeps dropping, you can sell your shares at a price agreed to in the contract at any time before it expires. So, in this case, a put option can be a form of insurance for a buyer that has invested in a lot of shares.

It's also possible for speculators to profit. The first case is where you really want to sell the stock. To do this, you wait until the stock price drops low enough so that making a move on the option would be profitable. So, you buy the 100 shares and then sell them to exercise your rights under the option. Of course, the way this would work is you would sell them to the originator of the options contract, who is obligated to honor the contract and buy the shares.

But just like call options, if prices are moving favorably, the value of put options themselves is going to be increasing. This means that if stock prices are dropping, the price of put options will be rising, all other things being equal. That provides many opportunities for traders to earn profits. You buy the put options when they are at a relatively high pricing point, and then you sell them when the stock price drops, for a profit. The buyer may be a speculator who is simply interested in trying to sell the option at a later date for a profit, or it may be someone who owns the shares and wants that insurance that we talked about earlier.

Selling Options and Options Strategies

Of course, there are all these options on the market to buy, but who sells them in the first place? Lots of people sell options. Options are not issued by the companies themselves, so in other words, Facebook does not issue options on its own stock. However, in some cases, big institutional traders might sell options. We say that the creator of an options contract *writes* the contract. Another way to put it is to say that they *sell to open*. As it turns out, not only can you buy options as an individual trader, you can sell to open options contracts as well.

This is a more advanced way to deal with options, so we will be talking about this later in the book after we've gotten a thorough understanding of trading options. Generally speaking, selling to open is an income strategy. So, people sell to open options and get paid when someone buys the option they are selling. They hope that this is the end of it (see below). Traders, on the other hand, will buy to open their positions, and then hope to make profits and trade away the option before it loses value. Trading is significantly riskier than selling options for income.

There are many strategies used when selling options. This can be used to reduced risk, but many experienced options traders sell what are called "naked" options. This is just straight up selling of options contracts to earn income. Of course, there is a risk with a naked option that you'll have to buy or sell the shares of stock. Since we are talking about 100 shares at a time (a single options contract covers 100 shares of stock), that can be a non-trivial amount of cash that you need to have on hand. It is also possible to sell options that are backed by either the full amount of cash or shares of stock that you already own. We will be talking more about this later.

Selling options can also be used in complex strategies in combination with buying options at the same time. This is done in multiple ways in order to minimize risk. These types of strategies also allow you to play different kinds of market situations. For example, many times, the stock doesn't go up or down very much. Instead, it stays trapped – often for very long periods – within a narrow range of prices. In that case, we say that the stock is "ranging". There are options strategies that allow you to earn profits when the price of a stock doesn't change very much. That may seem mysterious right now, but later in the book, you'll learn exactly how that works. An astute observer will note that this is a way to earn money that simply isn't possible investing in or trading stocks. This illustrates the explosive power that options provide.

Another strategy that can be used with options is you can sell options while limiting risks. These types of strategies are known as "spreads". Moreover, either selling naked options or trading in spreads, you can set up trades that make profit either when the stock price rises, or when it falls. This is another illustration of the power that options provide to traders, that is not available to stock traders. You might note that stock traders can "short" a stock to earn profits from market declines, however, to do that you have to be a major player with a large account. For most individual traders, shorting stock is going to be out of reach.

There are also strategies that can be used to earn profits if the stock goes up a large amount very quickly, or if it drops a large amount very quickly. So, you can make a profit no matter which way the stock moves, but there has to be a situation where there is going to be a large movement in stock price. A common time that this type of strategy is used is when there is an earnings call for a large company.

We are going to discuss all the details behind options trading strategies throughout the book so that you can become an expert in short order. You'll also learn all the meaning behind all the jargon behind these strategies that are probably floating around on the internet. For now, just be aware that there are many different ways that you can trade options as a buyer and a seller in order to earn money, and that you can do it under any condition that the market happens to be in. This type of flexibility is something that stock traders and investors, even "day traders", simply don't have access to.

Chapter 2: Options Basic Definitions

In the last chapter, we went over the basic concept of an options contract as a derivative that gets its value from some underlying financial asset. In this chapter and from now on, we will turn our attention strictly to options on stocks (and index funds trading as stocks). The purpose of this chapter is to define and explain all the basic properties of options and the basic terminology.

Strike Price

For a call option, there is a fixed price that is a part of the contract, which allows the buyer to purchase any amount of stock corresponding to a specific company at a pre-determined. The set price contained in the contract can be termed as the "strike price". The strike price of this kind of contract is one of its most important characteristics, and when you go to look for options to trade, you are going to see them listed in order by strike price. So, who do you purchase the shares from? You would buy the shares from the seller of the options contract. In the event they were not able to fulfill their end of the deal, the broker would step in and do it for them (with consequences to the seller). The strike price must be used independently of the stock's current market valuation. As such, if there is a strike price of $50, but the stock's current market valuation has risen to $350 per share, it's not relevant. The seller of the call option would still be required by law to sell you 100 shares at $50 a share.

The concept is the same for put options. In this case, the strike price of this kind of contract entitles the holder to trade a specific amount of a stock. As in the case of call options, you would be selling the shares to the originator of the put option. They would be legally bound to buy the shares of the stock whose valuation has been determined by the seller regardless of its perceived current market valuation.

Expiration Date

Next, we come to the other crucial piece of information, which is the date of the expiration date of the contract itself. Generally speaking, the most common way in which options can be traded are listed is first by expiration date. When you select a given expiration date, you will then see options listed by strike price. On some platforms, options are all listed on the same page but grouped according to type. So, you will see all the call options listed at the top, and then this will be followed by the put options. In other cases, you will see a tab that lets you move back and forth between call and put options for the same expiration date.

As we will see, the expiration date is very important for many reasons. As this critical deadline approaches, if the contract does not have an appropriate valuation with regard to stock's current market valuation, it's going to be rapidly losing value. Let's get some insight into this with this sample situation. Let's assume that you are looking to purchase a contract for a call option that has a current strike valuation of $10. With this trade, you are looking to make a profit when its price increases. As such, the option has the greatest value when its current market valuation exceeds $10. Consequently, you profit more, the higher the price gets. Now, let's assume that its current market valuation falls to $7 instead. Then that call option simply isn't worth anything. People can just buy shares for $7, so why would anyone enter into a contract that required them to buy shares at $10 a share? Of course, they wouldn't do that. The longer you have remaining on the deal, the greater the value it has. If there are three months left on the contract, then it might still have a little value, because there would be a chance that the stock could move significantly in that time frame. But, if there are only three days left on the contract, the chances of the stock increasing from $7 to above $10 are pretty much nil (unless an earnings call is coming up and it turns out to be unexpectedly rosy), so the option will be rapidly losing value.

The expiration date is also important because when an option expires, it may be in a position where it can be exercised. Of course, there are as many approaches to this situation as there are unique individuals. Some people are small traders and simply don't want to buy or sell stock, and they may not have the capital to do so even if they wanted to. Remember, we are talking about 100 shares for each options contract.

On the other hand, others may be looking to buy and sell the shares. So, they may want to exercise the option when it expires, or even beforehand. If you are not able to buy and sell shares, you'll probably want to get out of the option before it expires to avoid this situation. In other words, you'll want to get whatever profits you can from selling the option. So, you want to sell it prior to the expiration date.

The expiration date is closely associated with a concept called time decay (and time value), so let's go ahead and discuss that.

Time Decay

Time decay is an important factor to consider when trading options. For buyers, time decay works against them. For options sellers (that is people who sell to open options contracts), time decay works in their favor.

Earlier, we touched on the basic idea of time decay. When there is a long time until the option expires, there is a higher probability that the price of the option can move in one direction or the other. That means that the market price of the shares can move in such a way as to make the option profitable. On the other hand, as time passes, that probability that this is going to happen decreases. In fact, each day, that probability drops. This is known as time decay.

Time decay actually refers to a drop in the price of the option on the options market. Options pricing is complicated and described by mathematical formulas, and a part of that is value that comes from the time remaining until the option expires. This value is called time value, and time value translates into real dollars and cents. Again, as we will see, there are several elements that influence the valuation of an options contract, so it might so happen that an option is gaining overall value even as it loses time value. Down below, we'll discuss that a little bit more. In other cases, time value will be dropping rapidly, and the price of the option is going to be dropping with it.

Time value is also known as extrinsic value. Time value is extrinsic because it only relates to the time remaining on the options contract. We are simplifying a little bit, but this is generally the way to think of it. So, it's not derived from the underlying market valuation for this stock. Pricing of the option that comes from the underlying stock is known as intrinsic value.

Options Chain

The list in which options for stocks and even index funds that are up for sale is known as the options chain. Every option has a ticker, although many modern platforms don't bother with that anymore since options information can be displayed in a user-friendly manner using computer and mobile technology. The options ticker includes information on the option such as which underlying stock the option is for, the expiration date, type of option, and the strike price. It might look something like this:

AMZN200103C1530000

The first part of the options ticker is the stock ticker of the underlying stock or index fund for the option. This is followed by the expiration date, which is given in a 2-digit year, month, and day format. So here we see:

200103

This means January 3, 2020. So, the format is YYMMDD. Following this, we see a single letter representing the type of option. In the case of

AMZN200103C1530000, since we see a C in this position, that means that we are dealing with a call option. Had it been a put option, we'd see AMZN200103P1530000.

The last part pertaining to the contract is its strike price. This valuation (strike price) will have three decimal places and leading zeros if the strike price uses up all the digits. In other words, 1530000 represents a strike price of $1,530. If the strike price had been $851, the ticker would look like this:

AMZN200103C0851000

Tickers are displayed grouped by expiration date, with calls first, followed by put options, but probably with the ability to switch between them.

The options chain for Amazon.

As we said, many platforms no longer use the tickers and simply display the options by strike price in a user-friendly, readable format. Below, we see the contrast between the traditional display used by Yahoo Finance, and a newer user-friendly display used by the mobile trading platform Robin Hood:

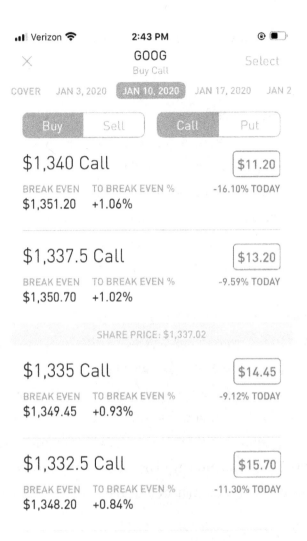

Here we see that you can simply click on a date at the top of the screen. For that date, we are able to move between call and put options with a single tap, and also between the purchase and sale. The options are listed in rows, going from highest strike price to lowest one, with the prevailing market valuation noted on the screen. The actual price of this contract is displayed on the right side of the screen, along with some other information.

How Options Are Priced

Options prices are quoted on a per-share basis. For the vast majority of options contracts, there are 100 underlying shares of stock. So, the quoted price is for one share, but to buy a single options contract, you'll be doing it for all 100 shares. Fractional purchases of options are not allowed. So, if you see the price of an option quoted as $2, that means to buy the option, you actually have to pay $200.

As you can see, some options are quite expensive, but the price varies considerably. In the example using Google above, the last option at the bottom has a price of $15.70. That means to actually buy this option. You must pay $1,570. Of course, looking at it another way, you could sell the option for $1,570, and that might clue you in as to why people are interested in selling options contracts. More on that later. Next, we are going to cover some industry jargon that refers to the relationship between the market valuation of the individual stock and its strike price.

In the Money

An option can be said to be *in the money* when it would be prudent to exercise it. In doing so, the transaction would generate a profit. As such, the term "in the money" means that the current valuation of a call options contract is greater than the current market price of the shares. The same can be said about a put options contract when its share price is below the valuation of the contract itself. But in reality, we need to take into account the price paid for the option. So, let's look at a more formal and more accurate definition.

In the case of a call option, this implies the market valuation of the shares is higher than its strike price in addition to the *breakeven* (note that in the options trading world, breakeven is two separate words). The breakeven price is simply the price paid to enter into the options contract. So, if the strike price of a call option is $100, and you buy that option for $1 (per share – so total of $100), the breakeven is $100 + $1 = $101. What this tells you is that its market valuation must increase to $101 in order for the option to be worth exercising.

For put options, remember that profit is earned from declining share prices. So, to get the breakeven price of a put option, you subtract the price per share spent on the option from the valuation of the contract. So, if we have a put contract containing a $90 valuation that costs $0.80, then the breakeven price would be $90 - $0.80 = $89.20.

Also, if the valuation of the stock drops below the strike valuation of a put contract minus the value paid, in other words, share valuation has fallen beneath the breakeven point. This is when the contract is said to be in the money.

At the Money

The term "at the money" means that the valuation of the shares is the same as the market valuation of the contract. We use the same definition for both call and put options. Keep in mind that in reality, you can basically consider an option as "at the money" when the valuation of the shares goes below its breakeven point, but at or above the market valuation for the contract in questions. For a put option, you would for practical purposes consider an option at the money in the event the valuation of the shares was over the breakeven point but below the strike valuation. An at the money option isn't really anything special, other than being close to the possibility of going in the money at some point. The more time remaining until the option expires, the more useful an at the money option is. If you have a strong reason to believe that a stock is going to move one way or the other, using the money options could be a lower-cost way to get into the trade.

Out of the Money

An out of the money option is one that is in a position relative to the market price of the stock such that it would not be worth exercising. For a call option, it will be out of the money when the strike price is above the strike price. Using the logic of the last section, in practice, you could consider it to be out of the money when it is above the stock price plus the break-even, but that is really a distinction without a difference when the option expires. An out of the money option will expire "worthless". Let's use a simple example to see why.

Remember the point of a call option. The purpose of a call option is to give someone the right to buy 100 shares of stock at a discount. So, let's say we buy a call option on some stock with a strike price that is $200 a share. Our speculation that the price of the stock was going to rise turns out wrong, and instead of going up, the price of the shares drops.

As the option is nearing the expiration date, the price of the shares drops to $195 a share.

You can ask yourself if it would be worth exercising an option that gave you the right to buy 100 shares at $200 a share. Of course, it wouldn't be worth doing this. So, nobody is going to do it, and fewer people will want to buy the option from you if you wanted to get rid of it by trading it. Of course, some people will still buy it, as some naïve traders (and there are a lot of them – but we are educating our dear readers) will buy out of the money options because they are cheap, and there is always the "hope" that the stock price will reverse and gain value.

In most cases, that hope is not realistic, so it is not advisable to buy out of the money options, except in a narrow situation that we will discuss in chapter 4.

Now let's turn our attention to put options. Since put options earn profit when the stock price drops, that means a put option is going to be out of the money if the strike price of the option is lower than the share price of the stock.

Open Interest

When you are looking for options to trade, there are other factors besides the strike price and expiration date that you should be looking at. One of these is called open interest. Open interest is the number of contracts that are on the market for a given stock, strike price, and expiration date. Some options are really popular, and you will see open interest in the tens of thousands. Others are not so popular – but could still be worth trading. A good rule of thumb that is used by professional options traders is you shouldn't get into options trades if the open interest is lower than 100.

There is a simple reason for this. You might need to find a buyer very quickly for an options contract to get out of a trade. This can happen when the price is moving in a favorable direction and when it's moving in a bad direction. The reason is that the relationship of the price of an option to the underlying shares is such that price movements of the stock are magnified in price movements of the option. Remember that there are 100 underlying shares of the option. So, a $1 price movement in the share price could, in theory, have up to 100 times the impact on the price of the option. We will discuss the actual values when we discuss the Greeks, but for in the money options, the relationship will be $0.50 to $1 per share, meaning that the price of the option can rise or fall $50 to $100 for in response to a $1 shift in the price of the underlying stock.

For at the money options, the relationship is $0.50 per share, so even at the money (or close thereto) options are massively impacted by price shifts in the underlying stock. It is this magnifying effect that makes options so attractive to many traders. In fact, although its operating at a lower level, large price shifts can even have a large impact on the prices of out of the money options, even a few days before expiration.

The bottom line here is that you can gain or lose money very quickly. When you've made a large profit, you're going to want to sell your options to someone else before the price moves in the opposite direction, and you end up losing money as fast as you've made it. These cuts both ways. Sometimes an option is destined to simply lose a lot of value. If you find yourself in a losing trade, you are going to want to cut your losses before they get too dramatic.

And if the open interest is too low, it's going to take a long time to find a buyer. To sell an option, although it seems like magic on the computer screen, you still have to find a real buyer to take an option off your hands. When open interest is only 30, that means there are only 30 contracts out there, and it might take you a long time to find someone to buy it. That can mean lost profits or catastrophic losses.

Check around, and you will find that there are plenty of options that have an open interest above 100, and some have very high levels of open interest.

Volume

Volume is another measure of an options popularity. Volume tells you the number of times per day the contracts were traded. The closer you get to expiration, the higher the volume is going to be. Volume can be higher or lower than open interest, but popular options such as on the index fund SPY can have a very high level of volume. A high volume isn't the only thing you are going to look for when deciding whether or not to trade an option, of course, but if the trading volume is high, this is an indicator in the options favor. Like open interest, a high trading volume indicates that it will be relatively easy to get in and out of trades quickly.

Options Exchanges

Options trading takes place on separate exchanges. They are not traded on the stock floors of the New York Stock Exchange or NASDAQ. Most options exchanges are located in Chicago, and there are several options exchanges. For an individual trader, indeed, for many large traders these days, that is all irrelevant. This is all hidden from you by the broker and by a computer interface. All you know is that you are placing an order to buy or sell an option, and the computer reports back on the trade. How it actually gets executed on the other end isn't that important. But you might want to keep it in the back of your mind that a real person is taking the other side of the trade. That can help you to make better trading decisions since you might think about whether a given trade would be something other people are going to be interested in. Usually, however, that isn't too much of a problem. The reason is that the options market is large, and although it is not as large as the stock market, there are enough people around to get the full range of different and competing interests represented. Sometimes when a trade seems like a disaster for you, someone else might feel they can do something with it. What their reasons are you can't possibly know, and it really doesn't matter anyway.

The Market Maker

Options markets have so-called "market makers". In the old days, these were high flying individuals that made large trades. Today they are likely people with large accounts that work for major institutions like major banks. The purpose of the market maker is to keep the options market running and running as smoothly as possible. Market makers will take the other side of many trades. The point of doing this is largely to keep the market as "liquid" as possible. If you are not sure what liquid means, basically liquid means how easy it is to convert an asset into cash. Something that takes six months to sell is less liquid than something you can sell in 1-2 days. As for options themselves, liquidity means you have the opportunity to purchase and trade options quickly. Sometimes, if you are doing lower volume trades, the market maker might help you by taking the other side of the trade. Once again, we can't always guess the motivations of the market maker or anyone else taking the other side of the trade, and it's not really worth worrying about it. The only thing to think about as an individual options trader is getting in and out of trades when you need to.

In the next chapter, we will discuss the topic pertaining to the so-called "Greeks". Learning about the Greeks will explain how options prices are determined. You will learn specific values and relationships that will tell you how much the price of an option will change in response to a variation in the asset underlying in the contract. You will also learn how much the price of an option will drop in response to "time decay" and some other factors that can influence option pricing.

Chapter 3: The Greeks

In this chapter, we are going to look at five important parameters that an option has that go by the name "the Greeks". Understanding these parameters will help you estimate where an options price is going to go when different factors that impact that price change. Options pricing is based on mathematical formulas, but you don't need to understand the details. The Greeks will help you make estimations at a glance once you understand what they are all about. Your brokerage trading platform will allow you to look up the Greeks for any option so that you can make the best choices for your investments.

Delta

The first Greek parameter that we are going to look at is called delta. In many cases, this is the most important of the Greeks. It describes the relationship between the valuation of the stock in question and the options contract. More specifically, it tells us how the price of the option changes in response to variations pertaining to the variation of the equities on the stock market. Consider call options first. The value is given in percentage terms, and if you think of the stock price rising or falling by a dollar, that means the price of the option will rise and fall by the fraction listed as delta. In other words, the option price will change by:

Delta x change in stock price x 100

So, if delta is 0.6, if the underlying price of the equity increased by $1, the price of the contract will rise by 60 cents per share, for a total of $60. If the stock price had only risen by 50 cents instead, then the option price would rise by 30 cents on a per-share basis, or by $30.

These figures show how dramatic options prices can change with small changes in share price. If you are trading options on Apple, Netflix, Tesla, or Google, for example, a one-dollar change in share price is not all that significant. And by extension, a 50-cent change in share price certainly isn't very significant.

Keep in mind, of course, that these cuts both ways. If the valuation of the equity drops by one dollar, the price of the option is going to drop by 60 cents per share if delta is 0.60. One thing this tells you is that you have to keep a close eye on your options trades so that you can get out of bad trades before they become disasters. However, trades can also change direction quickly, since we are talking about relatively small price movements on the stock market. In some of my trades, I had stuck it out when the price of an option dropped by $50 and then saw it rise by $120 in a matter of hours. Panic is not a reason to get out of a trade. We will be discussing this later.

Delta is not a fixed quantity. You will see that it changes depending on changing conditions in the markets. The more in the money an option is, the higher the delta is going to be. Options that are significantly in the money will have delta values that approach 1.0, so their prices can really move with changes in the stock price. If a contract happens to be out of the money, delta will be smaller. A rule of thumb you can use is that for an equity that is at the money, delta is 0.5. Then, for an options deal that is in the money, it will have delta higher than 0.5, while options contracts that are out of the money will have delta lower than 0.5. You can see how this will work to make out of the money options less lucrative. For example, and out of the money option might have a delta of 0.25, so that a $1 increase in the valuation of the equity might only bump the price up $25.

But this also raises the issue of tradeoffs. Options contracts with are out of the money are more affordable to buy, and you can still earn significant profits. Apple is trading at $293 a share as I am writing this, and you can buy a $302 call for $247. Delta is 0.2862. A $1 rise in the stock price is only a 0.34% change, so that is not something outlandish to expect. That would earn you a $29 profit on a $247 investment, a 12% ROI which isn't too shabby. Of course, you can earn more from in the money options, but a $290 call would require a $793 investment. So how much you can invest is obviously going to be a part of weighing what you trade.

Unfortunately, a lot of online articles, usually written by people who are financially trained but not active options traders, give a lot of bad advice. One thing you are going to see discussed on many websites is advice that you shouldn't trade out of the money options. The truth is that depends on the situation. Later we will discuss situations where trading out of the money options can be a viable strategy.

Now let's turn our attention briefly to put options. The concept is the same, but when you look at put options, you are going to see delta listed as a negative quantity. This is because of the inverse relationship between share price and a put option. Remember that with a contract for a put option, as the share valuation drops, the valuation of the contract increases. Conversely, when share prices rise, the valuation of the corresponding contract decreases. As such, the point of a put options contract is to be able to sell declining shares at a higher price, and the negative delta expresses this fact.

Otherwise, delta for a put option means the same thing. So, you can take a drop in share price and use delta to estimate how the price of the option would change, in the inverse manner described.

As the expiration date approaches, you'll see delta getting very small for out of the money options. Again, that doesn't mean you can't profit from out of the money options.

Remember that delta is dynamic. As the price shifts and time passes, delta might change as well. So, if you look up delta for an option today, it might be different three days from now. You need to keep track of these parameters on a regular basis, so you understand what is going on and what the possibilities are.

In the chart below, we show a perfect example of why these fluctuations are important for options traders. In a short time, frame after the market opened, the stock gained a dollar and twenty-four cents. So, with large, high volume stocks, one dollar or more fluctuations are easily going to happen, and this can cause big swings in options prices (and they might represent opportunities for profits). Notice that the stock also dropped back down but rose back up over $205 per share by the closing bell.

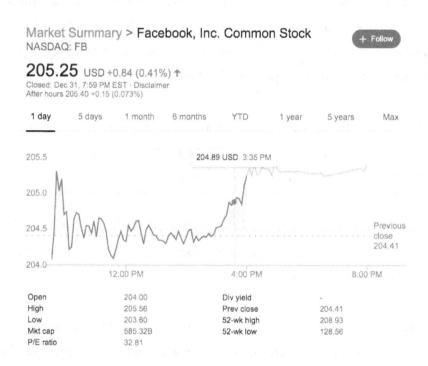

Theta

Next, we consider a parameter called theta. The purpose of this Greek is to tell you how much value the option is going to lose due to time decay. The losses that you will see from this occur every single day at the market open. So, once the decay happens at the market open, then theta won't impact the option again until the following day. The decline in options price due to theta can be significant, but it can also be overwhelmed by other factors impacting price. We just saw that delta can lead to large changes in options price, and if you have delta at 0.54, theta at -0.12, and the stock rises by $1 at market open, when all is said and done you actually have a 42-cent gain per share, or $42. Of course, if things are not moving your way with the stock, or the delta on an out of the money option is small, that means that theta is going to be working against you.

Theta is expressed as a negative value because it always means the price of the option is going to decline because of time decay when a new trading day opens. This is true for both call and put options, and so theta is always expressed as a negative number, ranging from 0.0 to -1.0. Realistic values range between -0.13 and -0.30. As time to expiration approaches, theta values tend to increase. Also, out of the money options tend to have smaller theta values. However, out of the money options get *all* of their pricing value from time value or extrinsic value, even though their price will fluctuate because of delta. To take an example, consider a stock trading at $220 per share, and suppose we have an out of the money call option with a strike price of $235. At 39 days to option expiration, the price of this option is $408. Theta is -0.105, and delta is 0.29. The extrinsic value is $408, and the intrinsic value is $0. Under the same conditions with 5 days to expiration, delta has dropped to 0.05, and theta has dropped to -0.082. The option is only priced at $160 at this point.

Let's compare values for an in the money call option. Suppose that we have the same $235 strike price, but with a share price of $240. At 39 days to expiration, the price of the option is $1,295. Delta is 0.60, theta is -0.129, and the option has $795 in extrinsic value with $500 in intrinsic value. At five days to expiration, the price is $670, delta is 0.71, and theta is -0.317. The extrinsic value of this option is $170, and the intrinsic value is $500 at this point.

This example shows us a few important things. The first is that without the money options, buying and holding them over a significant period is foolish. It is this fact that misleads many people that write about options trading to make a mistake to say you shouldn't trade out of the money options. In the trading strategies chapter for calls and puts, we will discuss this in more detail.

We also notice that the intrinsic value is the difference between the share price and the strike price. So close to expiration, as extrinsic value is declining, and in the money, option can make large profits from changing share prices as delta gets closer to 1.0.

The important thing about theta is to have an awareness of it and to be ready for it to work its wicked ways each morning when you hold the options overnight. As we said earlier, whether or not theta turns out to be important for your specific trades is going to be something that depends on the situation.

Gamma

Gamma is a bit of a more obscure Greek. For math geeks out there, it's a second derivative term. Or in English, it tells you the rate of change of another parameter. In this case, gamma tells us how delta is going to change, in response to a price change. Gamma is the same value for both calls and puts. It's also usually a small value.

Going back to our example, take call and put options with a strike price of $223, and an underlying share price of $220. Gamma for both the call and the put is 0.04. This means that if the share price goes up a dollar, delta for the call will rise by about 0.04, but delta for the put option will decline by 0.04. So, a rising share price will make delta grow for a call option, but it's going to make delta shrink for a put option. In this example that we are using, before the stock price increases, delta for the call is a bit more than 0.37, while for the put, it's -0.63. After the rise in share price by one dollar, delta for the call rises to 0.42, while for the put, it declines to -0.58.

It can be handy to know gamma depending on how deeply you're getting into the analysis. However, most individual traders don't pay much attention to it. I'd say that especially for a beginner spending time worrying about gamma isn't particularly productive. You should devote your time to delta and theta, which will help you focus on what is important for coming profits or losses.

Vega

The next Greek is Vega, which is related to the implied volatility of an option. Remember that with options, it is all about probabilities that the option is going to end up in the money. The higher the probability that this is going to happen, the higher the price of the option, and therefore more profits for options traders. Assuming that some readers are new to the world of options, let's explain volatility just briefly so that everyone knows what we are talking about.

You probably have a commonsense notion of volatility, and you can visualize it on any mathematical graph, and certainly on a stock chart. Volatility is a reference to the amount of fluctuation in the price when it comes to stock. If the price is making wild price swings, that is having large changes in price up and down for a given time period, then that's high volatility. Low volatility would be more of a smooth curve. Maybe the price is steadily going upward, but there isn't much fluctuation.

Of course, generally speaking, stock price charts are not smooth. There is an inherent amount of volatility baked into the system. This occurs from the random nature of the business. People are buying and selling shares, and fluctuating supply and demand is causing the price to move around basically in random ways, in addition to the overall price trend. But not all stocks fluctuate in the same manner. Stocks that are in heavy demand often have high amounts of volatility, since heavy demand can mean lots of buying and selling activity.

You can visualize volatility just looking at a stock chart, and it's pretty intuitive to determine which stocks are more volatile and which stocks are less volatile. At the same time, this is also precisely quantified. Each stock has a measure of its volatility, which is called Beta. You can look up beta for any stock using your brokerage provided trading platform or on free sites like Yahoo Finance.

Here is how to understand the values given for beta. The larger beta is, the more volatile the stock is. The way this is measured is that the average volatility for the entire market is calculated and assigned a value of 1.0. This means that any stock that has a beta that is higher than 1.0 is more volatile than the market average. If beta is 1.25, that means the stock is 25% more volatile than the market average. If beta were 1.4, that would mean the stock was 40% more volatile than average. When beta is less than 1.0, that means the stock is more quiescent, or less volatile than the market average. Beta can also be negative. That means that the stock is actually fluctuating against the market. So, when the overall market is increasing in price, that stock is decreasing, and vice versa. As you might imagine, negative beta values are actually pretty rare.

For options, it is implied volatility that we are interested in. This is a measure of what volatility is expected to be in the future. This can have a large impact on options prices. This goes back to that fundamental principle, which is that the higher the probability that the option ends up in the money, the higher the price of the option. More volatility means that probability is going to be higher. In fact, high levels of volatility can really cause options prices to rise. Implied volatility is expressed as a percentage.

Implied volatility tends to get large when there is an expectation of something that is going to impact the price of shares. The quintessential example of this is when there is an upcoming earnings call. Earnings calls are something that is big in the options world. If you are an options seller, you might want to avoid earnings calls. So maybe for that week, you don't trade. But for options buyers, earnings calls represent a big opportunity. The key here is to get in on your trade a couple of weeks prior to the earnings call of a big stock. Stock prices change a lot when there is an earnings call, depending on whether or not the company was profitable and more importantly, whether they managed to beat expectations or not. In the weeks leading up to the earnings call, implied volatility gets larger and larger. For some stocks like Tesla or Netflix, implied volatility can get quite large, over 50%. One strategy you can use is to buy an option a bit of time out before the earnings call and then sell it the afternoon before the earnings call.

Let's see how implied volatility impacts options pricing. We'll go with a $220 share price again and say that we are 10 days to expiration with a strike price of 223. We'll take a relatively average implied volatility of 18%. A call option is $141, and a put option is $439 under these conditions. To understand the impact of implied volatility, we'll keep everything else constant.

Now move to 5 days to expiration. If implied volatility hadn't changed, the call option would be worth $74, and the put option would be $373. That is due to the effects of time decay. However, if the implied volatility had risen to 35%, the call option would be $232, and the put option would be $531. So, you could sell either option for a profit just from the increase in implied volatility alone. And remember, the call option is out of the money, but despite 5 days of time decay, it has increased in value because of the increase in implied volatility.

Now let's go to 2 days left to expiration and suppose that implied volatility is 55%. Now the call option is $230, and the put option is $529, leaving everything else unchanged. The prices haven't changed much, but there has been a lot of time decay, and the increase in time decay is not impacting the options prices hardly at all because of the high level of implied volatility. In fact, at this point, theta is sitting at -0.85 for both the call and the put option. If implied volatility goes up to 65%, the price of the call goes up to $292 and the put to $592.

In some cases, with highly sought-after stocks, if big results are expected in an earnings call, implied volatility can go higher than 70%.

So, Vega is the parameter that tells us how the price of the option is going to change in response to a 1-point change in the implied volatility. You will find that Vega is the same for both calls and puts with the same strike price and expiration date.

Rho

Finally, we come to the last major Greek. This Greek goes by the name rho. It measures the sensitivity of options prices to interest rates. Specifically, a long-term "risk-free" interest rate is used. It changes in the interest rates that are important, and of course, in today's environment interest rates are pretty steady and only change by small amounts when they do. The best example that you can use to understand the "risk-free" interest rate is the interest rate on a ten-year U.S. Treasury. When interest rates rise, this can have a small but negative impact on options pricing. When interest rates fall, there will be a small but positive impact on options pricing. This is not really a

Greek to concern yourself within today's environment, where significant changes in interest rates are unlikely and infrequent. Also, it requires a pretty large change in interest rates to produce a measurable impact on options prices.

Minor Greeks

There are even more "Greeks". They are known as the minor Greeks. The vast majority of options traders don't pay much if any attention to the minor Greeks, so we aren't going to discuss them. Most options traders don't even pay attention to all of the major Greeks, focusing only on delta, theta, and Vega. If you understand delta, theta, and Vega, you have all the information you need in order to be a successful options trader.

Chapter 4: Swing Trading with Options

The most straightforward way to trade options is to make a bet on the direction of the stock market and buy call or put options accordingly. Most beginning options traders are going to have to start with this method because more advanced strategies are closed off to beginning options traders. That isn't all bad, however, because you should get a feel for the options market before attempting more complicated trades.

What is Swing Trading?

The type of trading that we are going to be discussing in this chapter can loosely be described as swing trading. If you are not familiar with it, swing trading is a simple trading philosophy, where the idea is to trade "swings" in market prices. In a commonsense kind of way, there is nothing special about swing trading because it's a buy-low and sell-high method of trading with stocks. You can also profit from a stock when the price is declining by "shorting" the stock.

So, what distinguishes swing trading from other types of trading and investing? The main distinction that is important is that swing trading is different from day trading. A day trader will enter their stock position and exit the position on the same trading day. Day traders never hold a position overnight.

Swing traders hold a position at least for a day, which means they will hold their position at a minimum overnight. Then they will wait for an anticipated "swing" in the stock price to exit the position. This time frame can be days to weeks, or out to a few months' maximum.

A swing trader also differs from an investor, since at the most, the swing trader is going to be getting out of a position in a few months. Investors are in it for the long haul and often put their money in companies that they strongly believe in. Alternatively, they are looking to build a "nest egg" over a time period of one to three decades or even more.

Swing traders don't particularly care about the companies they buy stock in. They are simply looking to make a short-term profit. So, although swing traders may not be hoping to make an instant profit like a day trader, they are not going to be hoping for profits from the long-term prospects of a company. A swing trader is only interested in changing stock prices. Even the reasons behind the changes in the stock prices may not be important. So, whether it's Apple or some unknown company, if it is in a big swing in stock prices, the swing trader will be interested.

The chart below shows the concept of swing trading. If you are betting on falling prices, you can earn profit following the red line in the chart. If you are betting on increasing prices, you would follow the upward trending blue line. A bet on falling prices is often referred to as being short, while a bet on rising prices means you are long on the stock. This, of course, is another difference between swing trading and investing; investors don't short stock.

Swing trading can be used in any financial market. In the chart above, we are actually showing a chart from the Forex (currency exchange) market. The principles are the same, so the specific market we are talking about doesn't really matter, which is why it works with options.

Support and Resistance

An important concept often used by swing traders is spotting support and resistance. Support refers to a local low price of the stock. It's basically a pricing floor that, for the time being, the stock price is not dropping below. To find support, you just draw straight lines on the stock chart. The share price should touch the support level at least twice in order for it to be a valid level of support.

Resistance is a local high price. So, this is a high price level that the stock is not able to break above. Again, expect it to touch the resistance level at least twice, and drop back down, before you consider a given share price for the resistance level.

As the share price moves in between support and resistance, there are opportunities to buy-low at the support level price and then sell-high at the resistance level. And you can do the reverse in the case of shorting stock. You can enter your position at the relatively high resistance level, then exit your position at the support level.

Of course, support and resistance are not going to be valid price levels for all time, and a stock will often "break out" of support or resistance. This happens when the share price starts a declining trend and goes below the support level, or if it breaks out above the resistance level in an uptrend. These can be more opportunities to make a profit. But, when a stock price is stuck between support and resistance levels, we say it is *ranging*.

Trade with the Trend

The best thing to happen to a swing trader (or a trader of straight call and put options) is for a stock to enter into a unidirectional trend. So, it could be a trend in upward prices, giving you a chance to make large profits before it starts reversing. Alternatively, of course, trends can head downwards, opening up opportunities for those who are shorting the stock.

Trends can exist in many different time frames. It might only last part of a day, or it could last weeks and even months. Learning to spot trends and take advantage of them, with a sense as to when the trends are going to come to an end, is something that comes with experience and education. A new options trader can benefit by studying educational materials related to both swing and day trading so they know what to look for in stock charts to spot not only trends worth getting into, but also how to spot a trend reversal which would eat up your profits.

The chart below of AutoZone stock is a simple example of this concept. It's a dream trade, with prices going steadily up with time. But remember nothing lasts forever.

Trading with a trend is definitely something you'll want to look for as an options trader. The time scale of the trend is going to be something important, of course, because you are going to be concerned about time decay when trading options. Time decay is a concept that a swing trader does not have to worry about.

So rather than being beholden to specific rules, like saying you are going to trade options like a day trader or like a swing trader, an options trader has to be flexible. You will need to be ready to take advantage of very short term moves in stock price that only last for a day or less, and you'll also want to be in trades that can last days to weeks or even months.

Swing Trading Options

Since options are time-limited, they are a natural fit for the concept of swing trading. Although many of the advanced strategies attempt to take out the direction of share price movement from the equation, if you are buying single call or put options in order to make a profit, then you're definitely behaving at least in a qualitative sense like a swing trader.

Since put options gain in value when stock prices are declining, buying put options is like shorting stock. It's actually quite a bit more accessible, however. In order to short stock, you must have a margin account so that you can borrow shares from the broker. The basic idea of shorting stock is to borrow shares from the broker when the stock price is at a relatively high point and sell them. After this, the trader will wait for the share price to drop. Then when the share price is low enough to make a profit, the trader will buy the shares back and return them to the broker.

Of course, shorting stock using options is far easier. The reason is you never have to buy the stock to make a profit from the declining price. You simply profit from prices of put options which will increase as the stock price goes down.

Going Long on a Stock

If you believe that the price of a stock is going to rise, then you want to buy call options. So, call options represent the most straightforward or common-sense way to trade options. When you buy a call option, you are betting on that stock. Another way to say this is that you are bullish on the stock.

A good way to go about trading options is to pick a few companies and limit yourself to trading them. The reason is that you are going to have to be paying attention to the markets, company news, and general financial news for any option that you invest in. If you spread yourself too thin, you are not going to be able to stay on top of things and will find yourself getting caught up in losing trades. The best approach is to keep your trading limited in scope so that you can know what is going on. That doesn't mean you only trade a single call option; you might trade a large number of them on the same stock.

There are two ways to go about swing trading options. The first way is to look for ranging stocks that are trapped in between support and resistance. Then you can trade call and put options that move with the swings. So, the idea of this type of trading is very simple. First, you need to study a stock of interest and determine what the price levels of support and resistance are. Then, when the price drops to the support level, you buy call options. Now hold them until the price goes back up near resistance. It can be a good idea to exit your trades before the price gets all the way to resistance so that you don't end up losing some of your potential profits if the price reverses before you get rid of the options.

Trend trading call options can also be very lucrative. In this case, you are looking for significant news and developments related to the stock or even the economy at large. For example, when a company announces that it had big profits, this can be an opportunity to earn money with call options, as the price will go up by large amounts as people start snapping up the stock. When trading in this fashion, you're going to need to know how to spot trend reversals. We will talk about that later in this chapter. The idea is basically the same when you identify a trend in the making, you buy call options, and then ride the trend until you are satisfied with the level of profit and sell the options.

Again, it can't be emphasized too much. You always need to take time to decay into account when trading options. So, remember that with each passing day, your options are going to automatically lose value. Check theta to find out how much value they are going to lose. And as we discussed before, often, other factors overwhelm time decay in the short term.

A big opportunity with call options is trading on index funds. SPY, which we mentioned earlier, is one of the top choices for trading call options. In the case of SPY, you are going to be paying attention to overall economic news to look for opportunities. Any information related to the economy at large can cause large moves with this index fund. This includes changes in interest rates (or even leaving them the same when that is what the market would prefer), announcements of GDP growth rates, changes in trade policy, or release of jobs numbers. One of the best things about options on SPY is that they are extremely liquid, making it very easy to get in and out of your trades. You can also trade many other index funds, tracking virtually anything financial.

Shorting Stock Using Put options

Put options may be one of the most powerful tools available to the individual trader. To earn profits from shorting stock, you have to be a big player in the market. That means you have to get a margin account and have enough financial resources that you are able to borrow large numbers of shares from the broker. Most new traders are not going to be at that point. Keep in mind that to earn profits from shorting stock, you'll have to be shorting 100 shares or more of stock in order to make money.

With put options, you can leverage the stock through the option. By investing in Put options, you get control of the stock and earn profits from the price movements in the stock without actually having to buy shares. A single put option might cost $30, $100, or $400, but you will control 100 shares.

Some traders actually hope to profit by selling the shares when they buy put options, but most traders simply want to get into a put option early when a downward trend in stock price is expected, and then sell the put option for a profit when stock prices have actually declined. The same basic things to look for apply, except you'll be doing it in reverse. So, you can trade put options for profits when stocks are ranging. In this case, you start the trade by purchasing put options when stock prices are relatively high, at the resistance level. Then you hold your put options until prices drop down again to support and sell them for a profit.

Likewise, for an options trader, downward trends in stock prices are just as nice as upward trends. When a downward trend is developing, you invest in Put options and then sell them when the stock price has dropped enough such that you are taking an acceptable profit. As with call options, traders using put options will need to learn about signals that indicate trend reversals so that you have some quantitative tools to help you make solid trades.

Keep in mind there are no guarantees on the options market. When trading options, we are really looking for probabilities. This means that you can expect to have some losing trades, and the goal is to be profitable overall without worrying about specific trades.

Tools to Spot Trend Reversals

Swing traders use tools that help them estimate changes in the direction of stock market prices. Some of these tools are more qualitative in nature and involve spotting particular chart patterns that usually indicate a trend reversal is coming. You can think of these tools more in the sense of being rules of thumb or even "art of trading".

Many other tools used by swing traders are more mathematically based. These tools go under the umbrella of *technical analysis*. We aren't going to have space in this book to delve into all the details and tools used, but we will cover the most fundamental tools which are enough to get you started, and in fact, are often all that you need. Let's get started looking at a few chart patterns.

Chart Patterns That Indicate Trend Reversals

A trend reversal is important for an options trader because it's a point that you will use to either enter a trade or exit a trade. Over the decades, traders have come to recognize certain chart patterns that will indicate a coming trend reversal. This is a bet, in a sense. The given chart pattern is no guarantee a reversal is coming, but most of the time that will be the case. Chart images below were created by Altaf Qadir on Wikipedia.

The first chart patter we are going to look at is the "head and shoulders". This pattern occurs at the top of an upward trend before the price begins declining. It is characterized by three peaks in the chart. The middle peak will be the highest, and it will be flanked by two smaller peaks that are generally the same height. The pattern emerges because there are still traders coming into the stock, but the numbers are such that not enough of them are still entering the position in order to push prices up further. So, as they enter their positions, these late arrivals push up prices a little bit, and then it drops back down again. When the pattern is forming, prices drop down to a level called the neckline. Then they rise back up.

By the point of the right shoulder, traders are going to be looking to take profits. So, they will be exiting their positions, and as the number of people selling increases, the increased supply of the stock on the market relative to willing buyers will start pushing prices down. So, if you are trading call options and the stock underlying the call shows this pattern, it is a good time to sell.

You can simply flip the chart over to see a trend reversal developing after declining stock prices.

A double top is the same type of phenomenon, but with only two price peaks.

Next, we consider a cup and handle. This takes place in an uptrending stock before there is a large breakout. In this case, the stock will rise to a peak, and then gradually drop down in a relatively smooth fashion, forming a bowl shape. So, it will drop to a minimum and then gradually start rising to the previous level, which forms the "cup" part of the pattern. Then there will be a period where the stock price is ranging between two values, not really doing much. This is the handle part of the pattern. After the handle, the stock is likely to break out to the upside.

There are many chart patterns like these used by traders, but we can only cover a few because there are large numbers of them, and it would be outside the scope of this book. There are many online resources available that can be used in order to study and learn chart patterns. Consider using the site Investopedia to learn all of them if you are so inclined.

Candlestick Charts

Candlestick charts show stock prices divided up into small trading periods. This is done so that you can determine changing investor behavior before there is a major trend reversal. Each trading period is a microcosm of the trading day, week, or month, with its own opening and closing price, and high and low price. This way, you can see whether or not investors are in a buying or selling mood, and how strong that mood actually is.

Candlesticks are colored according to whether or not the closing price for the trading period was above or below the opening price. If the closing price is higher than the opening price, that is a bullish candlestick, and these are normally green in color (although different trading platforms sometimes use different coloring schemes). Candlesticks have "wicks" that are sometimes called shadows that extend out of the top and bottom, indicating the high and low for the stock for that trading period. A candlestick chart is illustrated below.

By examining how candlesticks are forming in a series, it can be possible to spot trend reversals in price. Candlesticks can be used on many different time frames, from 1 minute to 5 minutes, to 1 hour, 4 hours and more. The time scale to use is going to depend on what your goals are at the moment. If the price of a stock is fast-moving and you are looking to sell options to make a profit by exiting your positions, you might want to go with a 5-minute time frame, for example.

There are many different patterns on candlestick charts that can indicate future direction in price. Remember that price is really a reflection of demand for a given security, so declining price means that fewer buyers are willing to close a sale for the given price, and the price must continually drop until an equilibrium between buyers and sellers is reached. As an options trader, you are looking for changes or reversals in the trend.

When you see three candlesticks in a row of the same type, this can be an indication of a trend reversal. We actually see this in two spots in the chart above. These have been marked to draw your attention to them in a reproduction of this chart here, showing a trend reversal turning into a significant downward trend in price:

This pattern goes by the name "three black crows" when there are three bearish (or red) candlesticks in a row. Although the sighting of a black crow may be taken by some to be an indication of bad luck, the term "black crow" in this context is really historical. Options trading began in the 1920s but was suspended in the Great Depression and not revived again until 1973. Prior to the widespread adaptation of colored printing, candlestick charts used solid black candlesticks to represent bearish trading sessions, thus the name "black crows". For stock traders, declining prices are always a bad sign, so that is another reason why "bearish" denotes a bad situation, but remember that as an options trader, you can profit in either case. If you saw a chart like the one above, the three red candlesticks in a row would be a very good indication that you should buy put options. Then, you hold your put options until either a) you have made a level of profit that you find acceptable, or b) you see signs in the charts of another trend reversal, which is going to start eating into possible profits and possibly even turn them into losses.

When you see three green or bullish candlesticks in a row, this is a sign of a coming uptrend, and in the business, it is known as "three white soldiers". Again, the name is historical. It comes from the fact that in the days before color printing and computer screens, bullish candlesticks were outlined and hence "white" in color.

Another important candlestick patterns every options trader should be aware of is the engulfing pattern. This can happen at the end of a downtrend in prices or at the end of an upward trend in prices. In either case, and engulfing pattern occurs when a candle of the dominant trend type is followed by a large candle of the opposite type, such that the following candle completely covers the length of the previous candle. This concept is illustrated below.

Let's focus on the bullish engulfing pattern to understand what is going on here. Notice that the closing price, which is indicated by the bearish candlestick to the left, is a bit higher than the opening price of the bullish candlestick immediately to its left. This indicates that at the start of the trading period, people were still selling off, pushing prices down lower. In fact, in the example given, you can see a wick sticking out the bottom indicating that prices continued to drop. However, by the end of the trading period, prices reversed and went much higher than the previous close, and also higher than the previous open. This indicates that the trend is reversing because buyers are now pushing prices up with increasing demand. In the given example, there is a follow up bullish candlestick, but that isn't strictly necessary although the appearance of one would increase confidence. It is the trend that starts to develop over the next few candlesticks that are important. In the example given, we see that at the next time period prices continue to be pushed higher. This kind of pattern would indicate that it's either a good time to buy call options on the underlying stock or a good time to sell put options if you've got some in your inventory.

In the bearish example, it's a similar situation but with everything reversed. In the engulfing candle, remember that the top of a red or bearish candle is the opening price for the trading session, while the bottom of the candle is the closing price. So, in this case, the trading session for the engulfing candle opened with a small continuation of the previous trend – and prices jumped higher. Then they were pushed down by a large amount, even further down than the opening price (and indeed for the low price) of the previous trading session. This indicates that the opening price of the bearish candle indicated only a slight increase in prices; in other words, demand was starting to peter out. The fact that the candle engulfs the previous one indicates that the selloff became overwhelming, as compared to the previous trading session.

Another important candlestick pattern that is often used is a "hammer". Depending on the orientation of the hammer, it can be a plain hammer or an inverted hammer. It is also called a shooting star if present at the start of an uptrend. A hammer has a wick that only comes out of one end of the candlestick and a relatively narrow body. This means first of all that opening and closing prices (regardless of whether we are talking about a bullish or bearish situation) were fairly close to each other. Second, it means that during the trading session, prices were pushed strongly in one direction, only to be pushed way back towards the opening price level for the trading session. A shooting star occurs when an inverted hammer occurs at the top of an uptrend, indicating that prices were pushed up high, only to drop down below the opening price (so for a shooting star you are looking for a bearish candlestick.

Here are two examples so that you understand what a hammer or inverted hammer actually looks like:

To get a hammer, you just flip it over.

While these are the main trend reversal signals with candlesticks, there are literally dozens of them. You can learn what they are and how to spot them using many resources, including free resources that are available online. A good options trader, however, is not going to rely on only using one or two techniques, so you don't need to devote your entire life to studying candlestick charts. Looking to spot the most compelling chart reversal signals is usually enough for most traders when used in conjunction with other tools.

Be calm when looking at stock charts. You don't need to enter or exit a trade in a matter of seconds when trading options in most situations. So, it isn't necessary to spend hours memorizing candlestick.

Moving Averages

One of the most powerful tools that you can use in order to spot trend reversals is using moving averages. Moving averages are used in conjunction with candlestick charts by most stock traders, but in my opinion moving averages are actually a stronger signal indicating a trend reversal, and it is even possible to rely only on moving averages in a lot of cases. But to play it safer, a typical approach would be to look at moving averages for a trend reversal and then confirm by looking at the candlestick patterns.

First, let's take a step back and make sure we understand what a moving average is. Anyone understands the concept of an average, we take a set of data points and add them up, and then divide by the number of data points. A moving average is like this, except at each point along the line, we compute the average at that point. So, the average at each point is going to be different and reflect market conditions at the point in question. Moving averages require that you specify the number of points used in the calculation. Note that stock charts extend far back in the past, so you could use 10 points, 30 points, 200 points or more.

For stocks, we can compute averages on nearly any time frame we desire. For the sake of simplicity, suppose that we are averaging daily, using the closing price. So, each point on our chart, assuming that we are using a candlestick chart is going to be one day. To compute the moving average for 9 days, we could create a 9-day moving average curve and add it to our chart. At each day along the chart, it would get the past 9 days of data and compute the average. So, you can see why it's "moving", as it goes to the next day on the chart, the first day used in the previous calculation drops off and is replaced with the current day.

If the stock prices used to calculate the average are just added up and then divided by the number of days in the calculation, then we call this a simple moving average. Many traders get by quite well using simple moving averages, and there really isn't an argument that you can frame against them. We are not looking for ultimate precision. We are looking for indicators that trader sentiment on a given stock is changing.

However, many traders argue against the use of simple moving averages. The reason that you might not want to use them is that notice the simple moving average treats all prices with equal relevance. That might be fine if you are only using a moving average over the course of a few days, but the longer the time frame you use in your moving average, the less relevant prices in the past are to the calculation. The simple moving average fails to recognize this basic fact.

To get around this, different types of moving averages were created to weight the data, so that more recent prices would get more "weight" in the calculations. The most popular type of moving average used for weighting is called an exponential moving average. Another popular method used is called a Hull moving average, after its creator. These types of moving averages are pretty accurate, and you will notice that they track the actual pricing trends quite closely.

One of the benefits of moving average curves is that they remove noise from a stock chart. Rather than seeing the typical jagged up and down zig-zag line that you are used to seeing, you will see a smooth curve that represents the real, underlying trend in stock prices.

To use moving averages to spot trend reversals, we will add two moving average curves to the stock chart. These moving averages will have different periods, or in plain English, they will use a different number of trading sessions. So, if you are using a chart of daily stock prices, the moving averages will use a different number of days for each curve. The point of doing this is to see whether or not the short-term price movements are going higher or lower than the long-term average at each point. When this type of event happens, this usually indicates a trend reversal. That apparent trend reversal can be compared to other indicators like candlestick patterns to confirm what you are seeing with the moving average curves. In most situations, you can be pretty confident that a crossover of moving average curves will mean a coming trend reversal.

Different choices are used to spot trend reversals with moving average curves. For example, a popular method is to use 50-day and 200-day moving averages. These curves work pretty well under a wide variety of circumstances, but I find the 200-day moving average too long. Let me tell you why.

When you are looking for a long-term moving average, you have to keep in mind that it's going to be impacted by many factors. For example, it might be impacted by earnings calls, and the more you extend the moving average into the past, the more impact moving averages are going to have. Earnings calls can have a pretty dramatic impact on stock prices. Over the past year, there have been earnings calls that have moved stock prices by $20, $40, and more in a single day or even in overnight after-hours trading. The impact of earnings calls can be long-lasting. For example, a boost in share prices from an earnings call might set a new support pricing floor for the stock in question. But it may not be long-lasting, and so it's an outlier data point that is distorting prices.

Also, no matter what, when it comes to tomorrow's stock price, recent events and stock prices are simply a lot more relevant. And trading options, unless you are investing in LEAPs, you're definitely interested in short-term price movements, often of 30 days or less. In fact, many options traders only trade on weekly time scales. So, what the stock was doing 200 days ago doesn't seem as relevant to what it's going to be doing in the next few days.

For this reason, I like to use a 9-day moving average in conjunction with a 20-day moving average, or you can use a 50-day moving average. My advice is to try different values and see how it works for you. Apply these moving averages to *past* stock market data, so that you can get a feel for how it really worked with real data. Your trading time frame will also be important. Shorter time frames that you are looking at to enter or exit trades are going to demand shorter moving averages.

So, what are we looking for? We are looking for the behavior of the short-term moving average curve with respect to the long-term moving average curve. Sticking to my preferred values, we are looking for the 9-day moving average curve to either move below or above the 20-day moving average curve. When the short-term moving average moves below the long-term moving average – this is a very strong signal that stock prices are going to decline in short order. On the other hand, when the short-term moving average goes above the long-term moving average, we have the reverse condition – so this is a strong indication that there is a coming uptrend in stock prices. Always confirm by looking at other signals, such as the candlestick chart, before entering or exiting a position.

When we see the short-term moving average drop below the long-term moving average, this is called a "death cross". Once again, the terminology used is reflective of the mentality of straightforward stock traders, where they view increasing stock prices as strictly positive, and declining stock prices as strictly negative. As an options trader, you should adopt a view that a particular move in one direction or the other is neutral. So, when you see a "death cross", you should consider investing in Put options. If you are already invested in call options, a death cross is a selling signal. Here is an example, via Market Watch, of a death cross for Apple stock prices:

Here, the green line represents the short-term moving average, while the red line represents the long-term moving average. Of course, prices are going to fluctuate up and down constantly, but by looking at the relationship between the two curves, you can not only spot buy and sell points but also false signals. For example, a bit after the death cross in the figure, we notice that the stock price started climbing, which may have led novice traders to buy calls or to sell put options. But if you are looking at the moving average curves, you'll see that the short-term moving average remained below the long-term moving average even as the stock prices momentarily rose to a higher level. Whenever you see the short-term moving average staying clearly below the long-term moving average, you should take the view that bearish conditions are still in existence no matter what the stock price is doing in the moment. Since the stock market is a pretty chaotic system, we can expect that it is going to be doing a lot of up and down movement that is not going to be significant at all over any time period of interest. And you can see clearly from the figure that the indication given to us by the death cross proved quite accurate, as the curve of stock prices continued to decline to a significantly lower value.

When the short-term moving average goes above the long-term average, this is called a golden cross, because it is an indicator of a coming upward trend in stock prices. A golden cross is, therefore, an indicator that represents a buy signal for call options and a sell signal for put options. The example below shows simple moving averages, using a 50-day simple moving average for the short-term curve, and a 200-day moving average for the long-term curve. This particular example is a textbook example, showing a very strong upward trend that followed the golden cross:

Pay attention to the slopes of the moving average curves. When one of the curves has a much stronger slope than the other curve, this can indicate that the trend is either going to be weak or strong. In the example above, the short-term moving average curve has a larger slope, and so it grows faster (for a time), indicating that this is a very strong upward trend in price. You can also note that at the marked entry point in the figure, the candlesticks certainly agree with the information that you are getting from the golden cross. There is a "three white soldiers" pattern just before the golden cross; in fact, there are more than three bullish candlesticks at that point. That is a strong confirmation signal that would give you confidence in using this moving average crossover as an indicator that you should go ahead and invest in call options.

Relative Strength Indicator

The next item we are going to look at, which can be used in swing trading, is called the relative strength indicator. This is a technical tool that can be used in order to estimate "overbought" and "oversold" conditions. In my opinion, it should not be used as a primary tool, but only to give confidence to the type of information that you are getting from your other tools. So, the general procedure you should utilize is to first look for moving average crossovers. Then confirm with the candlestick chart and then look at the relative strength indicator to solidify the information that you are getting.

The relative strength indicator will put a curve below your stock chart, and it will range over the values 0-100. If the relative strength index is between 30-70, it is considered neutral. If it is above 70, this represents "overbought" conditions. This means that buyers have been too enthusiastic about entering this stock and have pushed the price of the stock up to levels that aren't justified by external conditions. When a stock is overbought, this can be an indication that the price is going to start declining, since the only way out of an overbought stock is to sell it.

However, this technical indicator can only be described as suggestive. In many cases, I have seen stocks labeled as overbought, but the price kept going up and up. At least for a time. For this reason, my advice with the relative strength indicator is to only look at it when you are unsure even after looking at the candlestick charts and the moving averages. For example, you can come to a tentative conclusion with a crossover on the moving averages that the candlestick charts seem to confirm, and if you are still not confident, you can use the relative strength indicator to back up what you think your move should be.

When there are overbought conditions, this indicates that you should sell call options, or alternatively, buy put options. An overbought indicator is a bearish indicator. But again, it's no guarantee by any means.

Overbought conditions will form at the top of an upward trend in prices that are coming to an end.

When the relative strength indicator is 30 or below, this indicates oversold conditions. That means that people have been too active getting out of the stock, and prices are likely to start rising again soon. So oversold conditions are a strong indicator that you should be looking to exit your position if you have been investing input options. If you are looking for stock prices to rise, this could suggest an entry point for buying calls.

Oversold conditions are going to occur at the bottom of a downward trend.

Again, you are probably going to want to be using the relative strength index on a secondary basis. So if you see a golden cross and it seems to be confirmed by the candlestick patterns (which would indicate a trend reversal to the upside), if you can confirm this with an RSI below 30, that is a strong indication that you should be investing in call options or getting out of positions that are invested in Put options.

Bollinger Bands

Another very popular tool used in swing trading goes by the name of Bollinger bands after its creator. Bollinger bands involves defining some boundaries for a stock, using moving averages. It relies on simple moving averages by default, but you can customize it. It forms "bands" by using a simple moving average and then also plotting one standard deviation above the simple moving average, and one standard deviation below the moving average. The basic idea here is that under normal conditions, a stock is going to stay within a standard deviation of the mean. If it goes outside of this range, then that is an indication that there is going to be a trend reversal. Of course, there are special situations (again, think earnings calls) when this might not be true because breaking news can cause unusually large movements in stock price. However, under normal circumstances, the stock can be reasonably assured to stay within a standard deviation of the mean. After all, that is the meaning of standard deviation.

Bollinger bands are overlaid on the stock chart. Most traders are going to use Bollinger bands in conjunction with candlestick charts, and so you are looking for the candlesticks to fall above or below the Bollinger bands. So, if there has been an upward trend of the stock price and then the price touches or goes outside the upper Bollinger band, that is a point where you can expect a trend reversal in the price to the downside. This means that you would either be investing in puts or selling your positions that were invested in call options.

Alternatively, if prices have been dropping and then the candlesticks touch or go outside the lower Bollinger band, then we can expect a trend reversal to the upside. This is taken to be a signal that you should buy call positions or exit put options.

In short, Bollinger bands are a way to dynamically add support and resistance to your stock charts. So, we can take the lower Bollinger band to be supported, while the upper Bollinger band is taken to be supported.

Chapter 5: The Iron Condor and Iron Butterfly

In the previous chapter, we learned about straight trading of calls or puts. In short, this represents a style of trading that is something that goes along with swing trading stocks. You either want to short the stock, that is bet the price is going to be entering a decline or go long with call options and make profits from rising prices. This is a basic strategy that involves basically making a bet on which direction the stock price is going to move. The cold reality is that while there are certain circumstances when you can make bets on trends in stock prices, that is a very difficult game to play overall. Most professional options traders do not do straight trading of calls and puts, because it is a high-risk bet on stock direction. Instead, they use one or more of several advanced trading strategies.

Advanced trading strategies seek to do one or both of two things. The first thing that advanced trading strategies seek to do is to reduce your risk. This can be done by reducing the probability of engaging in a losing trade or by capping losses. And actually, there are more ways to reduce risk. For example, you can remove the direction of the stock market from the equation, which is something that we are going to talk about here.

Removing Direction from the Trade

The iron condor is a trading strategy that does something that is quite unusual. Rather than betting on the stock moving one way or the other, it bets instead that the stock is going to stay within a certain range of prices. Over short time periods, unless there is a dramatic event, be it something unpredictable or something expected like an earnings call, stocks are basically going to flail around within a certain narrow confine of pricing. In other words, most stocks will spend most of their time range.

This is where an iron condor comes in. An iron condor is a limited risk strategy that bets that the stock price is going to be trapped within two values over the lifetime of the trade. Now, of course, if you were to trade stocks over a matter of weeks or years, stock prices would probably be hard to pin down within a range. But most traders enter into iron condor positions with time frames of a maximum of 45 days all the way down to a single week.

An iron condor has four "legs". As a new options trader, it is important to become familiar with the jargon, and my legs, all this means is that there are four options involved in the trade. We will spell it out later in the chapter.

Central Goal of the Iron Condor

The central goal of an iron condor (or an iron butterfly) is that the stock price is going to stay within a bounded range of values over the lifetime of the options contracts. What the stock price does within that time frame really isn't of concern. It might go up, go down, or hardly move at all. For the trader, that isn't important.

All that matters to the trader of the iron condor or iron butterfly is that the stock doesn't move very much. Very much is a relative term for the iron condor, you can define any range you like. The narrower the range, the more money you are going to make. However, that means higher risk. If the stock's price goes outside of the range, this could end up being a losing trade, in the event that the options go to expiration. If you have a smaller range of values, that means that there is a higher probability that the stock is going to go outside the range. You can have a wider range to reduce risk, but that will decrease potential profits as well.

Iron Condors are Income Strategies

When you buy a call or a put, note that you are buying to open your position. This is a speculation strategy; you are speculating that you can earn profits from certain moves in the stock price. However, with an iron condor, we meet a new and different way to think about the stock markets and options trading. An iron condor is an income strategy.

This means that you are going to open a position in an iron condor by selling it for a credit. Since an iron condor has four legs, that means it's a trade that involves buying and selling four options simultaneously. But you will be buying options on net as we will see. But the point is not to speculate, although there is always a small amount of speculation in any stock or options trade. The point is to earn income. Many options traders sell iron condors on a revolving basis so that they can receive options premium on a regular basis. Options premium refers to the payments that are put in by people buying options.

As an income strategy, this means that you are going to be selling iron condors, rather than buying them. The idea is that you sell them for a credit, provided the stock price does not violate some conditions that you set on the trade; you get to pocket the credit as a profit.

The Lower Legs

The lower legs of an iron condor consist of two put options that form the lower boundary or support region for our trade. The boundary is formed using the strike prices of the options. So, we are hoping that the stock price never goes as low as the strike prices of our put options. There are two put options that form the lower boundary of the iron condor. We need the stock prices to be above the strike price of the higher put option at closing to make a profit.

We set this up using what is called a vertical spread. This just means that we have to options of the same type, that have different strike prices on the same stock and with the same expiration date. In this case, you are going to sell the put option that has a higher strike price. The idea with an iron condor is that you are going to be selling options that are out of the money.

Selling a put option can be lucrative, but it carries some risk. The risk is that we would be assigned, meaning that if the share price moved below the strike price of the option minus the breakeven price, a buyer out there might decide to exercise the option. In that case, we would be assigned, and we'd have to buy the shares from the buyer at the strike price on the options contract. Depending on circumstances, this could result in a substantial loss.

However, we can mitigate that loss substantially by simultaneously buying another put option. In this case, we buy another put option with a lower strike price. It's going to be cheaper, and if prices crash, while we will make profits, we will also reduce our risk since we can exercise that option in the event things don't work our way with the overall trade.

To understand how this works, let's make up a simple example. Suppose that a stock is trading at $200 a share, and there are 10 days to expiration. We could sell the $217 put option for $9.37 a share, for a total credit of $937. In the event that the share price moved low enough to make the $217 call profitable for a buyer, we might be assigned, which would mean that we'd have to come up with $217 x 100 = $21,700 in order to buy the shares of stock. That might be an unpleasant thought if the stock price was dropping substantially. For the sake of example, suppose the stock crashed to $200 a share.

However, we can cut our risk by purchasing another put option with a lower strike price. In fact, we could purchase the $210 put for $6.37. Since we are buying this while selling the other option, this means our total profit is cut substantially. In this case, our total profit would be $9.37 - $6.37 = $3. While that is a big cut in possible profits, we've also cut our risks massively. Suppose that the stock price drops below $210, also covering the breakeven price. If the option were exercised, we'd have to buy the 100 shares at $217 a share, resulting in a loss of $21,700. However, since we entered into the contract with the $210 put, we can turn around and sell the shares to someone else. Using the second options contract, we can sell the shares for $210 and make $2,100 back. Now we've reduced our loss to $21,700 - $21,000 = $700.

That may not sound good, but had we not bought the second option, we'd be stuck buying the shares at the sale price. At best, we could sell them on the open market. If they were trading at $200 a share, that means selling them for $20,000. So now our loss is $1,700. So, we've cut our losses by 41%.

The Other Legs

The upper legs of the trade are created by selling a call option and buying a call option with a higher strike price. The strike price of the lower call option forms the boundary of range for the stock to the upside. So if a stock is trading at $200, and we create an iron condor by selling a put option with a strike price of $195 and buying a put option with a strike price of $190, and then we sell a call option with a strike price of $205 and buy a call option with a strike price of $210, if the stock price stays in between $195-205, we earn profit. On the other hand, we lose if it goes above or below this range. So, with the legs involving the call options, you buy a call option with a certain strike price, and then sell one with a higher strike price.

The basic ideas are the same as compared to what we've looked at before, but in this case, we don't want the price to move very substantially. We are going to be in trouble if it breaks to the upside or the downside.

The Complete Iron Condor as a Single Trade

When you enter into an iron condor position, you are going to enter it as a single trade. So, you buy a call and a put, and you sell a call and a put, simultaneously. The important point here is that you are selling the position. You have to know that your inner strike prices set the acceptable range over which the price of the stock can move.

The following chart illustrates the iron condor:

The Iron Condor Relies on Time Decay

You can buy an iron condor with respect to any expiration date of options. However, the main strength of the iron condor is time decay. Put another way. You are going to earn more from an iron condor that expires further out in the future. However, most iron condor traders will work in a time frame that ranges between 30-45 days. Some traders will opt for shorter time frames. Many will take a mere week's time frame or 7-14 days. By reducing the amount of time until expiration, you also reduce the probability that the stock is going to move outside the bounded range. So, while buyers are hoping the stock is going to break one way or the other and get outside the range set up by the iron condor, you're playing the role of the house and making the opposite bet.

So, keep the following in mind:

- Less time left, lower risk to seller, but less possible income. In this case, with a shorter time frame on the contract, the probability of the stock exceeding the range set up by the strike prices is lower.
- More time left, higher risk to seller. This is because the stock has more chances to go above or below the range set by the iron condor. However, there is more possible income. With more time left until expiration, you will earn more money from time decay.

Since you are selling a call option with a lower strike price(relative to the call options that you buy) and selling a put option with a higher strike price(relative to a put option that you buy), you are going to get a net credit for the transaction.

The Iron Butterfly

The iron butterfly is essentially a derivative of the iron condor strategy. So, like the iron condor, the iron butterfly has four options, two puts, and two calls. It will have a put option with a relatively high strike price that you sell. It will have a put option with a relatively low strike price that you buy. Then it will have a call option with a relatively low strike price that you sell, and a call option with a relatively higher strike price that you sell. All options have the same expiration date.

In the case of the iron butterfly, however, you are going to have a call option and a put option that have the same strike prices. This means that for an iron butterfly to be profitable, the share price has to stay on the strike price, which defines the mid-value for the trade. You can see this in the graph for the iron butterfly shown below. It has a spike, rather than a range of prices over which the trade is profitable:

The Buyback Strategy

Now we are going to briefly mention an important advantage when selling options that can be used to mitigate risk. This is the buyback strategy. In short, if at any time it looks like an option or strategy that you have sold is not working out, or is likely to finish such that you would lose on the trade and have substantial financial obligations, you can buy the trade back. This doesn't mean you buy the trade back from the exact same person (who might not even have it anyway), you can buy it back from any trader on the market. Traders will buy positions back under two circumstances.

The first is that you have simply made a good profit, and the stock is still ranging within the values set by your inner strikes. In this case, you may buy the position back to exit the position, in order to protect yourself from the possibility that something unusual will happen on the last day of trading that could cause the stock to break out, and go below the strike prices of the put option or above the strike prices of the call option.

The second case is when your position is obviously not going to work. In this case, you could buy back your position in order to cap your losses. There is no requirement, as a seller, for you to hold onto the position if it is a losing position. The way that you get out of it is you tell your broker that you want to buy it back. This is done automatically by placing an order to buy that position.

Maximum Losses

Maximum losses are set to the upside and the downside. If the stock breaks toward the upside, the maximum loss is the difference in the strike prices of the call options plus the breakeven. On the other side, if the stock price collapses so that it ends up lower than the lower strike price of the put options, then the maximum loss is the difference between the strike prices less the breakeven price. The strategy does not require symmetry, but in most cases, traders construct symmetric iron condors or iron butterflies.

Summary

When do you get into an iron condor or iron butterfly? You do this when you don't expect the share price to move very much. In the case of an iron butterfly, you expect the stock to stay within a range of prices until the expiration date. For the iron butterfly, you expect the share price to stay at the strike price used for the inner call and put options in the trade.

Chapter 6: Strangles and Straddles

What if there was a strategy you could use to profit if the stock rose high, but you also earned profit if the stock crashed? It sounds too good to be true, but the reality is with options you can do this. The strategies used to accomplish this are called strangles and straddles. In this chapter, we will learn how to set them up, how they work, and when to use them.

Strangle Options Strategy

The strangle options strategy is designed in a way that is somewhat opposite that of an iron condor. While an iron condor is set up to earn profits if the stock price stays within a certain range, a strangle will earn profit only if the stock price breaks out of this range. It doesn't matter if the price rises or falls; a strangle makes a profit either way. So, this is an ideal strategy to use when you expect big price movements on the stock, but you are not sure which direction the price will go.

The classic situation where a strangle can be used is with an earnings call. Prior to an earnings call, it is not known for sure how the earnings of the company will be reported. The benchmark used by the markets is analyst expectations. If the earnings of the company exceed the predictions made by major analysts prior to the earnings call, this usually results in jubilation and rising stock prices. In many cases, the stock can rise 10-20% in value overnight.

Of course, companies often disappoint. In fact, it doesn't even matter if a company reports a profit, if they fail to meet the expectations of the market, this can lead to a crash in the stock share price. Movements in price can be as large as movements due to positive earnings reports. If the reports are actually bad, that is, they not only fail to meet expectations but also report a loss or some other negative news. This can lead to massive losses on the stock. This happened to Netflix and Tesla in recent earnings calls. Netflix reported a loss of subscribers, which caused a plunge in their stock price.

A strangle is a two-leg strategy, which is just another way of saying that we will use two different options to create the trade. Strangles are speculative trades, and therefore, we will buy to open these positions.

You might be asking how we can profit no matter which way the stock moves. The answer is that a strangle involves buying a call option and a put option simultaneously on the same stock. They will have the same expiration dates but different strike prices. The movement of the stock has to be large enough to exceed the cost of buying both options. If the stock price rises, this means that the Put Option which is a part of our trade, is going to expire worthless. If the stock price crashes, on the other hand, that means that the call option is going to expire worthless.

For our breakeven price, we need to take into account the total cost of entering into the position, so it will be the cost of the call option + the cost of the put option. So, if the stock were to break to the upside, the price would have to rise above the strike price of the call option + total cost of buying both options. If the strike price were $100 and we paid

$3 for the call option and $2 for the put option, then the price of the stock would have to go above $100 + $3 + 2 = $105 before we can make a profit.

To figure out the breakeven point for the put option, we start with the strike price used for the put option and then subtract the total cost for entering the position. Therefore, if our strike price for the put option on this hypothetical trade were $90, the breakeven point to the downside would just be $90 - $3 - $2 = $85.

In this hypothetical setup, we would not make any profit if the share price were to stay within the two strike prices. Specifically, this means that if the share price stayed between $90 and $100, we would lose on the trade. The total loss would be equal to the cost of the two options, or $3 + 42 = $5. Since there are 100 shares underlying the option, the total loss would be $5 x 100 = $500. The maximum loss occurs if the share price stays the same. Of course, the probability of a share price staying the same after an earnings call is practically nil. The stock is going to move somewhat, so the question is: will the stock price move enough so that you make a profit? If it doesn't, any movement in the share price will at least reduce your losses.

So how much can you make? To the upside, in theory, the maximum gain is unlimited. It depends on how high the stock price rises. Share prices on big stocks can rise $30 or $40 after an earnings call, and so it is possible to make thousands of dollars in profit. Of course, that doesn't mean you should go into these types of trades expecting that kind of profit. However, it is possible to earn substantial profits.

To the downside, the maximum gain is equal to the share price when you enter the position multiplied by 100. To earn the maximum gain to the downside, the share price would have to drop all the way down to zero. Of course, that is something that rarely happens, so don't expect it. But it is not uncommon to see share prices on big stocks drop $20, $30, or $40 a share after a bad earnings call. So, to the downside, very large profits are also possible.

How to Implement the Strategy

When there are big events like earnings calls, stock prices can even change dramatically after hours before the markets open the next morning. Therefore, it is important to plan ahead for using this type of strategy.

The first step is to identify an event that is coming up where the strategy might be appropriate. For stocks, the earnings call is the primary event to look for. Therefore, find stocks you are interested in and look up the dates of their upcoming earnings calls. These occur on a quarterly basis; therefore, we have four opportunities per year for each stock to employ the strategy.

Another opportunity might be the upcoming company announcements. For example, Apple has regular presentations it gives every year. They have a developer conference where the new operating system for the iPhone and iPad devices is unveiled to the public for the first time. This may or may not have a big impact on the viewpoint of major market analysts, and so it could cause a large shift in share prices of Apple if the changes to the operating system are viewed as having a possible impact on Apple's future bottom line. In the fall, Apple has presentations where they reveal their latest iPhones and changes to their computer line. If there are major changes and announcements by Apple, this can have a big impact on stock prices as well.

Apple is the quintessential example for using the strategy in this manner, but you can look up and follow different companies to see when and if they are going to make major announcements about their product line, or if there are going to be upcoming announcements on things that might impact the company's fortunes. For example, a pharmaceutical company might be seeking FDA approval for a major drug. If the drug is approved, the stock of the company could shoot up significantly. If the drug is rejected, the stock could decline by a large amount. This possibility suggests that a strangle might be an appropriate technique to use in order to earn profits from these events.

Index funds are also possible targets for the strategy. Any index fund on the blue-chip companies can be considered, most notably the S & P 500. You can also consider index funds on the Dow Jones Industrial Average, the NASDAQ 100, or the total market. In this case, major news events and releases of economic data will be important to consider. Of course, it is hard, if not impossible, to plan for unexpected events. But there are major scheduled events that occur on a monthly and quarterly basis. These include announcements of interest rate changes by the federal reserve, announcements on jobs and the unemployment rate, and announcements of the GDP growth rate.

Just like with stocks, the actual nature of the announcements may not be what drives changes in the share prices of index funds. Rather, it will be how the announcement compares to the expectations held by the market. For example, if the market expects the creation of 170,000 jobs, but it's announced that there were 190,000 jobs created, the market will be jubilant. This would mean that index funds like SPY would see large spikes in share price.

Once you have an event identified, you can buy one or more strangle contracts on the stock or index fund in question. A strangle is entered into as a single transaction, and so you will buy the call and put option simultaneously. Remember that options have time decay. This can mean that buying a strangle far ahead of time can be overly expensive. This can mean that some balance is going to be necessary. It is advisable that you get some experience trading straight call and put options for a few months before attempting this. As you are doing so, you should be studying the market behaviors and look at the prices of strangles on your trading platform to see how they change with time. In particular, look for earnings calls and see what happens.

The balance is going to come from the anticipation of the markets. Since people know that big movements in share price are possible when earnings calls are approaching, although the options have time decay, prices are going to be rising from increasing demand. So, it is a matter of balance, is there enough increasing demand to wipe out the time decay. The longer you wait to get into a position the more it is going to cost if there is a lot of interest swirling around the stock. This can happen with major stocks like Tesla, Facebook, Apple, and so on.

Once you've gotten in your position, you have to be ready to sell it at the right moment. Typically (but not always), what happens in these situations is that stock prices are going to rise very quickly. Companies may have a late afternoon earnings call. They often schedule these such that they take place after the markets close. Even though the markets are closed, there will be after-hours trading. Under normal circumstances, after-hours trading doesn't have significant impacts, but after earnings call, the impacts can be dramatic. Prices on a stock might rise or fall 20-30% even before the next market open.

What happens next is hard to say, as the market is inherently unpredictable. If there is going to be more movement, it is likely to occur in the first 30 minutes after the market open. At some point, the stock may stabilize at new levels of support and resistance. How quickly it does this will depend on the intensity of the earnings call. If the earnings call only mildly exceeded or failed to meet expectations, then the stock price might settle at a new level fairly quickly. If the announcement was dramatic, then a sell off or rush to buy the stock might last for a longer time period.

If you decide to implement the strategy, you should be prepared to be paying close attention to the market the morning after the earnings call or other announcement. Be ready to sell your position so that you can take an acceptable level of profit before the market stabilizes, and the demand for strangles on the stock starts to decline. The key here is to take advantage of latecomers to the marketplace. There are always people that come in late, but they eventually fizzle. However, buyers will come in late after noticing the large shift in share prices for the stock, and they will be interested in buying up strangles so that they can profit from any late hour movements in share price. But the key to being a successful options trader is to not be one of those late arrivals. You should plan these trades out and already be in your position before the earnings call. Remember, with a strangle you are going to be earning profit no matter which direction the stock moves, so if it goes up or down is not going to be your concern. The chart below graphically illustrates the way a strangle works.

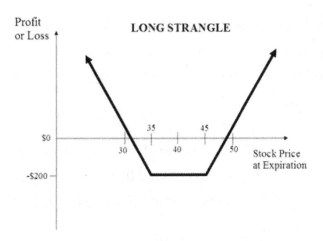

In the center of the chart, you see a flat line. This is the range in between the strike prices where you will have maximum loss. From here, on both sides, the line slopes upward to the breakeven point, which remember is the strike price + cost to enter the position on the upside, and the strike price minus the cost to enter the position on the downside. From there, the more the price moves past the strike prices of the options used to set up the position, the more profit that is earned. In the graph above, we see a hypothetical example with strike prices of $35 and $45, with a total cost to enter the position of around $5. The chart is for illustration purposes only and does not represent actual prices.

Let's look at a real example to see how much this would cost. Facebook is trading at $208 a share, and we can enter a strangle that expires in one week for a price of $2.10, or $210 in total. The strangle has strike prices of $212.50 for the call and $205 for the put.

The breakeven point for the upside is $214.60. This is computed by adding the cost to enter the position, which is $2.10, to the strike price of $212.50. To earn a profit with this trade, the share price of Facebook would have to rise above $214.50. If the share price rose to $216.50, you would earn a $190 profit. If it rose to $224, you could earn around $1,000 in profit.

Under normal conditions, you wouldn't expect the stock price of Facebook to rise to $224 a share. But if there was a very good earnings call, that is something that is definitely in the realm of possibility.

On the downside, the maximum possible profit on this trade is $20,200. To be profitable, it would have to drop below the strike price used for the put option, which is $205, less the cost of entering the position, which is $2.10, and so the breakeven point is $202.90. If there was a bad earnings call and the share price were to drop to $195 or so, you could earn a profit of $750.

Once the event has occurred, you can risk holding the position to expiration. If there are no other major movements in the share price, the options will expire, and you'll earn your profits. But a good strategy is to simply sell the position for a profit once the major movement in stock prices has occurred.

Straddle

Now we turn our attention to a related strategy that is called a straddle. This is also a two-legged strategy that is designed to take advantage of price breakouts of a stock, without regard to the direction that the breakout occurs. Like a strangle, a straddle will also involve buying a call option and a put option on the same stock, and with the same expiration date, simultaneously.

However, a straddle differs from a strangle in one key aspect. To set up a straddle, you will also set up the trade so that the call option and the put have the same expiration date. The chart for a straddle is shown below. This narrows down the range over which there are losses. Maximum loss on the trade would occur if the stock price were equal to the strike price at option expiration.

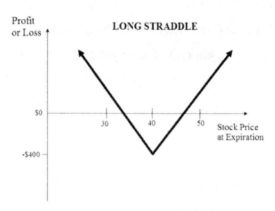

To summarize, both a strangle, and a straddle is set up in order to earn profit from large moves in the price of a stock. In either case, it doesn't matter if the stock moves up or down in price. No matter what direction the stock moves, they will earn a profit provided that the price move is large enough to overcome the breakeven points. Like a strangle, you can use straddles when there are big events or announcements coming up, such as earnings calls.

The same type of strategies should be employed when using straddles rather than strangles. This means that you want to enter your position over a time frame of a week up to maybe three or four weeks prior to a big event like an earnings call. Over the time period between your purchase and the earnings call, the straddle will gain in value from stock movements, regardless of whether or not the price of the stock moves up or it moves down. If the price of the stock increases, the value of the straddle will increase because of the call option that is a part of the trade. However, it could also lose value as a result of the put option that is a part of the trade. The price has to move one way or the other so that the share price is higher than the strike price + cost of the position, or lower than the strike price minus the cost of the position. Remember that for a straddle, the call option and the put option both have the same strike prices.

Let's say that the price of some stock is $234 per share. We create a straddle with a strike price of $235 a share. Although maximum loss occurs when the strike price is equal to the share price, we want to pick a strike price that meets that condition when entering the trade, because we are doing so expecting the share price to move off the strike price in one direction or the other at a later date before the options expire.

For our example, we are entering the trade 21 days before expiration. At this point, the call is $6.93, and the put is $7.89, and so the total cost to enter the position would be $14.92. Let's say that there is an earnings call when the option is five days to expiration.

Now, by 15 days to expiration, in anticipation of the upcoming earnings call, the share price might have moved a bit. Let's suppose that the market is expecting a good earnings call, and so share prices are going up. If the share price went up to $237, this is a modest gain that, despite time decay, will help the value of the call option. It has risen from $6.93 to $7.36. However, the put option has lost some value due to time decay combined with the modestly higher stock price, and it's now going for $5.33.

Our plan, however, is to hold the position until the earnings call. Remember that earnings call also impact volatility. We are setting the implied volatility at 33% for this exercise, but as we get closer to the earnings call, that value will rise.

Now 10 days to expiration, which would be five days to the earnings call in our scenario. The share price has risen to $240 share since the markets are expecting good news. Implied volatility has also increased to 37%. At this point, the call has jumped to $8.37, but the put is now down to $3.63.

Moving forward to just 7 days to expiration, there are only two days left until the earnings call. Now implied volatility has risen to 45%. The share price has increased steadily with the passing days and now stands at $245. Under these conditions, the call is $12.26, and the put is $2.25. The total value now is $14.51, and it cost $14.92 to enter the position, so we have a mild loss at this point – but it should be ignored. We need to hold the position until the earnings call.

Later that day, the stock is at $247, and the implied volatility has risen to 50%. The call is now $14.32, and the put is $2.30, so our position is now worth $16.62. Since it cost $14.92 to enter the position, we are now at a point of profitability to the tune of $16.62 - $14.92 = $1.70. If you wanted to, you could sell it now for a profit of $170. You'd find an eager buyer without a doubt because most traders would be anxious to get in on the trade prior to the actual earnings call.

Finally, we reach the earnings call. It beats expectations by a surprising margin, and the price of the stock jumps $23 a share in after-hours trading. At market open, the call option is worth $36.01, and the and the put is worth pennies on the dollar. At this point, the put option is worthless, but the call option has gone up so much in value that we are looking at a profit of $36.01 - $14.92 = $21.09 per share, putting us in a position where we can sell for a total profit of $2,109.

If the stock continued climbing the morning after the earnings call, which sometimes happens, we could earn even more profits. If it went to $280 a share by the afternoon, the call option would be worth $45. In that case, we'd have another $900 in total profits on the trade. Of course, you are taking some risk. The longer you hold the position. The stock might start declining a bit or stop rising. And if you hold it overnight, you are going to get hit with time decay. The put option is entirely worthless at this point, but it really doesn't matter.

Suppose that instead, the price had plummeted. Our hypothetical company might have missed expectations by a large margin, and rather than rising by a huge amount, it could drop to $210 a share instead. The beauty of the straddle is that in this scenario, we make a profit as well. This time, the call option would be completely worthless on the trading day after the earnings call, but the put option would be worth $24.99, giving us about a $1,000 profit. The more the stock drops, the more profit we would earn. The same holds true for a strangle but remember with the strangle the call and put options have different strike prices, and there might be a wider range over which the stock needs to move in order to earn profits. But in either case, the goals are the same.

Tips and Things to Watch Out For

There are a few things to watch out for with the strangle and straddle. For a strangle, you probably want to bracket the strike prices of your call and put such that the current share price is in the middle. For a straddle, you can use the current share price as your strike or pick a strike price that is very close to the current share price.

You can enter the position at any time, but depending on market conditions, costs might go up a lot in the days coming up to the earnings call. Prior to making your first trade, it is a good idea to simply watch from the sidelines and wait until the next quarter before actually doing trades. In fact, many trading platforms have demo accounts that let you go through the process of making trades, but without spending any money. In other words, they are pretending, simulated trades, but using the real data going on in the marketplace. New traders are often quite anxious and want to get in on the action, but it is worth spending one quarter going through the practice trades to get some experience doing it without risking real money. Since you are just observing, you can also keep an eye on multiple stocks to see how they and options prices are changing as their earnings date approaches, since all the major stocks are going to be doing earnings calls within a couple of weeks of each other.

Another thing to consider is liquidity, an issue that we've raised before. The bottom line here is that once the large shift in share price has occurred, you want to be able to get out of your position quickly. For this reason, you really need to focus on high volume, popular stocks if you are going to employ this strategy. So, you'll be checking the open interest and volume. It's good to focus on the big-name movers such as Amazon, Netflix, Facebook, Google, and Apple, the so-called FAANGS, at least as a beginner. These are not cheap stocks, of course, and that cuts both ways. It is more expensive to enter a position, but the potential profits are also quite large. These are the stocks that will experience very big moves in share price based on earnings calls, and they are also highly liquid and so you will have no problem selling a position when you need to.

For practice without risking money, you can try the technique out on lower priced stocks like AMD, which is trading at around $45 a share. We can enter a straddle on AMD for about $345. Apple is trading at $297 a share. A straddle choosing the closest strike price to the share price would cost $1,448. The Apple straddle is likely to earn far higher profits if the stocks moved a given percentage, so there are tradeoffs that have to be made. Of course, in the beginning, you are probably not going to want to risk large amounts of capital.

Chapter 7: Call and Put Spreads (Vertical Spreads)

In this chapter, we are going to discuss an advanced technique that can be used to speculate on stock price movements or as a method of generating regular income selling options. These techniques are called vertical spreads because they involve trading two options simultaneously of the same type which have a spread in strike prices, but the same expiration dates. There are two ways that you can set these trades up. They are going to involve two options of the same type. The trades also involving buying one option and selling another option with a different strike price, but the same expiration date, and of course, on the same underlying stock.

If you spend more on the option that you buy than you do on the option that you sell, this is going to create a net debit. The purpose of a debit spread is to trade on speculation as you would trading a single option. So, for example, if you thought that the stock price would go up, you'd buy a call option and sell a call option. This procedure will actually reduce your risk as opposed to buying a single call option. But the tradeoff of reducing your risk in this fashion is that you will cap the amount of profit you can make. For a single call option, the amount of possible profit you can earn is theoretically unlimited.

Keep in mind the jargon used in spreads by the industry. An option that you sell is short, while an option that you buy is long.

Debit Spreads

A debit spread is the purchase of one option and the sale of another option of the same type and with the same expiration date with different strike prices, such that the complete transaction results in a net debit. There are two types of debit spreads. You can do a call debit spread, which means buying a call and selling a call, or you can do a put debit spread, which means buying a put and selling a put simultaneously. The purpose of a debit spread is to reduce the amount of risk you face if the trade does not work, but this comes at the expense of capping profits below what you would get with an equivalent winning trade just buying a call or a put.

Let's consider the situation involving calls first. A call debit spread is also known as a bull debit spread or a bull call spread. The reason for the terminology is that this is a trade that you would enter into if you were bullish on the stock. In other words, you're expecting the share price of the stock to increase by the time the options expire.

This is a two-legged trade, meaning that we are going to trade two options simultaneously. The two options will have different strike prices, but the same expiration dates. This makes the trade a vertical spread, the vertical being along the strike prices. For a call debit spread, you are going to buy a call option with a lower strike price and sell an out of the money call option with a higher strike price.

Entering into this type of spread is going to change the Greeks associated with a position, as compared to simply buying a call option at a given strike price. It will reduce the delta and theta for the trade. This means that with a smaller delta, your position is going to be impacted less by changes in the underlying stock price. But that really isn't a concern. There is still enough delta that the trade can be profitable. Our position is also less sensitive to theta, which means it will be a little less sensitive to time decay as far as losing value. But don't rest on your laurels, any option position that you enter with a net debt (aka buying to enter the position) is impacted by time decay, and a call debit spread is no exception.

In order to make a profit, we need the underlying stock price to appreciate in value. The maximum profit that you can earn on a call debit spread is as follows:

Max profit = difference in strike prices − premium paid to enter the position

Looking at Apple, here are a couple of examples. We could enter into a call debit spread using two out of the money options by buying the $302.50 strike price and selling the $307.50 strike price. The cost to enter this position with one week to expiration is $1.19. The width of the strike prices is:

$307.50 - $302.50 = $5

Therefore, the maximum profit is found by subtracting the cost to enter the position from this value:

$5 - $1.19 = $3.81

Once again, there are 100 underlying shares, so it would cost $119 to enter the position and we could earn $381. Again, this is a capped amount. Maximum profit occurs if the share price goes above the strike price of the call option that we sell (the short call) in order to enter the position. If you had only bought a put option, your possible profits could be much higher. No matter how much higher the stock price goes above the strike price of the short option, your profit stays the same at a fixed amount. So, any time you enter into a call debit spread, if the share price of the underlying stock goes above the short strike price, sell the position to get out of it with your profits. If conditions warrant it, you can just let the options expire.

Maximum losses for a call debit spread are capped. The maximum loss that you can incur with a call debit spread is when the underlying stock price drops below the long strike price (that is the strike price of the option that you buy to enter into the position). Again, this is a fixed value. So, no matter how low the price of the underlying stock drops, even if it were to drop all the way to zero, the number of losses that you could incur would be limited to the premium paid to enter the position.

The breakeven point occurs at the strike price of the long call plus the premium paid to enter the position. Using the Apple example, the premium paid was $1.19, and the lower strike price (or the strike price of the long call) was $302.50. So, the breakeven point is $302.50 + $1.19 = $303.69. Let's summarize this for our example, and this will help you understand how these trades work:

- If the stock drops below $302.50, even by a penny, we incur the maximum loss. That is the premium paid to enter the position, which in this case would be $1.19 per share or $119 for the 100 shares in total.
- The breakeven point is $302.50 + $1.19 = $303.69. If the stock is between $302.50 and $303.69, we incur losses, but they will be less than the total premium paid. If it reaches $303.69, we neither lose nor earn money.
- In between $303.69 and the short strike price of $307.50, we would earn a small profit.
- If the underlying share price were to go above $307.50, then we'd earn a maximum profit of $381. Even if the share price were to go up to $500, it wouldn't matter, our profit is strictly capped in this trade.

A call debit spread is a smarter way to play rising stock prices as opposed to buying call options. You actually cut your risk, because when you sell a call option, you get paid premium for that call option. Since the strike price is higher than the strike price for the long call in this trade, the amount you get paid is lower than the amount spent to buy the long call. However, it reduces the amount you have to pay, as compared to buying the long call by itself.

Put Debit Spreads

Now let's consider a put debit spread. This trade also goes by the name of bear debit spread or bear put spread. The purpose of this trade is the same goal as you would have to buy a single put option; you are anticipating that the share price of the underlying stock is going to go down. The basic setup is the same as it is with a call debit spread. However, since we are looking at put options, we are going to be doing the reverse in our thinking. We will belong on a higher strike price and short on a lower strike price. Both put options that are a part of the trade are going to have the same expiration date.

Once again, the maximum profit will be the width of the strike prices minus the cost to enter the position. The maximum loss you can incur on the trade is the premium paid to enter the position.

From here, things are just reversed in the sense that we are looking for declining prices in the share price of the underlying stock. Therefore, the maximum profit is going to occur if the share price of the underlying stock goes below the strike price of the short put option. The breakeven point will be the strike price of the long-put option minus the premium paid to enter the position. Again, the long-put option will have a higher strike price than the short put option in this case. This is a strategy that can be employed to minimize risk when you believe that the share price of the underlying stock is going to decline.

Debit spreads are limited risk, limited reward strategies. They are set up in order to reduce the amount of risk (the amount of money you can lose) associated with a trade. The cost of doing this is that you also have a reduced profit potential for the trade. However, a lesson you should learn is that very few professional options traders just do straight trading of call and put options. That type of strategy is a high-risk strategy. But you can do the same type of speculating using debit spreads.

Put Credit Spreads

Now let's continue our investigation of vertical spreads but shift gears. This time we are going to talk about using options in order to generate income, rather than speculating on the direction of the stock. Of course, there is always a little bit of speculation, but in this case, we are only hoping that the price stays above a certain value, and not worry about what it is doing otherwise.

A put credit spread is created by trading two put options simultaneously. It can be said that this is set up just like the put debit spread, but we reverse the roles of which option is bought or sold. In this case, we are going to sell a put option with a higher strike price. The purpose of doing so is to generate a credit to our account that earns income. In order to reduce our overall risk of the trade, we are going to sell a put option with a lower strike price. A put option with a higher strike price is going to cost more than a put option with a lower strike price; therefore, there is a net credit on the trade.

There is only one rule to use when deciding to trade put credit spreads. You want to trade put credit spreads in good markets. It doesn't have to be a particularly strong bull market; it just has to be a market where prices are not declining. This applies to the individual stock as well, so you want to trade put credit spreads when the stock is doing well. A good rule of thumb is to avoid trading put credit spreads during the week of an earnings call when stock prices might suddenly plummet.

The main thing to learn about put credit spreads is that this is a selling position. You are going to sell to open, and therefore you will have the obligations of a seller associated with the short put with the higher strike price. That is, you could be "assigned". When a put option is exercised, the buyer will sell you 100 shares of stock at the strike price, no matter what the market price is. And theoretically, you need to have the cash on hand to cover the transaction. When you are assigned, you are required by law to buy the 100 shares.

But the good news about the put credit spread is you don't actually have to buy the shares, and your liability is capped. The reason is that you have covered yourself by purchasing a put option with a lower strike price. What happens is you are able to exercise the put option with the lower strike price. It works like this – you have to buy the 100 shares at the higher strike price. But you can turn around and sell them at the lower strike price by exercising the other put option. So, with a credit spread, you are assigned on one option and can exercise the other option. You would lose money in this situation; it would be the difference between the strike prices minus the net credit received. But at least it is a fixed amount of money.

In practice, you aren't going to have to do anything at all, because your broker takes care of all this automatically in the event the option expires in a situation where it could be exercised. As a trader, you won't know all this happened, the stocks will be bought and sold on your behalf, and you will only see the end result.

In order to sell put options, you are going to need some collateral. This is done by putting a cash deposit into your account. The purpose of doing so is to cover the theoretical loss that can occur if the trade does not work out for you. To see how this works, let's look at an example.

Consider a put credit spread on Apple that expires in one week. The strike prices are $297.50 and $295. The breakeven price is the strike price of the short put option, $297.50, less the net credit received. It is important to remember that with a credit spread, you don't actually pay anything to enter the position. You are actually receiving credit for it. But you won't actually see the credit materialize until the options expire or you buy it back.

In this case, the credit received is $1.12 per share, or $100. So, the breakeven point is $296.38. As long as the stock price stays above $296.38, you will make a profit (at the time of writing, it's $297.35). Maximum gain happens if the stock price stays or goes above the upper strike price. So, if it stays at or goes above $297.50 per share, a real possibility in this case, then you would earn the maximum credit of $112. Maximum loss is computed by taking the difference between the strike prices and subtracting the credit received. In this case, we have ($297.50 - $295) - $1.12 = $1.38, or $138.

In order to actually enter the trade, you would have to deposit some cash to cover that potential loss.

Put credit spreads are popular for generating regular income. Many professional options traders earn a living by selling put credit spreads at regular intervals. You can sell as many as you can back with collateral and can mix it up by using different stocks. The higher the share price on a stock, the more you can earn by selling put credit spreads. And at all times, the possible losses you can incur are known and fixed.

Call Credit Spreads

Put credit spreads sound great, but of course, the stock market is not going up and up all the time, even though it seems that way right now because we've been in a long-time bull market. What to do then? The answer is simple – you switch to selling call credit spreads in a bear market or when a stock is crashing. A call credit spread is designed to earn money when stock prices are dropping or staying below the lower strike price used in the spread.

In the call debit spread, we trade two call options with the same expiration date, and that is what we are going to be doing in this case. With the call debit spread, we bought a call option with a lower strike price and sold a call option with a higher strike price. Since call options with lower strike prices are worth more money, this results in a net debit to our account.

Now, we are going to do the reverse. So, we are going to sell a call option with a low strike price, and then buy one with a high strike price to reduce our risk. This will result in a net credit to our account. Other than the differences in the relationships of the strike prices and the fact these are calls rather than puts, the principles are exactly the same as a put credit spread.

In this case, the risk of assignment is that we would have to sell shares. But when using a credit spread, you don't actually have to own the shares. When a call option is exercised, the seller/writer of the option is required to sell 100 shares of stock at the strike price. In this case, if that were to happen to you with a spread, you don't have to do anything other than cry when you get your losses. The broker will sell the shares on your behalf and exercise the long option to recoup some of the losses.

If you decide to be an options seller, you can make a good living switching between call and put credit spreads as market conditions warrant. This is completely different than stock trading, as you will never have to worry about whether the stock market is bearish or bullish, you can earn money under any circumstances using these methods.

Time Decay and Buy Backs

Two things work in your favor as an options seller. For options buyers, time decay works against them because the option is losing value. As an options seller, that doesn't affect you – in fact, it helps you a great deal if you are selling out of the money options (and they stay out of the money). As a seller, time decay works in your favor as the options become less valuable to buyers. That makes it less likely they are going to be exercised as time passes.

The second key strategy is to buy your positions back either close to expiration, or in the event, they go in the money. If the options are not close to expiration, but they go in the money, there is a chance that they would be exercised. However, that is generally less likely. But if you feel there is a risk that the options are not going to go out of the money again prior to expiration, you can simply buy the contract back. When you buy an options contract back, you are freed of all obligations associated with that contract.

Chapter 8: Selling Options

In the last chapter, we actually touched on selling options, doing it by mitigating risk using credit spreads. In this case, we are going to talk about selling options without mitigating the risk, which is simply selling them alone. If the options are backed, we have covered calls and cash covered puts. If the options are not backed by anything, they are called "naked". Although it sounds crazy to sell naked options at first glance, the truth is many professional options traders make $500,000 and up per year selling naked options. Let's investigate each of these in turn in this chapter.

Covered Calls

The least risky option strategy is to sell covered calls. In order to sell a covered call, you must own 100 shares of stock. Many investors earn income from dividends, and covered calls provide an alternative and often more lucrative way to earn money from stock ownership. However, it does carry some risk in that your stock may be "called away". That is, if the stock price moves above the strike price of any option you sell + the premium received for the option, the buyer of the option may choose to exercise it, which means they have the legal right to buy 100 shares of stock from you at the strike price.

But, if you own 1,000 shares in Apple (actually any number of a specific stock of 100 shares or more), or some other good company that can fetch a good options premium, and you are willing to assume the risk of having your stock called away, this can be used to generate regular income from your stocks. Each option that you sell must be backed by 100 shares of stock.

When you sell an option, you get to keep the premium that is paid for the option. In fact, you can keep it no matter what happens. So that is cash in your pocket even if you have to sell the shares. And in many cases, you aren't going to lose anything in a fundamental sense. If you had purchased the shares in the past at a lower price, this means that you will actually be selling them at a profit, although the amount of profit you earn will be lower than what you could have earned on the stock market. That is because you will have to sell them at the strike price, no matter how high the stock price rises. But there is the possibility that you can still "lose" in the trade and come out financially ahead.

Different people have different risk tolerance, and for some people, this is going to be too much. They aren't going to be willing to risk losing their stock. But if you are willing to take on that risk, there are ways to minimize it. Although you will make less money, you can sell out of the money call options that have a low probability of being exercised. Suppose that we had 300 shares of Tesla stock. It is currently trading at $441.91 per share. We could sell a call option with a $450 strike price to receive a premium of $14.93 per share. This option is listed by the broker as having a 70% chance of profit. For 100 shares, that would be $1,493. If we did that for all 300 shares, the total premium received would be $4,479. So, you could make big money doing this.

Like with credit spreads, you can always buy your options back. In the situation where you sell a covered call and then buy it back later, you are freed of the obligation of having to sell your shares, and you get to keep your shares. So generally speaking, unless you are careless, it is a low-risk strategy. Keep in mind that if the option goes in the money, there is a chance that a buyer can exercise it and require you to sell the shares. But most options are not exercised until expiration. So, you can avoid the situation by selling in the money options prior to expiration.

Cash Protected Puts

Another way to sell single options is by selling cash protected puts. A cash protected put means that you deposit the money in your brokerage account that would be necessary to buy 100 shares of stock. This is a less popular strategy for a few reasons. If you have that kind of money lying around, there are better ways to utilize it in stock and options trading. Another reason is that you can sell put credit spreads and only tie up a small fraction of the capital.

This can be an expensive proposition. To sell the $437.50 put on Tesla expiring in one week, you would need to deposit $42,982.34 into your brokerage account. For the trouble, you would make $750. That would only be a 1.7% return on your money. If you have $42k to invest, I am sure you don't want to tie it up to make $750, especially when you could sell put credit spreads and make $750 tying up, maybe $1,200 or so.

The bottom line is that cash protected puts are not a favored strategy. In fact, they might be called pointless.

Naked Put Options

Finally, we come to the holy grail of income generation using options, which is selling naked options. This is a simpler strategy than selling vertical spreads, but the goals are the same. We have simply removed the risk mitigating factor. When you sell naked put options, you are selling one option in each trade. You receive the premium credit, and that's it.

In order to sell naked options, you are required to have a margin account and to deposit a certain amount of money to cover a trade. The amount of money is a fraction of the amount of money that you have to put in in order to sell a cash protected put. So, while you might be required to deposit $180,000 to sell cash protected puts against Amazon, you'd only have to deposit around $11,000 to sell naked Amazon puts.

The biggest risk of naked put options is assignment. That is, you are not paying attention, and the share price drops well below your strike price, and someone exercises the option. That would put you in a position of having to buy the shares. Then you could resell them on the market at the lower share price and take the loss.

This is why a margin account is necessary. A margin account is a type of account that lets you borrow money and shares from the broker. So, the required capital you must deposit helps cover your losses to some extent. You are going to have to borrow from the broker to buy the shares, and then after you sell them on the market the collateral you put up will cover the net loss.

You can also sell naked call options when stock market prices are declining. These are well-known winning strategies used by professionals. In the event that it looks like it is a losing trade, you use the same techniques you would use for credit spreads, that is you simply buy back the contracts.

Chapter 9: Tips for Successful Trading

In this chapter, we are going to run through some tips for successful options trading. These tips are based on years of experience trading options and come from many different people.

Set Stops on Your Trades

The biggest risk for an options trader is that they will get emotional during a trade. This can result in selling too early because of panic about declining options prices or staying in a trade too long because of greed. To avoid these problems, you can set a rule on the amount of loss you are willing to accept and the amount of profit you are willing to take on a trade. Many brokers allow you to hard code this with the trading software so that it gets implemented automatically. Then you don't have to worry about your trades. You just accept the end results. Another way to say this is to have a defined exit plan.

Letting Options Expire

Never let options expire, unless specific conditions are met. If you are buying call options and want to actually own the stock, then you can let an in the money option expire. If you are trading out of the money options, you should never let them expire. Sell them even it would mean a losing trade, a day or two before expiration. That way you can at least cut your losses.

Consider Rolling Out Trades That Aren't Working

Rolling out an option means closing the position and then entering the position again, but with a longer expiration date. This gives you more time to work the trade by pushing the expiration date to the future.

Avoid Options with Low Volume

Remember, you always want to look for liquidity. One of the biggest mistakes made by novice options traders is to trade options that are illiquid. Remember the rule for open interest, only trade options that have an open interest of 100 or higher. That will save you from getting into trouble trading options with low volume where you could get stuck in a trade.

Attempting to Make up for Past Failures

Don't try to trade using a higher volume in order to make up for past mistakes.

Conclusion

Thank you for making it through to the end of *Options Trading Crash Course*, let's hope it was informative and able to provide you with all of the tools you need to achieve your goals whatever they may be.

Options trading is a very exciting part of the stock market. With options trading, you can control large amounts of stock without actually owning it. This means that you can earn profits from movements in the stock price without risking huge amounts of capital. The return on investment on options is simply much better than the possible return on investment that you can earn trading options.

In this book, I have attempted to demystify options trading for you. We have explained what an option is, the difference between call and put options, and the strategies used by professional options traders when investing in options.

My hope is that rather than join the scare chorus that surrounds options from "financial advisors", I have shown you that options are actually a rational investment that can help you build your own successful trading business. Whether you engage in "speculation" or trading for investment income, options can help you read a six or even seven-figure income from your trading business, provided that you make careful trades and stick to the fundamental principles that are guaranteed to lead to success.

Your next steps are to actually get your feet wet with some trades. Start slowly, and spend some time trading small numbers of call and put options to build up some experience. Be sure to do both. Many novice traders are scared away from put options because they are not used to thinking in terms of earning money from declining stock prices. So, it's important to get over that and actually go through the experience of earning money while the company is having losses.

From there, you can start to employ options strategies after you've got a few months of experience making some trades. Before settling on a favorite, try the different strategies to see what you like best. Some people will end up focusing on only one trade. For example, many professional traders only trade iron condors, while others only sell put options. Others have a lot of variety and will engage in whatever trades suit them at the moment and what the market conditions are. This is a matter of personal taste, so you will have to figure out what works best for you.

I want to wish my readers good luck in the trading business!
Finally, if you found this book useful in any way, a review on Amazon is always appreciated!

CPSIA information can be obtained
at www.ICGtesting.com
Printed in the USA
LVHW021314301020
670160LV00001B/23